The Female Tradition in Southern Literature

The Female Tradition in Southern Literature

EDITED BY

Carol S. Manning

UNIVERSITY OF ILLINOIS PRESS
Urbana and Chicago

This book is printed on acid-free paper.

Library of Congress Cataloging-in-Publication Data

The Female tradition in southern literature / edited by Carol S. Manning.
        p.   cm.
    Includes bibliographical references and index.
    ISBN 0-252-01951-2 (cloth : alk. paper)
    1. American literature—Southern States—History and criticism.
    2. American literature—Women authors—History and criticism.
    3. Women and literature—Southern States.   4. Southern States in
    literature.   I. Manning, Carol S.
    PS261.F46   1992
    810.9'9287—dc20   92-9375
                                                           CIP

Contents

Carol S. Manning

Introduction: On Defining Themes and (Mis)Placing Women Writers

The literature of the American South has been an established area of study now for several decades. To help readers keep abreast of developments in the field, the Society for the Study of Southern Literature distributes a semiannual newsletter, now a quarter century old. According to a survey reported in the newsletter in 1978–79, responding colleges at that time offered over seven hundred courses in Southern literature, enrolling over eight thousand students annually. But the study of Southern literature is not just an American interest. In 1990 alone, there were at least two foreign symposiums in the field, one on the American South at the University of Genoa and the other on Eudora Welty at the A. M. Gorky Institute of World Literature in Moscow. By 1985, Southern literature had become such an established field of study that SSSL sponsored the creation of a six-hundred-page *History of Southern Literature,* edited by five prominent men of Southern letters.

As in any field of extended critical inquiry, there are patterns and recurring themes in the scholarship on Southern literature—patterns that developed early and have been perpetuated since, too often without challenge. These range from an overemphasis on the nostalgic, uncritical vein in the nineteenth-century literature to the way the so-called Southern Renaissance of the twentieth century is defined. During eighteen years of study of Southern literature, I have profited enormously from the extensive body of theory about it, but I long ago grew dissatisfied with more than one pattern in it. The time has come for an assessment of the critical literature and a reconsideration of terms, themes, and canons.

The contributors in this collection of essays attempt only a fraction of such a large undertaking. We expose limitations in accepted theory on Southern literature by examining one particular pattern in that theory: the pattern pertaining to how the South's women writers have been treated by reviewers and scholars. We give attention to women writers and their motifs and themes that have been slighted by established theory. And we look at threads that connect some writers—threads that reveal a female tradition in Southern literature. Given the limits of space and time, we necessarily leave much untouched that deserves attention.

The implications of the volume are revisionist and feminist. Despite the yearly proliferation of scholarship in the field, it was not until the 1980s—with works by such scholars as Anne Goodwyn Jones, Louise Westling, Kathryn Lee Seidel, Helen Taylor, and Minrose Gwin, and with special issues on Southern women writers by *The Southern Quarterly* (see Prenshaw)—that feminist murmurs about Southern literature began to be heard. Why did this body of literature escape the feminist critique for so long? No doubt the answer derives in part from the fact that quite a number of women writers *are* associated with the Southern canon: Ellen Glasgow is usually seen as a precursor of the Southern Renaissance; Katherine Anne Porter and Eudora Welty are identified with that renaissance; and Carson McCullers and Flannery O'Connor win favor as post-renaissance writers. The visibility of these writers and a few others has created the impression that somehow Southern literature has miraculously escaped the need for revision that feminists have sought for American literature in general.

But it is a false impression. Southern literature, in fact, epitomizes the need for revision that Paul Lauter describes in "Race and Gender in the Shaping of the American Literary Canon." Here, as elsewhere in American literature, the canonization processes that Lauter dates from the 1920s have created a literary map that privileges certain texts and themes and undervalues the contributions of minority and female writers.

The argument that the nineteenth-century Southern canon needs revising is easy to make. Until very recently, Southern women who wrote before the turn of the century were, with few exceptions, ignored by scholars. For example, according to Miriam J. Shillingsburg, during the eight years from 1968 to 1975 only two Southern women who wrote before the Civil War were the subject of study and only eight who published in the postbellum period "attracted even one scholarly nod" (128). Yet during the nineteenth century there were scores of women writing in the South. In 1865, Mary Forest (pseudonym for Julia Deane Freeman) published *Women of the South Distinguished in Literature*, containing biographical sketches of and selections by 34 Southern women. In 1869, James Wood Davidson published a volume on Southern literature titled *The Living Writers of the South,* in which 75 of the 241 writers—almost one-third of the total—are women. Three years later, in 1872, Mary T. Tardy put together *The Living Female Writers of the South,* an anthology of writings by 175 women. And in 1908 Kate Alma Orgain selected 11 women and 15 men for her text, *Southern Authors of Poetry and Prose.* Obviously, then, there was no shortage of women writers in the nineteenth-century South. Yet through the professionalization of the study of American literature that universities initiated in the 1920s (see Lauter), these writers all but disappeared.

For example, in the first modern historical survey of Southern literature, *The South in American Literature 1607–1900,* published by Duke University Press in 1954, Jay B. Hubbell lists one hundred male writers and only five female writers in his table of contents. He lumps together a number of additional female writers for brief attention in a nine-page subsection labeled "Women Writers." Women who wrote before 1900 are even less visible in two major anthologies of Southern literature. In *The Literature of the South,* edited by Richard Croom Beatty and others in 1952—the textbook that "largely shaped the teaching of Southern literature for over two decades" (Inge 594)—only one woman is included among forty-one writers representing Southern writing from Colonial days to the beginning of the Southern Renaissance. In the anthology that replaced the Beatty text in the classroom in 1979, Louis D. Rubin, Jr.'s *The Literary South,* the number of women representing the pre-renaissance centuries rose by 100 percent: not one but two of the forty writers are women.

In his book, Hubbell justifies his treatment of the women by explaining that while women writers were extremely numerous, prolific, and popular in the South during the nineteenth century, their writing was generally sentimental and inferior—not literature but a popular "sub-literature" (603). Yet whereas nineteenth-century women who allegedly wrote popular, sentimental, inferior fiction have been excluded from anthologies of Southern literature, nineteenth-century men who wrote popular, sentimental, inferior fiction are included. One need only think of the short stories of Thomas Nelson Page. In a handy anthology published in 1970, *Nineteenth-Century Southern Fiction,* John Caldwell Guilds includes Kate Chopin as the one female among eleven writers, praising her writing as superior to that of other women of her time, whose writing, in contrast, was characterized by "prolixity and embellished affectation" (7). Inconsistently, then, Guilds includes works by John Pendleton Kennedy and William Alexander Caruthers that show similar defects. Indeed, Guilds himself describes the selection by Caruthers, the nauseatingly sentimental story "Love and Consumption," as "didactic, moralistic, and bathetic" (3).

But it is simply not true that nineteenth-century Southern women wrote little of merit. Within the last twelve years, the nineteenth-century canon has begun to be revised through reassessments and rediscoveries of works by female and black writers. Some of these rediscoveries are making us aware that by ignoring the women we have previously neglected a whole genre of writing. For much of the best and most important writing these women did—moreover, much of the best and most important writing of the time and place—was in the form not of poetry and fiction but of letters, diaries, and journals. The resurrection of such works is not only enlarging the nineteenth-century Southern canon but also modifying our modern concept of what counts as literature.[1]

But this counting of heads is less significant than an examination of attitudes. For though women writers have fared better all along in the twentieth-century Southern canon, critics nonetheless frequently treat them as though they are outside the mainstream of Southern literature. For decades it was commonplace for critics to describe one or another woman writer as a "local colorist" whose works are merely picturesque, and even today they frequently assume women write books that appeal primarily to a female audience and reflect a feminine sensibility. Men's writings, on the other hand, presumably have universal appeal.

The twentieth century inherited from earlier times this attitude that writing by women is likely to be slight and frivolous. In an essay that Tardy includes in her 1872 anthology of writings by living Southern women, Mary E. Bryan of Florida expresses frustration over the way women writers were treated. She says that though men had finally given women liberty to write, they restricted what the women could write about: "With metaphysics [the women must] have nothing to do; it is too deep a sea for their lead to sound; nor must they grapple with those great social and moral problems with which every strong soul is now wrestling. They must not go beyond the surface of life, lest they should stir the impure sediment that lurks beneath." Bryan adds that when women do confine themselves to such acceptable female topics as nature and religion, the men then scorn their works as insignificant (336). Bryan's complaint not only anticipated Virginia Woolf's famous complaint by several decades but also foretold the treatment her Southern sisters of the twentieth century have received from critics.

For example, in early criticism on the Southern Renaissance, scholars who discuss female writers frequently do so apologetically. Two such essays appear in *Southern Renascence,* the path-breaking collection edited by Louis Rubin and Robert D. Jacobs in 1953. In an essay on Ellen Glasgow, John Edward Hardy insists that he is not advocating a Glasgow revival. Rather, a discussion of her works is for him merely a means to a more worthy end: "I might try to justify an essay on Miss Glasgow simply with the hope that it would help to furnish a clearer vocabulary for criticism of other novelists who are more exciting in their own right" (237). In the same text, Vivienne Koch seems to apologize for taking Caroline Gordon as her subject. She states that Gordon's work has not been appreciated sufficiently, but then she adds a qualification: Gordon's work has not been appreciated as much as it ought to be, as "compared to the lively admiration which has greeted the efforts of some other Southern women writers." Koch indicates that for a writer of her sex, Gordon is, to be sure, quite good, her prose perhaps "the most unaffected [of] . . . any American woman today" (325–26). The accomplishments, themes, and styles of the white male artists are taken as the standard, and the writings of the women are seen as an inferior strain.

A particularly outrageous example of this attitude appears in a review of Eudora Welty's fiction, published as recently as 1970 in *The Saturday Review.* The reviewer, noted critic John W. Aldridge, argues that in her early writing Welty was a little too precious or ladylike to be taken seriously. She lacked the sweep and mythic largeness of her fellow Mississippian William Faulkner, having "limit[ed] her own creative interests to the minor and peripheral." The result, Aldridge says, was that Welty seemed destined to remain the "most important minor female writer of fiction to come out of the South in the last thirty years." But, then, in 1970, Welty had dropped her long novel *Losing Battles* on the world, and Aldridge could now see her as capable of standing with the boys. Rather than implicitly condemning her with adjectives conventionally associated with women, he now praises her with adjectives conventionally seen as masculine: "She has ceased to be narrow and meticulous and become wide-ranging. . . . She has broken away from those patterns of response which made her too easily identifiable as a Southern lady writer, and has become simply—in the best sense—a writer" (22–23).

The prejudice against a so-called feminine style and interests of female writers that such examples illustrate has had serious consequences. The prejudice has, I submit, significantly affected the theoretical framework critics have created for the Southern Renaissance and hence has influenced the very way we think about and teach Southern literature. In looking for origins, causes, and major themes, scholars have tended to focus chiefly on the works of white male artists and to discount the contributions of women and blacks. Linking the origins of the Southern Renaissance to tensions in the South that surfaced after World War I, the commentators have identified certain cultural issues as central to the renaissance, issues they locate chiefly in the works of white males. The scant attention they give the women implies that they find the women not much interested in such weighty matters and thus as standing outside the mainstream of Southern literature.

Richard H. King's book *A Southern Renaissance: The Cultural Awakening of the South, 1930–1955,* published in 1980 by Oxford University Press, illustrates this pattern but with more gall than most. For King doesn't just slight the women; he blatantly excludes from his study all black writers and virtually all female writers, including Welty, Carson McCullers, Katherine Anne Porter, and Flannery O'Connor. He excludes the women, he explains, because he finds "they were not concerned primarily with the larger cultural, racial, and political themes that I take as my focus." They did not, he adds, "place the region at the center of their imaginative visions" (8–9).

Is this view, expressed straightforwardly here by King and hinted at by others, correct? Have the women in fact ignored the so-called larger cultural, racial, and political themes? Are their works—whatever their themes—less interesting and less significant to an understanding of the Southern culture, less in the mainstream of Southern literature, than those of the white male writers? I think these questions must, first of all, provoke a series of questions in reply. We need to ask: whose place is it to determine what are the so-called *larger* themes? Who decides what works are major and minor, who defines the canon?

During the last two decades, such questions have been raised by feminists and other revisionists about accepted truths of other literary canons. And the answer they have discovered with regard to those canons applies here as well: our perceptions of Southern writing and Southern writers have been shaped chiefly by white male academics. M. Thomas Inge's survey of the study of Southern literature in *The History of Southern Literature* supports this point. Of the numerous nineteenth- and twentieth-century anthologies of Southern literature and book-length studies Inge surveys, seventy-nine were written or edited by men, whereas only nine were written or edited by women. And all nine of the people Inge lists as the most influential of the modern critics are males. As a further example, in late 1972 the University of North Carolina at Chapel Hill assembled twenty-six "leading scholars," all men, for a three-day conference to discuss "problems, possibilities, and future directions in Southern literary study" (Rubin and Holman x).

As Louis Rubin explains after thanking twenty-two fellow male scholars in the preface to his 1979 anthology of Southern literature, "For in general the study of Southern literature has largely involved a community of scholars and gentlemen who are friends and fellow workers" (*The Literary South* vi).

These shapers of our perceptions of Southern literature—many of them Southern gentlemen—have not at all neglected the ladies. They have befriended them, aided them in getting published, praised their works. Judicious scholars, they appreciate the individual writer, male or female, and they write brilliantly about the individual work, whether its author is male or female. It is ironic, then, that in creating a framework for discussion of the Southern Renaissance, they *have* frequently unconsciously forgotten the women, or, in some cases, consciously excepted them from study. The scholars who have asserted that the Southern Renaissance ended or diminished following World War II because the major writers had died or their best work was behind them certainly ignore the continuing vitality of a Eudora Welty (see, for example, Sullivan). So does the critic who in 1977 lamented that there is no Southern writer today "to challenge comparison with Faulkner, or even Thomas Wolfe and Robert Penn Warren" (Gray 265). Even the best of scholars is guilty of forgetfulness. In an essay published in 1961, Rubin clearly forgot that some of the writers were female when he wrote that "change . . . was the keynote of Southern life when the writers of the Southern Renaissance were growing to manhood" ("Southern Literature" 34).

For a fuller example, let me return to Richard H. King's book on the Southern Renaissance. King describes the Southern Renaissance as an attempt by Southerners "to come to terms not only with the inherited values of the Southern tradition but also with a certain way of perceiving and dealing with the past." He adds that the writers were exploring "a tradition whose essential figures were the father and the grandfather and whose essential structure was the literal and symbolic family." Summarizing, he explains that the writers were seeking "to come to terms with what I call the 'Southern family romance.'" Through their efforts, "the Southern tradition was not only raised to awareness, it was also progressively demystified and rejected." According to King, with the exception of Lillian Smith, the female writers did not concern themselves with this theme and effort (7–8).

I think King is dead wrong here. Indeed, the very women he apologizes for excluding prove him wrong. As a careful reading of their works should reveal—and as recent scholarship surely suggests[2]—no one treats the Southern family romance more incisively than do Ellen

Glasgow in *The Sheltered Life,* Porter in *Old Mortality,* and Welty in a range of works but most notably in *Delta Wedding, The Golden Apples,* and *Losing Battles.* In these works the writers have (to borrow King's own words) "come to terms not only with the inherited values of the Southern tradition but also with a certain way of perceiving and dealing with the past." In sum, all three writers progressively demystify the Southern family romance and hence the Southern tradition; and in doing so, Welty, for one, undermines the male hero figure, whether his role in the family is as father, grandfather, brother, or husband (Manning chaps. 5–7 and 9).

Why or how has King overlooked or rejected the contributions of the women writers to his very theme? The explanation may lie in the way he has defined his theme. By defining the Southern family romance through the figures of the father and grandfather only, King has ignored fully one half of the Southern family romance itself; for the Southern woman is as essential to that romance as the Southern man. And just as the male writer, and critic, might tend to be obsessed with the father and grandfather figures, so is it natural for the female writer to react particularly to the dominant female images—to the mother and the grandmother, yes, but especially to the Southern belle, the Southern lady, the enduring mammy—and to the society's expectations of Southern womanhood.

This latter assumption is supported in recent scholarship by a few feminists who have brought a fresh perspective to the writings of Southern women. They are beginning to uncover a neglected tradition and theme in Southern literature. In *Tomorrow Is Another Day: The Woman Writer in the South, 1859–1936* (1981), Anne Goodwyn Jones argues that for seven white Southern women who wrote before the Southern Literary Renaissance, writing was a means of coming to terms with their experience as Southern women. In *Sacred Groves and Ravaged Gardens: The Fiction of Eudora Welty, Carson McCullers, and Flannery O'Connor* (1985), Louise Westling finds in the three writers' fiction the suggestion of a "distinctively feminine literary tradition" deriving from the authors' observations about women in the Southern society. Other scholars are adding to these investigations, including several with articles in the present volume that examine the ambivalence women authors have expressed, and women characters have exhibited, about their experience of growing up female in the South. Taken as a whole, the articles in this volume counter the orthodoxy's marginalizing of women writers' contributions to the Southern literary tradition.

Such feminist challenges suggest that a new day is dawning in the South. It is dawning, in fact, with such conviction that an establishment long deaf to rumblings from the hinterlands has begun to stir. In recent essays, C. Hugh Holman and Louis D. Rubin, two of the most prominent authors of the traditional interpretation of Southern literature, admit that the established views of Southern literature have been short-sighted and blind-sided, and they welcome the challenges to those views that "the structuralists and semiotics, . . . the feminists, and . . . the students of black culture" are bringing (Holman xviii). Confessing the sins of the fathers of Southern literary criticism, Holman writes in "No More Monoliths, Please: Continuities in the Multi-Souths" (1983):

> Most of us, by omitting a little that cannot be made to fit, selecting from the rest rather carefully, and, like Procrustes, fitting what we select to our particular narrow beds, arrive at conveniently simple answers to the question of what southern literature is all about. The result is usually a schema in which a sentimentalized version of Scott was used defensively in the antebellum period, an exploitative local colorism dominated the postbellum period, and a glorious, even sacramental, agrarianism illuminates the twentieth century. (xiv)

In "Of Literature and Yams" (1988), Rubin echoes Holman: "The bane of so much Southern literary scholarship has been cultural oversimplification. The South has been *this*, or *that*, and no other. Its literature is therefore supposed to exemplify the monolith. To study it has been to work at demonstrating that the monolith exists" (14). Holman encourages scholars to open their eyes and their minds, to recognize that "the cliches about southern writing, however skillfully presented, leave out aspects which we ignore at the peril of misunderstanding our subject matter" (xv).

Such words from two of the custodians of the traditional view are encouraging indeed. They leave quite a different impression from that evoked by Rubin in the preface to a book published only a few years earlier. Near the end of his preface to *A Gallery of Southerners* (1982), Rubin writes with seemingly amused surprise about his recognition that "the academic southern literature community" is a close group and, he admits some will think, a closed group:

> That is, almost all the more active participants tend to be personal as well as professional friends, to seek out each other's company, to share numerous interests that go beyond their common intellectual concerns, and to spend much of their time talking to each other about sports, outdoors activities, and the like. I had not thought of it that way, but upon reflection it is quite true. They do tend to think of themselves as a group; and in the way they go about things I suppose there is something resembling a coterie . . . . To an outsider I have no doubt that it has its aspects of smugness, even

clannishness; an unkind soul might even grumble about an establishment. But it does exist. Not only that, but it flourishes. What strikes me
about it is that it is really quite self-contained. One may call it insular, self-
congratulatory, pretentious if one likes, but it is an old southern custom. (xv)

We can admire and profit from the many contributions this orthodoxy has made to the study of Southern literature, at the same time that
we recognize—with the awakening Holman and Rubin—that much
remains to be discovered and to be said. Yesterday was another day;
fortunately tomorrow is with us now.

NOTES

Much of my work on this book was made possible by faculty development
grants from Mary Washington College and two resident fellowships from the
Virginia Center for the Humanities. I am grateful for the assistance.

1. Journals and diaries have long been included in the literary canons for
past eras, such as the American Colonial period, but those from the nineteenth
century and afterward have, until recently, been oddly ignored.
2. See, for example, Randisi, *Tissue of Lies;* Seidel, *The Southern Belle in the
American Novel* (1985); Prenshaw's and Schulz's articles in the present volume,
each of which covers a number of writers; and Manning, *With Ears Opening
Like Morning Glories.*

WORKS CITED

Aldridge, John W. "Eudora Welty: Metamorphosis of a Southern Lady Writer."
    Saturday Review. 11 April 1970: 21–23, 35–36.
Beatty, Richard Croom et al., eds. *The Literature of the South.* Chicago: Scott,
    Foresman, 1952.
Bryan, Mary E. "How Should Women Write?" In *The Living Female Writers of
    the South.* Ed. Mary Tardy. Philadelphia: Claxon, Rensen, and Haffelfinger,
    1872. 335–39.
Davidson, James Wood. *The Living Writers of the South.* New York: Carleton,
    1869.
Forest, Mary, ed. *Women of the South Distinguished in Literature.* New York:
    Charles B. Richardson, 1865.
Gray, Richard. *The Literature of Memory: Modern Writers of the American
    South.* Baltimore: Johns Hopkins University Press, 1977.
Guilds, John Caldwell, ed. *Nineteenth-Century Southern Fiction.* Columbus:
    Charles E. Merrill, 1970.
Gwin, Minrose C. *Black and White Women of the Old South: The Peculiar Sister-
    hood in American Literature.* Knoxville: University of Tennessee Press, 1985.

Hardy, John Edward. "Ellen Glasgow." In *Southern Renaissance: The Literature of the Modern South.* Ed. Louis D. Rubin, Jr., and Robert D. Jacobs. Baltimore: Johns Hopkins University Press, 1953. 236–50.

Holman, C. Hugh. "No More Monoliths, Please: Continuities in the Multi-Souths." In *Southern Literature in Transition: Heritage and Promise.* Ed. Philip Castille and William Osborne. Memphis: Memphis State University Press, 1983. xiii–xxiv.

Hubbell, Jay B. *The South in American Literature, 1607–1900.* Durham: Duke University Press, 1954.

Inge, M. Thomas. Appendix A: "The Study of Southern Literature." Rubin et al., eds., *The History of Southern Literature* 589–99.

Jones, Anne Goodwyn. *Tomorrow Is Another Day: The Woman Writer in the South, 1859–1936.* Baton Rouge: Louisiana State University Press, 1981.

King, Richard H. *A Southern Renaissance: The Cultural Awakening of the American South, 1930–1955.* New York: Oxford University Press, 1980.

Koch, Vivienne. "The Conservatism of Caroline Gordon." In *Southern Renascence: The Literature of the Modern South.* Ed. Louis D. Rubin, Jr., and Robert D. Jacobs. Baltimore: Johns Hopkins University Press, 1953. 325–37.

Lauter, Paul. "Race and Gender in the Shaping of the American Literary Canon: A Case Study from the Twenties." *Feminist Studies* 9 (Fall 1983): 435–63.

Manning, Carol S. *With Ears Opening Like Morning Glories: Eudora Welty and the Love of Storytelling.* Westport, Conn.: Greenwood Press, 1985.

Orgain, Kate Alma, ed. *Southern Authors in Poetry and Prose.* New York: Neale Publishing, 1908.

Prenshaw, Peggy Whitman, ed. *Women of the Contemporary South.* Jackson: University Press of Mississippi, 1984. (Largely from the summer and fall 1983 issues of *Southern Quarterly*).

Randisi, Jennifer Lynn. *A Tissue of Lies: Eudora Welty and the Southern Romance.* Washington: University Press of America, 1982.

Rubin, Louis D., Jr. *A Gallery of Southerners.* Baton Rouge: Louisiana State University Press, 1982.

——— ed. *The Literary South.* New York: John Wiley and Sons, 1979.

———. "Of Literature and Yams." *The Southern Literary Journal* 20 (Spring 1988): 12–15.

———. "Southern Literature: The Historical Imagination." In *South: Modern Southern Literature in Its Cultural Setting.* Ed. Louis Rubin, Jr., and Robert D. Jacobs. Garden City, N.Y.: Doubleday, 1961. 29–47.

Rubin, Louis D., Jr., et al., eds. *The History of Southern Literature.* Baton Rouge: Louisiana State University Press, 1985.

Rubin, Louis D., Jr., and C. Hugh Holman, eds. *Southern Literary Study: Problems and Possibilities.* Proc. of a conference on Southern literature at the University of North Carolina, Chapel Hill. 30 Nov.–2 Dec. 1972. Chapel Hill: University of North Carolina Press, 1975.

Seidel, Kathryn Lee. *The Southern Belle in the American Novel.* Tampa: University of South Florida Press, 1985.

Shillingsburg, Miriam J. "The Ascent of Woman, Southern Style: Hentz, King, Chopin." In *Southern Literature in Transition.* Ed. Philip Castille and William Soborne. Memphis: Memphis State University Press, 1983. 127–40.

Sullivan, Walter. *A Requiem for the Renaissance: The State of Fiction in the Modern South.* Athens: University of Georgia Press, 1976.

Tardy, Mary T., ed. *The Living Female Writers of the South.* Philadelphia: Claxon, Rensen, and Haffelfinger, 1872.

Taylor, Helen. *Gender, Race, and Region in the Writings of Grace King, Ruth McEnery Stuart, and Kate Chopin.* Baton Rouge: Louisiana State University Press, 1989.

Westling, Louise. *Sacred Groves and Ravaged Gardens: The Fiction of Eudora Welty, Carson McCullers, and Flannery O'Connor.* Athens: University of Georgia Press, 1985.

1. Challenges

Thadious M. Davis

Women's Art and Authorship
in the Southern Region: Connections

Currently, the process of recovering "lost" or "forgotten" authors is often linked primarily to issues of canon formation. I am not only sympathetic to this reconstruction but also active in it. In the 1970s, I researched several mislaid authors of the American South—Anna Julia Cooper, an ex-slave from North Carolina; Harriet Suddoth, a pioneer from Virginia; and Mollie Moore Davis, an upper-class Anglo from Louisiana. More recently, I have begun to think that the process of *connection* is the work that needs emphasis in the current paradigm of search and recovery. The work of connection is, fortunately, beginning to take precedence, perhaps for the obvious reason: now at least some of the lost or forgotten authors are more familiar names to scholars and students of American literature. This attention to connection, to exploring literary links and intertextuality and to formulating critical patterns, may be one major phase of scholarly work in the next decade.

I think of connection as another way of expressing what in *One Writer's Beginnings* Eudora Welty has termed "confluence": "our inward journey," she tells us, "leads us through time—forward or back, seldom in a straight line, most often spiraling. . . . As we discover, we remember; remembering, we discover; and most intensely do we experience this when our separate journeys converge." Confluence, she suggests, "exists as a reality and a symbol in one. . . . testifying to the pattern . . . of human experience" (102). Alice Walker, in "Saving the Life that is Your Own, puts it another way: "What is always needed," she says, "in . . . art, or life, is the larger perspective. Connections made, or at least attempted, where none existed before, the straining to encompass in one's glance at the varied world the common thread . . . through immense diversity, a fearlessness of growth . . . of looking that enlarges the private and the public world" (5). I take the work of connection, of what might be called literary confluence, to be a healthy sign, particularly at a time when some critics and theorists have somehow narrowed, perhaps unintentionally, the body of texts and authors for critical discussion, even while simultaneously they have supported the expansion of an American canon.

In discoursing on "Women's Art and Authorship in the Southern Region," I would like to pose as my subtext the significance of connection, especially for the larger work of sustaining our literature in both writing and teaching, in theory and application. If authors are uncovered or recovered and simply left in virtual isolation from discourses on theory, discussions of movements, trends, patterns, schools, traditions, and so forth, then in the next century they could well return to the ranks of the dead, buried, and ignored. And this prospect of augmenting the list of "also rans" is not what the enormous effort at canon formation is ultimately all about.

In the literature of the American South, for example, it has primarily been in the modern period that Louis D. Rubin, Jr., has termed the Southern Renascence that female authors have been treated in the context of the literary landscape, of larger movements, patterns, and other authors, whether in harmony or discord with them. The case of nineteenth-century female authors has begun to improve in recent years. For example, increasing attention to Kate Chopin, thanks to the research of Emily Toth, Barbara Ewell and others, to Augusta Jane King, in books such as Anne Goodwyn Jones's *Tomorrow Is Another Day*, and to other writers means not only that these women authors are better known but also that the way in which they fit into or relate to literary studies (women's, cultural, historical, regional, theoretical) is also becoming known. Yet nineteenth-century women such as Harriet Suddoth, whose writing appears under the name "Lumina Silvervale" and who has little chance of becoming a major author even after we know her name, can shed light on Southern literature, for instance, on the literature of westering experience, pioneering in the nineteenth-century South, women and education and careers, property and income, class and position, on the construction of culture and ideology—light that might prevent us from overextending a view of the Southern lady as the primary way of accessing relationships among female authors and of connecting their concerns to one another, and to those of male authors or to the more familiar readings of literature termed "culturally significant."

Few readers of the literature of the American South will recognize the name Lumina Silvervale, though many might immediately perceive it to be a pseudonym. As the pseudonymous identity of Harriet Almaria Baker Suddoth, author of *An Orphan of the Old Dominion: Her Trials and Travels, Embracing A History of Her Life Taken Principally from Her Journals and Letters* (1873), Lumina Silvervale has become for me a metaphor for the creative work of women writers in the American South and for the critical work needed to study and to reclaim those writers.

In the late 1970s, I set out to research Suddoth's life and career for the Frederick Ungar American Women Writers series. After months of work, I could find nothing other than the one book, *An Orphan of the Old Dominion;* nevertheless, I completed an essay designed for a text collecting critical information about both prominent and little-known women authors. The entry never appeared in print. Suddoth's lone book and shadowy life seemed somehow too insignificant even for the Ungar collection project. For years now, I have been troubled by the meaning and implication of that experience. Although the essay lay dormant, I did not completely forget it and, in fact, periodically searched for mentions of the author. She has not appeared, not even in the recent excellent bibliography *101 Virginia Women Writers;* nonetheless, I continue to think of her as significant in helping us to understand the function of writing in an "ordinary" Southern woman's life and the work of researching forgotten authors.

That Harriet Almaria Baker Suddoth, now a shadowy unlighted figure from the past, would choose "Lumina Silvervale" as a pseudonym seems ironically appropriate. "Lumina" not only derives from light but also refers symbolically to people as distinguished, glorious; "Silvervale," in one of its meanings, identifies a book or treatise describing trees of a certain area. Suddoth's choice of a name reveals an overarching sense of an identity and its function, which is primarily that of writer. Though she made no claims on writing as a profession for herself, in *An Orphan of the Old Dominion,* she set out to illuminate for others, and perhaps for herself as well, her formulative experiences. She presented them as a specific lived past that in total forged her character and her consciousness, and from the perspective of her present, the moment when she reflected and wrote, it seems that she used her experiences to validate her achieved identity and, importantly, its meaning.

In her title, *An Orphan of the Old Dominion: Her Trials and Travels, Embracing A History of Her Life Taken Principally from Her Journals and Letters,* and in her text itself, Suddoth assumes at once two important ideas: First, the writer herself is an independent, autonomous female, an "orphan," who has experienced both the private world of self, as well as its reflections in "trials," and the public world of others (places and people) in her "travels"; and second, as author she has a prerequisite background in writing itself to help assert her authority and control over the literary making of her "history." Her "journals," which are personal and private accounts, attest to her habit of observation and self-reflection, and her "letters," which are communal and public exchanges, document her practice of sharing and rendering.

The long autobiographical narrative traces the lives of Mary and Samuel Hobyn and their three children, Almaria, Willie, and Alonzo. While no specific dates or time references appear in the text, omissions that apparently are intended to expand the individual experiences to wide general applicability, the events begin before the Civil War when Mary Sterling, a girl not yet sixteen, marries Samuel Hobyn. After the war, the Hobyns leave the security of their Virginia birthplace for a homestead in Missouri. Their journey over the Virginia mountains westward to the south central region occupies the first third of the book and forms a detailed travelogue documenting landscapes, conditions, and accommodations, along with people. Here Suddoth's work forms a complement to those by writers such as Alice Carey, presented by Annette Kolodny in *The Land Before Her: Fantasy and Experience of the American Frontiers, 1630–1860* (1984), but there is a difference because Suddoth gives a portrait of westering that is exclusively Southern, as well as being specifically female. She renders what might be called the making of a Southern female pioneer; that is, for both Mary Sterling Hobyn and her daughter Almaria the experience of traveling for resettlement in the old Southwest challenges the more typical portraits of Southern females in a safe, sheltered domestic environment or in more familiar environs transfigured by war. Moreover, for Almaria the movement west is the start of a commitment to pioneering in a variety of modes.

Initially, the work appears intended as a memoir of the heroic and virtuous struggle of the Hobyns as pioneers in Alabama, Louisiana, and Arkansas. However, the central focus gradually shifts to their only daughter, Almaria, from whose perspective the third-person narrative is told. After mauraders murder her father and swindlers leave her mother destitute, she emerges as the main character. The narrative emphasis is neither a sentimental presentation of Southern life before the war nor a realistic account of the war years, nor yet a pre- and postwar comparison of life in the South, as is the case with works such as Sallie A. Putnam's *Richmond during the War: Four Years of Personal Observation* (1867), Judith W. McGuire's *Diary of a Southern Refugee during the War* (1867), Letitia M. Burwell's *A Girl's Life in Virginia before the War* (1895), or Constance Cary Harrison's *Recollections Grave and Gay* (1911).

The major portion of the book treats Almaria's efforts to overcome the sexism in her society, to receive an education, and to achieve her ambition of becoming a teacher-missionary. At first glance, this change of focus results in a disjointed narrative marred by a confusing sequential development; however, upon examination, it is immediately clear that the author is framing the contextual circumstances that made her "different" from many other females in her South, different especially in her dual ambition: to become more than literate, to be educated; and to travel and work in foreign lands. The desire for a formal education is the direct result of comprehending the meaning of her victimized mother's experiences, while that for travel is the indirect result of apprehending the varied configurations of the physical world, configurations imprinted in her earliest memories as freedom from the ordinary, the domestic, and the expected. Lumina Silvervale, then, would fit uneasily into the excellent study of the white woman writer in the South, *Tomorrow Is Another Day*, in which Jones rightly observes that the seven representative writers (Augusta Jane Evans, Grace King, Kate Chopin, Mary Johnston, Ellen Glasgow, Frances Newman, and Margaret Mitchell) "were raised to be southern ladies, physically pure, fragile and beautiful, socially dignified, clutivated and gracious, within the family sacrificial and submissive." Jones finds a source for these women's creativity in "the tension between the demands of this cultural image and their own human needs": "that tension is expressed thematically in their fiction, often as conflict between a public self and a private one, or in the image of veils and masks" (xi).

Examination of an author such as Harriet Suddoth, however, exhumes another portrait. One striking feature of Suddoth's work is the synthesis of her public and private being, her lack of veils and masks, despite her use of a pseudonym. In her unsentimental exposition of the victimization of women by male relatives who control their property, she questions both inheritance laws and family practice, especially the complicity of prosperous wives and daughters who ignore the mistreatment of their female relatives who, in the absence of fathers or husbands, must support themselves. Her societal and familial critiques are penetrating, revealing, and unflinching. These critiques strike a note of similarity with the slave narratives by black women such as Harriet Jacobs/Linda Brent's *Incidents in the Life of a Slave Girl* (1861), narratives that reveal the silent acquiescence of some mistresses to the male slaveowner's mistreatment of female slaves.

However, the structural form of *An Orphan of the Old Dominion* and its narrative insistence on telling one's own story, the truth of one's own life, are the aspects linking it more generally to the female slave narratives that came to prominence in the decade before the Civil War and that appeared periodically throughout the rest of the century. Among the best known today are those of Elizabeth Keckley, Silvia DuBois, and Susie King Taylor, whose slim volume, *Reminiscences of My Life in Camp with the U.S. 33rd Colored Troops, Late 1st South Carolina Volunteers* (1902), forms the working woman's counterpart of Mary Chesnut's cultivated and crafted Civil War diaries, *A Diary from Dixie* (1905), and C. Vann Woodward's massive edition *Mary Chesnut's Civil War* (1981). Suddoth's odyssey through unfamiliar and foreign territories also recalls *A Narrative of the Life and Travels of Mrs. Nancy Prince, Written by Herself* (1853). These texts speak to one another and perhaps take their authority to speak from the same sources. Further cross-racial study of the mid-nineteenth-century personal narrative and its fictional counterparts, in the manner of Minrose Gwin's *Black and White Women of the Old South* (1985), might prove particularly informative to a fuller picture of women and the South.

Suddoth treats Almaria's educational and missionary work in the context of her securing freedom from financial dependence upon her relatives. As a Christian missionary to China, Almaria endures illness and hardship, but she is almost entirely independent. Her journal entries and letters from China do not reveal a religious zeal, such as that which marked the accounts of nineteenth-century black women from the South; for example, evangelist Sojourner Truth's 1850 biography, or the testimonies of black women preachers Amanda Berry Smith, Rebecca Cox Jackson, Jarena Lee, Zilpha Elam, and Julia Foote—all of whom emphasized God's providential assistance in their religious missions. Rather, Almaria's personal records reflect her secular and practical concerns with building a life for herself by establishing a school for girls. Her discourse on self and society, on autonomy and empowerment connects gender identity to both work and class issues in Southern writing. Essentially, Suddoth becomes an early Southern emigre, much like the twentieth-century women expatriates Evelyn Scott, Frances Newman, and Laura Riding, all of whom sought to make a hospitable home for their lives and work in other countries.

It almost seems as though Almaria is determined to have the young Chinese girls break out of the cycle denying them an education because she herself has suffered so much in her own efforts to become literate and pursue academic subjects. In the women she meets and the girls she teaches, she sees the poverty and male domination that shaped her own formative experiences. She transfers her own needs to her pupils, a characteristic that also marked *The Journal of Charlotte Forten: A Free*

Negro in the Slave Era, which covered the period between 1854 and 1864 when Forten taught at Port Royal, South Carolina.

To focus on *An Orphan of the Old Dominion* is not to suggest that it is a found literary masterpiece. To call attention to this 1873 work is to remember that even what might appear to be an ordinary life of an ordinary Southern woman in the second half of the nineteenth century has a unique value. And it is to call into question typologies that confine writers solely within controlling images such as the Southern lady, whether born or elevated to the pedestal, who is often embodied in the representative plantation mistress; or such as the slave woman, whether mammy, maid, temptress or mulatto, who is always eager to serve; or such as the perennial belle or complacent cracker. Though we know from excellent historical studies—Anne Firor Scott's seminal *Southern Lady: From Pedestal to Politics* (1970), Margaret Jarman Hagood's pioneering *Mothers of the South: Portraiture of the White Tenant Farm Woman* (1939), and Deborah Gray White's groundbreaking *Ar'n't I A Woman: Female Slaves in the Plantation South* (1985)—that such types did exist, we also know that women in the South were multifaceted, complex, living beings.

Suddoth provides a paradigm to challenge wholesale acceptance of stereotypical views collapsing Southern women into a few types. It may seem incredible that a small girl from Virginia had experienced not only the excitement and the danger of pioneering west, of traveling to Asia, but also the struggle for changes in the laws and customs affecting the female's right to property and to education. (It is the stuff of a Jane Fonda or Meryl Streep movie.) But what is even more significant is that Lumina Silvervale wrote her own story, and clearly believed in its value for others. What could have brought her to such a belief? Was she herself so different from other women of the American South who wrote for publication in the nineteenth century? Let me pose answers to these questions by surveying some of the writers and their processes that are related to Suddoth and her authorship.

The Southern literary culture that helped produce *An Orphan of the Old Dominion* was coming into an identity of its own in the 1830s and 1840s, much like the larger American literary scene. Although women had little direct access to publication, some women published their letters, journals and diaries. Virginia Randolph Cary, a Virginian, published her advice to women in *Letters on Female Character* (1828), and Eliza Wilkerson of Charleston published her *Letters* in 1839. In the decade between these two publications, as Southern periodicals were emerging mainly in the larger urban areas (Charleston, Richmond, Baltimore, or New Orleans, where Francophone women published in

French), another Charlestonian, Caroline Howard Gilman, founded
Rose Bud in 1832. She later transformed the children's magazine into
Southern Rose (1835), a magazine for adults. Gilman wrote both poetry
and prose, including stories and novels, which tended to assert themselves as "real life" experiences; for example, *Recollections of a Housekeeper* (1834) and *Recollections of a Southern Matron* (1837) both
privilege representations of Southern customs and manners in the experiences of a young girl growing up on a plantation, and were, as Craig
Werner points out, the first Southern fiction on that popular and
enduring theme that comes into maturity in the Civil War period (87),
and that continued in the twentieth-century with historical novels such
as *Gone With the Wind* (1936) by Margaret Mitchell and the *Beulah
Quintet* by Mary Lee Settle. Gilman's poem "Mary Anna Gibbes, the
Young Heroine of Stono, S.C." (1837) is similar to Wilkinson's account
in her letters in treating the Revolution and the late 1770s, yet rarely is
her expression connected with the historical romances of the Revolution,
such as those of William Gilmore Simms.

Although slave narratives began to appear with increasing frequency
in the 1840s, works by females in that form come to prominence nearly
twenty years later on the eve of the Civil War. Jacobs's well-crafted
Incidents in the Life of a Slave Girl, edited by Lydia Maria Child, has
retained interest for readers today, particularly because of its self-conscious
attention to the specific difficulties of the female under the double
bondage of race and sex in slavery. Jacobs's text unfolds in any reading
incorporating not only domestic fiction of the period but also William
Wells Brown's earlier novel of women and slavery, *Clotel* (1853). The
slave narratives, like the "real life" accounts of Gilman and Wilkerson,
resulted in a greater demand for such works, in an audience eager to
match its personal experiences and vision to those of others, and in
models for the writing of additional, comparable works.

In the 1850s, however, as domestic fiction by and about women
reached its peak in America with the phenomenal successes of Susan
Warner's *The Wide, Wide World* (1850), a novel of a young girl's
maturation and education, and Harriet Beecher Stowe's *Uncle Tom's
Cabin* (1852), a novel of social protest with women's culture and ways of
knowing at its center, women of the South were, like Stowe and Warner,
charting courses as professional authors who could best express the
concerns and interests and needs of women. Because of the limited
opportunities for female wage earners, the new market for books and the
possibility of a decent livelihood spurred women into authorship. One
of the most prolific and popular was Emma Dorothy Eliza Nevitee
(E.D.E.N.) Southworth, a Virginian who, after her divorce in 1849,

supported herself and her two children by writing fiction, the first of which, *Retribution,* was serialized in *National Era,* the same journal that had first published Stowe's *Uncle Tom's Cabin.* The Hidden Hand (1859) with its cross-dressing, irrepressible heroine, Capitola, was the most successful of her approximately fifty romantic novels set in Maryland and Virginia; it spawned numerous imitations of "Mad Cap," the heroine who goes from rags to riches but who in the process retains her individuality and her determination to stamp out conventional restrictions and irrational limitations on the female and her development, and who all the while exhibits amazingly good humor. Horatio Alger's *Ragged Dick* (1868) and *Struggling Upward* (1890) surely owe something to Cap and *The Hidden Hand,* as does Mark Twain's *Adventures of Huckleberry Finn* (1884). More relevant here is that Southworth demonstrates how significant the mid-century turning to professional authorship was for Southern women, because though it has often been said that the societal view of the Southern lady and the ideal of Southern womanhood are major forces in the works of Southern women writers, it should also be added, in light of Southworth's texts, that the earliest of the popular authors wrote frequently of independent single women and rebellious young women who have little patience with unreasonable convention and less with ill-suited domestic roles; and that they saw the emergence of fiction as a popular form as an opportunity for self-expression and for a new career option.

Interestingly, Caroline Lee Whiting Hentz, like Southworth, turned to authorship as a means of supporting her family, but unlike Southworth, she emphasized what might be called "sense and sensibility" after Jane Austen. Though born in Massachusetts, Hentz began writing in 1846, after twenty years in the South. Her most commercially successful novel was *Linda* (1850), but her best known today is the proslavery *The Planter's Northern Bride* (1854), which, though atypical of her fiction, was considered an effective answer to *Uncle Tom's Cabin* in its defense of the South and plea to the North.

Maria Jane McIntosh also chose writing as a profession in the 1840s after managing her family's plantation for twelve years, but unlike Southworth and Hentz, McIntosh was born wealthy in Georgia. Her move to New York in 1835 gave her the perspective that defines her fiction: the contrast between the South and the North, a perspective evident in her first book, *Woman as Enigma* (1843), but fully realized in books such as *Two Lives; or, To Seem and To Be* (1846) and *The Lofty and the Lowly; or, Good in All and None All-Good* (1853).

What these popular early writers—Southworth, Hentz, and McIntosh—share is an insistence on literary expression, the remembering and telling of the individual story and general stories of women from the woman's perspective and, most often, for an audience of women. They assume an authority over their craft and an autonomy in their identity as author. Even Lillian Smith, the Georgia-born author who in the twentieth century was perhaps as responsible as anyone for forwarding the notion of the tension in the life of Southern women as an impetus for writing, has also said: "As is true of any writing that comes out of one's existence, the experiences themselves were transformed during the act of writing by awareness of new meanings which settled on them. . . . the writer transcends her material in the act of looking at it, and since part of that material is herself, a metamorphosis takes place: *something happens within;* a new chaos, and then slowly, a new being" (Foreword, *Killers of the Dream* 14).

While it may no longer be possible to determine what happened *within* Smith's female literary ancestors, study of Southern women's access to publishing houses in the North and to publishing outlets in the South, both private printers and small magazines, along with study of book circulation, such as the phenomenal dime novel, in the South might provide more information about sources, influences, incentives, authority as impetus for the Lumina Silvervales, the more shadowy Southern women, who became authors in the middle of the century. Because of the critical work on American domestic fiction, particularly Nina Baym's *Women's Fiction: A Guide to Novels By and About Women in America, 1820–1870* (1978), names such as Southworth, McIntosh, Hentz, Evans Wilson, and so on have become familiar to a new generation of readers; however, comparable systematic study specifically of Southern women's fiction during the period remains to be done.

If, for example, Augusta Jane Evans Wilson's novel *St. Elmo* (1866) were positioned next to Eudora Welty's *Ponder Heart* (1954), it might reveal added dimensions of Welty's thematic concerns and literary foremothers that she may have forgotten or neglected to tell us. Not by coincidence do the two texts share a heroine named Edna Earle and inscriptions of sexual anxiety. Welty's Edna Earle Ponder, incidentally, runs the Beulah Hotel, which is perhaps a chance naming, but speculation about the text within the text might be appropriate because of the encoding of Evans Wilson's *Beulah,* an 1859 novel. Welty's matrilineal heritage has yet to be identified, yet it is significant for the understanding of her consciousness of gender issues embedded in naming in her texts and for unknotting the theoretical underpinnings of sexuality and authority in those texts. (The difficulty of reading Welty's more oblique gender-specific references has led Carolyn Heilbrun in *Writing A*

Woman's Life [1988] to dismiss and misread the feminism of Welty's *One Writer's Beginnings.*)

While all of American literature experienced a renewed flowering during the period following the Civil War, the literature of women in the American South blossomed profusely. The tradition of eyewitness accounts flourished in local color writings. Local color, as Merrill Maguire Skaggs has observed, has "been used to denigrate the exceptional fiction of . . . twentieth-century women," perhaps because beginning in the nineteenth century, a great number of those writing it had been female (219).

Perhaps no place in the South was as prolific in this fictional genre as Louisiana, distinct in the nation and region because of its mixtures of heritages. Kate Chopin, Grace King, Ruth McEnery Stuart are the writers who mined the Louisiana experience and have already been rediscovered. But they were not the only women who achieved status as writers of Louisiana local color. The black writer Alice Dunbar-Nelson did as well with her two volumes of Creole stories. She too has begun to receive serious attention. One who has not is Mollie Moore Davis, a popular poet, novelist, and playwright from Alabama who spent the Civil War years in Texas but lived in the New Orleans French Quarter from 1880 until her death in 1909. Davis, an upper-class Anglo in Creole society, wrote about rural Texas folk, Louisiana Creoles and Cajuns (much like Chopin and Dunbar-Nelson), and plantation blacks. Her earliest book was the 1867 *Minding the Gap and Other Poems,* but in the 1880s her major genre was fiction, with *In War Times at La Rose Blanche* (1888), a semiautobiographical story sequence, being her best-known work, and *Under the Man-Fig* (1895), a Southwestern mystery, being her most fully realized novel. (All of her novels were published by a major Boston and New York company, Houghton Mifflin.) Her Creole stories and novels, *The Little Chevalier* (1903) and *The Price of Silence* (1907), merit reading and comparative treatment with those of King, Stuart, Chopin, and Dunbar-Nelson, and perhaps also George Washington Cable; her Texas stories might be read informatively with Evans Wilson's *Inez: A Tale of the Alamo* (1855).

But perhaps it is in her parlor plays, written for performance in her home and published in the *Saturday Evening Post* between 1899 and 1901 and reissued as performance pamphlets in 1907, that Davis illustrates the diversity of early Southern women writers and reminds us that Lula Vollmer, Lynn Riggs, Georgia Douglas Johnson, Zora Neale Hurston, Lillian Hellman, and Beth Henley had Southern dramatist foremothers, and also that the South long had drama included in its representative forms of writing. Parlor plays among the upper classes, like church pageants among the lower, were primarily written by women, both black and white. Of Davis's six published plays, several are of particular thematic interest: *The New System,* for its broad satire of a complete reversal of sex roles; *His Lordship,* for its attack on class pretensiousness; and *A Dress Rehearsal,* for its intricate play-within-a-play motif. More research into the public theatre and private performance of plays in the South, as well as of the publication of plays by women, may yield a different view of the place of drama in the cultural and literary history of the region, and may provide a way of further unearthing and documenting women's noncanonical, literary art in the South.

Let me illustrate one connection between creativity and recovery that is evident today. In 1892, Anna Julia Cooper, a black woman from North Carolina, recognized what she called the "muffled strain" in literature, the "mute . . . voiceless Black Woman of America." Cooper's book, *A Voice from the South by a Black Woman of the South,* identified the historical and social causes of the black woman's silence, and it attempted to rectify the condition by giving voice to the black woman's ideas and perspectives. At the end of the nineteenth century, Anna Julia Cooper did not receive attention; her message, though delivered in clear, intelligent, and forceful terms, did little to awaken interest in the lives and work of black women.

Yet Cooper, born a slave in Wake County, North Carolina, in 1858, remained determined to speak out. She followed in the path established by slave women such as Harriet Tubman, Ellen Craft, and Elizabeth Keckley, and continued by Northern-born free women such as Maria W. Stewart, Frances Watkins Harper and Charlotte Forten Grimké, all of whom spoke of their own lives, as well as of the lives of other blacks, and with the exception of Tubman, also wrote their stories. Like them, Cooper compiled an impressive record of addressing the position of women in America, both through her writings and her own life.

Though she herself was not a victim of silence, Cooper was relatively unknown a few decades ago. Fortunately, however, her book *A Voice from the South* was reprinted in 1969, and is available to contemporary readers. Historians Sharon Harley and Gerda Lerner committed themselves in the 1970s to drawing attention to Cooper and the meaning of her life and work. By 1981, the Smithsonian had published *Anna Julia Cooper,* a two-hundred-page book by Louise Daniel Hutchinson. Through these efforts Cooper's voice has been preserved for today and for the future: "The colored woman of to-day occupies . . . a unique position in this country. . . . She is confronted by both a woman question and a race problem" (134):

But no woman can possibly put herself or her sex outside of the interests that affect humanity. All departments in the new era are to be hers, in the sense that her interests are in all and through all; and it is incumbent on her to keep intelligently and sympathetically *en rapport* with all the great moments of her time.... In her hands must be moulded the strength, the wit, the statesmanship, the morality, all the psychic force, the social and economic intercourse of that era. To be alive at such an epoch is a privilege, to be a woman then is sublime....

But to be a woman of the Negro race in America, and to be able to grasp the deep significance of the possibilities ... is to have a heritage ... unique in the ages. (143–44)

Cooper's vision and literary articulation of that vision, then, inspired others to reclaim her life and work out of a buried corner of the past. These conjoined activities, those of the visionary foremother and those of the literary daughters reclaiming her, seem representative of much of the work underway and remaining in Southern American literature today.

In our own time, Alice Walker has portrayed the innovative ways in which silent African American women, artists by inclination and temperament, have expressed their creativity in environments inhospitable to their producing more traditional forms of art. Walker's now classic essay, "In Search of Our Mothers' Gardens," first published in 1974, asks the question, "What did it mean for a black woman to be an artist in our grandmothers' and great-grandmothers' day?" She believes that "It is a question with an answer cruel enough to stop the blood" (233).

A native of rural Georgia, Walker recounts the stories of her own mother, working among her flowers, and of other women, quilting, gardening, and even cleaning, who created art out of the ordinary fabric and duties of their lives. Even more than Anna Julia Cooper, Alice Walker celebrates the creativity of working-class black women. Her poem, "They Were Women Then," included in the essay and in her poetry volume *Revolutionary Petunias,* is a testimony to those earlier women, often illiterate, and to Walker herself, their literate and literary daughter.

Importantly, Walker has written her own stories, but in those works she has also recorded the sounds of women in the modern world, often in the language of Southern blacks, and she has recorded as well messages from a cultural past, the expressions of earlier artists. In this regard, she is akin to her fellow poet and novelist Margaret Walker, who paid tribute to Southern blacks in her 1942 volume of poems, *For My People,* and in the process celebrated her roots "deep in Southern life" and her "grandmothers ... strong ... full of memories," both of which culminated in her historical novel *Jublilee* (1966), dedicated to the memory of grandmothers, one of whom was her maternal great-grandmother, Margaret Duggans Ware Brown, whose story of enslavement she told in *Jubliee.*

Alice Walker, who calls herself a "womanist" while insisting on her Southern identity, is better known than Margaret Walker for her contributions to reclaiming the voices and lives of women artists. One of her earliest stories, "The Revenge of Hannah Kemhuff," was inspired not only by one of her mother's oral tales but also by the short fiction of Flannery O'Connor and the folklore collections of Zora Neale Hurston, who reached across race and class and time to influence Walker. In her essay "Saving the Life That Is Your Own," she has said of writing "The Revenge of Hannah Kemhuff": "I gathered up the historical and psychological threads of the life my ancestors lived, and in the writing . . . I felt joy and strength and my own continuity. I had that wonderful feeling writers get sometimes . . . of being *with* a great many people, ancient spirits, all very happy to see me consulting and acknowledging them, and eager to let me know, through the joy of their presence, that, indeed, I am not alone" (13).

Walker's search for the grave of one of her models, Zora Neale Hurston, a gifted writer who died penniless in a Florida welfare home, resulted in a moving essay that helped to rekindle interest in Hurston's works, especially in her 1937 novel *Their Eyes Were Watching God.* Janie, Hurston's heroine, is one of the most memorable Southern female fictional creations because she grows and develops into a truly sensitive woman who understands, loves, and accepts herself and who refuses to be limited by the restrictions her grandmother, her three husbands, and her community attempt to place on her. " 'You sho loves to tell me whut to do, but Ah can't tell you nothin' Ah see!' " Janie remarks to her second husband Joe, who answers, " 'It would be pitiful if I didn't. Somebody got to think for women and chillun and chickens and cows' " (110).

Janie emerges from silence to become one of the "wide picture talkers" in the process of telling and assuming narrative control over her story. One of her first steps is announcing to the men folk: " 'Sometimes God gets familiar wid us womenfolks too and talks His inside business. He told me how surprised He was 'bout y'all turning out so smart after Him makin' yuh different; and how surprised y'all is goin' tuh be if you ever find out you don't know half as much 'bout us as you think you do' " (117).

Through Janie's development and maturation from a child who cannot recognize her black self in a photograph to a woman who achieves a synthesis of her racial and gender identity, Hurston expresses what she had learned of Southern black folk life and female heritage. Janie realizes that male domination exists in a world in which only men sit on the porch and swap tales, where men view their wives as property, but she also realizes that the freedom to speak, to express her own female self, is a way to achieve personhood and independence from subjugation. Telling is a way to achieve authority and autonomy, and it is a way to make peace with the past. " 'Lawd!' [Janie's friend] Phoebe breathed out heavily, 'Ah done growed ten feet higher from jus' listenin' tuh you, Janie' " (284).

Hurston's recognition of the power of language and speech, specifically in Southern voices and tales, is at the center of the work of a now forgotten white writer, Kathleen Moore Morehouse, from the same period in the 1930s. In an afterword to her novel *Rain on the Just* (1936), recommended by the Book-of-the-Month Club and nominated for a Pulitzer Prize, Morehouse says that she was fortunate to be "in the presence as talk was passed" on Brushy Mountain, North Carolina, where her "narrative grew from my looking and listening" (312). The result was the preservation of something of Appalachia, its people, their customs, and their voices; it is a fictional feat comparable to that of Elizabeth Madox Roberts, Julia Peterkin, Harriet Arnow, Mary Naoilles Murfree, Edith Summers Kelly, and Zora Neale Hurston for their particular regions of the South, and it is an important extension of the local color tradition into the twentieth century.

Decades later, though she was deprived of access to a Kathleen Moore Morehouse, Alice Walker grew just listening to Hurston's voice, and Janie's, which she heard as posing an optimistic counterpoint to situations comparable to turn-of-the-century Kate Chopin's Edna in *The Awakening* ("Saving the Life" 6). Walker celebrates Hurston's voice in a poem, "Janie Crawford" (from *Goodnight, Willie Lee, I'll See You In the Morning*), which begins, "I love the way Janie Crawford / left her husbands." Hurston, a sassy and irrepressibly black Southerner, would perhaps have loved the way Walker popularized *Their Eyes Were Watching God* as well as her other works of fiction, folklore, anthropology, and storytelling (or "lies" as Hurston often called her oral tales). In a sense, Hurston's commitment to telling and to writing may have stemmed from an incident in her Florida childhood when her mother, who had urged her to "jump at de sun" and "to have spirit" so that she would never become "a mealy mouthed rag doll," lay dying. Hurston presents the scene in her 1942 autobiography, *Dust Tracks on a Road:* "I thought that she looked to me. . . . Her mouth was slightly open, but her breathing took up so much of her strength that she could not talk. But she looked up at me, or so I felt, to speak for her. She depended on me for a voice" (87).

Just as the mother Lucy depended upon her daughter Zora for a voice, so in turn Zora, the speaker and teller, came at least metaphorically to depend upon her literary daughter Alice Walker for reclaiming that voice in an ever-widening sphere of matrilineal literary work that is both creative and critical. Study of such cross-generational influences in the writings of Southern women remains to be undertaken, just as literary relations between writers, especially those from different races and sections of the South, also need study. For example, the relationship between Hurston's rendering of black folk life and that of the white Pulitzer Prize winner Julia Peterkin has yet to be explored, despite the fact that the South Carolinian Peterkin was a major established author, widely read and well-respected among writers during the Harlem Renaissance of the 1920s when Hurston was a struggling beginning writer. Such a study might uncover the relation between the writings by women in the white Southern Renascence (Peterkin or poet Laura Riding, for instance) and by Southerners in the black Harlem Renaissance (Hurston or poet Anne Spencer, for example).

Three of Hurston's Southern writer-sisters during the Harlem Renaissances of the 1920s and 1930s, Angelina Grimké, Georgia Douglas Johnson, and Alice Dunbar-Nelson, are the subjects of Gloria Hull's biographical and critical book, *Color, Sex, and Poetry: Three Women Writers of the Harlem Renaissance* (1987), which reveals the struggle for self-expression and for a racial and sexual identity that characterized these early modernist writers. In the preface Hull states: "From the very beginning [of the research], I saw myself as writing a book for those who could care about these three women not only because of their unique personalities, but also because of what they represent: black women/writers struggling against unfavorable odds to create their personal and artistic selves. Amid the current black female literary renaissance, we are moved to reclaim foremothers for the lessons and blessings that they give us" (xi). Indeed, Hull, herself a Louisianian who worked on her project for ten years, exhibits the kind of commitment necessary to remind us that these African American women artists lived, wrote, and mattered; that though Grimké, Johnson and Dunbar-Nelson may not have been part of a white and male-defined tradition of letters, they were nonetheless writers compelled to write.

One of the three, Georgia Douglas Johnson, a native of Atlanta who spent most of her adult life in Washington, displayed a wisdom in her 1918 poem "The Heart of a Woman" that is akin to the kind of gender recognition that feminists currently explore:

The heart of a woman falls back on the night,
And enters some alien cage in its plight,
And tries to forget it has dreamed of the stars
While it breaks, breaks, breaks on the sheltering bars.

Johnson's poem, addressing the soaring potential and the entrapping reality of a woman's life, became an inspiration for the contemporary author from Stamps, Arkansas, Maya Angelou, who used the title for one of her books and in so doing not only acknowledged a literary forerunner but also reiterated one aspect of the literary work of women writers: reclaiming voice. Though Angelou was born poor in the rural South and Johnson was born into the urban Southern middle class, the two are intricately connected. In her own career Angelou has become one of America's leading autobiographers with a series of books revealing the plain fact that reflective self-expression is a human necessity. That fact is the one that Angelou's foremother Johnson revealed in a 1927 statement for *Opportunity* magazine: "I write because I love to write. . . . If I might ask of some fairy godmother special favors, one would sure to be for a clearing space, elbow room in which to think and write and live beyond the reach of the wolf's fingers. However, much that we do and write about comes just because of the daily struggle for bread and breath—so perhaps it's just as well" (204). Because she struggled unsuccessfully to earn a living as an author, a tone of resignation is in her voice, yet it is not a note of defeat. It is an admission of the realities affecting the artist and the creation of her art, but it is, as well, an affirmation of her will to write and to tell.

Those realities and that affirmation mark the work of Mary Helen Washington in *Invented Lives* (1987), which treats ten black women authors, the majority of whom are Southern, and provides excerpts from their writings. In her introduction, " 'The Darkened Eye Restored,' " Washington states: "If there is a single distinguishing feature of the literature of black women—and this accounts for their lack of recognition—it is this: their literature is about black women; it takes the trouble to record the thoughts, words, feelings, and deeds of black women, experiences that make the realities of being black in America look very different from what men have written" (xxvii). Her statement, minus the descriptive adjective "black," applies to Southern women writers in general who have given us vision of the world from, as Lillian Hellman put it, "another part of the forest."

Significantly, Washington's statement also returns us to Anna Julia Cooper. The title for her introduction, " 'The Darkened Eye Restored,' " is from *A Voice from the South*, from an analogy in which Cooper observes "that a world in which the female is made subordinate is like a body with one eye bandaged. When the bandage is removed, the body is filled with light: 'It sees a circle where before it saw a segment. The darkened eye restored, every member rejoices with it' " (Washington xxvii). This is, and has been, the literary work of Southern women—black and white, poor and affluent, rural and urban—restoring the light, telling that which illuminates, and rejoicing in that restoration, sharing that which is essential. "The making of a literary history [a cultural history] in which . . . women are fully represented is a search for full vision, to create a circle where now we have but a segment" (Washington xxvii).

I began with the idea of connection as confluence in Eudora Welty's formulation, and I would like to end with another statement from Welty, who divided her 1984 writer's autobiography into three chapters ("Listening," "Learning to See," and "Finding a Voice"), in which she reminds her readers of the artist as a student of listening, of hearing the voices of others and of the inward self; of the artist as a student of seeing, of viewing with external and internal eyes the world and its inhabitants. Welty concludes in *One Writer's Beginnings:*

> Of course the greatest confluence of all is that which makes up the human memory—the individual human memory. My own is the treasure most dearly regarded by me, in my life and in my work as a writer. Here time, also, is subject to confluence. The memory is a living thing—it too is in transit. But during its moment, all that is remembered joins, and lives—the old and the young, the past and the present, the living and the dead.
>
> As you have seen, I am a writer who came of a sheltered life. A sheltered life can be a daring life as well. For all serious daring starts from within. (104)

Her conclusion draws us together in a confluence of understanding and memory and meaning and writing. Without ever telling us so directly, Welty evokes in her final sentences her sister-writer and ancestor Ellen Glasgow of Richmond, Virginia, who in the preface to her 1938 novel, *The Sheltered Life,* looked back over her nearly forty years of writing and saw in her work a method of constant renewal. The method, Glasgow maintained, included three ruling principles, the most important being: "Always, as far as it is possible, endeavor to touch life on every side; but keep the central vision of the mind, the inmost light, untouched and untouchable" (xxii). For students and critics of women's writings in the American South interested in an expansive approach to the literature, one that neither flattens the "central vision" of the authors nor obscures the essential subjectivity, the differences of race, gender, class, and region, Glasgow's words might be taken to apply to connections, to touching life on every side. And Welty also suggests Lillian Smith, who said in 1962, as Jacquelyn Dowd Hall tells us in the preface to *Speaking for Ourselves: Women of the South* (1984), "the time has come . . . for women to risk the 'great and daring creative act' of discovering and articulating their own identities" (xi). The resonances exist between Welty and Glasgow and Smith, as well as Walker, whose notion of connections "made, or at least attempted, where none existed before," I mentioned in the beginning. These resonances of confluence and connection suggest that the known and unknown Southern female authors share with the shadowy Lumina Silvervale a conception of authorship and of art, and with these two the recurrent, and perhaps a "great," theme of self-expression as a means of survival within the physical world, of the necessary remembering and telling of one's own life and of the lives of comparable others as a process of psychic renewal in a spatially defined landscape, which Eudora Welty has named "place," which Zora Neale Hurston actualized as Eatonville, and which Margaret Mitchell immortalized as "Tara." The irony, of course, is that much of the self-expression so faithfully rendered for contemporary and future generations has been lost or, perhaps to put it more optimistically, mislaid. Or, perhaps there is another possibility, as Kathleen Moore Morehouse reminds us:

> If anybody reading thus far wonders if the verbal sticks and stones produced a novelist manque, the lack of time to push through the mechanics of writing is probably the final reason. . . . The business of life became more demanding. Apples and children don't just grow. . . . But I wrote [radio plays]—and I read and I wrote. Somewhere in our attic are three first-draft book-length manuscripts. (328–29)

In recovering, reclaiming, and connecting those voices that told of what it meant to be female, and by extension to be human, in the American South, in a particular concrete world, we may have to search Morehouse's symbolic attic. In the process, we need not "suffer from a common human tendency to seek the controlling unity, the essential principle, the shaping archetype," as C. Hugh Holman put it in admonishing us who in "a profoundly pluralistic world want to lay hands on the simple key" (xiii–xiv). There is no simple key. Unpacking the attic is cross-generational, cross-racial, cross-class or socioeconomic status, and even cross-regional in a distinctly multiregional, diverse South, as I have attempted to demonstrate here. But it is also dependent upon our knowledge that many Lumina Silvervales wrote, and their visions and voices bear meaning for Southern writing and writing Southern women.

NOTE

A different version of this article appears in *A New Perspective: Southern Women's Cultural History from the Civil War to Civil Rights,* edited by Priscilla Cortelyou Little and Robert C. Vaughan (Charlottesville: Virginia Foundation for the Humanities, 1989). Reprinted by permission.

WORKS CITED

Baym, Nina. *Women's Fiction: A Guide to Novels by and about Women in America, 1820–1870.* Ithaca: Cornell University Press, 1978.
Burwell, Letitia M. *A Girl's Life in Virginia before the War.* New York: Frederick A. Stokes, 1895.
Cary, Virginia Randolph. *Letters on Female Character.* 1828.
Cooper, Anna Julia. *A Voice from the South by a Black Woman of the South.* Xenia, Ohio: Aldine Printing House, 1892.
Davis, Mary [Mollie] Moore. *A Dress Rhearsal: Comedy for 4 Males and 4 Females.* 1907.
————. *His Lordship: Romantic Comedy for 5 Males and 6 Females.* 1907.
————. *Minding the Gap and Other Poems.* 1867.
————. *The New System: Comedy for 4 Males and 4 Females.* 1907.
————. *Under the Man-Fig.* Boston and New York: Houghton Mifflin, 1895.
————. *In War Times at La Rose Blanche.* 1888.
Forten, Charlotte. *The Journal of Charlotte Forten: A Free Slave in the Slave Era.* Ed. Ray Allen Billington. New York: W. W. Norton, 1953.
Gilman, Caroline Howard. "Mary Anna Gibbs, the Young Heroine of Stono, S.C." 1837.
————. *Recollections of a Housekeeper.* 1834.
————. *Recollections of a Southern Matron.* 1837.
Glasgow, Ellen. *The Sheltered Life.* 1932. New York: Hill and Wang, 1979.
Gwin, Minrose. *Black and White Women of the Old South: The Peculiar Sisterhood in American Literature.* Knoxville: University of Tennessee Press, 1985.
Hagood, Margaret Jarman. *Mothers of the South: Portraiture of the White Tenant Farm Woman.* 1939. New York: W. W. Norton, 1977.
Hall, Jaquelyn Dowd. Preface. *Speaking for Ourselves: Women of the South.* Ed. Maxine Alexander. New York: Pantheon Books, 1984.
Harrison, Constance Cary. *Recollections Grave and Gay.* New York: Scribner's, 1911.
Heilbrun, Carolyn G. *Writing a Woman's Life.* New York: W. W. Norton, 1988.
Hentz, Caroline Lee Whiting. *Linda.* 1850.
————. *The Planter's Northern Bride.* 1854.

Holman, C. Hugh. "No More Monoliths, Please: Continuities in the Multi-Souths." In *Southern Literature in Transition: Heritage and Promise.* Ed. Philip Castille and William Osborne. Memphis: Memphis State University Press, 1983. xiii–xxiv.

Hull, Gloria T. *Color, Sex, and Poetry: Three Women Writers of the Harlem Renaissance.* Bloomington: University of Indiana Press, 1987.

———. *Give Us Each Day: The Diary of Alice Dunbar-Nelson.* New York: W. W. Norton, 1984.

Hurston, Zora Neale. *Dust Tracks on a Road: An Autobiography.* 1942. Urbana: University of Illinois Press, 1984.

———. *Their Eyes Were Watching God.* 1937. Urbana: University of Illinois Press, 1978.

Hutchinson, Louise Daniel. *Anna Julia Cooper: A Voice from the South.* Washington: Smithsonian Institution Press, 1981.

Jacobs, Harriet Ann [Linda Brent]. *Incidents in the Life of a Slave Girl, Written by Herself.* Ed. Linda Maria Child. Boston: Published for the Author, 1861.

Johnson, Georgia Douglas. "The Contest Spotlight." *Opportunity* (June 1927): 204.

———. *The Heart of a Woman and Other Poems.* Boston: Cornhill Publishing, 1918.

Jones, Anne Goodwyn. *Tomorrow Is Another Day: The Woman Writer in the South, 1859–1936.* Baton Rouge: Louisiana State University Press, 1981.

Kolodny, Annette. *The Land Before Her: Fantasy and Experience of the American Frontiers, 1630–1860.* Chapel Hill: University of North Carolina Press, 1984.

McGuire, Judith W. *Diary of a Southern Refugee during the War.* 1867. New York: Arno, 1972.

McIntosh, Maria Jane. *The Lofty and the Lowly; or, Good in All and None All-Good.* 1853.

———. *Two Lives; or, To Seem and to Be.* 1846.

———. *Woman as Enigma.* 1843.

Morehouse, Kathleen Moore. *Rain on the Just.* 1936. Carbondale: Southern Illinois University Press, 1980.

Prince, Nancy. *A Narrative of the Life and Travels of Mrs. Nancy Prince, Written by Herself.* 1853.

Putnam, Sallie A. *Richmond during the War: Four Years of Personal Observation.* New York: Carleton, 1867.

Rubin, Louis D., Jr., et al., eds. *The History of Southern Literature.* Baton Rouge: Louisiana State University Press, 1985.

Scott, Anne Firor. *The Southern Lady: From Pedestal to Politics, 1830–1930.* Chicago: University of Chicago Press, 1970.

Skaggs, Merrill Maguire. "Varieties of Local Color." Rubin et al., *The History of Southern Literature* 219–27.

Smith, Amanda. *An Autobiography: The Story of the Lord's Dealings with Mrs. Amanda Smith, the Colored Evangelist.* Chicago: Meyer & Brother, 1893.

Smith, Lillian. *Killers of the Dream.* 1949; 1961. Rev. ed. New York: W. W. Norton, 1978.

Southworth, E. D. E. N. *The Hidden Hand.* 1859.

Suddoth, Harriet Almaria Baker [Lumina Silvervale]. *An Orphan of the Old Dominion: Her Trials and Travels, Embracing A History of Her Life Taken Principally from Her Journals and Letters.* 1873.

Taylor, Susie King. *Reminiscences of My Life in Camp with the 33rd U.S. Colored Troops, Late 1st Carolina Volunteers: A Black Woman's Civil War Memoirs.* 1902. Ed. Patricia W. Romero and Willie Lee Rose. New York: Markus Wiener, 1988.

Walker, Alice. "In Search of Our Mothers' Gardens." In *In Search of Our Mothers' Gardens: Womanist Prose.* New York: Harcourt Brace Jovanovich, 1983. 231–43.

———. "Saving the Life That Is Your Own: The Importance of Models in the Artist's Life." In *In Search of Our Mothers' Gardens.* New York: Harcourt Brace Jovanovich, 1983. 3–14.

Walker, Margaret. *Jubilee.* Boston: Houghton Mifflin, 1966.

Washington, Mary Helen, ed. *Invented Lives: Narratives of Black Women, 1860–1960.* New York: Anchor Press, 1987.

Welty, Eudora. *One Writer's Beginnings.* Cambridge: Harvard University Press, 1984.

Werner, Craig. "The Old South, 1815–1840." Rubin et al., *The History of Southern Literature.* 81–91.

White, Deborah Gray. *Ar'n't I a Woman: Female Slaves in the Plantation South.* New York: W. W. Norton, 1985.

Wilkerson, Elizabeth. *Letters.* 1838.

Wilson, Augusta Jane Evans. *Beulah.* 1859.

Woodward, C. Vann, ed. *Mary Chesnut's Civil War.* New Haven: Yale University Press, 1981.

Carol S. Manning

The Real Beginning of the Southern Renaissance

One of the more significant publications in the field of Southern literature from the last decade is *Faulkner and the Southern Renaissance*, the collected papers from the 1981 Faulkner conference at the University of Mississippi. According to the book's introduction, the goal of the conference was to initiate the process of formulating the history of the Southern Renaissance. The speakers addressed the questions "What is the Southern Renaissance? Why did it happen? And what role did William Faulkner play in its inception?" (Fowler vii). What is significant about this volume is not the questions posed, for they had been posed many times before; or the answers offered, for most of them had been offered before (and would be made definitive four years later in *The History of Southern Literature*, a monumental undertaking of the Society for the Study of Southern Literature). Rather, what is significant here is that with this text the critical theory on the Southern Renaissance was itself acknowledged as an established tradition. In the lead essay, "Framework of a Renaissance," Richard H. King traces developments in the critical theory, finding that between the mid-1940s and the early 1960s the Southern Renaissance was defined and a canon of texts and writers established. The reputations of the scholars who have chiefly shaped our thinking about Southern literature—Allen Tate, Hugh Holman, Louis D. Rubin, Jr., Lewis P. Simpson, to name a few—rival the reputations of many of the artists about whom they write. We might safely say that the critical theory on the Southern Renaissance has itself become part of the Southern Renaissance.

There is striking unanimity among the theorists regarding the renaissance's parameters. The Southern Renaissance is taken to be a flowering of literature that emerged following World War I in a previously artistically barren South, to have had the Fugitives and Agrarians at its head and William Faulkner at its center, and to have declined (or, according to some critics, died) after World War II.[1] As for what occasioned this literary flowering, Tate's much-quoted explanation is generally accepted and is the starting point for anyone who begs to differ: "With the war of 1914–1918, the South re-entered the world—but gave a backward glance as it slepped over the border: that backward glance gave us the Southern renascence, a literature conscious of the past in the present" (292). In this orthodox view, as a consequence of the experience of World War I, the Southerner became conscious of a disparity between the South's traditional values and values developing out of a modern industrialism. That tension between the old and the new inspired the Southern Renaissance. Simpson largely accepts Tate's account but places the renaissance in the context of a broader literary secession. After World War I, he says, Western civilization saw an "upsurge of literary and artistic activity" as persons of sensitivity and talent tried to come to terms with "the abyss" following from the war (231).

Discussions of the Southern Renaissance usually start with reference to the Fugitive and Agrarian groups at Nashville in the 1920s and 1930s. Richard Gray says that any account of modern Southern literature "must begin" with the writers at Nashville (40). Rubin calls Nashville "the ideological headquarters" for the renaissance ("Dixie Special" 65). And Simpson sees the Agrarian manifesto *I'll Take My Stand,* published in 1930, as "the public and formal announcement" of the renaissance (243).

This orthodox view of the Southern Renaissance—as bounded by two wars, quarterbacked by the Fugitives/Agrarians at Nashville, and inspired by the South's attempt to move forward while looking backward—is neat and convenient, but it is hardly realistic. Like most definitions of literary movements, it provides content for literary journals and coherence for college literature courses, but the dating is arbitrary and the described canon constricted. What it slights in particular is the work of blacks and women. Indeed, it is a decidedly white male-focused view of Southern literature, as Richard M. Weaver makes explicit in his rendition of the renaissance's beginning:

> [I]t was the first World War which gave the South an opportunity to break out of a vicious circle in which it had long moved. Its young men had attended the poverty-ridden institutions of their section, or they had gone North to school. . . . This great upheaval and its aftermath caused numbers of them to spend periods abroad [some as Rhodes scholars]. . . . Following such experience, it was only natural that these voyagers should return home determined to take a fresh look at their inheritance. . . . In

effect, they brought to their interpretation of the Southern past a new realism. (31–32)

Weaver presents the Southern Renaissance as arising from the experience of Southern men, obviously meaning a select few Southern men. When he adds that these "young men" began their careers as poets (32), we see that he, too, takes the Southern Renaissance to have originated with the Fugitives at Nashville.

Perhaps it is legitimate to define the Southern Renaissance as emerging in the aftermath of World War I if we acknowledge that we are describing the beginning of a modern literature by Southern white men. But some Southerners, Southern women in particular, began to awaken earlier. Frequently described as artists ahead of their time, Ellen Glasgow and Kate Chopin are the best known examples. Thomas Bonner, Jr., says that Chopin "speaks not for the past but to the present" through " 'modern' characters who frequently break the bounds of tradition for the demands of the moment" (141–42); and Rubin calls Glasgow "the first really modern Southern novelist, the pioneer" who, years before Faulkner, "did her best to write about Southern experience as she actually saw it, not as her neighbors thought she ought to see it" (Intro., *Ellen Glasgow* 4). C. Vann Woodward points out that Glasgow anticipated virtually every theme that would inspire " 'the bold moderns' " of the Southern Renaissance (cited by Rubin, Intro., *EG* 4).

Yet despite such acknowledgments of Chopin's and Glasgow's modernity, neither writer is generally identified with the Southern Renaissance. Chopin is never even considered a candidate because her works predate the accepted time frame. But Glasgow, along with her contemporary in Richmond, James Branch Cabell, presents more of a problem for the canon-makers, for she had a long career that continued into that time frame. Yet Glasgow, according to many critics, lacks either modernity or merit or both. Allen Tate once described her as "one of the worst novelists in the world" and her prose style as "abominable" (Waldron 105), and Daniel Joseph Singal says she "plainly belongs to the nineteenth century" (xi). Moreover, that her career began before World War I is itself taken by many to be sufficient grounds for excluding her from the modern canon. Thomas Daniel Young makes that practice official in *The History of Southern Literature*: "Ellen Glasgow and James Branch Cabell, because their literary careers were launched before World War I, are not included in the Southern Renascence, though some of their most important work was done in the twenties, thirties, and even later" (Intro. to Part III 262).[2]

The examples of Chopin, Glasgow, and Cabell should suggest that we need to reconsider the way we date and perceive the Southern Renaissance. To mark the boundaries of this literary phenomenon by two wars is a characteristic historical, and masculine, conceit that ill fits the territory. In fact, if we look objectively for first signs of a modern Southern literature, we will discover that the Southern Renaissance did not wait for World War I and the Fugitives and Agrarians at Nashville but dawned instead with scattered individuals, perhaps chiefly women, writing alone in the last decades of the nineteenth century. In this essay, I want to offer this alternative view of the Southern Renaissance's beginning and to identify a female tradition in Southern literature that has followed from that beginning.

It has been said that significant literary movements are most likely to develop in times of tension. As we have seen, tension is crucial to established explanations of the Southern Renaissance's origins—tension between an agrarian past and a growing industrialization, tension resulting from the Southerner's experience of World War I and decreasing isolation. The region's artists would express that tension through their writing, often by holding to the past while simultaneously questioning inherited values. In a recent reexamination of the Southern Renaissance, Singal also stresses cultural tension following World War I as crucial to the renaissance's birth: "Southern intellectuals had moved toward a new mode of culture largely by way of rebellion against the culture they had inherited" (xiii). If, as I want to suggest, the Southern Renaissance began for women well before World War I, the reason may be that the women encountered intense cultural tension decades earlier. Toward the end of the nineteenth century, many Southern women—like American women elsewhere—would grow dissatisfied with traditional values and assumptions, and would move toward a new mode of culture by way of questioning the culture they had inherited. Out of their questioning would develop a serious Southern literature.

Throughout the nineteenth century, hundreds of Southern women—indeed, hundreds of American women—wrote and published fiction and poetry. While much of this writing does not merit resurrection, some of it, along with their more personal writing, is of historical, cultural, and artistic interest, as revisionists are even now discovering. Among the more valuable of these discoveries are journals, letters, and diaries from the mid-century and postbellum decades. In these private modes of writing—modes to which women of the time readily turned—the authors discuss their everyday lives and issues of personal as well as often of national concern. Many hint at dissatisfaction with some of their culture's values and conventions. Toward the end of the nineteenth century, such expressions would begin to receive larger, public expression.

With the slaves emancipated, the nation growing more urbanized and mobile, and immigration, the middle class, and reform movements on the rise, the late nineteenth century brought rapid change and tension to America. For many women, it was a time of organization, action, and awakening. "These were the years," Hazel V. Carby writes in her book *Reconstructing Womanhood: The Emergence of the Afro-American Woman Novelist* (1987), "of the first flowering of black women's autonomous organizations and a period of intense intellectual activity and productivity [for black women]" (7). Elizabeth Ammons writes similarly of middle-class women of the time, black and white alike. In *Conflicting Stories: American Women Writers at the Turn into the Twentieth Century* (1991), she says such women "used various means—women's clubs, settlement house work, temperance agitation, antilynching crusades, and the campaign for suffrage—to assert their right to direct, active participation in the public affairs of the country" (6). In sum, these decades saw women getting out of the home more frequently, taking a more active and personal interest in local and national affairs, finding their voices. These experiences led many to become more conscious of and less satisfied with traditional values and behaviors expected of women.

Given the special emphasis in the South on conventional male and female roles, epitomized in the pervasiveness of the Southern belle and Southern lady concepts as ideals of Southern womanhood, it might seem unlikely that Southern women would take part in the more radical aspects of this women's movement. Whereas they might embrace philanthropic work and social club engagements as consistent with the ideal of Southern womanhood, they might be inclined to shy away from publicly questioning traditional values. Many did, nonetheless, feel intensely the discrepancy between the conventional female role, so exaggerated in the South, and their enlarged desires. Some eventually took to the lecture circuit to protest the double standard; others took up the pen.

Two who did both were Anna Julia Cooper and Belle Kearney. Though little known today,[3] they deserve a place in Southern intellectual and literary history. Their lives illustrate well the struggle of late nineteenth-century women for voice and opportunities, and their writings express themes central to a then-emerging female tradition in American literature in general and Southern literature in particular. Indeed, Cooper and Kearney—along with other aggressive or reluctant spokeswomen— helped create the climate for, and participated in, a renaissance for Southern women, both personal and literary.

On the surface, these two women would seem to have nothing in common except the time in which they lived. Anna Julia Haywood (later Cooper) was born in 1858 near Raleigh, North Carolina, the daughter of a slave woman and her white master. Belle Kearney was born five years later to slaveholding plantation owners near Vernon, Mississippi. But despite one's being born a slave and classified as black and the other's having all the advantages of being white, their lives would follow similar routes. Most importantly, both would, in some way, be liberated by the Civil War; both would early recognize the sexism in their societies and would protest that sexism; both would become teachers and through their teaching develop confidence and a sense of mission; both would lead women's organizations and become spokeswomen for their sex; and both would leave a legacy of their time and their ideas in significant written works.

The Civil War liberated Anna Julia Haywood directly and Belle Kearney indirectly. In 1868, at age nine, Anna Julia entered a newly established school for the freed slaves and began a life-long pursuit of education, a pursuit she could never have accomplished so impressively without Emancipation. By 1887, she had earned B.A. and M.A. degrees from Oberlin College; and in 1925, at the age of 67, she became only "the fourth American black woman to receive a Ph.D." when she finished her doctorate at the University of Paris (Washington, Intro. xxxix). The Civil War liberated Belle Kearney in a different way: it freed her from the confined life of the Southern belle (for which she was named) and Southern lady that would have likely been her destiny otherwise. As a result of the war, her father, a Confederate officer, experienced economic defeat, and his family's lot changed. In her autobiography, *A Slaveholder's Daughter* (1900), Kearney remembers that, after the war, her family's former slaves drifted away, and her parents were left rudderless, neither of them knowing "how to work, nor how to manage so as to make a dollar" (21). Thus, as a child Belle had to assume many household chores, and as a teenager she privately took up dressmaking in her home, her customers including some of the family's former slaves. The need to help her family and to support herself developed in Belle an independence, a capability, and a desire for education that she almost surely would not otherwise have known. In her autobiography, Kearney generalizes that the Civil War had a similar effect on many other Southern women. At the close of the war, she says, with their men killed, defeated, or just in need of assistance, the women of the South had to rise from that devastation and "put their hands figuratively and literally to the plow and have never faltered or looked back" (112).

Early experiences with sexism would make Cooper and Kearney incipient feminists. Cooper's awakening occurred when, as a teenager, she realized that the black school she was attending encouraged males to pursue serious study (theology and the classics) but made no provision for females with the same desires (Washington, Intro. xxxii). Kearney's experience was similar. She was keenly disappointed when, at age fifteen, she had to drop out of school, her education being curtailed so that her parents could afford to send a son to the university, which, of course, was not open to females (Kearney 40–41). A few years later, when she saw her younger brothers ride off to vote while she had no such privilege, she became a suffragist (Kearney 112).

In a time in which employment for middle-class Southern women was uncommon, due to the cult of domesticity and the influence of the Southern lady ideal, both Cooper and Kearney became teachers. In an introductory essay about Cooper, Mary Helen Washington says that Cooper's being left a widow at age twenty-one was her ticket to a career in teaching, for "no married woman—black or white—could continue to teach" (Intro. xxxii). Being single, Kearney too could seek a teaching position, but she had to do so over the objection of her father, who was embarrassed to have his daughter working outside the home. Cooper taught for several decades at a black high school in Washington, D.C.—Washington's now-famous Dunbar High School—where she also served as principal for a number of years. Kearney taught for six years in small schools in Mississippi, until recruited by the Women's Christian Temperance Union.

Through teaching, both women acquired a sense of self-worth and a mission. Remembering their own encounters with the double standard in education, they spoke out for the education of women. In "The Higher Education of Women," a stirring essay in her book *A Voice from the South* (1892), Cooper stresses the education of black women. In obedience to her society's view of woman's role as supportive (for the conventional ideals for womanhood permeated the black society too), Cooper argues for the education of women on the grounds not of personal fulfillment but of women's better service to the human race: education would make women better wives and better mothers. Moreover, the educated woman would provide a "tender and sympathetic chord" to balance the chord "of mere strength and might" that characterizes "the world of thought" under men (53–54). But when Cooper undertakes to answer those who had argued that woman's higher education would conflict with marriage, she acknowledges—almost gleefully—that education does enrich and empower the woman:

I grant you that intellectual development, with the self-reliance and capacity for earning a living which it gives, renders woman less dependent on the marriage relation for physical support (which, by the way, does not always accompany it). Neither is she compelled to look to sexual love as the one sensation capable of giving tone and relish, movement and vim to the life she leads. Her horizon is extended. Her sympathies are broadened and deepened and multiplied. (68–69)

In a satiric thrust, Cooper adds that the educated woman need not ask, " 'How shall I so cramp, stunt, simplify and nullify myself as to make me eligible to the honor of being swallowed up into some little man?' " Rather, the problem is the man's: how will he reach the ideal this new woman now expects of him? (70–71).

In two chapters of her autobiography, Kearney also campaigns for equitable education for women. In "The Young Ladies' Academy," she laments the lack of opportunity she had had, being a girl, for a full education. In "The Evolution of Southern Woman," she compares the improved education and the greater job opportunities available to young women of 1900 to those available two decades earlier, criticizes the South for paying female teachers less than male teachers, and indicates that teaching had fueled her feminist spirit: "Since beginning to teach, every question that related to the attainment and possibilities of women was of intense interest to me; but especially her [sic] developed power of bread-winning" (107).

In their books, both Cooper and Kearney proclaim women's organizations, many of which were founded in the last decades of the nineteenth century, the real educators and liberators of Southern women. Kearney says, "Modern reformations have gained a foothold in the hearts and lives of Southern women that is astonishing to all who realize the intense conservation that fettered them in other days" (118). And Cooper writes that "it is pre-eminently an age of organizations" through which women have a chance to influence public affairs (85). Both women point to the Women's Christian Temperance Union as particularly opening up possibilities for women, Cooper calling the organization a grand "prophesy of the new era and of woman's place in it" (134) and Kearney dubbing it "the generous liberator, the joyous iconoclast, the discoverer, the developer of Southern women" (118). Kearney illustrates this claim by listing activities of the Young Women's Christian Temperance Union (YWCTU), through which young women had developed goals, experience of the larger world, a sense of self-worth, and independence—activities such as assisting in campaigns for constitutional amendments, rest homes, and clubs for working girls; distributing charities to prisoners and the poor; and forming hygiene clubs and loan libraries (167).

Cooper and Kearney themselves exemplify the raised horizons and growing independence and power of women of their time. Born a slave, Cooper rose to be not only one of the leading educators of blacks of her day, becoming the second president of Frelinghuysen University in 1930, but also a recognized spokeswoman invited to address international conferences of women and of blacks. She helped found the Colored Woman's YWCA in 1905 and the Y's Camp Fire Girls in 1912 (Washington, Intro. xxvii). Kearney left behind a sheltered childhood on a declining plantation when she became, in 1889, Mississippi superintendent of the juvenile society of the YWCTU, subsequently traveled across the states and to Europe and Asia organizing chapters of the WCTU and the YWCTU, served as president of the Mississippi Woman Suffrage Association, and was elected the first woman to the Mississippi Senate (Gullette).

Despite their achievements, Cooper and Kearney remained in some ways conventional Southern women, "never able," as Mary Helen Washington says of Cooper, "to discard totally the ethics of true womanhood" (Intro. xlvi). Like many women of their time—and of ours—they were torn between desire for independence and the pressure of gender role expectations. That tension is reflected in their lives and written works. Cooper, for example, prefaces *A Voice from the South* with a stanza by George Eliot that exalts conventional feminine values:

> For they the *Royal-hearted Women* are
> Who nobly love the noblest, yet have grace
> For needy, suffering lives in lowliest place;
> Carrying a choicer sunlight in their smile,
> The heavenliest ray that pitieth the vile. (n.p.)

She embraces this image of the good woman as nurturing, sacrificing, and angelic. At age 57, she adopted five grandchildren of her half-brother; and as Washington has pointed out, she encouraged, complimented, and fed ideas to the black male intellectuals of her day (especially W. E. B. Du Bois) without expecting, or receiving, similar support from them (Washington, Intro. xl–xliii). However, she rejects the other half of that conventional ideal of womanhood, the expectation that Southern women "stand on pedestals" and be decorative. She boldly accuses Southern black men of hampering black women's progress by expecting the women to mold themselves to that ideal:

> [The men] . . . do not seem sometimes to have outgrown . . . the idea that women may stand on pedestals or live in doll houses, (if they happen to

have them) but they must not furrow their brows with thought or attempt to help men tug at the great questions of the world. I fear the majority of colored men do not yet think it worth while that women aspire to higher education. . . . The three R's, a little music and a good deal of dancing, a first-rate dress-maker and a bottle of magnolia balm, are quite enough generally to render charming any woman possessed of tact and the capacity for worshipping masculinity. (75)

Kearney shows that she too has not escaped the influence of the Southern lady ideal at the same time that she, like Cooper, speaks out against it. Though her prose is usually graceful and straightforward, she tends to shift to the passive voice whenever she narrates her own actions and achievements, thereby reflecting the self-effacement of the well-trained Southern woman: "On my return from St. Louis a lengthy visit was made to Canton. My mathematical studies under Mrs. Drane were resumed and examination taken, . . . in both of which first-grade certificates were obtained" (125–26). Moreover, she at times deliberately perpetuates the image of the Southern woman as selfless. Southern women have not sought equality and a life outside the home, she says, but have had this position forced upon them by the times:

> The women of the South have not sought work because they loved it; they have not gone before the public because it was desirable for themselves; they have not arrived at the wish for political equality with men simply by a process of reasoning; all this has been thrust upon them by a changed social and economic environment. It is the result of the evolution of events which was set in motion by the bombardment of Fort Sumter. (112)

She contradicts this view of the Southern woman, however, when she says that for years "there had been a profound unrest in the heart of the girlhood of the New South" as these youth longed for "a higher, stronger life" and "the right to do and to dare" (166), and when she says that the women of the South hungrily seized on the idea of women's suffrage: "It is the natural outcome of their desperate struggle for individual freedom" (118). Furthermore, Kearney, like Cooper, describes the Southern belle/ Southern lady mystique as handicapping women: "All the women who were known to me personally, or through books, or tradition, had their bills paid by male relatives, and made fancy work, and visited, and danced, and played on the piano, or did something else equally feminine and equally conventional, and all were equally dependent and equally contented,—at any rate, asked no questions" (40). With these models and images before her, Kearney as a teenager had given up her aspirations for a higher education: "I was fairly bound . . . by the cankered chains of a false conventionality, and sacrificed for the lack of a precedent" (41).

Cooper and Kearney are important figures in the cultural and intellectual history of the South, and their books, published eight years apart—Cooper's *A Voice from the South* (1892), which she signs, "By a Black Woman of the South," and Kearney's *A Slaveholder's Daughter* (1900)—are well written and important documents of their time.[4] They would deserve to be read for that reason alone. But they are additionally interesting and important when recognized as early documents in an emerging renaissance of Southern women: these books reveal the rebirth that Southern women themselves were experiencing as they struggled for freedom and voice, and they also are evidence of a parallel rebirth (or birth) of a serious Southern literature.[5] The tension between adherence to and defiance of the cult of Southern womanhood reflected in these works of nonfiction motivates as well many worthy creative works—and/or characters in such works—written in the late decades of the nineteenth century and after.

And that brings us back to Ellen Glasgow and Kate Chopin, who have been seen as precursors of the post–World War I Southern Literary Renaissance, modernists and realists ahead of their time. My reading of Southern literary history tells me that Glasgow and Chopin were, indeed, modernists and realists, but rather than being ahead of their time, they were squarely of their time: a time of questioning, awakening, and challenge for increasing numbers of Southern women. Near-contemporaries of Cooper and Kearney (Chopin was born in 1851, seven years before Cooper, and Glasgow in 1874, eleven years after Kearney), they too grew up influenced by the cult of true womanhood, and they too would soon strain at that bridle. Glasgow in her prefaces and essays and both Glasgow and Chopin in their fiction examine the position of the Southern woman, suggesting that traditional values stifle the woman. Many of their female characters are torn between adherence to and defiance of the role expected of them.

But Chopin and Glasgow are only the best known of turn-of-the-century Southern women whose writing is motivated by this tension. In *Tomorrow Is Another Day: The Woman Writer in the South, 1859–1936* (1981), Anne Goodwyn Jones discusses seven Southern women from the time span cited by her title who, she finds, turned to the writing of fiction in an effort to work through the tension they were experiencing in their roles as Southern ladies: "All seven were raised to be southern ladies, physically pure, fragile, and beautiful, socially dignified, cultured and gracious, within the family sacrificial and submissive, yet, if the occasion required, intelligent and brave. The tension between the demands of this cultural image and their own human needs lay close to the source of their creativity" (xi). In addition to Glasgow and Chopin, Jones discusses Augusta Jane Evans, Grace King, Mary Johnston, Frances Newman, and Margaret Mitchell. In her much-cited study, she finds that through their fiction all seven of these authors "criticize the ideal of southern womanhood" though "some ultimately retreat from the critique" (xii).

In her study Jones accepts the usual dating of the Southern Literary Renaissance and places the women she discusses outside of it. Her study and similar ones, however, lend themselves to an argument for revision. By their nature, studies that seek to reclaim neglected or slighted writers implicitly challenge orthodox definitions and canons. The case for revision is heightened when we see recurring in many of these studies the discovery of the same neglected theme. That theme: Southern women writers, or their characters, are motivated by tension between personal desire and the demands of the Southern ideal of womanhood. Decades before the Fugitives put pen to paper in Nashville, that tension would inspire a flurry of writing by women and provide the basis for the development of a modern Southern literature.

Miriam J. Shillingsburg discusses works by three such women in her article "The Ascent of Woman, Southern Style" (1983): Caroline Lee Hentz's *Eoline* (1852), Grace King's *Monsieur Motte* (1888), and Kate Chopin's *The Awakening* (1899). These works, Shillingsburg says, "show the ways in which three female characters bucked convention and their 'place' in society, the reactions of those societies to their rebellions, and the degree of success each heroine (and quite likely each author) felt in being her own self in spite of the circumscriptions of being a female in the South" (128). Though it would take the liberating experiences of the late nineteenth century to inspire a proliferation of works treating this theme, Hentz's novel is evidence that, even earlier, some writers turned to the theme.

Long neglected, Grace King (1852–1932) is beginning to get the attention she deserves. She not only is included in Jones's and Shillingsburg's studies but also is the subject of a particularly relevant essay by Clara Juncker, "Grace King: Feminist, Southern Style" (1988). Drawing on King's memoirs and stories, Juncker sees King as "inadvertently" a feminist—an apt description for many other Southern women writers of her day as well. Being a Southern lady, King frowned on women's addressing issues publicly, so she was not a feminist advocate. Yet she expressed feminist sentiments in her fiction through her exposure of women's limited choices.

These early signs of a Southern Renaissance have not been recognized as such for two reasons. The obvious reason is that which feminist-revisionists have argued in other cases: for centuries, women's activities and accomplishments have tended to be ignored or denigrated because male experience, male accomplishments have been taken to be the standard of what is valuable. In *Reconstructing Womanhood,* Carby makes this point with regard to the neglect of the accomplishments of black women at the turn of the nineteenth century: "Afro-American cultural and literary history commonly regards the late nineteenth and early twentieth centuries in terms of great men, as the Age of [Booker T.] Washington and [W. E. B.] Du Bois" and "marginaliz[es]" the literary and political achievements of black women (6–7). In the introduction to the present text, I show that scholarship on Southern literature has likewise valued male experience and writing over those considered characteristically feminine.

But there is a second, less obvious reason for the neglect of this emerging Southern Renaissance around the turn of the century. It is that the writers were not only females but chiefly individuals writing alone, publishing alone, in scattered places across the South. There was no central circle of writers or central locale to draw the critics' spotlight. And being women, and Southern women at that, these writers did not advertise themselves and thus were more easily overlooked. In the second decade of the new century, the Fugitives at Nashville presented a different case. They met together regularly, discussed each others' works, created a journal specifically for the publication of their poetry, and attracted attention as a center of (male) intellectualism and creativity. They thereby offer critics a point of coherence to latch onto, a visible starting point—to repeat Rubin's words, "an ideological headquarters" for the Southern Renaissance ("Dixie Special" 65). Writing about the Fugitives in 1958, Donald Davidson, who had himself been a member of that group, describes them as a literary circle comparable to the literary circles of earlier centuries in New England and England ("The Thankless Muse"), and Lewis P. Simpson in 1973 refers to the Fugitives-turned-Agrarians similarly, as "the most intense and coherent literary group in America since the Transcendentalists" (243). Hence Richard Gray's ultimatum that "any account of the modern literature of the South must begin with [the Fugitives and the Agrarians]" is grounded in his finding a coherent starting point for the renaissance at Nashville: "their work offers the most coherent demonstration possible of the impulses which helped generate the 'renaissance' of regional literature during the period between the two World Wars" (40). Moreover, the core group of Fugitives and Agrarians at Vanderbilt were among the literary scholars who first defined the Southern Renaissance. According to Richard King in his essay "Framework of a Renaissance," the "notion of a regional renaissance was a brainchild of . . . Allen Tate," himself a Fugitive and an Agrarian, who "used the term in 1936 and again in 1945 when he declared that the Renaissance was over" (11, 12). As King says, "The literature about the Southern Renaissance was a kind of home industry" (15).

Thus, while the women writing in the late nineteenth and early twentieth centuries were lone and isolated voices in that South described by H. L. Mencken as "the Sahara of the Bozart," the Fugitives and after them the Agrarians at Nashville were voices speaking in unison and consciously proclaiming a new day for Southern letters. But in another sense, these women, though scattered across the South, were themselves speaking unconsciously in unison, motivated, as we have seen, by the same tension of time and place. To hear their chorus, and hence to recognize this earlier beginning of the Southern Renaissance, we must give credence to that tension. It links black women with white women and educator-reformers with literary artists. As such a connection, it, fortunately, can answer our need for coherent classroom discussion and manageable literary history.

To locate the beginning of the Southern Renaissance, then, in a circle of male friends at Nashville is to be blind to the meritorious writing that emerged in the last decades of the nineteenth century as women such as Anna Julia Cooper, Belle Kearney, Grace King, Glasgow, and Chopin began to examine and question women's conventional roles and place. As though gaining strength from the success of the women's suffrage movement, this nascent female tradition would grow more confident in the 1920s and afterward, at the same time that the Southern Renaissance was expanding and gaining visibility with the arrival of the Fugitives, Faulkner, Thomas Wolfe, and others. A constant of this female tradition would be a close look at family relationships and Southern conventions and how these touched on women's lives; and a central theme of this tradition—the demythologizing of the cult of Southern womanhood and, by extension, of the Southern hero and Southern traditions—would attract many male writers as well.[6]

This theme found expression especially in some of the little magazines of the 1920s, particularly *The Reviewer,* which was begun in Richmond in 1921 and moved to Chapel Hill in 1924 and, though little known today, during its five-year life won international acclaim for its promotion of a modern Southern literature.[7] Roughly 40 percent of its contributors were women, whose topics and skills ranged widely but whose best writing included incisive examinations of women's lives and satires of the myth of the Southern lady. For example, in her poem "The Misses Poar Drive to Church" in the April 1925 issue, Josephine Pinckney of Charleston satirizes the Southern lady as an anachronism, a role and image past its time. The Misses Poar keep up appearances of aristocratic gentility despite the dilapidated circumstances they have lived in since 1864. Wearing neatly darned black silk mitts, they ride to church in an oxen-driven wagon, yet as they issue from the plantation gate they exhibit the proud bearing of queens. In church, at the mention of President Grant's name, they bury their "noses' patrician hook" in great-grandfather's prayer book: "Better to pray for the Restoration / Than the overseer of a patchwork Nation!" (59). Representing the Southern society through one of its major images, the Southern lady, the Misses Poar are pathetic figures frozen in time.

This feminist vein in *The Reviewer* is apparent also in the works of another neglected writer, Sara Haardt of Montgomery, Alabama. In the July 1924 *Reviewer*, she published "Miss Rebecca," a sensitive story about the relationships between three women: an invalid mother, her spinster daughter, Miss Rebecca, and the invalid's nurse, Miss Connor. The story gradually reveals that both Miss Rebecca and the nurse feel trapped in roles forced upon them as single women in a male-centered world. One has become a companion to her mother, while the other has chosen one of the few respectable careers then open to a woman who had to work to support herself. In another piece, "The Southern Lady Says Grace," in the October 1925 *Reviewer*, Haardt satirizes the Southern lady concept, exposing what that idea had done to women who tried to live up to it. The Southern lady, Haardt writes, "is still, and rather proudly, a slave of the conventions": "She shrinks from the shrillness, the vulgarity, above all, the pettiness of 'taking her own stand.' It is easier and more convenient to follow the old order: it saves her from thinking; and she has witnessed the utter impossibility of thinking intently and looking pretty at the same time" (57).

Among other writers moved to question traditional expectations for Southern women are many of those whom Kathryn Lee Seidel discusses in *The Southern Belle in the American Novel* (1985), where she argues that by the 1920s writers had begun to use the Southern belle "not to praise the South [as she finds antebellum writers had done] but to criticize and at times condemn" the South for its restrictive codes of behavior for men and women (26). Her illustrations include the previously mentioned Sara Haardt and many other little-known writers and works, such as Evelyn Scott, *Narcissa* (1922); Edith Everett Taylor Pope, *Not Magnolia* (1928); and Isa Glenn, *Southern Charm* (1928). This female tradition encompasses further such forgotten but interesting works as Emma

Speed Sampson's novel *The Comings of Cousin Ann* (1923), which contrasts two women, Cousin Ann, a product of the Old South who is now an aging spinster grotesquely stuck in the role of the Southern belle, and young Judith Buck, the new Southern woman, independent, self-supporting, and full of initiative. It includes as well such rediscovered works as Edith Summers Kelley's *Weeds* (1923), a bluntly realistic novel about life on Kentucky tobacco farms, especially the life of monotony, toil, and deprivation as experienced by the women; Zora Neale Hurston's *Their Eyes Were Watching God* (1937), a poetic novel that traces Janie Starks's gradual rejection of the roles others would impose on her, including the role of the Southern lady, and her discovery of and acceptance of her own identity; and Frances Newman's *The Hard-Boiled Virgin* (1926), which Seidel praises for its "bold assessments of the place of women in the South and shrewd probings into feminine psychology" (41–42).

The trail from the Coopers, Kearneys, Glasgows, and Chopins runs also to such well known writers as Katherine Anne Porter, Lillian Hellman, Caroline Gordon (who isn't as well known as she should be), Eudora Welty, Flannery O'Connor, Carson McCullers, and Peter Taylor. As Louise Westling shows in *Sacred Groves and Ravaged Gardens,* Welty, McCullers, and O'Connor investigate "the identity and the experience of women in their unique Southern world" (7). Peter Taylor does the same, with stellar sensitivity and insight. Contemporary writers of the South—Ellen Douglas, Elizabeth Spencer, Doris Betts, Alice Walker, Lee Smith, Anne Tyler, Gail Godwin, and others—are fortunate inheritors of this rich tradition, and they are keeping it vital.

The Southern Renaissance did not begin after all, then, in the aftermath of World War I with the Fugitives and Agrarians at Nashville; rather, it began in the midst of the turn-of-the-century women's movement with the voices and writings of scattered women, and it lives today in the works of men and women who continue to examine the nature of the Southern family and community and the South's expectations— changing though those expectations may be—for womanhood and manhood.

To recognize this earlier beginning for the Southern Renaissance is, of course, to recognize a neglected feminist vein in Southern literature. Yet recognition of the earlier beginning takes nothing away from the writers who came to the forefront following World War I, except the distinction of being first. In fact, there is a continuity between the earlier beginning and the orthodox beginning in the 1920s. For just as literary historians have credited tension between the past and the present with inspiring the excellent writing that followed World War I, so apparently did tension between the past and the present influence the excellent writing at the turn of the century. Kearney and Cooper, Glasgow and Chopin, Grace King and others were drawn to the South's time-worn ideal of Southern womanhood and to other traditional values at the same time that they were moved to question that ideal and those values. Slightly modifying Allen Tate's well-known theory, then, we might explain what I am calling the real beginning of the Southern Renaissance this way: With the women's movement of the late nineteenth century, Southern women began to enter the modern world—but gave a backward glance as they stepped over the border; that backward glance introduced the Southern Renaissance, a literature that not infrequently has exhibited a consciousness of the past in the present.

NOTES

A portion of this article appears, in different form, in "The Case for Female Writers of the South, Known and Unknown" in the *Virginia English Bulletin* 40 (Fall 1990): 51–63.

1. In 1952, in the first major modern anthology of Southern literature for classroom use, Richard Croom Beatty and his co-editors dated the renaissance's beginning from 1918. In a more recent anthology, *The Literary South* (1979), Rubin frames the renaissance by the two world wars, as do recent critics, such as Daniel Joseph Singal in his *The War Within: From Victorian to Modernist Thought in the South, 1919–1945* (1982). The authors of *The History of Southern Literature* (1985) date the period similarly, and King revises the standard dates only slightly in *A Southern Renaissance: The Cultural Awakening of the American South, 1930–1955* (1980).

2. Rubin is unusual in placing Glasgow with the renaissance, as he does in *The Literary South.* Young's practice in *The History of Southern Literature,* of which Rubin is general editor, is the standard.

3. Neither author is mentioned in *The History of Southern Literature* (1985), but Cooper's *A Voice from the South* is now back in print, with an introduction by Mary Helen Washington, and is drawing some attention. It is also the subject of an article by Washington in *Legacy* (Fall 1987) and is discussed by Carby in *Reconstructing Womanhood.* Louise Daniel Hutchinson has written *Anna Julia Cooper: A Voice from the South* (1981).

In addition to *A Voice from the South,* her only full-length book, Cooper wrote numerous letters, speeches, and articles, as did Kearney. Kearney wrote two books, *A Slaveholder's Daughter,* discussed in this article, and *Conqueror or Conquered; or the Sex Challenge Answered* (1921), a novel designed to warn readers about venereal diseases, or, in words from the title page, to educate readers about "the Tragic Results of Ignorance Surrounding the Mysteries of Sex."

4. Understandably, they are not, by today's standards, always "politically correct" documents. Cooper, in Washington's view, was elitist as a feminist: "while she speaks *for* ordinary black women, she rarely, if ever, speaks *to* them" (Intro. xxx). And Kearney is not able to escape entirely the racism of her culture: she frequently portrays blacks as children in need of moral uplifting, and she uses Southerner whites' fear of the power of black voters in arguing for the enfranchisement of women.

5. In a study of American women writers (rather than Southern women writers in particular) at the turn of the century, Ammons directly credits the women's movements of the time with causing a renaissance in writing by American women. She argues, "Women writers at the beginning of the twentieth century flourished in large part—as they do as I write in the 1980s—because of an intensified and pervasive feminist political climate. Whether consciously acknowledged or not, this political climate had the effect of empowering women, including writers" (vii).

6. In *The Southern Belle in the American Novel,* Kathryn Lee Seidel discusses the treatment of the Southern belle by both male and female writers. In an article in the present text Peggy W. Prenshaw refers to male and female writers' treatments of the Southern lady.

7. *The Reviewer* is a neglected gem of the Southern Renaissance, progressive where *I'll Take My Stand* is conservative. Besides *Innocence Abroad* (1931), Emily Clark's history of the journal she helped create and edit, and *Ingenue among the Lions* (1965), Clark's letters to Joseph Hergesheimer as collected and edited by Gerald Langford, the most extensive treatments of *The Reviewer* are two unpublished Master's theses by Elizabeth Spindler Scott (completed in 1977 and 1985) and an article by Scott, " 'In fame, not specie': *The Reviewer,* Richmond's Oasis in 'The Sahara of the Bozart' " (1978). Fred C. Hobson, Jr., devotes part of a chapter on the little magazines of the 1920s to *The Reviewer* in his *Serpent in Eden: H. L. Mencken and the South* (1974), where he describes the journal as having been "at the center of the first phase of the Southern Literary Renaissance" (45–46). An unpublished paper by Dorothy Scura spurred my interest in *The Reviewer.*

WORKS CITED

Ammons, Elizabeth. *Conflicting Stories: American Women Writers at the Turn into the Twentieth Century.* New York: Oxford University Press, 1991.
Beatty, Richard Croom, et al., eds. *The Literature of the South.* Chicago: Scott, Foresman, 1952.
Bonner, Thomas, Jr. "Kate Chopin: Tradition and the Moment." In *Southern Literature in Transition.* Ed. Philip Castille and William Osborne. Memphis State University Press, 1983. 141–49.
Carby, Hazel V. *Reconstructing Womanhood: The Emergence of the Afro-American Woman Novelist.* New York: Oxford University Press, 1987.

Clark, Emily. *Innocence Abroad.* New York: Alfred A. Knopf, 1931.

Cooper, Anna Julia. *A Voice from the South. By a Black Woman of the South.* 1892. The Schomburg Library of Nineteenth-Century Black Women Writers. New York: Oxford University Press, 1988.

Davidson, Donald. "The Thankless Muse and Her Fugitive Poets." *Southern Writers in the Modern World.* Eugenia Dorothy Blount Lamar Memorial Lectures, 1957. Athens: University of Georgia Press, 1958. 1–30.

Fowler, Doreen, and Ann J. Abadie, eds. *Faulkner and the Southern Renaissance.* Proc. of the Faulkner and Yoknapatawpha Conference, 1981. Jackson: University Press of Mississippi, 1982.

Gray, Richard. *The Literature of Memory: Modern Writers of the American South.* Baltimore: Johns Hopkins University Press, 1977.

Gullette, Charles A. "The Career of Belle Kearney: A Study in Reform." Master's thesis. Mississippi College, 1967.

Haardt, Sara. "Miss Rebecca." *The Reviewer* 5 (July 1924): 276–84.

———. "The Southern Lady Says Grace." *The Reviewer* n.v. (October 1925): 57–63.

Hobson, Fred C., Jr. *Serpent in Eden: H. L. Mencken and the South.* Baton Rouge: Louisiana State University Press, 1974.

Hurston, Zora Neale. *Their Eyes Were Watching God.* 1937. Urbana: University of Illinois Press, 1978.

Hutchinson, Louise Daniel. *Anna Julia Cooper: A Voice from the South.* Washington: Smithsonian Institution Press, 1981.

Jones, Anne Goodwyn. *Tomorrow Is Another Day: The Woman Writer in the South, 1859–1936.* Baton Rouge: Louisiana State University Press, 1981.

Juncker, Clara. "Grace King: Feminist, Southern Style." *Southern Quarterly* 26 (Spring 1988): 15–29.

Kearney, Belle. *Conqueror or Conquered; or the Sex Challenge Answered.* Cincinnati: S. A. Mullikin Co., 1921.

———. *A Slaveholder's Daughter.* New York: Abbey Press, 1900.

Kelley, Edith Summers. *Weeds.* 1923. Old Westbury, N.Y.: Feminist Press, 1982.

King, Richard H. "Framework of a Renaissance." Fowler and Abadie 3–21.

———. *A Southern Renaissance: The Cultural Awakening of the American South, 1930–1955.* New York: Oxford University Press, 1980.

Langford, Gerald, ed. *Ingenue among the Lions: The Letters of Emily Clark to Joseph Hergesheimer.* Austin: University of Texas Press, 1965.

Newman, Frances. *The Hard-Boiled Virgin.* 1926. Athens: University of Georgia Press, 1980.

Pinckney, Josephine. "The Misses Poar Drive to Church." *The Reviewer* n.v. (April 1925): 59.

Rubin, Louis D., Jr. "The Dixie Special: William Faulkner and the Southern Literary Renascence." Fowler and Abadie 63–92.

———. Introduction. *Ellen Glasgow: Centennial Essays.* Ed. M. Thomas Inge. Charlottesville: University Press of Virginia, 1976. 1–4.

———, ed. *The Literary South.* New York: John Wiley and Sons, 1979.

Rubin, Louis D., Jr., et al., eds. *The History of Southern Literature.* Baton Rouge: Louisiana State University Press, 1985.

Sampson, Emma Speed. *The Comings of Cousin Ann.* Chicago: Reilly and Lee Co., 1923.

Scott, Elizabeth Spindler. "An Experiment in Southern Letters: *The Reviewer,* 1921–1925." Master's thesis. University of Richmond, 1985.

———. " 'In fame, not specie': *The Reviewer,* Richmond's Oasis in 'The Sahara of the Bozart.' " *Virginia Cavalcade* 27 (Winter 1978): 128–43.

———. "Richmond and *The Reviewer.* " Master's thesis, University of Richmond, 1977.

Scura, Dorothy M. " 'An Improbable Literary Experiment': *The Reviewer,* 1921–24." 1983. Unpublished paper.

Seidel, Kathryn Lee. *The Southern Belle in the American Novel.* Tampa: University of South Florida Press, 1985.

Shillingsburg, Miriam J. "The Ascent of Woman, Southern Style: Hentz, King, Chopin." In *Southern Literature in Transition.* Ed. Philip Castille and William Soborne. Memphis State University Press, 1983. 127–40.

Simpson, Lewis P. "The Southern Writer and the Great Literary Secession." In *The Man of Letters in New England and the South: Essays on the History of the Literary Vocation in America.* Baton Rouge: Louisiana State University Press, 1973. 229–55.

Singal, Daniel Joseph. *The War Within: From Victorian to Modernist Thought in the South, 1919–1945.* Chapel Hill: University of North Carolina Press, 1982.

Tate, Allen. "The New Provincialism." 1945. Rpt. in *Collected Essays.* Denver: Alan Swallow, 1959. 282–93.

Twelve Southerners. *I'll Take My Stand: The South and the Agrarian Tradition.* 1930. New York: Harper Torchbooks, 1962.

Waldron, Ann. *Close Connections: Caroline Gordon and the Southern Renaissance.* New York: G. P. Putnam's Sons, 1987.

Washington, Mary Helen. "Anna Julia Cooper: The Black Feminist Voice of the 1890s." *Legacy* 4 (Fall 1987): 3–15.

———. Introduction. Cooper xxvii–liv.

Weaver, Richard M. "Agrarianism in Exile." 1950. Rpt. in *The Southern Essays of Richard M. Weaver.* Ed. George M. Curtis, III, and James J. Thompson, Jr. Indianapolis: Liberty Press, 1987. 29–49.

Westling, Louise. *Sacred Groves and Ravaged Gardens: The Fiction of Eudora Welty, Carson McCullers, and Flannery O'Connor.* Athens: University of Georgia Press, 1985.

Young, Thomas Daniel. Introduction to Part III: "The Southern Renascence, 1920–1950." Rubin, et al., *The History of Southern Literature* 261–63.

Jan Cooper

Zora Neale Hurston Was Always a Southerner Too

Recently, Thadious M. Davis has remarked on the "black return migration" that appears to be occurring in the southern United States. Not only are African Americans moving back to the South in a modified reversal of the great black migration north of the first half of the twentieth century, but more African American writers than ever before are imaginatively returning in their works to the southern roots of the African presence in North America. Davis recognizes that the tendency to dichotomize race and region in the South persists, that the adjective "Southern," with no racial marker, is still applied exclusively to white Southern culture, while black Southern culture continues to be designated as simply "black" or "African American," with no mention of region. Nevertheless, she applauds the generation of black American writers, from Sherley Anne Williams of California to David Bradley of Pennsylvania, who are engaged in an "expansion of the definition of Southern culture based upon an insistence that race and region are inextricable in defining a Southern self, society, or culture" (5).

Of course some observers of the South, particularly those who have read abolitionists like Frederick Douglass and Harriet Beecher Stowe, have always defined it as the heart of racial conflict and guilt in America. But the present generation of African American artists are undertaking a different task, the rehabilitation of the black South's cultural reputation. Davis notes in passing that this phenomenon "has, of course, antecedents, not merely in the ritual of hundreds of black family reunions and homecomings held annually from Virginia to Texas or in the group political activism of the 1960s, but also in the individual self-assertions of other black Southerners, some of whom are prominent and others not" (11).

One Southerner, now prominent in some circles, who asserted herself in precisely this way is Zora Neale Hurston. Born probably in 1891, raised in Eatonville, Florida, the anthropologist, essayist, manicurist, librarian, playwright, impresario, domestic worker, and novelist died in poverty in Fort Pierce, Florida, in 1960. Since the mid-1970s, feminist critics who needed a representative woman of color to racially balance their texts have promoted Hurston's reputation as a writer who dared to portray strong, questing women. Other scholars have also singled her out as a primary participant in the Harlem Renaissance of the 1920s, the woman most flamboyantly capable of standing shoulder to shoulder with the likes of Langston Hughes and Jean Toomer. Henry Louis Gates, Jr., credits Hurston, along with Richard Wright and Ralph Ellison, with having articulated "the cardinal points of a triangle of influence, with their attendant ramifications upon the ideology of form and its relation to knowledge and power, [that] comprise a matrix of issues to which subsequent black fictions, by definition, must respond" (184). Gates does not, however, recognize the extent to which Hurston's need to define and use the crucial African American literary trope he names "signifyin(g)" may have been the product of her regional consciousness, elements of which she shared with European American contemporaries.

Most critics, in fact, have ignored the relation of Hurston's work, as well as the work of other Southern blacks, to another group of twentieth-century American writers, also credited with a reawakening, called the Southern Renaissance. This exclusion is unfortunate, because Hurston's life and writing demonstrate that the Southern Renaissance wasn't just a white Southern literary phenomenon. The conditions that produced most of the South's best white writers have affected Southern black writers as well. The editors of *The History of Southern Literature,* published in 1985, have begun to rectify the assumption that the Southern Renaissance was an exclusively European American phenomenon by including three chapters on African American writers in the third part of their book, entitled "The Southern Renascence, 1920–1950." But in all three chapters these writers are discussed primarily in relation to other black writers or other black Southerners, with no sustained attempt to examine their relation to their white contemporaries. It is a shame that such separate but equal—or, more defensible from a black critic's point of view, such separatist—attitudes still prevail in the discussion of Southern literature. We are starting to acquire a knowledge of the African heritage of the American South and the critical tools to discuss cross-cultural influences. It is time to question exactly how "white" previously assumed European American traditions may be.

One or more of three kinds of criteria have frequently been used to identify Southern Renaissance writers: (1) historical/biographical information, that is, when these writers wrote and what it was in the world they knew that moved them to write; (2) thematic similarities in their work, namely an adherence to an agrarian myth that challenged the rise of industrialism in the South and the alienation of modern society; and (3) the quality of the writing itself, its freshness of language, its critical distance from the culture, usually checked by an acutely ironic sense of its values and their frailty in the face of modern encroachments. Zora Neale Hurston's work exemplifies all three of these criteria equally as well as it fulfills the expectations of feminist critics or scholars of the Harlem Renaissance. It also suggests that African American cultural values may be among the Southern traditions drawn on by other Southern Renaissance writers, black and white.

The Southern Renaissance is a label given to a flourishing of (white) Southern literature in the first half of the twentieth century that seemed to be a turning point in the region's literary history. Scholars hypothesize that in part this development was a Southern answer to a more widespread American phenomenon. C. Hugh Holman has said, "One of the most obvious characteristics of the period is that it was an age of protest against certain aspects of the American present which seemed to many to violate the American ideal" (89). According to this view, Southern men who had survived World War I, who had seen both the glory and then the massive destruction of Europe, came back saying to themselves what William Alexander Percy could never bring himself to write home:

It's over, the only great thing you were ever part of. It's over, the only heroic thing we all did together. What can you do now? Nothing, nothing. You can't go back to the old petty things without purpose, direction, or unity—defending the railroad for killing a cow, drawing deeds of trust, suing someone for money, coping again, all over, with that bright rascal who rehearses his witnesses. You can't go on with that kind of thing till you die. (223)

Some women, too, experienced life beyond their traditional Southern roles. The loss and disablement of men in the First World War made it less likely that every woman could expect to marry a husband who would support her for life; later the Great Depression convinced many parents that their daughters, as well as their sons, needed some kind of occupational training to fall back on to support themselves. Therefore, for the first time Southern women could aspire to higher education and artistic careers, although the social imperatives to marry and raise a family remained powerful in their lives. As a result, someone like Eudora Welty could decide to leave Mississippi to study art at the University of Wisconsin (although her father also convinced her to study business at Columbia University), just as eighteen years later Flannery O'Connor would board a train in Georgia bound for Iowa City and the University of Iowa Creative Writer's Workshop.

Women and men who left the South during this time naturally encountered as much to challenge their traditional values as anyone in America; their reactions, however, tended to be different, according to the interpreters of the Southern Renaissance. Although the Southern writer "responded to the same impulses," Holman found that "the middle-western writer called for social reform and pleaded for a utopia of the future, but his southern cousin, bound by the past, looked backward for his answers" (89–90). In *William Elliot Shoots a Bear*, Louis D. Rubin, Jr., describing the experience of the Nashville Fugitives, observes:

> they were the first generation of young southerners since early in the nineteenth century to be brought into direct contact and confrontation with the vanguard of the most advanced thought and feeling of their times. . . . But they did not go into confrontation with that world unarmed. They took with them the experience of the southern community and the southern past, and such experience was, all in all, a formidable legacy of attitudes, presuppositions, and habits of feeling and belief, which was not to be violated without resistance. (161, 162)

In 1959 Allen Tate felt his generation's break with the past more sharply. He thought that, thanks to the social change that had occurred, traditional Southern rhetoric was being diverted into an altered "mode of discourse." The traditional mode, he said, had been rhetorical, based on Aristotelian categories of meaning that were never intended for dialectal give-and-take. After about 1920, however, such an unquestioning frame of mind became increasingly impossible for intelligent young Southerners. And so they turned to another Southern verbal tradition— "Was it not said that Southerners were the best storytellers in America? Perhaps they still are," he claimed. Looking even further back, Tate saw forerunners for this change. Augustus Baldwin Longstreet's *Georgia Scenes* was "the art of the rhetorician applied to the anecdote . . . the minor secular myth which just succeeds in skirting the suprahuman myth of religion," he declared, and *Huckleberry Finn* was "the first modern novel by a Southerner," although "not quite fully developed and clean in outline" (591).

Tate saw in Southern fiction (by white writers) of his time the first widespread intimations of a genuinely artistic Southern use of myth. These writers had reached back into the past for that myth because they had a past that applied to their present. The moral complexities of the Southern slaveholding system, the rebellion that stirred in white Southerners' hearts as the country drifted toward the Civil War, and the thorough social and moral upheaval that occurred after the war all had provided intellectual precedents for the post–World War I Depression Era malcontents' very modern sense of guilt and alienation. Holman, Rubin, and Tate (as well as other critics) agree that a profound change took place in Southern literature around 1920, a shift from two dimensional, sentimental, primarily rhetorical works to a literature of universal significance.

These critics base such observations almost exclusively on the writing of white Southerners. At the same time, however, a number of African American writers were also reaching back into a Southern tradition for a critical reshaping of their literature. Black Americans had more cause than anyone for disillusionment after the First World War. Historian David Levering Lewis points out: "The year 1919 was less than seven weeks old when the [all black] 369th Infantry Regiment marched proudly up Fifth Avenue. By the end of 1919 there had been race riots in two dozen cities, towns or counties, rampant lynchings and resurrection of the Ku Klux Klan, and a dismal falling off of jobs in the North for Afro-Americans" (23). Black women also suffered during the demobilization period after World War I. Writing about their experience, historian Jacqueline Jones quotes a *World Outlook* writer's assessment of the American labor situation in October 1919: "in most cases, the colored woman is the 'marginal worker.' . . . the last to be hired, the first to go" (167). As the great numbers of African Americans who migrated north failed to find the economic security and sociopolitical parity they dreamed of, some black writers looked back at the black South to examine the cultural foundations of their present experiences—at what resources, as well as what deprivations, African Americans had brought from the South. Jean Toomer, the most innovative of these, used a brief stint as the head of a school for blacks in Georgia as the basis of the hauntingly complex *Cane,* but others, such as Richard Wright and Langston Hughes, also drew on Southern life as they had known or seen it. Naturally these writers did not view the Southern mythic past in the same way as their white contemporaries. Nevertheless, at least one pervasive mythic image used by many modern white Southern writers—that of the agrarian community—can also be seen in Zora Neale Hurston's work.

As Robert Hemenway, Hurston's biographer, has pointed out, Hurston was one of the few members of the Harlem group who intimately knew the rural South that provided much of the movement's best folk sources (61). In fact she spent more time in the South than she ever did in Harlem. Raised in a small Florida town entirely populated and governed by blacks, Hurston was steeped in the language of the gossip and "lying sessions" she heard on the front porches of her hometown. After her mother died and her stepmother's jealousy drove her out on her own, Hurston drifted through a series of odd jobs, first to Baltimore and then to Washington, D.C., where she resumed her education and began the short story writing that eventually took her to New York City. Thanks to her own high energy and white America's temporary fascination for "Negro art" in the 1920s, Hurston was able to pursue a career in writing and anthropology. There were few times in her life when she could count on a steady income for more than several months; one passage in her autobiography eloquently reveals how closely she had observed destitution: "There is something about poverty that smells like death. Dead dreams dropping off the heart like leaves in a dry season and rotting around the feet; impulses smothered too long in the fetid air of underground caves. The soul lives in a sickly air. People can be slave-ships in shoes" (*Dust Tracks* 116). But before she died, Hurston's mother had taught her children to "jump at de sun" (*Dust Tracks* 21), and Hurston never forgot the lesson.

Like other Southerners of her time, she found that her contact with the misapprehending world beyond the South clarified and made more intense her need to document her culture. As well as any of her European American contemporaries, Hurston sensed the erosion of the unique Southern culture she had come from and the pathos of the loss of its special values and rituals. She devoted her life to preserving some record of the Southern life she'd known or seen, whether it be in anthropological folklore collections like *Mules and Men* (1935) or *Tell My Horse* (1938), or in her several short stories, or in the novels *Jonah's Gourd Vine* (1934), *Their Eyes Were Watching God* (1937), *Moses, Man of the Mountain* (1939), and a novel primarily about white Southerners, *Seraph on the Suwanee* (1948). As early as 1934, writing to Carl Van Vechten, Hurston clearly saw the struggle she'd chosen to participate in, one that would occupy the rest of her life: "The major problem in my field as I see it is, the collection of Negro folk material in as thorough a manner as possible, as soon as possible. In order for the collection to [be] exhaustive, it must be done by individuals feeling the materials as well as seeing it objectively. In order to feel it and appreciate the nuances one must be of the group" (Hemenway 207). But Hurston didn't just leave the South, realize the worth of what she'd left, and return to work to preserve it, like a museum piece, by recording it. She felt that what she was trying to preserve had a certain usefulness for the modern world. As she told Van Vechten, "In my humble opinion, it is almost useless to collect material to lie upon the shelves of scientific societies. . . . the world and America in particular needs [*sic*] what this folk material holds" (Hemenway 207).

This urge to preserve a traditional Southern culture because it might contain healing powers for the future is more commonly associated with the Nashville Fugitive-Agrarians than with the Harlem Renaissance. Twelve white Southern men, most of them associated with the Nashville Agrarians (and among them such well known Southern writers as Robert Penn Warren, John Crowe Ransome, and Andrew Lytle), contributed to *I'll Take My Stand: The South and the Agrarian Tradition,* often cited as the classic statement of Southern agrarian philosophy and the major creed of the Southern Renaissance. Yet *I'll Take My Stand* is curiously silent at the moments when one might expect it to be most explicit. Its authors seem able to define Southern agrarianism only in contrast to the inhuman, mechanical forces of modern industrial capitalism that they felt were threatening its destruction. In the introduction, for example, after a long critique of industrialism, they can only conclude, "Opposed to the industrial society is the agrarian, which does not stand in particular need of definition" (xxviii), although they do add that the "theory of agrarianism is that the culture of the soil is the best and most sensitive of vocations, and that therefore it should have the economic preference and enlist the maximum number of workers" (xxix).

Scattered throughout the book, however, are vignettes of life pictured according to the various authors' image of an agrarian model. Memory, or the imagined reconstruction of what had existed for their ancestors, was all they could summon as a definition of what they asserted to be the traditional Southern community in need of defense against the Northern industrial onslaught. Thus, one must look at John Donald Wade's "The Life and Death of Cousin Lucius" or Henry Blue Kline's "William Remington: A Study in Individualism" or the sections in the other essays where an exemplary generic "he" is invoked, to catch the essence of the life the professional Southern agrarians feared was about to be lost. Numerous writers (including those among the "Twelve Southerners") portrayed the Southern agrarian myth of community better in fiction. Whether it was Faulkner's Yoknapatawpha county or Wolfe's Pulpit Hill or even Welty's Shellmound or O'Connor's unspecified rural Georgia farming neighbors, the communities found in white Southern Renaissance fiction share certain agrarian assumptions.

A community, in these works, is a hierarchical structure in which some mobility is possible but potentially damaging to individuals. That community is also intimately attached to "the soil," the natural environment of its geographical location, but distinctly separate from the world beyond its borders, not linked in any significant way to national or global forces that exist outside. The members of the community, while they may have knowledge of the outer world, finally can identify themselves only within their original circle of kin and neighbors. Whereas in the work of other American writers of the time—Hemingway and Fitzgerald come most quickly to mind—characters negotiate their places among a circle of acquaintances of equal status or between classes in a broader, urban social order, white Southern Renaissance writers often retained in their fiction the setting of the small farming communities inherited from both the plantation romancers and Southwest humorists who preceded them, adding, however, a twist of angle or view, a self-critical awareness of choices that went far beyond the insularity of earlier Southern fictional communities.

Both Hurston's fiction and her nonfictional anthropological writings are informed by this modern Southern agrarian sense of community. Whether it be the Eatonville residents of *Jonah's Gourd Vine* and *Their Eyes Were Watching God* or the barely disguised black slaves of *Moses, Man of the Mountain,* the characters of Hurston's novels populate a very specific kind of black Southern community. These towns tend to be small, relatively newly formed, thus giving their inhabitants a sense of history that is an inspiration, rather than a Faulknerian burden; but they contain a sense of history and thus an inherited social order nonetheless. Each member of these communities still matters and has a separate, unique (if predetermined) identity recognized by the whole community. The human inhabitants are equally well acquainted with the flora and fauna of their location in nature and sometimes anthropomorphize features of the environment into the human community.

What seems to have fascinated Hurston about these agrarian collections of people is the way individuals become active members of such communities, specifically the ways in which such joining could be represented in the storytelling of the community. In *Their Eyes Were Watching God,* some of the most memorable stories are told on the porch of Joe Starks's general store, where the inhabitants of a fictional version of Eatonville gather every day to exchange "the pictures of their thoughts for others to look at and see" (81).

A frequent object of the Eatonville discussions is Matt Bonner's yellow mule, who becomes a kind of mascot for the community, a totem figure representing their meager resources but also their endurance. The mule is pitied because he is skinny and old. Storytellers claim they've seen the women of the town using his ribs for a washboard, his hocks as a place to hang clothes out to dry. But he is also admired for his defiance, for being "mean" and "ornery," and his owner is despised for overworking and underfeeding him. Everyone enjoys the "mule talk"—the "stories about how poor the brute was; his age; his evil disposition and his latest caper" (85). The townspeople identify with the animal's poverty and rebellion, and they constantly ridicule Matt Bonner, whose behavior parallels the insensitivity of white authority in their world. When Matt Bonner's demands and the town's taunts threaten to kill the mule, Joe Starks rescues the beast by buying him and turning him loose. Like Starks's original land purchases and his leadership in the formation of the town government, this act challenges the townspeople to see how magnanimous a black man can be, to enlarge their standards of human dignity, demonstrating for them their own relative freedom from white authority.

But the "mule talk" also invokes the dissatisfaction that Janie, Joe's wife, feels. Although "sometimes she thought up good stories on the mule," she is prevented from joining the communal circle on the porch because "Joe had forbidden her to indulge" (85). He thinks she should remember at all times that she is "Mrs. Mayor Starks," and in his attempt to assert his own dignity he thwarts her impulses to join the verbal life of the community. Ironically, instead of telling stories about Matt Bonner's mule, Janie becomes a superficially pampered kind of " 'mule uh de world,' " the fate her grandmother had warned her was the birthright of black women. It is she who first gives Joe the idea of buying the animal when she tells him she wishes someone would put the animal out of its misery. But Janie too has been bought in a sense, rescued from Killicks's schemes for the use of her labor by Joe Starks's flashy clothes and promises of glittering change.

The "mule talk" may look like a folklorist indulgence in the novel and has been the source of some African American male critics' severest negative comments. In a review of the novel for *New Masses* in 1937, Richard Wright was one of the first critics to condemn *Their Eyes* for perpetuating what he thought was a demeaning "minstrel technique" (23); and in a later issue of the same publication Ralph Ellison commented that the book, "though possessing technical competence, retains the blight of calculated burlesque that has marred most of her [Hurston's] writing" (24). More recently Darwin T. Turner has thoroughly attacked the inclusion of this material, calling it Hurston's "most serious structural blunder" (107). All three critics seem to have been too embarrassed by Hurston's trope of the mule (always a figure of self-parodying pride in her work) to recognize its contribution to larger ideas in the book. The down-to-earth agrarian imagery of the yellow mule prefigures for the "yellow," or mulatto, woman Janie what is wrong in her marriage to Joe—its lack of playfulness, Joe's enforcement of a monotonous existence that does not acknowledge her identity in any way except as a possession. Once she stands up for the yellow mule, she can also find the strength to stand up for herself. Classic African American values of stubbornness in adversity and self-determination, as well as agrarian imagery, are bound up in the act of telling a story. Storytelling itself then becomes a theater for the drama of an individual seeking an authentic place in a community where participatory rhetoric, as in the call and response mode of African American Christian preaching, is highly valued. As Maria Tai Wolff has observed, "This kind of [story] telling does not necessarily formulate material, but becomes material for formulation by the listener" (32).

Most of the unhappiness in Janie's life occurs as the result of some exclusion from normal communal life. But what she suffers is usually an exclusion caused by someone else's Snopesian greed. By marrying Janie off to Killicks, Janie's grandmother in effect exiles her to "a lonesome place like a stump in the middle of the woods where nobody had ever been" (39). Despite Killicks's sixty acres and the parlor organ that Janie's grandmother so admires, Joe Starks easily seduces Janie away only a year later with promises of change that she mistakes for her adolescent vision of sexual communion. She sadly discovers all he can really give her is a new form of isolation, the pedestal of "Mrs. Mayor Starks." In Tea Cake, however, Janie at last finds a husband who is not preoccupied with the materialism of a nascent industrial society. A propertyless man, albeit with major flaws (as Michael Awkward points out), Tea Cake encourages Janie to reenter the life of her community, to join in the "game," whether it be checkers or Sunday School picnics. Briefly with Tea Cake and the other workers in "the muck," as they call the Florida Everglades, Janie regains something as close to the agrarian ideal as a modern Southern writer could imagine, a community in which all members have a well-defined role and are fundamentally at harmony with the luxuriant natural world surrounding them.

Some scholars have warned against idealizing the communal life pictured in this book. Mary Helen Washington has observed, "*Their Eyes* has often been described as a novel about a woman in a folk community, but it might be more accurately described as a novel about a woman outside of the folk community" (237). It is true that each of the communities Janie lives in is too quick to judge her when for some reason she doesn't fit their expectations—the children who tease her at school because she lives on white people's property, the Eatonville neighbors who can't understand her attraction to Tea Cake, her friends on the muck who condemn her for killing Tea Cake before they hear her story. The first short scene that frames Janie's narrative is an unforgettable dramatization of the viciousness of small town talk. Sitting on their porches in the late afternoon, the people of Eatonville watch Janie's return, their former "Mrs. Mayor" now wearily heading for home in worn overalls, and we are told: "Seeing the woman as she was made them remember the envy they had stored up from other times. So they chewed up the back parts of their minds and swallowed with relish. They made burning statements with questions, and killing tools out of laughs. It was mass cruelty. A mood come alive. Words walking without masters; walking together like harmony in a song" (10). There is more in this passage than a simple evocation of local color. Its author knows the habits of the people she describes, their petty sense of their past, the way they nurse old jealousies. And more than anything she appreciates the ugly dignity that such traits take on when amplified in a communal ritual. She is making neither an unqualified defense of their point of view nor a totally unsympathetic attack on their way of life. Instead, Hurston is revealing them from a critical perspective that is made at a knowing distance, far enough away to show their complexities, but near enough to see the heart of their motives.

As a result, the novel is more than a romantic look at a "primitive" community or the life of a "tragic mulatto," that staple of melodramatic novels of both the pre-renaissance South and the "New Negro" 1920s North. Instead, it is a vibrant, complex representation of a distinctive Southern agrarian culture, told in a regional version of American English that hums with the full mythic tension of its characters. It carries equal debts to its author's identity as an African American woman and a Southerner living in the first half of the twentieth century, and discussions of neither the Harlem Renaissance nor the Southern Renaissance are sufficient to understand it.

And so this novel and its author raise questions about literary categories, especially categories in the study of Southern literature. The wealth of excellent black Southern writers now publishing has made it imperative to reexamine what racial assumptions underlie our discussions of region in literature. Some readers might argue that it is inexact and dangerous to use the label "Southern" at all without a qualifying racial adjective, that the black and white Southern literary traditions are parallel but distinct from each other, never overlapping or intersecting. Certainly it's only prudent to make explicit racial identity whenever it exists, but that is not the same thing as saying that a generic term "Southern," meant to include a wide range of racial identifications, is not possible. Hurston's case suggests that position may be too limiting because it tends to close off examinations of how black and white Southern traditions (and red, brown, and yellow ones too, for that matter) have interacted and transformed each other. Before Hurston's time, white Southern regional writers like John Pendleton Kennedy showed signs of being aware that they were writing in response to black abolitionist literature like William Wells Brown's *Clotel; or, The President's Daughter.* Looking closely at the mule stories section in *Their Eyes Were Watching God,* for example, leads the reader to wonder exactly how much the communal values in Southern Renaissance agrarianism owe to Pan-African world views, whether or not a non-white, non-Western cosmology is the ultimate source of a passage like this in one of white Southerner Wendell Berry's recent environmentalist essays:

> The local community must understand itself finally as a community of interest—a common dependence on a common life and a common ground. And because a community is, by definition, *placed,* its success cannot be divided from the success of its place, its natural setting and surroundings; its soils, forests, grasslands, plants, and animals, water, light, and air. The two economies, the natural and the human, support each other; each is the other's hope of a durable and a liveable life. (192)

How many of their agrarian ideals may have been instilled in the "Twelve Southerners" by the black women who may have tended them as children or the black men with whom they may have fished and hunted or sowed and reaped? In other words, exactly to what extent was the Southern Renaissance a transracial, cross-cultural product of the South itself, as well of Southerners' encountering the world beyond the Southern United States? It's time to stop treating such questions as if they are a literary miscegenation taboo, pretending that anything in the South is racially pure. Might the African American literary return migration Davis cites also represent a continuation of the examination of Southern agrarian values? Most surely, Hurston's work tests the value of critical labeling of literary works. The failure of scholars of the Southern Renaissance to examine her place in their category indicates that a label can obscure as well as identify.

WORKS CITED

Awkward, Michael. *Inspiriting Influences: Tradition, Revision and Afro-American Women's Novels.* New York: Columbia University Press, 1989.

Berry, Wendell. "Does Community Have a Value?" In *Home Economics: Four-teen Essays by Wendell Berry.* San Francisco: North Point Press, 1987. 179–92.

Davis, Thadious M. "Expanding the Limits: The Intersection of Race and Region." *The Southern Literary Journal* 20 (1988): 3–11.

Ellison, Ralph. "Recent Negro Fiction." *New Masses* 5 Aug. 1941: 22–26.

Gates, Henry Louis, Jr. *The Signifying Monkey: A Theory of Afro-American Literary Criticism.* New York: Oxford University Press, 1988.

Hemenway, Robert E. *Zora Neale Hurston: A Literary Biography.* Urbana: University of Illinois Press, 1978.

Holman, C. Hugh. *The Roots of Southern Writing: Essays on the Literature of the American South.* Athens: University of Georgia Press, 1972.

Hurston, Zora Neale. *Dust Tracks on a Road: An Autobiography.* 2d ed. Ed. and intro. by Robert Hemenway. Urbana: University of Illinois Press, 1984.

———. *Their Eyes Were Watching God.* 1937. Urbana: University of Illinois Press, 1978.

Jones, Jacqueline. *Labor of Love, Labor of Sorrow: Black Women, Work, and the Family from Slavery to the Present.* New York: Basic Books, 1985.

Lewis, David Levering. *When Harlem Was in Vogue.* New York: Vintage, 1982.

Percy, William Alexander. *Lanterns on the Levee: Recollections of a Planter's Son.* Baton Rouge: Louisiana State University Press, 1977.

Rubin, Louis D., Jr., et al., eds. *The History of Southern Literature.* Baton Rouge: Louisiana State University Press, 1985.

Rubin, Louis D., Jr. *William Elliott Shoots a Bear: Essays on the Southern Literary Imagination.* Baton Rouge: Louisiana State University Press, 1975.

Tate, Allen. "A Southern Mode of the Imagination." In *Essays of Four Decades.* Chicago: Swallow Press, 1968. 577–92.

Turner, Darwin T. *In a Minor Chord: Three Afro-American Writers and Their Search for Identity.* Carbondale: Southern Illinois University Press, 1971.

Twelve Southerners. *I'll Take My Stand: The South and the Agrarian Tradition.* 1930. Gloucester, Mass.: Peter Smith, 1976.

Washington, Mary Helen. " 'I Love the Way Janie Crawford Left Her Husbands': Zora Neale Hurston's Emergent Female Hero." In *Invented Lives: Narratives of Black Women, 1860–1960.* Ed. Mary Helen Washington. Garden City, N.Y.: Anchor Press, 1987. 235–54.

Wolff, Maria Tai. "Listening and Living: Reading and Experience in *Their Eyes Were Watching God.*" *Black American Literature Forum.* 16 (1982): 29–33.

Wright, Richard. "Between Laughter and Tears." *New Masses* 5 Oct. 1937: 22–23.

2. Connections

Peggy Whitman Prenshaw

Southern Ladies and the Southern Literary Renaissance

In her 1970 study, *The Southern Lady,* Anne Firor Scott delineated the image of the nineteenth-century lady as she emerged from the sermons, newspapers, commencement addresses, diaries, literary journals and novels of the period. Exorbitantly praised, the antebellum Southern white woman of the upper class would have been the happiest and most nearly perfect specimen of womanhood ever seen on this earth, Scott notes, if words could have made her so (4). In earlier studies of the South, W. J. Cash, Clement Eaton, William Taylor and others all commented upon the South's romantic exaltation of woman, but few scholars before Scott focused their research on the experience of Southern women—white or black—in the nineteenth-century South. Since the early 1980s, especially with the work of Anne Goodwyn Jones and Catherine Clinton, and more recently with the studies of Suzanne Lebsock, Minrose Gwin and Elizabeth Fox-Genovese, we have begun to add significantly to what we know of these women's lives and to broaden our understanding of the significance of white Southern womanhood as a shaping symbol of the patriarchal Old South.

In "Dixie's Diadem," the opening chapter of her book *Tomorrow Is Another Day,* Jones notes that "as an image, southern womanhood has been the crown of Dixie at least since the early nineteenth century. . . . Roughly interchangeable with the image of the southern lady or (for the young unmarried) that of the southern belle, southern womanhood was born in the imaginations of white slaveholding men." Jones views the image of the lady as having served two key historical roles, as the central embodiment of "the values by which southerners have defined the region's character through Civil War and Reconstruction, New

South and modernism," and as a compelling pattern of behavior that has exerted incalculable influence upon the daily lives of actual women (8–9). "More than just a fragile flower," Jones writes, "the image of the southern lady represents her culture's idea of religious, moral, sexual, racial, and social perfection" (9). Particularly in the view of nineteenth-century writers, this image was extolled not only as an ideal but an attainable one, and in countless ways the Southern white woman was encouraged to shape, repress, modify, and monitor her behavior to create her own perfectness.

In the twentieth century, the Old South paragon who was in every way good and beautiful has been subjected to widespread skepticism, although the mythology of ladyhood has continued, paradoxically, to maintain a spirited vitality. At times defended, but more often repudiated, the myth of the ideal Southern white lady has challenged the imagination of male and female writers alike. Furthermore, the profound historical consciousness that distinguishes the Southern writers who ushered in a literary renaissance in the first half of the twentieth century has been significantly formed by their effort to understand and come to terms with the dominating image of the "lady."

In his 1832 *Swallow Barn*, John Pendleton Kennedy depicts prototypical ladies—Lucretia Meriwether, the efficient but delicate mistress of the plantation, and the youthful, vivacious Bel Tracy. Nearly fifty years later, George Washington Cable's Aurora Nancanou and daughter Clotilde illustrate in *The Grandissimes* (1880) the same alluring modesty that typifies both older matron and innocent belle. In these and other nineteenth-century Southern novels the lady is curiously enigmatic—shy, delicate, patient, and vivacious, teasing, restless. She is ruled by a tender heart easily aroused and an endearing foolishness that undermines her orderly management of household affairs. At the same time, she is the moral center of the home, the pious bulwark of Christianity who molds the next generation, the stabilizing force who calms the unruly passions of sons and husbands.

The writer who perhaps most fully states and uncritically accepts this extraordinary combination of qualities is Thomas Nelson Page, especially in his nostalgic 1897 work, *Social Life in Old Virginia Before the War*. Interestingly, he reserves the dramatic conclusion of his description of the plantation family for a tribute to the older daughters, the awesome belles who epitomize for him the grace and chivalrous aristocracy of the antebellum South. "They held by a universal consent the first place in the system, all social life revolving around them," he writes. Once started on the hymn of praise, Page gathers force, asserting what would seem to be ludicrous contradictions in any but a description of a courtly lady fair—or the mythic Southern lady. For example, the girl's manners are as perfectly formed as her mother's, but she is described as the more "self-possessed." Page extols her daintiness and sweetness, noting the "pure, clean, sweet atmosphere of her country home," and then concludes that "she was generally a coquette, often an outrageous flirt." After three pages of such praise, he admits, "Truly, she was a strange being." Accepting the strangeness, he uses it to explain how it was that, in time of war, the "most supine suddenly appeared as the most efficient and the most indomitable" (52–57).

No doubt it was tempting for Page to conclude with the familiar lauding of the courage and sacrifice of Southern womanhood during the Civil War, but this is not the conclusion he chooses. Instead, he returns to the curious paradox of the lady's nature, as if credence required one more attempt to explain her. "She was indeed a strange creature, that delicate, dainty, mischievous, tender, God-fearing, inexplicable Southern girl. With her fine grain, her silken hair, her satiny skin, her musical speech; pleasure-loving, saucy, bewitching—deep down lay the bedrock foundation of innate virtue, piety, and womanliness, on which are planted all for which human nature can hope, and all to which it can aspire. Words fail to convey an idea of what she was. . . . To appreciate her one must have seen her, have known her, have loved her" (58). The enigma remains unresolved except for one lucky enough to have lived in the mythic golden age and to have known such a girl. The modern Southerner, even the modern Southerner of 1897, must be content with the hazy memory or the active faith that this marvelous creature, the belle, once actually graced the Old South.

In *The Southern Belle in the American Novel*, Kathryn Lee Seidel has explored the manifold traits of the belle in the figure's characterization in nineteenth- and twentieth-century fiction. Although the belle represents only one aspect of the Southern lady, Seidel maintains that the belle epitomizes the most salient features of the symbolism served by the mythic white woman. She argues that in American fiction, especially Southern fiction, the belle is the symbol of the South, and "the belle's personality traits and the plot or life story an author invents are roughly reflective of the author's attitude toward the South itself" (xiii).

Of course, the idealized image of the lady, the perfection of womanhood that reconciled the most extreme contradictions, was neither uniquely of the nineteenth century nor of the American South. The courtly lover or, later, the cavalier tradition in Western literature had idolized the lady fair. Certainly the early nineteenth-century romantics, especially Sir Walter Scott, had revived the interest in the age of chivalry.

And in Victorian England, as well as in the United States generally, the idealized version of the lady was ubiquitous. As Anne Scott, Anne Jones, and Kathryn Seidel all show, however, the image assumed peculiar force in the South.

The effort to understand how and why the Southern lady incarnated the central ideology of the patriarchal, slaveholding, plantation South and, in fact, continued to represent distinctly Southern values in the postbellum and twentieth-century South has, as I have noted, preoccupied many Southern historians and literary scholars in the past decade. Even in works like Bertram Wyatt-Brown's *Southern Honor* and Richard King's *A Southern Renaissance,* studies that take for their central subject the male code of honor in the nineteenth century and the figures of the father and the grandfather in the "Southern family romance," the presence and potent symbolism of the lady are inescapable.

In order to understand the mythos of the Southern lady, it is well to remember that in the last century not only the South but the country as a whole largely perceived the culture of the Southern states to be distinctly different from that of the North. In *Cavalier and Yankee,* William R. Taylor traced the development of the idea of the divided culture, showing how the idea took hold and flourished in the nineteenth century. By 1860, most of the country had come to regard the South as an aristocratic, agrarian society and the North as democratic and commercial. Furthermore, the differences were thought to be not only political and economic but ethnic as well. One popular theory held that the Yankee was descended from the English Puritan, a "Saxon" or "Anglo-Saxon" type, whereas the Southern gentleman was descended from the English Cavalier, a "Norman" type, who bequeathed to the region the manner of the English gentry (Taylor xv). The passages from Page's *Social Life* clearly illustrate his assumption of the South's "blue-blood."

The role of the lady was thus viewed not merely as genteel refinement but as integral to the aristocratic social structure. The image of the beautiful, pious and obedient lady of the chivalric tradition, popularized in the Scott novels beloved by the South, was appropriated as the fitting model for the mistress of the plantation. As Barbara Welter shows in her study of the nineteenth-century American woman, *Dimity Convictions,* the image of the woman as the ladylike queen of the home was common throughout most of the English-speaking world in the middle of the nineteenth century (21–41). The invocation of the medieval fair lady and the avowed loyalty to aristocratic values show up in the United States, however, principally in Southern writings.

In the 1840s and 1850s, when the South came to defend its way of life with its peculiar institution of slavery, or even later, after the worst of the Reconstruction years, when Southern writers like Page looked backward to glorify antebellum days, it is not surprising to find the patriarchal system, which was argued to be in the best interests of the slaves, logically extended and justified as the necessary protection of helpless women and children. In fact, many nineteenth-century writers explicitly state the link between slavery, the patriarchal system and the image of the Southern lady. George Fitzhugh, for example, in his 1854 *Sociology of the South,* describes the Southern woman precisely in terms of her dependency: "So long as she is nervous, fickle, capricious, delicate, diffident and dependent, man will worship and adore her. Her weakness is her strength, and her true art is to cultivate and improve that weakness. . . . Woman, like children, has but one right and that is the right to protection. A husband, a lord and master, whom she should love, honor and obey, nature designed for every woman. . . . If she be obedient she stands little danger of maltreatment" (214–15). Women, like children and slaves, were expected to recognize their proper and subordinate place. According to Fitzhugh, any assertion of independence threatened the whole system.

That such sentiments as Fitzhugh's were patently contradicted by the facts of the plantation mistress's life has been shown in great detail by Catherine Clinton in *The Plantation Mistress.* That one's urging such a restrictive role, proscribing any sense of a separate self or initiative for action on the part of the lady, constitutes more a hostile threat than proferred protection has been pointed out by Scott, Jones, Seidel, and, more recently, by Louise Westling in "The Blight of Southern Womanhood," the opening chapter of *Sacred Groves and Ravaged Gardens,* her insightful study of Eudora Welty, Carson McCullers, and Flannery O'Connor. Citing the Fitzhugh passage, Westling also notes that "if the lordliness and mastery of the husband required that she cultivate and improve her weakness, there must have been serious danger of feminine strength" (17).

What is evident in the paeans to Southern womanhood is the transparent and deconstructing "doublespeak." As Wyatt-Brown points out, "Southern male honor required that women be burdened with a multitude of negatives, a not very subtle way to preserve male initiative in the never-ending battle of the sexes" (227). If not subtle, at least ingenious was the Southern male's exaggerated praise of the female's topsy-turvy virtue, which Wyatt-Brown notes served to make the "ascriptive disadvantages of the gender more bearable. They elevated the negative features into admirable qualities" (234).

Ultimately, the most oppressive and damaging result of the codifica-tion of subservience as the essential requisite of the lady was the in-junction that she be silent. Closely related in many respects to the anxiety of authorship that Susan Gilbert and Sandra Gubar explored in *The Madwoman in the Attic,* the Southern woman's anxiety of voice arose directly from the proscription of female self expression. The hopeless bind was nearly absolute: to remain silent was to acquiesce to voicelessness and invisibility; to speak in one's own behalf, to assert one's view or conviction, was not only to forfeit the respect and atten-tion of powerful men, as well as that of most women, but to threaten the foundation of the South itself. In Cash's inimitable words in *The Mind of the South,* "She was the South's Palladium, this Southern woman—the shield-bearing Athena gleaming whitely in the clouds, the standard for its rallying, the mystic symbol of its nationality in face of the foe. She was the lily-pure maid of Astolat and . . . the pitiful Mother of God. Merely to mention her was to send strong men into tears—or shouts. . . . At last, I verily believe, the ranks of the Confederacy went rolling into battle in the misty conviction that it was wholly for her that they fought" (86).

I have dwelt at length on the image of the nineteenth-century lady because it is crucial to an understanding of female protagonists in twentieth-century Southern literature and, especially, to a more inclu-sive analysis of the literary movement we designate the Southern Renaissance. There have been, of course, a great many explanations advanced for the origins of the extraordinary literary activity that occurred in the South beginning in the late 1920s, but most literary scholars, whatever other theory they may advance, agree with the central premise articulated by Allen Tate in his 1945 essay, "The New Provin-cialism," that it seemed after World War I the South paused, just before moving into the modern world, to take a backward glance, to see what life had been like, and to measure its present and future against its past.

The focus on the Southern past, so central in the works of Faulkner, Warren, and Tate, concentrates typically on slavery, the Civil War, and the tragic blend in nineteenth-century leaders of guilt, courage, moral blindness, and honor. I would argue that the image of the Southern lady, no less than that of the black and the Confederate dead, has pervaded the mind of the South, powerfully evoking its literary imagina-tion. For the female character in modern Southern literature, the effort to interpret her history and discover her place in the world has led inevitably back to the role of the lady with all its ironic contradictions. Perhaps women, who have experienced firsthand the pressure of recon-ciling their lives with the old ideal, have written more frequently of such characters, but many male writers have also portrayed women characters whose chief conflicts grow out of the tension between the social archetype and their own striving for individuality.

In her study of the belle figure, Seidel maintains that it is precisely the nineteenth-century virtues of purity, loveliness, and modesty that are shown to be the attributes most harmful to the belle and destructive to others in the fiction of Glasgow, Faulkner, and other twentieth-century Southern novelists. "The belle as a symbol of the South's beauty and purity is parodied and inverted so that she represents many of the worst qualities of the South when she appears in the fiction of the Southern Renaissance" (146). Seidel is persuasive, but she does not fully account, I think, for the deep ambivalence that Southern writers, especially male writers, have brought to their characterizations of the Southern lady. Faulkner's Quentin Compson, for example, concentrates on two human beings in his search for a life of meaning and purpose—Thomas Sutpen from the nineteenth century and sister Caddy from the twentieth. With great expense of will and emotion he understands the history of Sutpen and penetrates the myth, seeing the failure as well as the honor of the Old South. But he does not see, as Faulkner's male characters rarely see, that the vision he has of Caddy, beautiful and innocent, is bedrock illusion. His vision of the "lady" signifies a desperate heroic compromise: the admission that, though blemish may taint active, ambitious, and violent men, moral purity is yet attainable on this earth in the character of the Southern lady. The Quentin-like longing for the reality of the lady, which marks so many heroes in twentieth-century fiction (Gowan Stevens, Jack Burden, and Eugene Gant come to mind), the longing for proof that she can exist, is perhaps the last vestige of the romantic idealization of the past. Westling makes a similar point, noting Faulkner's comment that "he felt he would reduce Caddy's beauty by letting her talk." She writes: "For him as for other men of his heritage, women were perhaps too potent. . . . Southern white men . . . needed the vision of their inviolate women to sustain their elaborate fiction of aristocratic civilization, and when women like Caddy began to openly reject the game and live as independent warm-blooded beings who asserted their sexuality—New Women, Southern style—the loss of the myth was insupportable. It was really the loss of a goddess incarnate, the end of a religion which, despite their trespasses and hypocrisies, these men loved" (39).

When female characters are given voice in Southern fiction, however, we often hear expressed a quite different attitude toward the idealized image of the lady. There is the same obsessive regard for the role as the embodiment of the cherished past and the same pervasiveness of the myth, but the experiences of these characters inevitably abrogate the old ideal. Some characters, such as Peyton Loftis of William Styron's *Lie Down in Darkness,* adopt the fatalistic view that the old mode is simply irretrievable; others like Cousin Eva of Katherine Anne Porter's "Old Mortality" deny that there is anything of value in the ideal and dismiss it as irreconcilable with the present. Such characters as Ellen Glasgow's Dorinda Oakley suspect, and become themselves proof of, the profound unreality of the myth. They find that it cannot be lived and grow suspicious that it ever was. Looking at the characters of twentieth-century Southern literature, one finds endless studies of the figure of the lady, denials and defenses of the ideal, analyses of the myth. Invariably the figure complicates and shapes the destiny of the characters, who try to contend with its paradoxes and contradictions. What stands revealed in this literature is the enormous psychic cost to women of a role absurdly inconsistent with life, and yet rigidly defined and extolled with religious fervor. As Anne Jones wryly notes, "Whereas southern manhood could be demonstrated by obtaining an ideal southern woman, southern womanhood had to be shown by becoming one" (22).

Many of Glasgow's heroines try vainly to live the myth of the Southern lady, but among her many novels none so starkly exposes the limitations and inherent dangers of the myth as does *The Sheltered Life.* Principally the story of Jenny Blair Archbald, who grows to adulthood during the course of the novel, the book unmasks the naiveté that accompanies a sheltered life, an innocence that is really moral blindness. Spoiled and guarded from the knowledge that a bold reaching for happiness can have disastrous consequences, Jenny Blair at seventeen is much like one of the older daughters described by Page. But Glasgow develops the effects of such a disposition realistically. When Jenny becomes infatuated with George Birdsong, an old family friend and husband of the beautiful Eva, she acts the coquette, selfishly disregarding everyone affected by her action, especially Eva, whom she deeply admires.

Eva Birdsong, who most fully embodies the myth of the beautiful lady and at last most completely exposes its pretense, has been the town's reigning beauty for forty years. Her only flaw, it would seem, is that as a handsome and talented woman she "gave up too much" to marry George. With unsparing irony Glasgow shows her to be a tragically unfulfilled human being. Just before the violent conclusion of the novel, Eva tells Jenny of frequent feelings of terror, moments when she rushes from the house. "Unless I go alone, I can never find myself. When you've never been yourself for forty years, you've forgotten what you are really. . . . I'm worn out with being somebody else—with being somebody's ideal. I want to turn round and be myself for a little while before it is too late, before it is all over" (385–86). But it is shortly over for Eva, who, finding George embracing Jenny Blair, kills him and retreats into a silent, deadened self. The portrait of a lady that closes the novel is chilling, resembling less an Isabel Archer than a Madeline Usher: "[She] sat very erect, and gazed, with her fixed smile, into the twilight beyond the window. Her face was so vacant that her expression and even her features were like wax. The waves of her hair clung to her scalp; her skin was as colourless as the skin of the dead; and her eyes and mouth were mere hollows of darkness" (393).

There are many other evidences of the repudiated myth in Southern fiction and drama. Kathryn Seidel discusses the Southern Renaissance as a period of sustained "demythologizing" of the belle, noting the emphasis in the novels of the 1920s upon the belle's narcissism, sexuality, and masochistic self-abnegation. She observes that, beginning with the title, such novels as Evelyn Scott's *Narcissus,* Frances Newman's *The Hard-Boiled Virgin,* Edith Everett Taylor Pope's *Not Magnolia,* and Isa Glenn's *Southern Charm* all give evidence of their authors' self-conscious attack on the nineteenth-century image of the belle (26).

Among the more subtle evidences of the repudiated myth of the lady is the frequent appearance of paired characters, a fictional device that allows for the contradictions within the role—that is, the willful coquette or the efficient manager of worldly affairs and the submissive, obedient innocent—to be realistically resolved. The Southern writer repeatedly "divides" the heroine in a doppelgänger motif to create a parade of Scarletts and Melanies, or variants of the pair. Of course, the strong-willed protagonist and her dependent foil are familiar in dramatic and prose literature. One thinks of Shakespeare's heroines or of Becky Sharp and Amelia of *Vanity Fair.* But the paired type is pervasive in Southern literature—Cassie Morrison and Virgie Rainey of Eudora Welty's *The Golden Apples,* or, much earlier, Georgiana and Sylvia Cobb of James Lane Allen's *A Kentucky Cardinal.* Georgiana claims she does not belong to the "rose order of Southern women . . . Sylvia does" (99). One may see a radical example in Lena Grove and Joanna Burden of Faulkner's *Light in August,* an oversimplified version and thereby one of considerable dramatic clarity in Lillian Hellman's Regina Giddens and Birdie Hubbard. Regina in *The Little Foxes* is darkly beautiful, alluring and as hard and unflinching as Birdie is delicate and birdlike. Birdie watches helplessly as her husband and Regina conspire for power and personal wealth in their attempts to raise money for a partnership in a new industry. Birdie retains the old, idealized innocence, but her dialogue, for all its evidence of generosity, is a melancholy parody of the sweet, simple belle: "I should like to have Lionnet back. . . . I'd like to see it fixed up again, the way Mama and Papa had it. Every year it used to get a nice new coat of paint. . . . Papa used to say that *nobody* had ever lost their temper at Lionnet, and *nobody* ever would. Papa would never let anybody be nasty-spoken or mean. No, sir. He just didn't like it" (145–46).

The characterization of the plantation daughter and mother so admired by Page does not quietly fade away. Female characters confront the full weight of the myth, the promise from the past and from society that approval and fulfillment reside in the role. And they contend with the popular assumption that the admired traits are compatible, an assumption based largely on the uncritical acceptance of the nineteenth-century stereotypes. But time after time they fail when measured against the mythic Southern lady. Indeed, there is an endless gallery of failed types who strive to emulate the ideal, usually succeeding in one respect or another but who finally either desert the role or fall victim to its impossible contradictions.

There are childlike women who cannot cope with life: Birdie, Laura Wingfield in *The Glass Menagerie,* Ellen Coldfield in *Absalom, Absalom!* There are restless, sexual women like Edna Pontellier in Kate Chopin's *The Awakening* and Blanche DuBois in *A Streetcar Named Desire,* who are undone by their passionate desire for life; there are vital women like Maggie of *Cat on a Hot Tin Roof* or Stella of *Streetcar,* who simply relinquish "ladyhood." There are strong matriarchs who gain their strength at the expense of submissiveness and innocence: Faulkner's Rosa Millard and Addie Bundren, Wolfe's Eliza Gant. There are the conscious pretenders who with great control live lives of duplicity, carefully making up their public faces according to the myth, but privately doubting or rejecting it. For a character like Temple Drake in *Requiem for a Nun,* the double life at last is so divided and contradictory that it proves unlivable. And, like Temple, Julia Garrett of Elizabeth Spencer's *The Snare* rejects the shelter of an artificial innocence, refusing to repress her affinity for the sensual and destructive world.

Despite this endless array of questionings and repudiations of the myth of the lady in twentieth-century literature, there are also examples of a more profound examination of the myth or, more precisely, of the mythmaking impulse that has produced the Southern lady. As conclusion to these observations about the relation of the lady to the Southern Literary Renaissance, I should like briefly to discuss the portrayal of the female protagonist who consciously examines the traditional role in her search for a rich life and comes to understand on the one hand the unreality of the image of the lady and, on the other, the vitality and grandeur of the myth. Many examples are available here, but three characters will illustrate the way in which the role of the lady defines and locates the past for the protagonist, then forces her to search out the truth—and lies—of the past, and ultimately to measure herself against it. Having made the journey backwards in time, the protagonist comes to regard herself as a person in history, as one who has been shaped by images and myths she only partly apprehends and controls, and, at last, as one who in her turn will be a shaper of myths to come.

Katherine Anne Porter's Miranda embodies the kind of intellectual and moral complexity that distinguishes these women. In the stories of *The Old Order,* the author portrays the family background that works upon Miranda. "The Source" introduces the Grandmother, who like a plantation mistress directs the life around her, passing judgment on her own inherited past and decreeing what memories, values, and rituals are to be maintained. She is a "caretaker" of the past, and her value to her grandchildren's generation is principally in furnishing a code of values, clear cut and firmly believed in. To Miranda, she was "the only reality . . . in a world that seemed otherwise without fixed authority or refuge" (8). Miranda, like Quentin Compson, is compelled to search out the reality of the past and—just as her grandmother had once done—to perform her own act of judging what is worthy of reverence and respect, and what is possible (and necessary) to hold on to.

Perhaps Miranda's mother might have guided and helped ease the clash of old and new orders. She is described as the kind of woman whose "idea of a honeymoon would be to follow the chuck-wagon on the round-up, and help in the cattle-branding on her father's ranch." In the Grandmother's view, she was "altogether too Western, too modern, something like the 'new' woman who was beginning to run wild, asking for the vote, leaving her home and going out in the world to earn her own living" (22). But her mother has died before Miranda ever begins her search to know the family and the culture she has been born to, and thus she must confront the old order, reconstructing and interpreting it from various witnesses' stories, largely on her own. For Miranda, understanding the past is delayed until her adult experience gives her emotional sympathy, as in "The Grave" when, walking by the stalls in a Mexican market, she finally comprehends the treasures she and her brother had discovered years before in two open graves. In "Old Mortality," Miranda as a young wife seems very much like the "modern woman" her mother had been. Returning home for the funeral of her uncle, she undertakes to discover the truths of her father's and her grandmother's generations and, by doing so, to interpret society's uses of the past.

She hears repeatedly that her Aunt Amy had been the quintessential belle, belonging to the world of music and poetry. Her story was filled with romantic excitement: a host of gentlemen callers, a duel of sorts, a mad horseback trip to the border, marriage to handsome, reckless Gabriel, even a youthful, tubercular death just six weeks after her marriage. All "charm and vivacity," as Amanda Wingfield would say—in short, a beauty. In this family there was no equivocation or uncertainty about what sort of person "a beauty" described. It is a familiar portrait: "First, a beauty must be tall; . . . the hair must be dark . . . the skin must be pale and smooth. . . . A beauty must be a good dancer, superb on horseback, with a serene manner, an amiable gaiety tempered with dignity at all hours. Beautiful teeth and hands, of course, and over and above all this, some mysterious crown of enchantment that attracted and held the heart" (112). As a child, Miranda and her sister had searched in vain among the family pictures and mementos for some evidence of this glamor and had found only a disappointing ordinariness. Miranda's suffragist cousin Eva further contradicts the Amy legend and the myth of the beautiful, innocent lady. To her the family's stories are silly illusions, or worse—malicious, destructive distortions.

At the conclusion of the story, recalling her own experiences as well as the stories she has been told, Miranda recognizes that her psyche has been shaped by her grandmother, Aunt Amy, and Cousin Eva. She also recognizes that her determination to know *the* truth about them is a childish expectation, and she gives it up as pointless. She does not give up the illusion, however, that she can know *the* truth about herself, nor does she ever quite understand that she will be the next generation's mythmaker and the object of its puzzlement and confusion. Porter makes sure the reader understands, however, her subtle irony richly exposing Miranda's brash egoism. At the same time, Porter communicates her own admiration for both family legends and family facts. As Richard Gray remarks, Porter embodies in "Old Mortality" a "measure of equilibrium between our sympathy for the myth-making impulse and our recognition of the recalcitrant facts" (191).

Resembling Miranda, Dicey Hastings in Eudora Welty's story "Kin" returns from her home in the North to her family's homestead in Mississippi. Engaged to a Northerner, she decides that before she can set her own direction she must revisit the models of her past, take account of her kin, and try thereby to understand what lies ahead for her as a woman. With her cousin Kate she drives out to the old family place, site of large family gatherings she remembers from her childhood. It is the home of her great uncle Felix, who, as her Aunt Ethel recalls, "always made us be ladies out there" (117). The house is very much alive, filled with mementos and, on the day of Dicey's visit, brimming with the whole countryside who have come to have pictures made by an itinerant photographer set up in the parlor. She tries to talk to Uncle Felix, but too ill to speak, he writes instead a cryptic message: "River—Daisy—Midnight—Please" (148). The note intrigues Dicey (Felix's wife had been Beck, not Daisy), suggesting a man very different from the "real" Uncle Felix that Dicey sees and remembers.

Although Uncle Felix does not give her the sense of direction that she has come such a long way for, Dicey does at last glimpse what lies ahead for her. As she watches the busy procession of country people having photographs made, she is amused to think how artificial and vain is their effort to capture the moment. The young man in a borrowed soldier's uniform, standing against a painted backdrop hung over the parlor wall, gives unmistakable evidence that the images of the past handed to later generations will be false. But the falsity, Dicey suspects, also obliquely points to a deeper truth, a paradox that is in fact enacted in the parlor—a picture behind the picture.

Dicey notices an old portrait hanging on the wall behind the photographer's artificial backdrop, one well remembered from her childhood for it was the only picture in the whole house. It showed "the romantic figure of a young lady seated on a fallen tree under brooding skies," Dicey's "Great-Grandmother Jerrold, who had been Evelina Mackaill." Like a coded message, the portrait tells her what truth *is* handed from the past: "I remembered—rather, more warmly, *knew*, like a secret of the family—that the head of this black-haired, black-eyed lady who always looked the right, mysterious age to be my sister, had been fitted to the ready-made portrait by the painter who had called at the door—he had taken the family off guard, I was sure of it, and had spoken to their pride" (147).

Welty suggests that the portraits and mementos—and the myths—reveal the human effort to preserve and honor an ideal of itself, the impulse of civilization. The factual inaccuracy of the record is of little matter. As Dicey thinks, "The yellow skirt spread fanlike, straw hat held ribbon-in-hand, orange beads big as peach pits (to conceal the joining at the neck)—none of that, any more than the forest scene so unlike the Mississippi wilderness . . . or the melancholy clouds obscuring the sky behind the passive figure with the small crossed feet—none of it, world or body, was really hers. *She* had eaten bear meat, seen Indians, she had married into the wilderness at Mingo, to what unknown feelings" (147–48).

Dicey gives up the hope of really possessing the elusive past. She acknowledges that she is a link among the kin, but she understands that she will have to make her separate place in her own time, just as she is sure Evelina once had done: "those eyes, opaque, all pupil, belonged to Evelina—I knew, because they saw out, as mine did; weren't warned, as mine weren't and never shut before the end, as mine would not. I, her divided sister, knew who had felt the wildness of the world behind the ladies' view. We were homesick for somewhere that was the same place" (148).

Laura McKelva Hand in Welty's *The Optimist's Daughter* is also homesick for some place that is her own, of her own time. Like Miranda and Dicey she journeys homeward and explores the myths transmitted to her from the past. At home in Mount Salus, Mississippi, she faces the funeral of her father, an ordeal that is intensified by the presence of a vulgar, empty-headed young stepmother who exists as a perfect betrayal of every possession and attribute of Laurel's mother, Becky, who by the town's reckoning was the epitome of the "lady." On the surface, as Carol S. Manning points out, the novel might seem, in fact, to be Welty's "traditional Southern novel," but *The Optimist's Daughter* "does not suppose that the weaknesses observable in members of the Old Order are products of the changing times, nor does it suggest that once upon a time people were better" (175).

Laurel Hand, a widow in her early forties, is a woman who struggles with the hard, eternal lessons: the inescapable dependency of human experience, that we are ever as children and like the pigeons she had watched as a child: "sticking their beaks down each other's throats, gagging each other, eating out of each other's craws, swallowing down all over again what had been swallowed before" (140). Laurel thought, too, she already knew the lesson of mortality, that death is inevitable and the past, irretrievable. She had given up a handsome young husband to the war and her mother to a slow, agonizing death ten years earlier. As a child Laurel had imagined her mother powerful and unalterable, knowing, as Becky did, where back in West Virginia the choicest strawberries grew, knowing how to *command* roses to grow, to make life proceed with order. But Laurel had eventually learned that Becky was not immune to time. She had built her own life, created her own myth out of the values gained from the past, but, as Laurel discovers, she had finally left no pattern of living a daughter could follow. In the end her mother's power to order the daily activity of life was as vulnerable as a rosebed neglected for a season. With all this knowledge carried to the heart, Laurel confronts the inevitable dilemma manifest in her early lessons: she must maintain her ties to the past, and yet she must constantly struggle to free herself sufficiently to create a separate self.

The only escape from constant memory and ambitious hopes is offered by Fay, an escape wholly repugnant to Laurel. Healthy, lusty, brash Fay is the antithesis of the lady. With green shoes clicking, she is eternal nature, like the weather, Laurel thinks at one point. Fay is *outside* history. "The past isn't a thing to me," she says, "I belong to the future" (179). She offers no troubling, unrealistic historical myth; she embodies raw life force and is heedless of human efforts to cherish and preserve fine moments in time. Horrified by what she sees in Fay, that is, oblivion, Laurel gratefully acquiesces to the burden of history, to her place as Southern daughter of a great lady. She does not "adopt" the past, nor does she reject it. She consents to remember. She thinks at the conclusion, "The past is no more open to help or hurt than was Father in his coffin. The past is like him, impervious, and can never be awakened. It is memory that . . . will come back . . . , calling us by our names and demanding its rightful tears. It will never be impervious" (179).

Memory, one might say, is for Laurel "myth recovered." She consents to live with a fictionalized past because it is her human inheritance, including the falsified ideal of her mother Becky. Welty has created characters who see unmistakably that myths are constructed of paradoxes and contradictions, built upon falsity and repression as much as candor and openness, but deserving respectful attention because they are legacies of an idealized vision of human possibility. Even the fantastic exaltation of the Southern lady attests finally to the human imagination. The "lady" is no more nor less a human fiction than is the past itself. And, as Welty shows, human fictions are the glory of the human race, creations of spunky men and women who reach out, prize what they discover, aggrandize it, and transform the reality of their lives to beget a heightened version of themselves for their sons and daughters.

WORKS CITED

Allen, James Lane. *A Kentucky Cardinal.* New York: Macmillan, 1906.

Cash, Wilbur J. *The Mind of the South.* New York: Alfred A. Knopf, 1941.

Clinton, Catherine. *The Plantation Mistress: Woman's World in the Old South.* New York: Pantheon, 1982.

Eaton, Clement. *The Growth of the Southern Civilization, 1790–1860.* New York: Harper and Row, 1961.

Fitzhugh, George. *Sociology for the South.* Richmond: A. Morris, 1854.

Fox-Genovese, Elizabeth. *Within the Plantation Household: Black and White Women of the Old South.* Chapel Hill: University of North Carolina Press, 1988.

Gilbert, Sandra M., and Susan Gubar. *The Madwoman in the Attic: The Woman Writer and the Nineteenth-Century Literary Imagination.* New Haven: Yale University Press, 1979.

Glasgow, Ellen. *The Sheltered Life.* Garden City, N.Y.: Doubleday, 1932.

Gray, Richard. *The Literature of Memory: Modern Writers of the American South.* Baltimore: Johns Hopkins University Press, 1977.

Gwin, Minrose C. *Black and White Women of the Old South: The Peculiar Sisterhood in American Literature.* Knoxville: University of Tennessee Press, 1985.

Hellman, Lillian. *Collected Plays.* Boston: Little, Brown, 1972.

Jones, Anne Goodwyn. *Tomorrow Is Another Day: The Woman Writer in the South, 1859–1936.* Baton Rouge: Louisiana State University Press, 1981.

Kennedy, John Pendleton. *Swallow Barn; or, A Sojourn in the Old Dominion.* 1832. Baton Rouge: Louisiana State University Press, 1986.

King, Richard H. *A Southern Renaissance: The Cultural Awakening of the American South, 1930–1955.* New York: Oxford University Press, 1980.

Lebsock, Suzanne. *The Free Women of Petersburg: Status and Culture in a Southern Town, 1784–1860.* New York: W. W. Norton, 1984.

Manning, Carol S. *With Ears Opening Like Morning Glories: Eudora Welty and the Love of Storytelling.* Westport, Conn.: Greenwood Press, 1985.

Page, Thomas Nelson. *Social Life in Old Virginia Before the War.* New York: Charles Scribner's Sons, 1897.

Porter, Katherine Anne. *The Old Order.* New York: Harvest Books, 1958.

Scott, Anne Firor. *The Southern Lady: From Pedestal to Politics 1830–1930.* Chicago: University of Chicago Press, 1970.

Seidel, Kathryn Lee. *The Southern Belle in the American Novel.* Tampa: University of South Florida Press, 1985.

Tate, Allen. "The New Provincialism." 1945. Rpt. in *Collected Essays.* Denver: Alan Swallow, 1959. 282–93

Taylor, William R. *Cavalier and Yankee: The Old South and American National Character.* 1961. Garden City, N.Y.: Doubleday, 1963.

Welter, Barbara. *Dimity Convictions.* Athens: Ohio University Press, 1976.

Welty, Eudora. "Kin." In *The Bride of the Innisfallen and Other Stories.* New York: Harcourt, Brace and World, 1955. 112–55.

———. *The Optimist's Daughter.* New York: Random House, 1972.

Westling, Louise. *Sacred Groves and Ravaged Gardens: The Fiction of Eudora Welty, Carson McCullers, and Flannery O'Connor.* Athens: University of Georgia Press, 1985.

Wyatt-Brown, Bertram. *Southern Honor: Ethics and Behavior in the Old South.* New York: Oxford University Press, 1982.

Joan Schulz

Orphaning as Resistance

The literature of the American South is—or, perhaps, more aptly, has until fairly recently been—distinctly and distinctively a regional literature, a product of a regional consciousness that Allen Tate describes in "The New Provincialism": "that consciousness or that habit of men in a given locality which influences them to certain patterns of thought and conduct [and, he adds elsewhere, "a quality of judgment"] handed to them by their ancestors." Without that regional consciousness, says Tate, "no literature can be mature" (325, 322). According to the South's proponents in, for example, their famous manifesto *I'll Take My Stand* (1930), and according to many of its fictional recreators and critics in the twentieth century, the values inherent in the Southern tradition—place, past, community, and especially family—are enormously important features of the regionalism Tate and others describe; taken together, they form an image of an ideal life and, understood mythically, they become enabling acts for poets and fictionalists. Furthermore, discussion and analyses of the crucial significance of all four—place, past, community, and family—comprise a substantial portion of the critical and other nonfictional literature of the Southern Renaissance. And Anne Firor Scott tells us in *The Southern Lady* that the family remained the center of most Southern women's lives well into the twentieth century: "More than other Americans, perhaps, southerners had put their faith in the family as the central institution of society, faith that was slow to change" (213).

In its twentieth-century fictional embodiment, the South has been frequently portrayed as a society in which one's identity is determined by who one's family is or who one's father is or was. As a friend once said to me, New England college women identify themselves on the basis of where their father attended college, Westerners on how big the ranch was, and Southerners on who their father was.[1] Stark Young's novel *So Red The Rose,* published in 1934, offers a prime example of this characteristic mode of self-identification. It is true, of course, as Louis Rubin, Jr., makes clear in several of his early writings, that writers of the Southern Renaissance have maintained a certain distance and detachment from the values thought to have inhered in the Old South; nonetheless, the decay of those values is often portrayed as a loss of the wholeness of life—and the decay of the family remains instrumentally uppermost in much of the male fiction as central to that loss. In addition to this primary identification with and location of value in a stable family and kinship structure, the search for the father, as in Robert Penn Warren's *All the King's Men* (1946)—or the search for *a* father, as in Allen Tate's *The Fathers* (1938) and even in Truman Capote's *Other Voices, Other Rooms* (1948)—is the motive force behind many of the more familiar men's novels having male protagonists.

That this search for a father should be considered coextensive with the location of meaning and identity in the family can be demonstrated, I think, by noting that in an exaggeratedly masculinist society, such as the South has been, the term *father* becomes a synecdoche for the family and for one's place in the community and society.[2] The nexus I am suggesting among father, family, kin, community, and society—so that to speak of family is to imply community and even the culture as a whole—has not always been spelled out in explicit ways, but it is implicit in the commentary on the South of historians, sociologists, literary and social critics, and even of novelists themselves. The links may often be implicit or only partially formulated, but they are pervasive. Walker Percy is, interestingly, one of the few who makes the connection between the public and private explicit and extreme. Postulating the "absence of a truly public zone" in the South, Percy suggests in "Mississippi: The Fallen Paradise" that the family "came to coincide with the actual public space which it inhabited" (230). And, in *A Requiem for the Renascence,* Walter Sullivan says of Katherine Anne Porter's *Old Mortality,* "The family is the microcosmic representation of Southern society" (7); so, too, is Southern society often treated as a macrocosm of the family.

Throughout the critical literature, commentators return again and again to the sense of the larger South as a community—"a group of people held together by shared values"—and of the local community (of past and present) as an embodiment of values having their roots and significance in kinship structures. In a panel discussion on Southern literature, Cleanth Brooks put it succinctly: "Another, though a related way to look at the South, is to regard it as a kinship society. . . . No wonder that the family bulks large in the southern 'society.' No wonder that in southern literature the family occupies so important a place" (Rubin and Holman 201–2). And Brooks has said elsewhere, "The southern writers of our century present a culture in which interpersonal relationships are close and important. The family still exists as a normative and stabilizing force" (Brooks 10).[3]

It is also the case that whatever similarly pervasive obeisance may be made to Southern ladyhood, and to the moral and familial power of the woman as wife and mother, both the community and the family as concepts are singularly male in Southern life and letters. Rubin succinctly, though probably unconsciously, demonstrates the equation between community and maleness: "The essence of membership in the old Southern community was the sense of belonging, of being able to define one's place, one's identity as a *man* through one's role in the community's life" (*Faraway Country* 11—italics mine). And when historian Bertram Wyatt-Brown points to the crucial "community values of honor and reputation" (127), it is clear from the whole of his book, *Southern Honor,* that *male* should modify that phrase. So, too, when Hugh Holman in *Three Modes of Modern Southern Fiction* speaks of the entire Southern social order (read "larger community") as in large measure resting upon "a concept of honor" (13), one understands male honor to be determinative and the community to be male.

Inadvertently demonstrating the same point, Louis Rubin tells an anecdote about John Donald Wade and "two of his colleagues from the University of Georgia," swapping good-old-boy stories, the point of which was that they were "demonstrating to each other, but most of all to themselves, that they were still southern boys. They were, to put a more formal construction upon it, asserting their community identity" (*The Writer in the Modern South* 83, 85). Several pages later, Rubin adds, "The South's version of the harmonious community had tradi-tionally been for whites only" (95), and, I would suggest, in its most cherished freedoms and meanings, for white *men* only. One under-stands readily from these examples Wyatt-Brown's comment: "All ranks of men agreed that women, like other dependents upon male leadership and livelihood, should be subordinate, docile" (228).

In "The Profession of Letters in the South," Allen Tate asks two questions in the same paragraph, and the juxtaposition underscores the conceptual equation of community and family with men: "And, where, outside the South, is there a society that believes even covertly in the Code of Honor? . . . Where else in the modern world is the patriarchal family still innocent of the rise and power of other forms of society?" (308). Faulkner's *Absalom, Absalom!* provides us with probably the clearest fictional portrayal of the connections among fatherhood, family, and community in the older South: As Walter Sullivan says, Sutpen's "design . . . —that of establishing a family, a name to be passed from father to son and to accrue respectability in the passing, is the only way possible for him to succeed. Sutpen's character is such—his dimensions so exaggerated, his accomplishments so vast—that he can properly be extrapolated into an image of the South" (10–11).

Although both are widely taken for granted as true for women by critics who are (in the main) male, neither the exaggerated valuation of the traditional family nor the connection of family and community operates in a significant group of works by women writers in which female characters are central. A substantial—and at first glance, surprising—number of women in novels and short stories by Southern women authors "orphan" themselves. Some few are orphans to begin with, remain so by choice, and appear to be none the worse for it. More importantly, a larger number are women who either have or are offered families and who choose to orphan themselves—literally or metaphorically. In doing so, they signal themselves as resisting, refusing, or rejecting the kind of family identity, family roles, and family ties with the past or the present considered so vital to the Southern way of life, sought after or lamented with such vigor and obsessiveness by male figures in Southern literature, and treated as the central response by male critics.[4] Donald Davidson singled out what he referred to as "a moment of extreme consciousness" after World War I when the decay of Southern society and its values was at last acutely perceived. While Southern male writers were busily responding with a literary renaissance that reexamined the values inhering in the Southern tradition, and frequently mourned the loss of them, some of the women writers of the renaissance were establishing an alternative tradition of dissent respecting the values and virtues of family. Women writers knew the same sense of loss and privation as their male counterparts, but they also must be presumed to have seen how little traditional family life had offered to women. Hence the orphaning phenomenon found in many of their works. Frequently their female characters suggest by their words or actions that they prefer to risk solitariness, exclusion, estrangement, even isolation; that they prefer deracination—or even death—to absorption in the family of the past or the present.[5]

In brief, the oppressive nature of the family for Southern women rests on its denial to them of a separate and self-determined existence and on its demand that they live out the dictates of the family's past. Southern women in particular are expected to adulate and emulate the family's past as it is conveyed to them in legends, stories, and clichés, despite their awareness of its destructive potential for their lives. As women, they are condemned to hearing, accepting, and living by the self-destructive myths of the nature and role of women as passive, submissive, obedient, compliant, pious, and so on. They have enforced on them a role that is limited in action and activities, restrictive in behavior and conduct—that is, they must be beautiful, charming ornaments; must support the double standard of sexual conduct; must heed the imperatives of self-abnegation and duty to their families; and must limit their sphere of action to the home and family. Lastly, they are taught that, unlike a man's, a woman's source of happiness is singular and total, and is to be found only in marriage and family. In all this, they are not unlike other women in the United States, except that the demands and expectations are more exaggerated in the South because it is such an extravagantly patriarchal society.

Miranda, in Katharine Anne Porter's *Old Mortality* (1937), provides probably the most familiar example of the pattern I am exploring. Born in the last decade of the nineteenth century and growing up in the first decade of the twentieth, Miranda orphans herself, deliberately and consciously rejecting her past-intoxicated family, whose legend making centers on her ideally-beautiful Cousin Amy, conveniently dead and therefore available for fond reinterpretation by her family. Miranda chooses homelessness over the family, whose lies and destructive myths at once exalted Amy, caused her death, and would, at the very least, cripple Miranda as they crippled her ugly (because chinless) Cousin Eva.

In *Sartoris* (1929), William Faulkner shows how family myths can be equally destructive to young men. Like Miranda, young Bayard appears to be breaking his ties with the family past when, in fact, he is actually acting under the compulsion to re-create these myths under modern conditions, and he commits suicide in the attempt to live within the family's male tradition of reckless violence and false heroics. Miranda, however, instead elects orphaning as necessary to survival, and by refusing to believe or act in terms of the family mythology, she improves her chances that she will manage her life, albeit perhaps not gloriously.[6]

An equally important aspect of Miranda's defection from the family and her self-conscious orphaning rests in her rejecting the role of listener (and worshipper) at the shrine of the family legends of past glories: "Let them tell their stories to each other. Let them go on explaining how things happened. I don't care" (182). By this gesture Miranda repudiates another past, when Southern women were enjoined to be silent and listen—and to be all else that that entailed—that is, acquiescent, submissive, obedient, passive, reticent. In refusing the role of listener, Miranda protects herself against being "smothered" and forbidden "to make her own discoveries" (180).

Milly Burden, of Ellen Glasgow's *They Stooped to Folly* (1929), is another in the continually lengthening list of young women who likewise shut their ears to the voices from the family and community past, insisting on the right to selfhood involved in making their own discoveries about themselves and their world. Milly resists not only her own immediate family in the form of her mother but also the empty, restrictive, "conventional" behavior demanded of women in that society. Though Milly is not the central character in the novel, Glasgow makes her an important figure in several ways, one aspect of which is her implicit relation to two similarly "fallen women" from earlier generations. Of the three women who "stooped to folly," only Milly seems to yearn for— or even to imagine—"something" beyond living in the attic or beyond amusement, trifling, sweets, or volunteer work. For Milly (as for those other women), it is the family that serves as the repository and transmitter of those conventions against which Milly is rebelling, and it is the family, therefore, that remains the focal point of her orphaning.

Within this framework, then, both the language of Milly's rebellion and its motivation to self-determination seen in her ignoring the limiting, oppressive voices of the past and what are called in this novel, its "ideals," are strikingly similar to Miranda's in her interior reflections, as is her breaking the primary law for young women, obedience. Milly's conversation with Virginius Littlepage, a super-conservative holdover from Victorian America, who tries to play the role of surrogate father to a fatherless young woman, exemplifies the connection between the two young women. Virginius tells her:

> "The trouble is that you have learned nothing from the past, nothing from the experience of other women. . . . You have set out to demolish conventions before you have tested them."
>
> Her eyes had mocked him. "But you have tested them haven't you? And where have they led you? Could anything that we do or think end in a greater calamity? No, we'll have to learn the truth for ourselves. Nothing that the older generation can tell us will do any good. We refuse to accept your theories because we saw them all break to pieces. The truth is we are determined to think for ourselves and to make our own sort of ideals. Even if everything you say to me is true, I shouldn't consent to take my experience from you secondhand. I want to find out myself. I want the freedom to live my life as I please. I want to choose the things I believe in. . . . " (58)

Near the end of *Old Mortality*, Miranda reflects on her past and future in similar language and tone:

> Miranda walked along beside her father, feeling homeless, but not
> sorry for it. He had not forgiven her, she knew that. When would he? She
> could not guess, but she felt it would come of itself.... Surely old people
> cannot hold their grudges forever because the young want to live, too, she
> thought, in her arrogance, her pride. I will make my own mistakes, not
> yours; I cannot depend upon you beyond a certain point, why depend at
> all?... She resented, slowly and deeply and in profound silence, the
> presence of these aliens [i.e., her father and cousin Eva] who lectured and
> admonished her, who loved her with bitterness and denied her the right
> to look at the world with her own eyes, who demanded that she accept
> their version of life and yet could not tell her the truth, not in the smallest
> thing. "I hate them both," her most inner and secret mind said plainly, "I
> will be free of them, I shall not even remember them." (178–79)

And then comes Porter's famous final, ironic sentence: "At least, I can
know the truth about what happens to me, she assured herself silently,
making a promise to herself, in her hopefulness, her ignorance" (182).
While Porter questions Miranda's ability simply to walk out on the past,
she does nothing to suggest that that young woman won't bravely
attempt to be her own person.

Psychologists define the act of separating one's ego from one's family
as an identity-forming developmental task of adolescence and recognize
that girls often do not complete the separation and hence remain
"daughters" forever. Miranda and Milly, both young women, demonstrate that they are determined to make this separation, but it is noteworthy that in both cases, the language, feelings, and commitment to
estrangement, even deracination, go well beyond anything required of
young men who make that separation almost imperceptibly and whose
reintegration is far simpler in most cases.

In Eudora Welty's *Losing Battles* (1970), Gloria Short Renfro battles
to be her own person as dramatically as do Milly and Miranda, even
though her battle takes place within a different context. Choosing to
believe that the orphan Gloria is in fact a blood relative of the family
into which she marries, the clan, gathered for its annual celebration of
Grannie's birthday, tries to initiate her into the tribe, absorb her, and
deny her a separate existence. But Gloria, who to this point has been
fighting spiritually and verbally against being considered a member of
the family simply because she married into the Beecham-Renfro clan,
now physically resists (in the memorable watermelon battle) being
drawn into the Beecham family against her will and in spite of her
sense of what is "good enough" for her.

Orphan by chance and then orphan by choice, Gloria is yet another
of those women like Miranda who likewise refuse their attention to

family mythology, this time to the Renfro family's storytelling: " 'The way your family loves to tell stories, they wouldn't hear the Crack of Doom' " (128), she says to her husband, Jack, and, later, " 'They're all up there just sitting and listening to themselves talk' " (132). Gloria's resolute stance against her husband's family is in part determined by her view that the family's backward-tending storytelling is a sign of their futility; and so she is adamantly opposed to Jack's wanting merely to pick "up living right where he left off" (113) when he was sent to jail for, in effect, acting out the family's verbalized conception of him. It is noteworthy that young Bayard Sartoris also lands in jail following a similar attempt to match his actions to his family's conception of the life appropriate to a male Sartoris.

The women in these novels generally do not "act out" quite so outrageously—that is, in societal, not psychological, terms. Their rebellions are mainly quieter, though not less dramatic ones. Gloria's stubborn refusal to let the family determine her life and Jack's as well is spelled out very clearly for Jack (who feels her words as "a sudden danger") near the end of the novel, significantly at one of the few times they are alone: " 'We're to ourselves, Jack. . . . Oh, this is the way it could always be. It's just what I've dreamed of. . . . I've got you all to myself, Jack Renfro. Nobody talking, nobody listening, nobody coming—nobody about to call you or walk in on us—there's nobody left but you and me, and nothing to be in our way. . . . If we could stay this way always' " (411–12). At this time Gloria briefly outlines her future-oriented planning and resolution. From hints she has thrown out earlier in the novel, we understand that her plan involves saving Jack from his family-inspired foolishness and his pride in his own unaided power. As important, Gloria intends to protect Jack from his family's failure to do more than just talk. Like Miranda, Gloria, too, wants to make her own discoveries about life. She does not want to listen to the prideful voices of a dirt-poor past, and she is prepared to drag a still unconvinced and unsuspecting Jack along with her, away from the family. As she says, " 'I never will let you escape from me, Jack Renfro. Remember it' " (412). And as she has just said, " 'I'll never change!' " (412), we can be sure of the strength of her resistance and her resolution. That her future plans are vague and perhaps even conventional should not vitiate for us the power of her "No, in Thunder." She perceives herself as an outsider in that family and is intent upon remaining so, and she is equally intent upon remaining steadfastly loyal to her own vision of her identity and future.[7]

Dorinda Oakley, the protagonist of Ellen Glasgow's *Barren Ground* (1925), is equally "inflexible" in her purpose to be her own person and win over the odds against her at whatever cost. As was true for Milly Burden, her lover's betrayal initially forced on Dorinda the need to make her own discoveries about herself and her world. Dorinda, however, is both more prosaic and less romantic than either Milly or Miranda in her assumptions about life's possibilities. Dorinda is equally more specific about her goals—she intends to make the family land productive—and more dependent on her own physical energies than she is on the strong will and imagination she shares with the others. More prosaic also and less dramatic than the others in the form her protest takes, Dorinda is nonetheless like them in her refusal to heed the voices of the family and community past, which in her case would counsel working hard in ways familiar to all, but then stoically accepting monotony, failure, and defeat as the lot of most people.

Instead, Dorinda borrows money, learns and then employs newer methods of farming, and is rewarded not merely by being financially successful but also by achieving self-realization. Her orphaning of herself thus resides in her being, unlike her family and against their wishes and judgment, risk taking and future-directed. Her resistance to and departures from her family can be best seen in the light of what she shares with them: like her father, Dorinda feels an "intimate kinship" with nature, but his is described in terms of the body and hers of the soul, so that while he can never rise above the dumb, patient, suffering, toiling beasts he so much resembles, Dorinda survives betrayal, recovers from defeat, and succeeds in wresting a good living and a good life from the barren soil, because what Glasgow conceives of as Dorinda's essential self, like nature's, and unlike her father's, is stronger and more durable than what has happened or can happen to her.

Like her mother, Dorinda has tireless energy; unlike her mother, however, who is "driven" by it, Dorinda manages to gain control over her energy and thereby to gain "contentment" through what she refers to as "breathless activity." Of Dorinda's mother Glasgow says, "She had worked so hard for so many years that the habit had degenerated into a disease, and thrift had become a tyrant instead of a slave in her life. . . . Though she spent every bit of her strength there was nothing to show for her struggle. Like the land, which took everything and gave back nothing, the farm had drained her activity without altering its general aspect of decay" (31). The thrift the mother practices becomes a kind of metaphor for her family's unwillingness to take the necessary financial risks in order to improve the farm and their lives. Their whole existence is governed not only by their penury but by their cautiousness; Dorinda, driven by her lover Jason's defection and by her own need to achieve, is willing to gamble in ways that her family has always feared and shunned. As Dorinda and then Glasgow express it, " 'I was able to take risks because I was too unhappy to be afraid.' Yes, she had had the courage of desperation and that had saved her from failure" (269).

Dorinda may not, then, in fact be made of sterner stuff than her mother, as the vein of iron imagery Glasgow uses on the younger woman suggests; nonetheless, in paradoxical fashion, she grows healthier and more successful—though not happier—as a result of the betrayal of her adolescent dreams, and she therefore has her strength and her vitality available to her and can pit them against nature and win by her superior means. In so doing, she transcends her family and triumphs by obliterating the effects on the land of her family's past encounters with it.

Dorinda's orphaning of herself is demonstrated further by another aspect of her response to her romantic betrayal. Unlike various of her female ancestors or of female characters in fiction generally, Dorinda neither tries to commit suicide nor goes mad following Jason's betrayal of her; instead, she first takes a shot at Jason, then takes a train out of town, and finally takes her own measure of herself. Although for a time it would appear that Anna Russell's wonderful line about Brunhilda, "Well, love has certainly taken the ginger out of her," would seem to apply equally to Dorinda, finally it is her "fierce self-determination" that enables her to find satisfaction and self-realization in a life devoid of love and the kind of marriage and family that is conventionally supposed to make women happy. Dorinda does marry, but for companionship, not for either romantic love or family, and only after she has found her own way to be in the world.

Not only Dorinda Oakley, but Milly Burden, Alabama Beggs (of Zelda Fitzgerald's *Save Me the Waltz*), and Miranda—all are at first victimized by the myth of romantic love. Following their disillusionment, Dorinda and Alabama locate their selfhood in self-actualizing work of their own, Dorinda in farming and Alabama in ballet dancing. Milly's response is very like Dorinda's early focusing on her need to get away, except that Milly feels that need more directly as an alienating response to what she thinks of as her mother's continual nagging, the nagging that comes from a mother who thinks it her duty to counsel her daughter to be ashamed and penitent over her "ruin" and to sacrifice herself on the altar of woman's duty. In fact, it is Mrs. Burden's religious sense, translated into the conventional secular duties and proprieties for women, whose rehearsal so oppresses Milly and convinces her of the necessity to orphan herself. Having been betrayed by the romantic love-marriage-happiness equation, and rejecting her mother's idea of duty, Milly stubbornly asserts her right to her own life and to freedom, which is her version of her duty, and at the end of the novel she is about to leave the South to go to New York City, determined to find outside the confines of the family "some*thing* worth loving" (italics mine).[8]

Milly—who has said she despises that sacrosanct word from the old tradition, "duty," mouthed so often by her mother—nonetheless has remained with her mother out of her own sense of duty until Mrs. Burden, aided by the Littlepages, has been relieved of some of her financial burdens and her loneliness by being offered a position as matron in the charity House of Hope. Only then does Milly feel free to leave, making her strikingly similar to Virgie Rainey in Welty's *The Golden Apples* who, with the same impulses to flee family and past and the same vagueness about what the "something" outside both might be, remains at home, faithful to her mother and her family responsibilities until her mother dies. Virgie, however, like Milly, has spiritually orphaned herself from the community much earlier, never having been able to find that "something" in Morgana. Virgie is, at the same time, unlike Milly in that she has always been a rebel and a wanderer (one of the few such women to be found in Southern fiction until very recently). A breaker of rules, Virgie has already run away once before, returning presumably to care for her mother.

Milly repeats the formulation, "something worth loving," several times in the novel, which suggests that, for her, neither romantic love nor familial, conventional duties have proved to be durable or worthy enough for her. Like Dorinda, who also expresses that need for "something worth loving," Milly feels she must leave, if only long enough to experience some freedom from the dead hand of the past and her mother. Milly, however, may finally be leaving the (Southern) family forever, whereas Dorinda, following a different trajectory, returns to transcend past and family.

That "stubborn resolution, which," we are told by Glasgow, "was the controlling motive in [Dorinda's] character [and] shot through her like a bolt" (134), is equally an aspect of Molly Bolt, Rita Mae Brown's protagonist in *Rubyfruit Jungle* (1973). Molly Bolt, whose name suggests not only the resoluteness she shares with Dorinda but also her primary impulse, which is always to leave, insists on living her life her own way and proves as inflexible as Dorinda in her purposefulness. Thus, for example, Molly flatly ignores—where she doesn't ridicule—her adopted mother's and aunt's continual remonstrances that she be a lady and model herself on Cheryl Speigelglass, who wears dresses and looks like Shirley Temple. There are, of course, significant differences between Molly Bolt's rebelliousness and resoluteness and those of the earlier fictional protagonists so far surveyed. Perhaps the most significant difference is that Molly is a lesbian, and Brown seems to be suggesting that her lesbianism accounts for her willingness to take risks, her determination to live as she sees fit, and, in general, her more fully developed sense of self. At the same time, Molly's learning that she is not only an orphan but a bastard to boot is the efficient cause of her decision to be herself at all costs—and that self is centrally a lesbian. At first shocked and then frightened when her "mother" flings her true heritage in her face, Molly runs off to the wheat fields near her house, significantly vowing, "Well, I ain't going back into that house for them to laugh at me and look at me like I'm a freak" and, as significantly deciding, "I can't see why it's such a big deal. Who cares how you got here? . . . I got myself born, that's what counts" (8, 9).

It is equally the case that *Rubyfruit Jungle* postdates the resurgence of the women's movement, and Molly may also be seen as responding to more contemporary possibilities for women. The result is that Molly Bolt both shares attitudes with her predecessors and, at the same time, moves well beyond them in the vehemence of her defiance. For example, whereas Dorinda's resistance to her family is muted, Molly's is as flamboyant as her denial of the importance of her familial origins—"It makes no difference where I came from. I'm here ain't I?" (7). Molly's self-definition and goals are as future-oriented as are those of the others, and like theirs, require rejecting the familiar roles and models available to her as a woman. Molly, for example, rejects her family's implicit desire that she elect the typical female, private, and silenced role of sexual ornament and object rather than any public, vocal one: "Carrie and Florence [her adopted mother and aunt] were scandalized that I had been elected student council president. Carrie had her heart set on me being prom queen" (78). Except that Molly comes to her decision about herself and her future earlier than Miranda and that she is literally an orphan, Molly's determination about herself could be Miranda's updated:

> I had never thought I had much in common with anybody. I had no mother, no father, no roots, no biological similarities called sisters and brothers. And for a future I didn't want a split-level home with a station wagon, pastel refrigerator, and a houseful of blonde children evenly spaced through the years. I didn't want to walk into the pages of McCall's magazine and become the model housewife. I didn't even want a husband or any man for that matter. I wanted to go my own way. That's all I think I ever wanted, to go my own way and maybe find some love here and there. Love, but not the now and forever kind with chains around your vagina and a short circuit in your brain. I'd rather be alone. (88)

And one suspects that Molly is not only correct about her family's motive for their rehearsal of the past but that it might apply in some ways to Miranda's family as well: "Mothers and aunts tell us about infancy and early childhood, hoping we won't forget the past when they had total control over our lives and secretly praying that because of it, we'll include them in our future" (3).

As a matter of fact, Molly does include her adoptive mother in her future. Having been disowned by Carrie, Molly moves from Florida to New York City, enrolls in NYU, studies photography, and for her senior project visits Carrie in the South and makes a very successful short documentary film of her mother's random talk. Despite this rapprochement, however, Molly is forced to deny her own memory and her own sense of their mutual family past in order to maintain the recently established good feeling between them. As she leaves her mother, it is clear that she will continue to resist the kind of family identity and societal roles her mother, in her reconstruction of the past and desire to negotiate a lien on the future, would force her to accept. And it is similarly clear at the end of the novel that Molly intends to continue fighting the world until it allows her selfhood on her own terms. After graduating from college summa cum laude and Phi Beta Kappa, Molly goes job hunting and runs up against a certain typicality of woman's experience: secretarial jobs or low-paying offers to grind out PR for the latest releases of other people's movies. As she says, "No, I wasn't surprised but it still brought me down." And she concludes, "Damn, I wished the world would let me be myself"—that is, a lesbian with a mind and the ambition to achieve in the public sphere: "One way or another I'll make those movies and I don't feel like having to fight until I'm fifty. But if it does take that long then watch out world because I'm going to be the hottest fifty-year-old this side of Mississippi" (245–46).

For the moment, however, "the hottest fifty-year-old this side of Mississippi" has to be Su McCulvey, like Molly a lesbian and like her willing to risk exclusion and estrangement from her family and society rather than submit to its combined dictates about woman's nature and role. Su, June Arnold's protagonist in *Sister Gin* (1975), is like these other female protagonists in that she, too, refuses to listen, in this instance not to family legends but to the equally dishonest and evasive clichés that pass for family wisdom, and in that she, too, refuses to submit to others' demands on her life or to accept their versions of the world.

Su's case is a rather complicated one. Her resistance to the family begins early in a rather conventionally adolescent rebellion; later, she resists the family-encouraged female role and opts for what she calls "Fame." Additionally, she diverges from her family and separates herself from the male-dominated culture in which she has been raised by living with another woman for years. Their physical relationship is, however, kept secret, and the result is that, for all her resistance to family and society, Su has generally lived publicly *within* the culture to a large extent. Thus, unlike Molly, it is not until Su is fifty years old that her real orphaning process begins, but it is no less crucial and conclusive for all that. It is, in fact, a tribute to the power of that family-inspired, female-inhibiting culture that Su is fifty and menopausal rather than fifteen and menstrual before she finally discovers her sense of selfhood and is ready to act on that discovery. That action initially takes the form of a "daring" decision to speak and live out the truth, instead of silently living out the clichés, lies, and deceits she has learned from her family.

Su's decision to be no longer quiet, compliant, and acquiescent but instead to speak the truth loses her an influential job as a book-reviewer, temporarily makes an alcoholic of her, and, most importantly, fails to get her the genuine, open, and honest relationship with her mother that she seeks. Su's mother wants neither to talk about herself nor to hear about Su's life, and she simply refuses to believe Su's open avowal of her lesbianism. Paradoxically, Su's attempt to speak openly to her mother about her lesbianism measures both her desire to separate her life from her mother's and to forge family ties that never existed. But her mother won't have it; she is too threatened by the truth. Having maintained her own family relationships and identity by living out women's lies about her feelings toward men, marriage, and family, Su's mother cannot, at seventy-seven years old, reverse a whole lifetime. So it is left to another seventy-seven-year-old woman, Mamie Carter, to help Su complete both her orphaning and her self-actualizing. Mamie accomplishes this by releasing Su from fear, making her "bold,"—a term of opprobrium for women in her mother's generation—kindling her anger against the male culture and the deceptions it forces on women, and rekindling her determination to write. Su resolves that whatever happens, she will not abort the "baby"—that is, her identity—growing inside her, and will, instead, allow that baby to express itself in the form of a book. Not the book she once wanted to write for "Fame," but a book that speaks to and for other women, "so that all the women could hear, even those who didn't listen any more: All out come in free! That would be her play; Or book. Or . . . " (205).

Whatever Su's final "or" means, it is a long way both in time and in tone from the fate of the much-earlier Edna Pontellier of Kate Chopin's *The Awakening* (1899). Edna's ultimate self-actualization, unlike that of the others, takes the form of suicide. Having earlier orphaned herself from her husband and children, and from her father, who believed that if wives or daughters disobey their husbands or fathers they should be beaten, Edna finally elects to commit suicide rather than submit to the circumscribed and, for her, unfulfilling role of wife and mother. Edna feels passionately that the institutions of marriage and family do not allow her a separate and sustaining identity any more than love affairs would. And even though Kate Chopin treats Edna's suicide as an affirmative gesture, summoning up all the positive imagery associated with the sea in the novel to support this depiction, the implications of her act are clear: Edna's society has failed to provide her with either positive models or internal resources that would enable her to live a self-determined life; therefore, she must die to confirm her selfhood.

And die she does, unlike the more recent Ginny Babcock, the protagonist of Lisa Alther's *Kinflicks* (1975), whose many unsuccessful attempts both to orphan herself and to realize and actualize her identity eventuate in a series of comically treated, but ultimately ironic, attempts at suicide. For contemporary women, Alther seems to be saying, suicide is no answer, and if the alternative is merely a never-ending search for selfhood and self-actualization, so be it. Ginny will just have to keep picking up her knapsack and moving on, as she does at the end of the novel.

Ginny initially left her hometown in Tennessee with a clear intent to remove herself as far from town and family as possible. As Mary Anne Ferguson says, "She has escaped . . . in the hope that she would not replicate the experience of her mother and of her mother's mother who had played to the hilt the traditional role of mother/wife who gave all to husband and family" (105). Near the end of the novel, Ginny reluctantly returns because her widowed mother is very ill. Though ambivalent about her relationship with her mother, she resolves to help her mother, but we soon understand that Ginny also wants her mother to help her. In a partial reversal of her earlier orphaning, Ginny turns to her mother, hoping that the older woman will reveal something that will help Ginny live. Her mother refuses. Having decided that her lifetime commitment to nurturing others was meaningless and now focused solely on herself, Mrs. Babcock will not be nurturer to Ginny. Oddly enough, by so refusing, she helps complete Ginny's orphaning. At first distraught, Ginny finally understands that, as Ferguson concludes, "her mother's refusal was a gift to her, the gift of freedom from role-playing and guilt" (106).

The forces motivating the resistance of these female characters to family values and morés and to the centrality and synecdochical quality of family to the good life—Southern style—are more fully explored in these novels than are the solutions the women seek. The novelists are compelling in their depiction of their characters' quests for self-determination and self-actualization, of women who recognize themselves as essentially outsiders in their culture and who hence determine to discover or create their own cultural visions and versions of themselves. The sense of the narrow and narrowing rewards for women of family life in an extravagantly realized and self-proclaimed patriarchal society and the failure to find satisfaction in the roles available to women in Southern society are convincingly portrayed, as are these characters' refusals to be silent.

At the same time, we do not often get specific answers to the question, "What new ways of living have women writers discovered for their characters to replace acceptance of Southern society's assigned roles and behavioral models for women?" For the most part, what we get are powerfully enacted statements of a woman's right to live for herself and not for her family or within the usual family sphere. For these women characters, for whom marriage is the only career and source of happiness culturally validated, and for whom "duty" is the prescribed motive for action, merely refusing these forms for their lives is plainly subversive. To expect women who have not been encouraged to be goal-oriented and who have almost no positive models for alternative life patterns to be other than vague in their sense of what that "something worth loving" is, is to demand too much. For most, as a friend said to me recently, "They just knew they had to get the hell out."[9]

Postscript

The forms that women's "orphaning" take in these novels and stories are various, but can be subsumed under the categories of separation and reinvention. The former, separation, includes inattentiveness, refusal, and departure. The latter, reinvention, involves intellectual and spiritual reconstitution, experimenting with new forms and directions for their lives, risk taking, future-orientation, and, as importantly, finding their voices.

Perhaps it is this last, finding their voices, that is finally the most important step women characters take in many of these novels. In an article entitled "The Woman's War," written in 1910, Mary Johnston wrote, "In the South we are not used to woman's speaking"; and in 1913 in her essay "Feminism," Ellen Glasgow said, "Woman has become at last not only human but articulate."[10] Since, as Anne Goodwyn Jones points out, "The word 'inarticulate' appears repeatedly, almost repetitiously, in [Glasgow's] *The Woman Within*" and is indirectly connected with suffering and womanhood (230, 231), the movement toward speaking oneself and one's desires is momentous.[11] Discourse materializes possibility, and the orphaning enacted through constructing the self as a speaking subject prepares the ground for contemporary women writers and their female characters.

NOTES

1. In *Southern Honor,* Bertram Wyatt-Brown cites studies of Southerners' "adherence to family names"—that is, male first names—through the generations as suggesting that this custom of "naming sons for paternal forebears . . . helped to make everyone feel loyal not to an immediate father alone, but to a whole weighty series of fathers" (125). The most confusing and most destructive example of this practice is, of course, in William Faulkner's *Sartoris,* but even in Eudora Welty's *The Golden Apples* "Morgana judges everyone according to who his or her parents are" (Manning 129).

2. It should be noted that the Freudian implications of a search for the father are not primarily or necessarily what is at issue or uppermost in these male novels. Richard H. King reads the whole Southern Renaissance as a playing out of the Oedipal family romance, but not only does this position mandate King's avoidance of women writers, but it also severely limits the terms of the male quest in these novels, the significance of which involves a determination of who and what the self is in relation to community, society, history, and place.

3. Neither the family as "normative . . . force" nor its particular Southern configurations are, of course, unique to the South. What is peculiar to the South and to Southern literature as seen through male critics and commentators is the strength of what Wilbur Cash calls the "domestic sentiment" (88). From John Crowe Ransom's "Statement of Principles" in *I'll Take My Stand* (xxv), where he refers to "family living" as one of the "amenities" of life (amenities being crucial to the life worth living), to articles by Sullivan and Brooks in *Southern Renascence* (edited by Rubin and Robert D. Jacobs), the centrality and significance of family to Southern literature is repeatedly underlined.

4. The list of (mostly Southern) male literary critics who do not cite, discuss, or even mention women writers much less distinguish and address any issues that might be called particularly theirs is legion. Nearly always and everywhere, the Southern writer is spoken of as man, with the context making it clear that this "man" is sex-specific, not generic. A telling instance is to be found in *Southern Literary Study* (Rubin and Holman), the proceedings of a conference held at Chapel Hill in late 1972. Except for Rubin's praise of Eudora Welty as "marvellous" and "not just another good southern woman writer" but "a major writer" (154, 155), and a nod to Flannery O'Connor and Elizabeth Spencer by other panelists, in not one of the three moderated discussions does any one of the all-male panelists ever mention a Southern woman writer, much less consider women's issues—as writers or characters—and all this from a group devoting its attention to the themes, problems, continuities and discontinuities

in Southern literature and literary history. In an Appendix to this volume, the editors list 128 "Topics for Further Study": Although several suggestions refer to very minor writers and issues, only three propose work on Southern women writers, two on individual writers, McCullers and Gordon, and one on diaries and memoirs.

5. I say "establishing an alternative tradition of dissent" while knowing that several Southern women writers of the nineteenth century had challenged earlier the traditional pieties and expectations surrounding women. The difference is that in the earlier novels the writers and female characters either did not challenge the traditional family or backed off at the end. (Louise Westling calls it having "finally capitulated to the traditional expectations for the lady" [37].) The earliest literary critic who approached this material appears to have been Nina Baym, who studied women in popular literature from 1790–1870, among them several Southern writers. These novels are forerunners of the ones I study to the extent that, as Baym found, "In no case ... does the male provide validation for feminine existence.... The marriage-and-motherhood syndrome is presented as the most desirable life for a woman, *but it is not required to complete her as a human being*" (229, 230). Though many of the female characters in these novels are orphans, they do not orphan themselves. In fact, being an orphan in *these* novels engages the pathos of the reader and/or is the motive force for the character to achieve "self-control and self-dependence" and, only then, domesticity.

Studying some of the same women writers a little later, Miriam Shillingsburg and Anne Goodwyn Jones take different and more fully marked paths to conclusions fairly similar to Baym's. Shillingsburg, for example, found "an undercurrent of discontent among nineteenth-century Southern women" that found a voice in the "extremely popular fiction ... they wrote and read" (127). See also Westling's extremely useful study of O'Connor, Welty, and McCullers, in which she wrestles with the problem of women writers "growing up in the 1920s [who] inherited an acute consciousness of what they could not be, of how the past had jilted their mothers and grandmothers. They would take the more difficult step to discover who they were" (37).

6. The grandmother's story in the sketches called "The Old Order" could have been an inverted cautionary tale for Miranda, had silence not reigned so supreme in the family. For us, the grandmother's story suggests why later generations of women would be forced to make so powerful, open, and vocal a break as can be seen in their impulse to orphan themselves.

7. Looking at Welty's work as a whole, one sees that there are other orphans in it—and that Welty does not always use them to challenge the family "system" as it were. Easter, for example, in *The Golden Apples,* is an orphan who appears to be an orphan by choice as well, but looking more closely, one understands her to be not only someone without the opportunity to evaluate the family or community as value systems but, finally, a little girl who, as Carol S. Manning points out, asks to be "carried" back to her tent after her near-drowning (110). The point is that though Easter is presented as defiant, Welty does not set her in

a context of any kind of family that attempts either to smother or socialize her. Wanda Fay, Judge McKelva's second wife in *The Optimist's Daughter*, is another of Welty's characters who seems quite clearly to orphan herself, denying she even has a family until they show up for the Judge's funeral. However, although Fay dismisses virtually the whole Southern tradition, referring to herself as futuristic—" 'The past isn't a thing to me. I belong to the future, didn't you know that?' " (179)—when her family's values begin to emerge at the funeral of Judge McKelva, it is clear that she is one of them and even demonstrates positive family feeling. She has not looked at the family in its restrictive role of socializer of women and then orphaned herself. No, Fay's orphaning is pure upward mobility and has none of the implications of any other character I study. Nor is Laurel's orphanhood in the same novel a rejection, despite her having moved away from her family and community to live and work in the North. Sometimes an orphan is just an orphan.

8. In Milly's wanting to find "something worth loving," Glasgow is engaging a version of the dialectic mode Rubin and others pose as modern Southern— that is, she suggests the antithesis to the usual Southern value of family being the only center for love, heroism, activity. As Manning reads Dabney's response (in *Delta Wedding*) to George's hugging the little black boys: "The family forms the center and the circumference of the world of the Fairchilds, and George as family hero is expected to devote his heroism [and his "caring"] to them. . . . In this incident, as in . . . others, George has stepped outside the family code" (133). As a man, however, George can, on occasion, flout that code without having to orphan himself from the family.

9. To put this in more contemporary and elegant terms, I quote from Nelly Furman, who is describing the work of the textual critic, but whose words may be adapted to describe the situation of the women in the novels I have studied: "To refuse the authority of the signified [i.e., father/phallus] means rejecting the status of a defined object in favor of the dynamics of becoming, and privileging the freedom of process rather than the permanence of product" (49). Further, to refuse the family is to refuse the most powerful and important of the culture's inscriptions. It is to think oneself, say oneself, write oneself in a nearly unthinkable way, especially in Southern society.

10. I am indebted to Jones (190, 253) for the quotations from Johnston's article in the *Atlantic Monthly* 105 (April 1910) and Glasgow's in the *New York Times Book Review*, 30 November 1913.

11. Lucinda MacKethan has recently published *Daughters of Time: Creating Woman's Voice in Southern Story*, which deals essentially with Southern women finding or constructing their voices as writers.

WORKS CITED

Alther, Lisa. *Kinflicks.* 1975. New York: Alfred A. Knopf, 1976.
Arnold, June. *Sister Gin.* Plainfield, Vt.: Daughters, 1975.

Baym, Nina. "Portrayal of Women in American Literature." In *What Manner of Woman: Essays on English and American Life and Literature.* Ed. Marlene Springer. New York: New York University Press, 1977. 211–34.

Brooks, Cleanth. "Southern Literature: The Past, History, and the Timeless." In *Southern Literature in Transition: Heritage and Promise.* Ed. Philip Castille and William Osborne. Memphis: Memphis State University Press, 1983. 3–16.

Brown, Rita Mae. *Rubyfruit Jungle.* 1973. New York: Bantam Books, 1977.

Cash, Wilbur. *The Mind of the South.* New York: Alfred A. Knopf, 1941.

Davidson, Donald. *Still Rebels, Still Yankees.* Baton Rouge: Louisiana State University Press, 1957.

Ferguson, Mary Anne. "Lisa Alther: The Irony of Return?" In *Women Writers of the Contemporary South.* Ed. Peggy Whitman Prenshaw. Jackson: University Press of Mississippi, 1984. 103–16.

Furman, Nelly. "Textual Feminism." In *Women and Language in Literature and Society.* Ed. Sally McConnell-Ginet, Ruth Borker, and Nelly Furman. New York: Praeger, 1980. 45–54.

Glasgow, Ellen. *Barren Ground.* 1925. New York: Hill and Wang, 1966.

———. *They Stooped to Folly.* 1928. Garden City, N.Y.: Doubleday, 1961.

Holman, C. Hugh. "The Southerner as American Writer." In *The Southerner as American.* Ed. Charles Grier Sellers. New York: E. P. Dutton, 1966.

———. *Three Modes of Modern Southern Fiction: Ellen Glasgow, William Faulkner, Thomas Wolfe.* Athens: University of Georgia Press, 1966.

Jones, Ann Goodwyn. *Tomorrow Is Another Day: The Woman Writer in the South, 1859–1936.* Baton Rouge: Louisiana State University Press, 1981.

King, Richard H. *A Southern Renaissance: The Cultural Awakening of the American South, 1930–1955.* New York: Oxford University Press, 1980.

MacKethan, Lucinda. *Daughters of Time: Creating Woman's Voice in Southern Story.* Athens: The University of Georgia Press, 1990.

Manning, Carol S. *With Ears Opening Like Morning Glories: Eudora Welty and the Love of Storytelling.* Westport, Conn.: Greenwood Press, 1985.

Percy, Walker. "Mississippi: The Fallen Paradise." *Harper's* 230 (1965): 230.

Porter, Katherine Anne. *Old Mortality.* 1937. In *The Old Order.* New York: Harcourt Brace Jovanovich, 1969.

Ransom, John Crowe. "Statement of Principles." In *I'll Take My Stand,* by Twelve Southerners. 1930. Rpt. Baton Rouge: Louisiana State University Press, 1977. xix–xxx.

Rubin, Louis D., Jr. *The Faraway Country: Writers of the Modern South.* Seattle: University of Washington Press, 1963.

———. *The Writer in the Modern South: Studies in a Literary Community.* Athens: University of Georgia Press, 1972.

Rubin, Louis D., Jr., and C. Hugh Holman, eds. "Thematic Problems in Southern Literature." In *Southern Literary Study: Problems and Possibilities.* Proc. of a conference on Southern Literature, University of North Carolina, Chapel Hill, 30 Nov.–2 Dec. 1972. Chapel Hill: University of North Carolina Press, 1975. 199–222.

Rubin, Louis D., Jr., and Robert D. Jacobs, eds. *Southern Renascence: The Literature of the Modern South.* Baltimore: Johns Hopkins University Press, 1953.

Scott, Anne Firor. *The Southern Lady: From Pedestal to Politics, 1830–1930.* Chicago: University of Chicago Press, 1970.

Shillingsburg, Miriam. "The Ascent of Woman, Southern Style: Hentz, King, Chopin." In *Southern Literature in Transition: Heritage and Promise.* Eds. Philip Castille and William Osborne. Memphis: Memphis State University Press, 1983. 127–40.

Sullivan, Walter. *A Requiem for the Renascence: The State of Fiction in the Modern South.* Athens: University of Georgia Press, 1976.

Tate, Allen. *Reason in Madness.* New York: G.P. Putnam's Sons, 1941.

———. "The New Provincialism." In *The Man of Letters in the Modern World: Selected Essays: 1928–1955.* New York: World Publishing, 1964. 321–31.

———. "The Profession of Letters in the South." In *The Man of Letters in the Modern World: Selected Essays: 1928–1955.* New York: World Publishing, 1964. 305–20.

Twelve Southerners. *I'll Take My Stand: The South and the Agrarian Tradition.* 1930. Baton Rouge: Louisiana State University Press, 1977.

Welty, Eudora. *Delta Wedding.* New York: Harcourt Brace and World, 1946.

———. *Losing Battles.* 1970. New York: Vintage, 1978.

———. *The Optimist's Daughter.* New York: Random House, 1969.

Westling, Louise. *Sacred Groves and Ravaged Gardens: The Fiction of Eudora Welty, Carson McCullers, and Flannery O'Connor.* Athens: University of Georgia Press, 1985.

Wyatt-Brown, Bertram. *Southern Honor: Ethics and Behavior in the Old South.* New York: Oxford University Press, 1982.

Young, Thomas Daniel. "A Second Generation of Novelists." In *The History of Southern Literature.* Ed. Louis D. Rubin, Jr. et al. Baton Rouge: Louisiana State University Press, 1985. 466–69.

Louise Westling

Fathers and Daughters in Welty and O'Connor

Both Eudora Welty and Flannery O'Connor grew up in the heart of the privileged minority who dominated the South's economic life and preserved its heroic masculine myth of the Lost Cause. Critics have spent volumes discussing the relation of male writers to this tradition. In the most systematic of these studies, *A Southern Renaissance,* Richard King has explored the debilitating consequences of that patriarchal heritage for the sons and grandsons of the Civil War heroes. However, King leaves women writers out of his account, and relatively little attention has been paid elsewhere to the position of daughters and granddaughters like Kate Chopin, Ellen Glasgow, Katherine Anne Porter, Margaret Mitchell, Carson McCullers, Caroline Gordon, Eudora Welty, and Flannery O'Connor. Anne Goodwyn Jones has helped to remedy this omission with her work on Southern women writers from 1859–1936, and I have offered a general description of the Southern daughter's dilemma,[1] but we continue to need specific analysis of the literary daughter's reaction to the father's power.

In her article "The Daughter's Seduction: Sexual Violence and Literary History," Christine Froula has moved beyond Sandra Gilbert and Susan Gubar's challenge to Harold Bloom's exclusively masculine definition of the anxiety of influence,[2] showing that women writers have not simply suffered from being left out of patriarchal traditions of literary authority but have been actively and sometimes violently coerced to tell their stories from the father's point of view. Froula describes what she calls "the hysterical cultural script" that "dictates to males and females alike the necessity of silencing woman's speech when it threatens the father's power" (623). By following this text, women remain muted and suppressed daughters, manipulated by the power of fathers who define culture and history in their own image.

I believe, however, that Welty and O'Connor, writing from within the domain of the supposedly patriarchal establishment, testify to alternative forms of power in their culture. Welty depicts fathers and daughters in ways that profoundly challenge "the hysterical cultural script" described by Froula as having been revealed in central cultural materials from the Homeric epics to the psycholanalytic writings of Sigmund Freud. For Eudora Welty, the father is always human and vulnerable. He is a beloved man on the periphery of the daughter's life, seldom intruding and always Other. Welty's daughters confidently assert their right to self-determination. Flannery O'Connor, in contrast, dramatizes the punitive action of the father, crushing and silencing the assertive daughter. Yet the obsessive repetition of this action reveals a strong habit of rebellion and more particularly a pattern of female authority and assertion that continually requires patriarchal attack. In O'Connor's fiction, most families are actually mother-dominated, and repeatedly the action of the stories moves toward some sort of violent chastisement of the mother's authority by agents of an absent patriarch. Flannery O'Connor's ultimate identification is with this paternal authority, the Judeo-Christian God. In many of her short stories, this God is a rapist, asserting his will by sexual violence, in a Christianized rewriting of the archaic Zeus, who gained dominance over the Greek pantheon by raping, incinerating, and eating female deities and mortal daughters whose independent power stood in the way of his rise to supremacy.[3]

As educated Southern ladies, Eudora Welty and Flannery O'Connor absorbed their culture's classical orientation in childhood and read widely in collections of myths and fairy tales. Later in their literary educations at Midwestern universities, they were initiated into the modernist fascination with Sir James Frazer's *The Golden Bough* and with the metaphoric adaptation of myth popularized by Eliot's "Wasteland," Joyce's *Ulysses*, and Yeats's Celtic Twilight poetry. Welty has often testified to her love of mythology, and many critics have commented on the ways she has saturated her fiction with it.[4] Flannery O'Connor's personal library contains several well-used volumes of mythography, and critics have also shown how she uses it for a symbolic base in stories like "Greenleaf" (see Asals 317–30 and Westling 156–66).

Like other modernist writers, each woman revives a myth or group of myths particularly appropriate to her fiction and expressive of an essential orientation to experience. Here, the difference between Welty's comic vision of daughters and their fathers, and O'Connor's tragic one is clearly defined.

As Cuchulain functioned for Yeats to symbolize Celtic heroism and Odysseus seemed to Joyce the complete man representing all facets of human experience, so fertility myths represent a vital system of values for Welty. In "The Wide Net," for example, fishing and ritual drownings bring a fertilizing rain and the reunion of an estranged man and wife. In *The Golden Apples,* the Celtic myth of Aengus is mingled with allusions to Zeus's appearance to Danae as a fertilizing shower of gold in her lap.

The most dramatic and sustained adaptation of mythology in Welty's fiction, however, and to me the most revealing of her orientation toward parental authority and sexuality, is her complex adaptation of the story of Demeter and Persephone in *Delta Wedding.* Because I have previously discussed this hypothesis at considerable length (Westling 65–93), I will not repeat it here. The crucial point about this myth is that it is the archetypal mother-daughter story in which father Zeus, who has authorized the rape of his daughter by his brother Hades or Pluton, must eventually relent and allow her to return to her mother because Demeter has laid waste to the earth in her mourning. The mother-daughter bond remains primary, while the father's attempt at control is ultimately denied. Classical scholars have argued about the provenance of this myth for many years, but archaeological evidence has established that the myth goes back at least to Mycenaen times, around 1500 B.C. Comparative studies suggest that Demeter is the great mother goddess of Minoan civilization and the other great Neolithic civilizations of Anatolia and Old Europe, predating by thousands of years the establishment of the father gods in the Western world.[5]

While the myth of Demeter and Persephone serves as a unifying metaphor for the action of *Delta Wedding,* on the realistic surface of the novel Welty is telling the story of the mother-centered Fairchild family in the Mississippi Delta as it prepares and enacts a daughter's wedding. This daughter, Dabney, defies her father's wishes and determines her own destiny at the age of 17, by choosing the plantation overseer as her husband and vowing never to live by the Civil War code of masculine honor that had caused so much bloodshed in her family's and region's history. Dabney's father, ironically named Battle, must stand helplessly by, watching his daughter "marry down" on the social scale. He is a reliable fertilizing agent (his wife Ellen is pregnant with her ninth child), a kindly man, and a good provider for his huge clan, but he cannot control his daughters. "I am the first thing Papa has ever given up," Dabney thinks on the eve of her wedding. "Oh, he hates it!" (122). Battle teases his daughters, using a bluff, jesting manner to express his hurt at Dabney's precipitous wedding and to wheedle his daughters for expressions of their affection for him. At one particularly frustrating moment, he groans hopelessly, "A man's daughters!" (22, 106, 180).

Another vulnerable father, always offstage in *Delta Wedding,* belongs to nine-year-old Laura McRaven, the character whose point of view opens and closes the novel. He is a lonely widower in Jackson, having lost his wife the previous winter and sent his only child on the train down to her aunt and uncle's plantation for the wedding. As a sign of his daughter's clear sense of her father's need, Welty tells us that Laura keenly pities his attempts to fold her clothes in preparation for the journey. She senses and shares the pain he feels when such activities recall his wife (9).

After the wedding, Laura is invited to stay at Shellmound by her aunt Ellen, to become one more in the gaggle of Fairchild children, for after all, her dead mother was a Fairchild. But Laura realizes that she would lose her father if she stayed. Not long before the wedding, in a scene set appropriately in the graveyard where her mother lies buried, Laura tries to remember her father and realizes that he is slipping away from her.

> She suffered from the homesickness of having almost forgotten home. She scarcely ever thought, there wasn't time, of the house in Jackson, of her father, who had every single morning now gone to the office and come home, through the New Capitol which was the coolest way, walked down the hill so that only his legs could be seen under the branches of trees, reading the *Jackson Daily News* so that only his straw hat could be seen above it, *seen from a spot on their front walk where nobody watched for him now. . . .*
>
> She tried to see her father coming home from the office, first his body hidden by leaves, then his face hidden behind his paper. If she could not think of that, she was doomed; and she was doomed, *for the memory was only a flicker, gone now.* (133–34, my emphasis)

In Laura's mind, the father ceases to exist without a loving woman to watch his daily return from his office. As long as his daughter can call this vision to her mind, he exists. But in the graveyard where her mother lies with the other dead Fairchilds, Laura cannot retain his image and knows she has lost him unless she soon returns to Jackson. We should also notice that she feels herself *doomed* if this loss occurs. The father's well-being seems to require his being watched or *looked after* by women, and the daughter's vision is privileged so that her father's reality depends on it. But the daughter's life somehow depends as much on her relation to her father as his reality does on her presence and attention.

Unlike the privileged "gaze" of male writers and their narrative per-
sonae, which typically objectifies female characters and freezes them into
powerless stereotypes that serve the needs of the observer, the gaze of this
daughter assumes the father's subjective need and yearns for a restoration of relationship. We have only this glimpse of the father from a distance, and the previous image of his folding his daughter's clothes for her
journey, but they are enough to suggest sympathetic interdependence.
Elsewhere in *Delta Wedding*, Welty makes a point of distinguishing
between the family definition of Laura's uncle George Fairchild as a
romantic hero and his wife Robbie's insistence on seeing him as a complex
person in need of her subjective understanding. Similarly Dabney, her
mother, Ellen, and Laura all appreciate George's subjective life, refusing
the objectification the rest of the family practices for their communal
need. Thus Welty's brief treatment of the father-daughter bond in Laura's
consciousness is typical of her creation of a female narrative perspective
on males in *Delta Wedding*, which grants them individuality, mystery,
and power (see Westling 70–71 and Kaplan 309–27).

Welty's most strikingly self-reliant daughter, and her favorite among
her characters, is Virgie Rainey of *The Golden Apples*. She lives in total
independence of social proprieties in her little town of Morgana,
Mississippi, enjoying sex with various partners as the years go by, and
ignoring any pressures toward marriage or disapproval of clucking
church ladies. The primary bond with her mother seems her only
sustained relationship; indeed, Virgie lives with and cares for her
mother until the old lady's death (see Westling 98–104). Virgie's name
refers to a Spenserian kind of virginity—connoting freedom from male
control—and she is virtually fatherless, "Old Man Rainey" having died
when she was a small girl. In an important scene at her mother's wake,
however, there is a suggestion that she has another father, at least in
terms of sympathy if not in fact. He is King MacLain, the Zeus figure in
the novel, or "Sir Rabbit" as he is more humorously called in one
section. As the second name suggests, he is a light-footed philanderer,
an elusive satyr figure who appears on his wife's doorstep from time to
time to get her with child, but then disappears afterward, only to pop up
again in the woods to seduce a poor farmer's young wife or in another
town to appear to some other young woman. It is he who provides the
shower of gold in maidens' laps and then skips away to other conquests.
Given Virgie's sexual independence and similarly promiscuous ways,
we might reasonably wonder whether her mother Katie Rainey might
not have been one of King's "victims."

In any case, as the guests circulate and gossip around the feast-laden
tables of her mother's dining room after the funeral, Virgie looks out

from her mother's bedroom at the now shrivelled and obscene old King and shares a moment of recógnition.

> While Mamie C. Loomis, a child in peach, sang "O Love That Will Not Let Me Go," Mr. King sucked a little marrow bone and lifted his wobbly head and looked arrogantly at Virgie through the two open doors of her mother's bedroom. . . . Mr. King pushed out his stained lip. Then he made a hideous face at Virgie, like a silent yell. It was a yell at everything— including death, not leaving it out—and he did not mind taking his present animosity out on Virgie Rainey; indeed he chose her. Then he cracked the little bone in his teeth. She felt refreshed all of a sudden at that tiny but sharp sound. (446)

Welty goes on to define more specifically the kinship Virgie recognizes in this moment of alliance: "it lacked future as well as past; but she knew when even [such] a rarefied thing had become a matter of loyalty and alliance" (446–47). For the reader, King has been established as a kind of father for Virgie, a Zeus to her Athena or Aphrodite. Both of them are determined to suck the marrow out of life and pay no attention to the pieties of small town behavior (see also Yeager). The remarkable qualities of this symbolic father-daughter bond are its mutual validation, equality, and freedom from coercion. Even more than Dabney Fairchild, Virgie decides her own fate outside the patriarchal system of control. The only father figure in her life is a shriveled old reprobate who chooses her to witness his obscene protest against his own powerlessness in the face of time and death and then relieves her as he does himself with the life-affirming crack of the marrow bone. The act is both terrifying and reassuring in the funeral setting, with our knowledge that the sweet marrow comes from the bones of creatures we have killed to sustain our own lives.

With *The Optimist's Daughter*, we come much closer to Eudora Welty's own life, for even she has admitted its closeness to her parents' lives and her own childhood (see Capers 116 and Freeman 174–75). The novel is dedicated to C. A. W.—Chestina Andrews Welty—Eudora Welty's mother, although the story is ostensibly focused on a daughter's loss of her father. The father's death is a door through which the daughter moves to confront the deeper mysteries of her parents' relationship, her mother's powerful character and apallingly long and painful death, and finally the daughter's own long-suppressed grief for the husband she lost in the war.

Laurel Hand has come back to the South from her independent professional life in Chicago to be with her elderly father while he undergoes a serious eye operation. Unexpectedly he begins to fail, and no encouragement from his doctor or his daughter can keep him from drifting toward death. After her father's funeral, Laura spends a night alone in the family home. Her lonely wanderings through the house take her ultimately to her mother's sewing room, where she opens her father's desk and pores through old photographs and her parents' love letters.

Her thoughts move from her lost father to her parents' relationship and come to rest on her long-dead mother, Becky, the shadowy figure whose presence has been felt but not really confronted throughout the novel. Her mother was the real center of the family, the strong parent with whom Laurel identified. This part of the novel is intensely autobiographical, for Welty almost directly transposes memories of her own mother into the novel for Laurel Hand (see Welty, *Beginnings* 46–60; and Freeman 174–75). At the age of fifteen, Eudora Welty's mother, Chestina Andrews, bravely accompanied her gravely ill father alone across an icy West Virginia river on a raft and then by train to Baltimore to a hospital where he died of a ruptured appendix, just as Becky McKelva is said to have done in *The Optimist's Daughter*. Laurel comes to see that she and her mother had both tried to save their fathers and failed. The father had been the optimist, just as Welty said her own father was, but the mother was the heroic one who faced the horrible truths of experience. The fathers end up needing the protection of their daughters and wives, just as Laura McRaven understood in *Delta Wedding*.

We have moved from the mythic undercurrents of ordinary experience in *Delta Wedding* and *The Golden Apples* to a starker realism in *The Optimist's Daughter*, finding nevertheless a common emphasis upon strong daughters and vulnerable fathers. The basic orientation of these texts is maternal and seems to rest on an unquestioned assumption of feminine autonomy. There is no hostility to males, but they are always seen from outside; fathers are beloved but peripheral or dead or dying. For Welty, fertility myth provides a rich tradition for dramatizing the daughter's secure grounding in the Southern matriarchy behind the patriarchal facade.

Flannery O'Connor's mythic orientation was radically different. She found a key in Oedipus very early in her career, when she was living with Robert and Sally Fitzgerald in rural Connecticut and was struggling to conclude her first major work, *Wise Blood*. Robert Fitzgerald remembered that when she had reached an impasse with her main character, Hazel Motes, "and didn't know how to finish him off, she read for the first time the Oedipus plays. She went on then to end her story with the self-blinding of Motes, and she had to rework the body of the novel to prepare for it" (xv, xvi).

That was not the first time she had reworked the novel, for its writing was an agonizing process of revision that covered four years and produced some 1000 pages of manuscript that fill 130 folders in the O'Connor Collection at Georgia College. Sarah Gordon has discovered some remarkable changes over the course of these revisions—a gradual diminishing of a powerful and disturbing female prophet, accompanied by an increasingly focused investment of power in the male protagonist, Hazel Motes. In early versions of the novel, Sabbath Lily Hawkes is a large, ugly woman with mysterious outsized feet and a fierce devotion to God. She is an obvious competitor to Haze for prophetic vocation. By the final version of *Wise Blood*, however, she has been reduced to "little more than . . . the child-temptress whom Haze uses at first to get to her father and then uses to demonstrate to himself that fornication is not a sin" (Gordon n.p.).

Such an evolution disciplines and represses an assertive daughter figure absorbed in an all-demanding relationship with the father God. Her competing presence is removed so that the whole focus can fall upon the son's relation to this father. O'Connor's identification with the father's power is clearly revealed in her discovery of the consummation for Haze's struggle against God's calling in the story of Oedipus. Here she found a Greek prototype in which the hero mutilates himself for his sacrilege in destroying the father and assuming his power.

A similar pattern of the daughter's diminishment and identification with patriarchal authority occurs in many other stories, most obviously in "Good Country People," "A Circle in the Fire," "A Temple of the Holy Ghost," and "A View of the Woods." The sexual nature of the daughter's humiliation by the father God is always displaced, so that some excavation is required to unearth the subtext that carries this message (Westling 149–74). As an example we need only remember "Good Country People," in which the thirty-two-year-old daughter's wooden leg is stolen in a hayloft by the traveling Bible salesman she has naively planned to "seduce." His name is Manley Pointer, and his phallic lesson in humility is more of a rape than mere physical penetration could be. The wooden leg is Joy-Hulga's prop, the crutch that gives the crippled woman a modicum of physical independence. When she last glimpses the Bible salesman, he appears to be walking on water like Jesus. Thus the cynical young pervert is meant to function as Christ did for His Father—as an agent of grace for God's human children. The perverse "grace" that Manley Pointer supplies is a destruction of the daughter's dignity and ability to walk alone.

Again and again in O'Connor's stories women are chastized by satanic male agents of the Heavenly Father, who demands allegiance and submission. If we accept O'Connor's Christian premise, all these women are daughters of the Divine Patriarch. Hence, when Mrs. May of "Greenleaf" is gored to death by a bull representing Jesus, we can see another divine rape that brings a recalcitrant daughter to her knees. When three vicious boys invade the female preserve of Mrs. Cope's farm in "A Circle in the Fire," they too end up performing a rape in the name of the Father, claiming, "Gawd owns them woods" that Mrs. Cope prizes and burning them down to teach her a lesson (Westling 167–70). An especially disturbing example of the daughter's humiliation is "A View of the Woods," for the daughter is beaten repeatedly by her father, even though she supports his determination to save his land from her rapacious grandfather. On the symbolic level the woods represent Christ (see O'Connor, *Habit of Being* 190), and she is therefore defending something sacred. Nevertheless her father continues to beat her, and she is ultimately killed in a fight with her grandfather, still upholding her father's values. The point in all these stories seems to be that daughters must be punished by fathers for any kind of assertion or claim of authority.

Some years ago, Claire Katz Kahane pointed out that "the literal or figurative penetration of characters reveals their destiny to them" (57) and went on to discuss the unresolved relation to the father of many characters: "Actual fathers rarely appear in O'Connor's fiction; when they do, they are usually sadistic figures, their aggressiveness associated with the sexual role of the male as penetrator" (63). O'Connor has clearly alligned herself with this punishing father in her fiction and used sexual violence as a means of abasement for women like herself and her mother.

As the repetition of the pattern attests, the mother's power is so great that it must be crushed again and again. Sons like Thomas of "The Comforts of Home" or Julian of "Everything That Rises Must Converge" are allowed to overthrow their mothers—to kill them, in fact. Although these sons suffer anguish and remorse for doing so, they are nevertheless reasserting masculine domination. We see this motive quite literally in "The Comforts of Home," where the ghost of Thomas's father eggs him on to prove his manhood by putting his mother in her place, and he ends up shooting her. Sons are granted the power of action, for maternal dominance is seen as unnatural and debilitating. Even in *The Violent Bear It Away*, where a son is the victim of rape by an agent of God's humiliating grace, the abasement only prepares the boy for his prophetic mission. Daughters, in contrast, are forced into alliance with their mothers, as passive victims of invading males.

Flannery O'Connor's practice stands in a venerable literary tradition, which we see exhibited in the character Athena in Aeschylus's *Eumedides*. While Athena is only a character created by the playwright, she models the behavior a male world expects of women by accepting the divine father's violent appropriation of the mother's power. The play is a masculine version of mythic history in which the daughter denies even her mother's existence and agrees with a male version of her origins as a completely father-born and father-identified being.

At the famous trial scene in Athens, where Orestes's matricide is being judged, Apollo represents the father's claims of true parenthood and is opposed by the ancient representatives of mother-right, the Furies or Eumedides. Apollo is the more recent deity, while the Furies are the primordial agents of Gaea, Mother Earth, who ruled Delphi long before Apollo became its resident deity. Athena must judge whether the murder of father Agamemnon by mother Clytemnaestra could legitimately be avenged by the son Orestes, or whether mother-right should prevail and Orestes be punished.

Apollo argues that the father is the true parent whose authority must be upheld, and the god points to Athena as proof of his argument. "The mother is no parent of that which is called her child, but only nurse of the new-planted seed that grows. The parent is he who mounts. A stranger she preserves a stranger's seed, if no god interfere. . . . I will show you proof of what I have explained. There can be a father without any mother. There she stands, the living witness, daughter of Olympian Zeus, she who was never fostered in the dark of the womb yet such a child as no goddess could bring to birth" (158).

Athena cheerfully agrees with this biography and its male claims to reproductive power, casting the deciding vote in Orestes' favor and testifying, "There is no mother anywhere who gave me birth, / and, but for marriage, I am always for the male / with all my heart, and strongly on my father's side" (161).

But if we remember the story of Metis, Athena's mother, we see how transparent this fiction is and how the daughter has been forced to deny her female heritage and the most obvious facts of biology. Hesiod tells the story in the *Theogony*.

> Zeus, king of the gods, made Metis his wife first, and *she was wisest among gods and mortal men.* But when she was about to bring forth the goddess bright-eyed Athene, Zeus craftily deceived her with cunning words and put her in his own belly, as Earth and starry Heaven advised. For they advised him so, to the end that no other should hold royal sway over the eternal gods in place of Zeus; for very wise children were destined to be born of her [Metis], *first the maiden bright-eyed [Athene], equal to her father in strength and in wise understanding.* . . .

> But Zeus put her [Metis] into his own belly first, that the goddess might devise for him both good and evil. . . .
>
> And she remained hidden beneath the inward parts of Zeus, even Metis, *Athena's mother, worker of righteousness, who was wiser than gods and mortal men. There the goddess (Athena) received that whereby she excelled in strength.* (143–47, emphasis added)

What followed this peculiar gestation was the famous birth of the daughter from the father's forehead, the "proof" Apollo cites for his claim to masculine reproductive autonomy. Yet even in Hesiod's patriarchal version of the story we can clearly see that "the father of the gods" had been afraid of Metis because of her superior wisdom and the threat to his authority, which her offspring would represent. Metis remained alive inside Zeus, empowering him with her wisdom, and there she gave birth to a daughter who still had to undergo another birth to be rendered submissive to patriarchal culture. The story is a perfect metaphor for the culture's attempt to surround and control the mother's power and erase her existence in the daughter's life.

We have historical evidence of this process in Freud's treatment of female hysterics. The case of Dora has become the classic example of Freud's swerving away from the implications of his seduction theory. Instead of validating the daughter's testimony of sexual violence and the guilt of the father or a father-figure, Nancy Armstrong writes, Freud "does not concede her the right either to declare her own feelings or to pass judgement upon the sordid business taking place in her household" (240). This case came at a crucial point in Freud's career as he began to realize how profoundly the implications of seduction theory challenged patriarchal power. Froula believes Freud saw that "if he credited the daughters, he would risk sharing their fate of being silenced and ignored." Thus he began to make "subtle war on woman's desire and on the credibility of her language in order to avert its perceived threat to the father's cultural preeminence." And most important of all for the development of psychoanalysis, Freud turned to the myth of Oedipus to explain the psychic distresses of his patients (Froula 629–32). The true voices of women in his practice were effectively silenced, their testimony to patriarchal hypocrisy and abuse of power erased.

It would be difficult to overemphasize the power of the Freudian, Oedipal perspective in our culture since psychoanalysis established itself in England and the United States during the 1930s and 1940s. For forty years, students have been taught that *Oedipus the King* is the greatest of the Greek tragedies. The Oedipal Complex has become the basic Western myth of family life and psychic development. Yet this theory is a skewed one, intended, as Armstrong argues, to squash the emerging power of women in Western culture, to deny their stories and thus ignore their very existence. Flannery O'Connor's fiction shows us the disastrous consequences for women who accept it and identify with the father's power. As a daughter in a mother-dominated world, powerful in her intellect and imagination and fully equipped to challenge the cultural fathers, O'Connor was nevertheless constrained to find her allegiance in the father's power and destroy her mother's authority.

O'Connor's case is undoubtedly an extreme and unusual one, for the disease that killed her father when she was thirteen struck her at the age of twenty-five and rendered her an invalid captive in her mother's house for the remaining thirteen years of her life. She had had only five years of freedom at the University of Iowa, in New York, and in rural Connecticut, after she left home and began her writing career. When disseminated lupus ended her independence and threw her back into the claustrophobic conventionality of her mother's control in her small Georgia hometown, she could only express her forbidden rage through the violent and rebellious characters in her fiction, and then escape from culpability by siding with the Father who punishes it. Claire Katz Kahane sees the process as reflecting regressive, almost infantile resentment of the mother, which works itself out in destructive masochism in her fiction. As Kahane explains, O'Connor implies that to act "is to assume the male role and the power associated with the father" (61–64). The only way for O'Connor as a writer to break free and achieve autonomy was paradoxically to deny the female self and the relation to her mother, and instead identify with the divine Father. Despite her acceptance of "the hysterical cultural script," O'Connor could not escape the tensions that it was meant to resolve. Her fiction can therefore be seen as a stage on which that script had to be dramatized again and again to defend its legitimacy. The obsessive repetition of the father's punitive action in the stories reveals its insufficiency, and the mother/daughter stories become ironic testimony to female power at the same time that they expose the sexual violence against it which Froula sees at the heart of the patriarchy.

Eudora Welty's fiction, on the other hand, simply ignores "the hysterical cultural script" altogether. We may never know how Welty was able to accomplish this feat, though we do know from her autobiographical *One Writer's Beginnings* how appreciative she was of many strong women in her life. The broad circumstances of her life resemble those of O'Connor's with respect to her life with her mother. After four years of independence in the North as a student at the University of Wisconsin and at Columbia, Welty suddenly returned home to help her mother when her father died. She lived with her mother for the rest of the latter's life and still resides in the family home. But somehow Welty was able to maintain her intellectual and creative autonomy under these circumstances, to find a source of strength in the feminine rather than in the patriarchal version of legitimate power.

Eudora Welty's fiction quietly and confidently returns to ancient sources of female authority in myth. She presents an alternative, comic vision that acknowledges the reality of pain and loss but dramatizes a pre-Oedipal world where daughters can grow to independent maturity, secure in their identification with strong mothers and indulgent or protective toward vulnerable, human fathers who are powerless to direct their daughters' lives. Her fiction turns away from "the hysterical cultural script" encoded in the Freudian interpretation of the Oedipal myth and rests instead upon the myth of the Great Mother who sustains all life and who has been the real image of power and vitality for most of human history (Kirk 249 and Burkert 138). We live in a time when the old powers of the feminine are reasserting themselves and causing reactions in some respects far more dangerous than Freud's. Flannery O'Connor's stories dramatize the cost of identification with the violent reassertion of the father's power, but Eudora Welty uses the myths of mothers and daughters as the basis for stories of human cooperation and renewal that can serve as models for a future dominated by neither sex and freed from violent compulsion.

NOTES

1. See Jones, *Tomorrow Is Another Day,* and her unpublished paper "Katherine Du Pre Lumpkin"; and Westling, *Sacred Groves and Ravaged Gardens* 8–64.

2. See Gilbert and Gubar's *The Madwoman in the Attic* and Bloom's *The Anxiety of Influence.*

3. *Oxford Classical Dictionary* 324, 497, 679, 972, 1146, 1147. Zeus raped scores of female deities and mortal maidens including Semele, Metis, Demeter, and his wife Hera; the unfortunate Semele was burnt to death by his thunderbolt when she insisted on seeing her lover in his divine form; and the god swallowed Metis because he feared her power and that of her offspring.

4. See Freeman, "An Interview with Eudora Welty" 189, and Gretlund, "An Interview with Eudora Welty" 224; Allen, "The Other Way to Live" 26–55; Phillips, "A Structural Approach to Myth in the Fiction of Eudora Welty" 56–67; and Westling, *Sacred Groves and Ravaged Gardens* 65–93.

5. See Burkert, *Structure and History in Greek Mythology and Ritual* 102–4, 123–42; Gimbutas, *The Goddesses and Gods of Old Europe 6500–3500 B.C.: Myths and Cult Images* 112–215, 236–38; Kirk, *The Nature of Greek Myths*

249–58; Lincoln, *Emerging from the Chrysalis* 72–73; Mylonas, *Mycenae and the Mycenaean Age* 141–61; and Nilsson, *The Mycenaean Origin of Greek Mythology* 20–34, 74–79.

WORKS CITED

Aeschylus. *The Eumenides. Oresteia.* Trans. Richard Lattimore. Ed. David Grene and Richard Lattimore. Chicago: University of Chicago Press, 1953. 133–71.

Allen, John Alexander. "The Other Way to Live: Demigods in Eudora Welty's Fiction." In *Eudora Welty: Critical Essays.* Ed. Peggy Whitman Prenshaw. Jackson: University Press of Mississippi, 1979. 26–55.

Armstrong, Nancy. *Desire and Domestic Fiction.* New York: Oxford University Press, 1987.

Asals, Frederick. "The Mythic Dimensions of Flannery O'Connor's 'Greenleaf.'" *Studies in Short Fiction* 5 (Summer 1968): 317–30.

Bloom, Harold. *The Anxiety of Influence.* New York: Oxford University Press, 1973.

Burkert, Walter. *Structure and History in Greek Mythology and Ritual.* Berkeley: University of California Press, 1979.

Capers, Charlotte. "An Interview with Eudora Welty." Prenshaw 115–30.

Fitzgerald, Robert. Introduction *Everything That Rises Must Converge,* by Flannery O'Connor. New York: Farrar, Straus, and Giroux, 1965. vii–xxxiv.

Freeman, Jean Todd. "An Interview with Eudora Welty." Prenshaw 172–99.

Froula, Christine. "The Daughter's Seduction: Sexual Violence and Literary History." *Signs* 11 (Summer 1986): 621–44.

Gilbert, Sandra, and Susan Gubar. *The Madwoman in the Attic.* New Haven: Yale University Press, 1973.

Gimbutas, Marija. *The Goddesses and Gods of Old Europe 6500–3500 B.C.: Myths and Cult Images.* Berkeley: University of California Press, 1982.

Gordon, Sarah. "The Early Sabbath and the Ultimate Sin: The Drafts of *Wise Blood.*" Unpublished paper presented at MLA convention, 1984.

Gretlund, Jan Nordby. "An Interview with Eudora Welty." Prenshaw 211–29.

Hammond, N. G. L., and H. H. Scullard, eds. *The Oxford Classical Dictionary.* 2d ed. Oxford: Clarendon Press, 1970.

Hesiod. "To Demeter." *Hesiod, the Homeric Hymns, and Homerica.* Trans. H.G. Evelyn-White. Cambridge: Harvard University Press, 1977. 289–325.

Jones, Anne Goodwyn. "Katharine Du Pre Lumpkin: Her Father's Daughter." Unpublished paper presented at MLA convention, 1986.

———. *Tomorrow Is Another Day: The Woman Writer in the South, 1839–1936.* Baton Rouge: Louisiana State University Press, 1981.

Kahane, Claire Katz. "Flannery O'Connor's Rage of Vision." *American Literature* 46 (March 1974): 54–67.

Kaplan, E. Ann. "Is the Gaze Male?" In *Powers of Desire: The Politics of Sexuality.* Ed. Ann Snitow, Christine Stansell, and Sharon Thompson. New York: Monthly Review Press, 1983. 309–27.

King, Richard. *A Southern Renaissance: The Cultural Awakening of the American South, 1930–1955.* New York: Oxford University Press, 1980.

Kirk, Geoffrey Stephen. *The Nature of Greek Myths.* New York: Penguin Books, 1980.

Lincoln, Bruce. *Emerging from the Chrysalis.* Cambridge: Harvard University Press, 1981.

Mylonas, George E. *Mycenae and the Mycenaean Age.* Princeton: Princeton University Press, 1966.

Nilsson, Martin. *The Mycenaean Origin of Greek Mythology.* Berkeley: University of California Press, 1979.

O'Connor, Flannery. "A Circle in the Fire." In *The Complete Stories* 175–93.

————. "The Comforts of Home." In *The Complete Stories.* 383–404.

————. *The Complete Stories.* New York: Farrar, Straus, and Giroux, 1971.

————. "Everything That Rises Must Converge." In *The Complete Stories* 405–20.

————. *The Habit of Being: The Letters of Flannery O'Connor.* Ed. Sally Fitzgerald. New York: Farrar, Straus, and Giroux, 1979.

Phillips, Robert L. "A Structural Approach to Myth in the Fiction of Eudora Welty." In *Eudora Welty: Critical Essays.* Ed. Peggy Whitman Prenshaw. Jackson: University Press of Mississippi, 1979.

Prenshaw, Peggy Whitman, ed. *Conversations with Eudora Welty.* Jackson: University Press of Mississippi, 1984. 56–67

Welty, Eudora. *Delta Wedding.* New York: Harcourt Brace Jovanovich, 1946.

————. *The Golden Apples.* 1949. Rpt. in *The Collected Stories of Eudora Welty.* New York: Harcourt Brace Jovanovich, 1980.

————. *One Writer's Beginnings.* Cambridge: Harvard University Press, 1984.

————. *The Optimist's Daughter.* New York: Random House, 1969.

Westling, Louise. *Sacred Groves and Ravaged Gardens: The Fiction of Eudora Welty, Carson McCullers, and Flannery O'Connor.* Athens: University of Georgia Press, 1985.

Yeager, Patricia. " 'Because a Fire Was in My Head': Eudora Welty and the Dialogic Imagination." *PMLA* 99 (October 1984): 959–70.

Mary Hughes Brookhart

Spiritual Daughters of the Black American South

In 1927, Alain Locke lamented the black writer's "somewhat expatriated position" in the North because of the South's inhospitable environment: "And if I were asked to name one factor for the anemic . . . quality of so much Negro expression up to the present, I would cite . . . the pathetic exile of the Negro writer from his best material, the fact that he cannot get cultural breathing space on his own soil" (117). As Thadious M. Davis discusses in her essay, "Expanding the Limits: The Intersection of Race and Region," more and more black Americans are reclaiming their Southern soil and in the process their heritage. Davis points to such media events as the phenomenal success of Alex Haley's *Roots* and the massive family reunions at the plantations where ancestors were once slaves. And she considers several black American novelists who have never lived in the South yet are making the region the locus for their creative imagination and the means of affirming personal and cultural identity.

The Ohio-raised Toni Morrison is probably the best known of these "outsiders" to reclaim the region through such novels as *Song of Solomon* (1977) and *Beloved* (1987). In those novels, as in Ntozake Shange's *Sassafrass, Cypress & Indigo* (1982) and Gloria Naylor's *Mama Day* (1988), the South is more than a physical location; it is a psychological space where those who have been made anemic by their exile can come in contact with mystical powers and be rejuvenated. As in the African tradition, which is their ultimate source, those powers may come from ancestors still capable of effecting action or from special people in tune with supernatural forces. In either case, when we look at contemporary African American fiction by women, the region to get in touch with such powers is not Africa but the southern United States—the region of their characters' internalized history. And in a specifically female tradition, those powers reside in women. In this essay, I will consider four novels in which mysteriously endowed Southern black women reach out to their would-be heirs: Ellease Southerland's *Let the Lion Eat Straw* (1979), Linda Beatrice Brown's *Rainbow Roun Mah Shoulder* (1984), Paule Marshall's *Praisesong for the Widow* (1983), and Toni Cade Bambara's *The Salt Eaters* (1980).

Of these four African American authors, none is indisputably Southern in the sense of having grown up in the South. Paule Marshall is the furthest from being Southern; although she now teaches at Virginia Commonwealth University, both her parents came to the United States from Barbados, and she has lived most of her life in New York. Also from New York, Ellease Southerland never got to the South until she was twenty-three. Toni Cade Bambara grew up in New York and relocated to Atlanta only in 1974. While Linda Beatrice Brown went to college in North Carolina and has lived in Greensboro since 1966, she was raised in Ohio. Yet, when asked if she considered herself Southern, Brown answered emphatically, "I am Southern," and gave the simple explanation, "My mother was born in Jackson, Mississippi," before amplifying that she was raised with Southern traditions and her grandparents and other relatives were Southern (telephone interview, 15 Jan. 1989). To be Southern for Brown is certainly more internal than a fact of where she lives. It has to do with her maternal heritage.

For Southerland and Bambara, a Southern heritage also influences their sense of themselves. As though to account for her presence as one of eleven authors in *A World Unsuspected: Portraits of Southern Childhood,* Southerland begins her essay, "Although I was born in the North . . . , the South was more than an equal presence in my girlhood years. My two older brothers had been born in Florida, our father's birthplace. The South as a state of mind, the black South with its sometimes latent but unmistakable ties to Africa, would shape our lives" (175). Although Southerland goes on to illustrate how her family and most of their neighbors maintained Southern traditions, the South as "a state of mind" is the most important factor in her sense of being Southern. Bambara's move to the South in 1974 was probably in part political, a conscious act after having been active in the civil rights movement and continuing her commitment to community action. Still, she too recalls her Southern roots and is accountable to her Southern heritage. In "What It Is I Think I'm Doing Anyhow," Bambara lists as one of her mentors her "grandmother, Annie, whom folks in Atlanta still remember as an early Rosa Parks." She illustrates her grandmother's enduring presence and influence when she accounts for two of her characters whom she could not allow to be defeated by circumstances: "Were I to do them in, my granny would no doubt visit me in the night to batter me gingerly about the head and shoulders with an ancestral bone pulled out of the Ethiopic Ocean called the Atlantic" (163).

In keeping with the affirmation of heritage, each author acknowledges through her novel an older woman to whom she is indebted. Bambara dedicates *The Salt Eaters* to her mother, "my first friend, teacher, map maker, landscape aide/Mama/Helen Brent Henderson Cade Brehon"; and Marshall's dedication in *Praisesong for the Widow* reads, "For my grandmother, Alberta Jane Clement ('Da-duh')." In her dedication "to Yvonne and Elizabeth, the Keepers of the rainbow," Brown refers to her classmate and friend from Bennett College and to her former teacher at Bennett, who is both friend and mentor (telephone interview). While Southerland dedicates *Let the Lion Eat Straw* to the youngest of her fourteen brothers and sisters after their mother's death from cancer, the dedication again suggests a keeping of memory and heritage alive, particularly since the heroine, Abeba Williams Lavoisier Torch, so closely resembles their own mother. Southerland writes of *Let the Lion Eat Straw:* "It was a book planned before my mother's death, she sketched a lion and child in pencil as a possible cover design, and her quiet and respectful confidence that I would complete the work was important in sustaining me" (Southerland, letter to the author, 30 Dec. 1981). In finding her novel's starting place with Abeba's early childhood in North Carolina, she also finds the source of her own mother's remarkable strength in an old woman her mother called Mamma Habersham: "She would give my mother water from the bell of a cow to cure her stuttering. She was the protective spirit during my mother's formative years" (Southerland, "I Got a Horn," 178).

Mamma Habblesham of Southerland's *Let the Lion Eat Straw* is clearly modeled after Mamma Habersham. She is the first, and the gentlest, of the fictional "protective spirits" this paper considers. "Half Indian, half African" (3), she seems to draw her strength from ancient lore and powers. She knows when babies are about to be born. She and the child sleep together and dream each other's dreams. It is she who names the child Abeba for an African flower. Mamma Habblesham remains spiritually present for Abeba even after the child's "natural mother" (30), the woman she first distinguishes as her "New York Mamma" (5), takes her to live in the North. "Home" will remain for the woman Abeba back in North Carolina with Mamma Habblesham, her playmate Jackson, and the rooster (85). At the novel's conclusion, after Abeba, like Southerland's own mother, has died of cancer and left a grief-stricken family, Southerland writes, "They didn't know that four days ago, at three in the morning, an old midwife had slipped into Abeba's room, had taken her hand and gone up the hill" (163). The number three reinforces the magical nature of their relationship. It had been 3:00 A.M. when the child Abeba awakened in her new Northern home, "shouting 'Mamma Habblesham'" and knowing the old woman back home had died (17). As Southerland points out in reference to Hurston's *Their Eyes Were Watching God,* the number three is used "to signal the conclusion of things" ("The Influence of Voodoo" 175). Still a spiritual presence at Abeba's funeral, Mamma Habblesham studies Abeba's fifteen children, her husband, and her mother: "And the midwife said ever so quietly, 'Hush your mouth'" (164). Beginning and ending the novel with Mamma Habblesham, Southerland affirms the sustaining influence of Abeba's, and her own mother's, Southern past. The midwife will still be there for those in the family who perceive her. By implication, so her spiritual daughter Abeba will be also.

Paule Marshall's Great-aunt Cuney in *Praisesong for the Widow* has even less time with Avey Johnson as a child than Mamma Habblesham does with Abeba, but she too returns decades later to direct the woman. While others in Aunt Cuney's community of Tatem, South Carolina, thought she was crazy, events in *Praisesong for the Widow* make clear that she was/is not. For example, she knew from a dream months before the event that her great-great niece would be born. "It's my gran' done sent her. She's her little girl" (42), Aunt Cuney informed the expectant parents, who were to name the child Avatara after Aunt Cuney's grandmother.

On Aunt Cuney's insistence, Avey's parents would send the child from New York for Augusts in Tatem. Every few days the two would walk down to a place called on maps Ibo Landing, and in "the voice that possessed her," the woman would slowly and skillfully tell the eager child the miracle her own grandmother had witnessed there as a child: how the Ibos were brought in chains to that very spot, took one look at the white people waiting for them, and knew of the grief ahead. "Even seen you and me standing here talking about 'em" (38). She would describe how every one of the chained Ibos turned, walked back across the river, past the little boats and the ship: "When they realized there wasn't nothing between them and home but some water and that wasn't giving 'em no trouble they got so tickled they started in to singing" (39). It was that vision of the Ibos that gave the grandmother power—"Her body she always usta say might be in Tatem but her mind, her mind was long gone with the Ibos" (39)—and the same vision has empowered Aunt Cuney. It is a power that the child begins to question by the time she is ten.

Decades after Avey Johnson has thought seriously of the woman or Ibo Landing, her aunt comes to her in a dream with all the fierce insistence that Bambara imagines her actual grandmother would come to her should she fail to be accountable to her heritage. Now a well-off widow, Avey is taking a Caribbean cruise. In the dream, Aunt Cuney is dressed in the eccentric garb she wore in Tatem. She appears at Avey's New York home, to invite, then coax, and finally drag the well-dressed and resisting Avey out in order to take her to the Landing. To Avey's mortification, they fight in front of her horrified North White Plains neighbors. That disturbing dream precipitates Avey Johnson's decision to leave her ship, *Bianca Pride.* The names *Bianca Pride* and North White Plains suggest how closely Marshall associates Avey's malaise with her cultural expatriation. Avey gradually will understand that since she first rejected her great-aunt's story, she has been in exile: "Hadn't she found it increasingly difficult as the years passed to think of herself as 'Avey' or even 'Avatara'? The woman to whom those names belonged had gone away, had been banished along with her feelings and passions to some far-off place—not unlike the Eskimo woman . . . who had been cast out to await her death alone in the snow" (141). The novel traces her repatriation, her physical and then her spiritual recovery. It ends appropriately with Avey Johnson planning to sell the North White Plains house, build in that little South Carolina community, and from there take her grandchildren and others to the Landing where she will recount the miracle entrusted to her to tell.

For the Northern-born novelists Marshall and Southerland, the South takes on symbolic dimensions in *Praisesong for the Widow* and *Let the Lion Eat Straw.* Their characters' strength depends upon their spiritual closeness to the region of their African American past. Southerland's Abeba, dying of cancer, stays strong because she is never spiritually estranged. She proudly bears the name of the African flower Mamma Habblesham somehow knew to give her; she internalizes her Southern home and the spirit of Mamma Habblesham. Avey Johnson, with nothing more objectively identifiable than indigestion and sea sickness, is desperately ill until she realizes and reclaims her heritage. The South recalls the sufferings and legacy of slavery at the same time that it links the twice expatriated African American of the North to folk traditions and those heroic and sometimes magically endowed ancestors who manage to survive: " 'Cause those pure-born Africans was peoples my gran' said could see in more ways than one. The kind can tell you 'bout things happened long before they was born and things to come along after they's dead' " (*Praisesong for the Widow* 37–38).

The South itself does not function symbolically in *Rainbow Roun Mah Shoulder* or *The Salt Eaters,* two novels written by women who have made the region their home and the home of their characters. Brown and especially Bambara allow supernatural events to happen without feeling the need to couch them in dreams. The magical black women in these novels appear in the flesh, call upon ancient lore in exercising their powers, move into others' minds, and perform healings before our eyes. It is as though the closer the author is to her Southern roots, the more secure she is in the validity of such women.

Bambara's Minnie Ransom is the most colorful and outrageous of all these mysteriously endowed Southern black women. The course of this complex novel is the time it takes Minnie Ransom to heal Velma Henry, who sits on a stool at the Southwest Community Infirmary in Claybourne, Georgia, after having tried to commit suicide. The fabled healer's showy clothes, her appearance of doing nothing but humming and "playing to the gallery" (7), and her earthy language distract visitors who do not believe in spiritual healings. When she says, "I can feel, sweetheart, that you're not quite ready to dump that shit," there are "gasps, the rib nudges against starchy jackets, and shuffling of feet" (16). But Minnie Ransom is legitimate and her next audible words—"got to give it all up, the pain, the hurt, the anger and make room for lovely things to rush in and fill you full. Nature abhors a so-called vacuum, don't you know?"— elicit a nod from Velma. Even though visitors are skeptical, the others there have "witnessed the miracle of Minnie Ransom's laying on the hands over the years" (9).

Minnie Ransom has her own spirit guide, Old Wife, no longer alive and, consequently, invisible to others. When Minnie Ransom's healing of Velma seems hopeless, her conversations with her sassy spirit guide lighten her load and restore her perspective. For example, Old Wife teases her that she "ain't learned to quit casting a voluptuous eye on the young mens." Minnie Ransom answers, "When you gonna learn, you ole stick in the mud, that 'good' ain't got nothing to do with it [her gift]?" (54). Minnie Ransom complains that Old Wife is not helping her with "the Henry gal": "Ain't you omniscient yet, Old Wife? Don't frown up. All knowing. Ain't you all knowing? What's the point of being in all-when and all-where if you not going to take advantage of the situation and become all knowing?" (49).

Bambara's amazingly encompassing book asserts a reality far beyond the everyday. As Gloria T. Hull explains in " 'What It Is I Think She's Doing Anyhow': A Reading of Toni Cade Bambara's *The Salt Eaters,* " "Without addressing the issue of belief in healing or giving anyone else a chance to do so, Bambara posits its authenticity and describes it with the same faithful nonchalance that she accords to every other human activity" (219). From telepathy to the Tarot to throwing cowrie shells to conjuring and to prayer, Hull catalogues a dizzying number of "spiritual arts" drawn on by the characters as a part of Bambara's method and vision.

The novel places serious demands on the readers, both in its style and its revision of reality. Even Velma's healing does not come from Minnie Ransom alone. For example, Velma Henry's godmother, Mrs. Sophie Heywood, off by herself in Doc Serge's office, is deeply involved: "she'd waited a long time for the godchild's gift to unfold," and it is she who will train Velma once she is healed (293). Furthermore, Velma Henry is not the only character to be healed.

The spiritual healer, Miss Rebecca Letenielle Florice, occupies an uneasy center stage in Brown's *Rainbow Roun Mah Shoulder.* The novel reads like a saint's life as it conveys with equal attention the subjective and objective experiences of this troubled and earthy visionary. As a young married woman in New Orleans, Florice receives the words: "Heal and love. You are blessed with power" (7). Though a blessing, the power will mean loneliness and onerous responsibility. For much of the novel, Florice lives with her friend Alice Wine in Greensboro near the black women's college where they serve as cooks and friends to some of the students. Ardently Christian, this Southern black woman knows hoodoo and conjure, and in this book the powers derived from those sources are dangerous. Once, in her despair, for example, Florice consciously turns to the Petro loa, gods "who were wicked and terrible and trafficked in sacrifices" (67). Only Alice Wine, with her Sea Islands background, can recognize what is happening and know the ritual to counter Florice's "unholy" attempt to destroy herself. Unlike Minnie Ransom, Florice applies her healing powers quietly and reluctantly. Her faith and love are inextricable components of her mysterious powers and equally remarkable.

Two images for Florice's gift—the rainbow and the butterfly—suggest that her powers derive from two religious traditions in the New Orleans of her young adulthood: Christianity and hoodoo, with hoodoo having originated in Africa but, as Zora Neale Hurston explains, having adapted "itself like Christianity to its locale, reclaiming some of its borrowed characteristics to itself" (193). The rainbow first appears the night "the words were given" concerning her power to the devoutly Christian Florice. The butterfly first appears with Florice's early recollection of a hoodoo ceremonial in New Orleans. Frightened by the ceremony, the young woman protested: "This had nothing to do with her, this scene of fire and seduction. These weren't her people after all." But shortly after, she "felt herself being called; . . . the shadow flapped over her, a gorgeous bat, like the princely scarab beetle. The wings turned and the shadow moved into a butterfly shape and rose and rose from her head" (9).

The magnificent butterfly rising from her head reveals Florice's special mission as surely as do her more readily understood words from God and the "gift of the rainbow . . . , a sign that the light inside was burning like a private sun" (8). The butterfly image also reinforces what the plot illustrates, that such power emerges gradually. Short sections concerning the metamorphosis of a butterfly follow many scenes and serve as commentary on Florice's and, later, her goddaughter Ronnie's spiritual growth. For while *Rainbow Roun Mah Shoulder* focuses on the Southern woman with magical power rather than on her reluctant heir, transmitting that power is as crucial here as it is in *Praisesong for the Widow* and *The Salt Eaters.* In her farewell letter before going off to die, Florice explains to sixteen-year-old Ronnie that Ronnie is her "special child, blessed with some of God's most wonderful and dangerous gifts." Just as Florice has had, now Ronnie has "a rainbow tied all roun" her shoulder. "It's yours now. . . . From God to me; from me to you" (166–68).

Brown's *Rainbow Roun Mah Shoulder* tracks the female heritage through two generations. Marshall's *Praisesong for the Widow* traces five, with Great-great Aunt Cuney carrying out her own grandmother's charge. This old woman "by instilling the story of the Ibos in [young Avey's] mind had entrusted her with a mission" (42), the same as Aunt Cuney's gran' had entrusted her. Only by Aunt Cuney's vigilance from beyond the grave and then not until Avey Johnson is on the island of Carricou will Avey again accept that heritage. During the islanders' "Beg Pardon" to their ancestors, she begins dancing the Carricou Tramp, the same steps she had seen long before and far away in that Tatem church, "the shuffle designed to stay the course of history" (250). A silent young woman charged with remaining at her side strangely makes her think of Great-aunt Cuney. Avey imagines that she is still the little girl who stands by her great-great-aunt in the darkness, looking in on the church congregation and secretly duplicating their steps. What follows is metaphor, but it is also miracle:

> And for the first time since she was a girl, she felt the threads, that myriad of shiny, silken, brightly colored threads . . . which were thin to the point of invisibility yet as strong as the ropes at Coney Island. Looking on outside the church in Tatem, standing waiting for the *Robert Fulton . . .* , she used to feel them streaming out of everyone there to enter her, making her part of what seemed a far-reaching, wide-ranging confraternity.

> Now, suddenly, as if she were that girl again, with her entire life yet to live, she felt the threads streaming out from the old people around her. (249)

One by one the islanders bow to her, and finally one old woman looks closely, "searching for whatever it was she possessed that required her to defer despite her greater age" (251). When she gives her name, she remembers her great-aunt Cuney's insistence, "Avatara." What Great-aunt Cuney began, special people on this island complete, but Aunt Cuney's spirit is there just as her gran's has been for her. The novel ends with Avey imagining herself taking her grandchildren to the Landing: " 'It was here that they brought them,' she would begin—*as had been ordained*" (256, emphasis added).

Velma Henry, the "ordained" inheritor in Bambara's *The Salt Eaters*, is that novel's central character, and the acceptance of her heritage brings the healing that culminates the novel. She too must learn from an older woman whom many dismiss as crazy. As in *Praisesong*, so in *Salt Eaters*, the protagonist is not the first to be guided by an older woman specially endowed. When Minnie Ransom despairs of reaching Velma, her own spirit guide, Old Wife, reminds her, "Just like you for the world, Min" (56). It had been Old Wife who once helped the deeply disturbed Minnie know about her "gift unfolding" (53).

The novel opens with the words, "Are you sure, sweetheart, you want to be well?" Minnie Ransom offers this arresting question to Velma Henry, a young woman who has been deeply involved both in spiritual movements and the civil rights struggles and is now caught, so her godmother thinks, in "the chasm that divided the two camps" (147). Discouraged by factions, setbacks, and destructive powers that seem insurmountable, she has attempted suicide. Through her gift, Minnie Ransom eventually succeeds with this most resistant patient; the gift involves mystical healing and communication with spirits but, like Rebecca Florice's gift, just as importantly relies on her exceptional common sense and humanity.

With their visions of empowered women passing on their gifts to succeeding generations, *Rainbow Roun Mah Shoulder*, *Praisesong for the Widow*, and *The Salt Eaters* share motifs and images. For instance, both Bambara's and Marshall's novels describe life-affirming contacts between people as though there were actually physical strands connecting them. Similar to the wonderful sensation of "confraternity" that Avey Johnson used to experience as a child and later at Carricou—the sensation of being connected to everyone else by a "myriad of shiny, silken . . . threads" that stream out of the people—Velma at the beginning of *Salt*

Eaters is "caught up . . . in the silvery tendrils that extended from the healer's neck and hands" (4). As both Avey and Velma recall the music of their people, they recover their wholeness. The authors use the term "centered" (Bambara 115; Marshall 254). Both *The Salt Eaters* and *Rainbow Roun Mah Shoulder* conclude with the same positive image of a butterfly. Realizing that Velma Henry no longer needs her healing hands, Minnie Ransom "withdraws them, drops them in her lap just as Velma, rising on steady legs, throws off the shawl that drops down on the stool a burst cocoon" (295). The butterfly at the end of Brown's novel has long since emerged from its cocoon; instead, Brown juxta-poses Florice's impending death with the butterfly's potential for great migrations.

In both Brown's and Marshall's novels, the protagonist's ultimate arrival at a certain spot in the South seems to fulfill her destiny and signal her final achievement of wholeness. Florice is as deliberate in her movement to the coastal Southeast as Avey Johnson will be. After settling her accounts in Pittsburgh, Rebecca Florice returns not to Greensboro but to Bear Island, North Carolina, a place she has been only once before. "Searching for something specific on this beach which was her home" (168), she finds it—the nearly fitting other half of a sand dollar she picked up there almost forty years ago. The novel closes with one last account of the butterfly—its potential *"to fly more than a thousand miles, . . . even to cross oceans"* (169)—a veritable transmigra-tion. One is reminded of Great-aunt Cuney's comment about her grandmother, the woman for whom Avatara Johnson is named: "Her body she always usta say might be in Tatem but her mind, her mind was long gone with the Ibos." In Tatem and Bear Island, where Avatara Johnson and Rebecca Florice can best connect with their complex heritage, they are spiritually "home."

By the end of *Praisesong for the Widow, Rainbow Roun Mah Shoulder,* and *The Salt Eaters,* the older Southern woman has succeeded in finding and preparing her heir. Southerland's *Let the Lion Eat Straw* also has an inheritor but only by implication. It is Kora, Abeba's eldest daughter, who recognizes and therefore can partake of the magic present for her mother through old Mamma Habblesham. As Southerland explains, "The 'kora' (or 'cora') is a West African instrument used to accompany the telling of a story. It was my hidden way to identify the story teller present" (Brookhart 243). While the "daughters" may face the loneliness of not being understood and their mission may entail sacrifice and pain, each has emerged from a community and tradition that allow for such specially empowered individuals, and each will direct her gifts to the survival and health of that community. Furthermore, the "magical" woman, who has personally claimed her, will continue to guide. Just as Minnie Ransom has Old Wife, she will have one or many "spirit guides" from her Southern past.

The nature of the protagonists' supernatural gifts is certainly familiar in African American folklore and literature, from Charles W. Chesnutt's *The Conjure Woman* (1899) and Zora Neale Hurston's accounts of hoodoo in *Mules and Men* (1935) to such "modern" characters as Alice Walker's Hannah Kemhuff in "The Revenge of Hannah Kemhuff" (*In Love and Trouble*, 1973) and Toni Morrison's Pilate in *Song of Solomon* (1977). "Magical" black women of the South persist. Nevertheless, however literally Southerland, Brown, Marshall, and Bambara expect readers to take the supernatural associated with the older women, all make clear that these women are great in the most familiar ways.[1] As impressive as any "magic" are the healers' endurance and depth of humanity. They may cajole and chide or gather the "daughters" in need of healing into their arms.[2] They understand and help overcome spiritual and physical loneliness, the feeling that the young Rebecca Florice expresses of being "sometime . . . like a motherless chile, a *long* way from home; so far away that I won't never get home" (44). They restore for the "motherless chile" her home, her past, and her present, and they give her a vision for the future.

Even though the tradition of such women is familiar, how can we account for the fact that contemporary black women novelists have made the transmission of magical power from one generation to the next central to their plots? The answer seems to lie in two directions: the readers' needs and the novelist's needs.

Toni Morrison recalls the novel's history of functioning for the class that wrote it and describes a current crisis for African Americans that novels may be serving to alleviate: "We don't live in places where we can hear those stories anymore; parents don't sit around and tell their children those classical, mythological archetypal stories that we heard years ago" (340). Not so coincidentally as it turns out, Morrison believes the African American novel requires the presence of ancestors—"timeless people whose relationships to the characters are benevolent, instructive, and protective" (343). Although she does not specify the South, Morrison associates the necessary and once available stories with a former place and time.

The critics Joanne V. Gabbin and Joanne M. Braxton also accept the novel's function in meeting its readers' needs in their analysis of literature by black women. Referring to Morrison's belief in the novel's capacity to heal, Braxton states, "Much of the contemporary fiction by Afra-American writers performs this important healing function" (305).

Gabbin considers the "laying on of hands" present in a number of works by black women to be a metaphor for the function of the writings themselves. The writings bring readers who have been wounded by "racism, oppression and indifference" toward self-definition as they convey cultural traditions "too long silenced by a male-centered literary tradition" (246). For Gabbin and Braxton, what happens in certain works relates to what happens to their readers. Indeed, in the novels discussed in this essay, the reader too is an inheritor, a spiritual "daughter" to this powerful legacy of Southern women.

Yet the remarkable similarities of these novels, all of which trace women becoming empowered through a mysteriously endowed older woman, strongly suggest the subject serves another function besides meeting the readers' needs. Marjorie Pryse, in her introductory essay to *Conjuring: Black Women, Fiction, and Literary Tradition* (1985), leads us to the most plausible explanation. Discussing primarily Zora Neale Hurston and Alice Walker and their antecedents, she argues that the "emergence of the Southern black woman as major novelist" may have something to do with her having found her own literary models from the women in her past, among them the traditional "magical" black women. She writes,

> In the 1970s and 1980s, black women novelists have become metaphorical conjure women, "mediums" like Alice Walker who make it possible for their readers and for each other to recognize their common literary ancestors (gardeners, quilt makers, grandmothers, rootworkers, and women who wrote autobiographies) and to name each other as a community of inheritors. By their combined recognition and mutual naming, based on magic, oral inheritance, and the need to struggle against oppression, black women writers enlarge our conventional assumptions about the nature and function of literary tradition. (5)

Southerland's, Brown's, Marshall's, and Bambara's novels support Pryse's sense of a black female "community of inheritors." Each novelist portrays remarkable strengths, both magical and human, in individual black women and proclaims a continuity between "ancient power" still residing in the South and the power inherent in contemporary black women who are free to move about once they have internalized this region, its history, and its female tradition. Each of the novels ends with fulfillment and promise—the fulfillment of one generation and the promise of its successor.

The authors of *Rainbow Roun Mah Shoulder, Praisesong for the Widow,* and *The Salt Eaters* make the process of locating and then accepting one's power the central issue of the novel. In each case, the result is a specifically female African American version of the *Künstler-roman*, that is, "an artist of some sort who struggles from childhood to maturity against an inhospitable environment and within himself toward an understanding of his creative mission" (Holman 271). Although none of these novelists calls herself a medium or conjurer (as Pryse points out that Alice Walker in fact does in her Afterword to *The Color Purple* when Walker writes, "I thank everybody in this book for coming./ A. W., author and medium"), the connection between herself as writer/artist and her magically endowed characters is implicit. It is not surprising that the three younger women whose gifts unfold—Brown's Ronnie, Marshall's Avey Johnson, and Bambara's Velma Henry—are roughly the ages of their authors. It is also not surprising that the novels end at the point that they do: they make clear a destiny for Ronnie, Avey Johnson, and Velma Henry without following them beyond their moment of empowerment.

These female characters have located at last their role models and their own authority. So have their authors, the "metaphorical conjure women" behind the texts. Brown, Marshall, and Bambara, as well as Southerland, link traditional and sometimes ancient Southern black healers, mystics, and storytellers to modern black women who also have special visionary gifts. In doing so, they redefine our notion of the artist. And in tracing the conflicts, the suffering and sacrifice, and the growth of artist figures in their novels, they have written *Künstlerromane—Künstlerromane* that have been envisioned and shaped by a female tradition of the African American South.

NOTES

1. In "Artists without Art Form," Renita Weems comments on critics who are uncomfortable with characters who seem "bigger than life": "I suspect that those who feel this way know nothing of the sheer miracle it is that black people, and black women especially, have survived all these years. There is nothing commonplace about a people who have survived, and continue surviving, some of the most brutal oppression that human beings can inflict upon one another" (100).

2. Carole Boyce Davies, in an essay that considers *The Salt Eaters* and *Praisesong for the Widow* as well as Alice Walker's *The Color Purple*, Naylor's *The Women of Brewster Place*, and Shange's *Sassafrass, Cypress and Indigo*, discusses black female healers who, though not biological mothers, take on that nurturing role in order to rid these "daughters" of their self-destructive behavior brought on by various forms of oppression.

WORKS CITED

Bambara, Toni Cade. *The Salt Eaters.* New York: Random House, 1980.

————. "What It Is I Think I Am Doing Anyhow." In *The Writer on Her Work.* Ed. Janet Sternburg. New York: W. W. Norton, 1980. 153–68.

Braxton, Joanne M. "Ancestral Presence: The Outraged Mother Figure in Contemporary Afra-American Writing." In *Wild Women in the Whirlwind: Afra-American Culture and the Contemporary Literary Renaissance.* Ed. Joanne M. Braxton and Andree Nicola McLaughlin. New Brunswick, N.J.: Rutgers University Press, 1990. 299–315.

Brookhart, Mary Hughes. "Ellease Southerland." In *Afro-American Fiction Writers after 1955.* Ed. Thadious M. Davis and Trudier Harris. Vol. 33 of *Dictionary of Literary Biography.* Gen. ed. Richard Layman. Detroit: Gale Research Company, 1985. 239–44.

Brown, Linda Beatrice. Telephone interview with Mary Hughes Brookhart. 15 Jan. 1989.

————. *Rainbow Roun Mah Shoulder.* 1984. New York: Ballantine Books, 1989.

Davies, Carole Boyce. "Mothering and Healing in Recent Black Women's Fiction." *Sage: A Scholarly Journal of Black Women* 2 (Spring 1985): 41–43.

Davis, Thadious M. "Expanding the Limits: The Intersection of Race and Region." *The Southern Literary Journal* 20 (Spring 1988): 3–11.

Gabbin, Joanne V. "A Laying On of Hands: Black Women Writers Exploring the Roots of Their Folk and Cultural Tradition." In *Wild Women in the Whirlwind: Afra-American Culture and the Contemporary Literary Renaissance.* Eds. Joanne M. Braxton and Andree Nicola McLaughlin. New Brunswick, N.J.: Rutgers University Press, 1990. 246–63.

Holman, C. Hugh, and William Harmon. *A Handbook to Literature.* 5th ed. New York: Macmillan, 1986.

Hull, Gloria T. " 'What It Is I Think She's Doing Anyhow': A Reading of Toni Cade Bambara's *The Salt Eaters.* " In *Conjuring: Black Women, Fiction, and Literary Tradition.* Eds. Marjorie Pryse and Hortense J. Spillers. Bloomington: Indiana University Press, 1985. 216–32.

Hurston, Zora Neale. "Origin of Hoodoo." In *Mules and Men.* Bloomington: Indiana University Press, 1978. 193–97.

Locke, Alain. "Our Little Renaissance." In *Ebony and Topaz: A Collectanea.* Ed. Charles S. Johnson. New York: National Urban League, 1927. 117–18.

Marshall, Paule. *Praisesong for the Widow.* New York: Putnam's, 1983.

Morrison, Toni. "Rootedness: The Ancestor as Foundation." In *Black Women Writers (1950–1980).* Ed. Mari Evans. Garden City, N.Y.: Doubleday, 1984. 339–45.

Pryse, Marjorie T. Introduction: "Zora Neale Hurston, Alice Walker, and the 'Ancient Power' of Black Women." In *Conjuring: Black Women, Fiction, and Literary Tradition.* Ed. Marjorie Pryse and Hortense J. Spillers. Bloomington: Indiana University Press, 1985. 1–24.

Southerland, Ellease. "I Got a Horn, You Got a Horn." In *A World Unsuspected:*

Portraits of Southern Childhood. Ed. Alex Harris. Chapel Hill: University of North Carolina Press, 1987. 175–209.

————. "The Influence of Voodoo on the Fiction of Zora Neale Hurston." In *Sturdy Black Bridges.* Ed. Roseann P. Bell, Bettye J. Parker, and Beverly Guy-Sheftall. Garden City, N.Y.: Doubleday, 1979. 172–83.

————. *Let the Lion Eat Straw.* New York, Scribner's, 1979.

————. Letter to Mary Hughes Brookhart. 30 Dec. 1981.

Walker, Alice. *The Color Purple.* New York: Harcourt Brace Jovanovich, 1982.

Weems, Renita. "Artists without Art Form." *Home Girls: A Black Feminist Anthology.* New York: Kitchen Table Press, 1983. 94–105.

Suzanne W. Jones

Dismantling Stereotypes: Interracial Friendships in *Meridian* and *A Mother and Two Daughters*

> For various reasons, the average, struggling, non-morbid Negro is the best-kept secret in America. His revelation to the public is the thing needed to do away with that feeling of difference which inspires fear and which ever expresses itself in dislike.
>
> —Zora Neale Hurston, "What White Publishers Won't Print"

> We must recognize differences among women who are our equals, neither inferior nor superior, and devise ways to use each other's difference to enrich our vision and our joint struggles.
>
> —Audre Lorde, "Age, Race, Class, and Sex"

When pondered together, these meditations on difference raise some perplexing questions. How do we discover a shared humanity without erasing difference? How do we use difference to enrich our vision if we fear it? How can we come to understand difference differently? When Zora Neale Hurston wrote "What White Publishers Won't Print" in 1950 before the civil rights movement began, she believed literature could help reduce white prejudice by proving blacks to be "just like everybody else" (171). When Audre Lorde called for new patterns of relating across differences at Amherst College in 1980, she ended her powerful plea with lines from an unpublished poem, "we seek beyond history/for a new and more possible meaning" (358), lines that suggest the power and importance of imaginative literature in producing change. Currently Henry Louis Gates, Jr., writing when racism is once again on the rise, continues to insist on the power of language to shape perception:

"Race has become a trope of ultimate, irreducible difference. . . . we carelessly use language in such a way as to *will* this sense of *natural* difference into our formulations. To do so is to engage in a pernicious act of language, one which exacerbates the complex problem of cultural or ethnic difference, rather than to assuage it or redress it" (5). Several contemporary Southern novelists are attempting to assuage and redress this complex problem in their fiction, to deal with difference in the way Audre Lorde calls for. I am limiting my discussion to two novels written by Southern women after it was obvious that desegregation, in and of itself, would not eliminate prejudice—*Meridian* (1976), by Alice Walker, and *A Mother and Two Daughters* (1982), by Gail Godwin. I am interested in the literary techniques they employ to dismantle the stereotypes of Southern womanhood produced by the patriarchy of the Old South—stereotypes that persisted after the Civil War ended slavery and after the civil rights movement ended legal segregation. Both Walker and Godwin imagine shared experiences for their black and white characters, calling attention not only to their common interests and common humanity but also to other similarities that the South's preoccupation with racial differences overshadowed: gender and class. Walker and Godwin do not attempt to erase difference so much as to assure that difference is not misread or misnamed, to show that it is not biologically determined but culturally conditioned.

Recognition of any similarities between black and white women has been rendered difficult in the South by a history of slavery and segregation, which caused blacks and whites to define themselves in opposition to each other, to see difference as innate rather than socially constructed. Though not representative of the majority of Southerners, the white plantation society, because of its economic and social dominance, established conventions of behavior for women, both white and black.[1] The white woman was expected to be a "lady"—physically pure, socially correct, culturally refined, and dutiful to family. Lower-class white women were less-refined, more hardworking versions of this same ideal of the dutiful wife. In contrast, plantation society defined black women as promiscuous wenches, prolific breeders, hardworking mules, or nurturing mammies. Irving H. Bartlett and C. Glenn Cambor contend that "each image was paradoxical and something far less than that of a mature, autonomous, and well-integrated woman" (19). The white "lady" was deprived of her full sexual and maternal identity while the black woman was deprived of her equality and her humanity. Literary critic Minrose Gwin argues that "just as black women were forced to be strong, white southern women often were compelled to appear weak" (4). Even though these racial stereotypes were inaccurate, as historians

Catherine Clinton, Paula Giddings, and Anne Firor Scott have shown, they have affected black and white women's images of themselves as well as their images of each other. Psychologist Mark Snyder has observed the power of stereotypes to become self-fulfilling: "In inter-racial encounters, racial stereotypes may constrain behavior in ways to cause both blacks and whites to behave in accordance with those stereotypes" (266). He also points out that when people have adopted stereotypical ways of thinking about another person, they "tend to notice and remember the ways in which that person seems to fit the stereotype while resisting evidence that contradicts the stereotype" (266).

The difficulty of realizing that racial differences are socially constructed rather than biologically determined is evident from the following passage of Mary Chestnut's Civil War diary. An aristocratic white woman, Chesnut can see the brutality of slavery, but the ideology of plantation society blinds her to the fact that it is the system that degrades the female slave, rather than the female slave who is naturally inferior:

> Under slavery we live surrounded by prostitutes, yet an abandoned woman is sent out of any decent house. Who thinks any worse of a Negro or mulatto woman for being a thing we can't name? God forgive us, but ours is a monstrous system, a wrong and an iniquity! Like the patriarchs of old, our men live all in one house with their wives and their concubines; and the mulattoes one sees in every family partly resemble the white children. . . . My disgust sometimes is boiling over. Thank God for my country women, but alas for the men! They are probably no worse than men everywhere, but the lower their mistresses the more degraded they must be. (21)

Such reasoning, the literary critic Hazel Carby argues, was part of the nineteenth-century ideology of Southern womanhood, which held that the white man was "merely prey to the rampant sexuality of his female slaves" (27). This dichotomous thinking shows not only that stereotypes falsify the causes of behavior but that they are also used to bolster self-esteem.

For years white women have defined themselves in opposition to their black sisters, but black women have done the same. One hundred years after Chesnut confessed these strong feelings, Toni Morrison wrote an article for the *New York Times Magazine* rightly questioning the relevance of the women's liberation movement for black women and proudly affirming her identity as a black woman by delineating the differences between the races. She reminisces about a trip to Charlotte, North Carolina, where she was struck by the "accuracy and fine distinctions" of the labels "White Ladies" and "Colored Women" on bathroom doors: "The difference between white and black females seemed to me an eminently satisfactory one. White females were *ladies,* said the sign maker, worthy of respect. And the quality that made ladyhood worthy? Softness, willingness to let others do their labor and their thinking. Colored females, on the other hand, were *women* — unworthy of respect because they were tough, capable, independent and immodest" (15). Morrison's perspective allows her to question the ideology of Southern womanhood and to reverse its positive and negative attributes. The following description, however, still bears evidence of stereotypical thinking:

> Black women have always considered themselves superior to white women. Not racially superior, just superior in terms of their ability to function healthily in the world. . . . Black women have no abiding admiration of white women as competent, complete people. Whether vying with them for the few professional slots available to women in general, or moving their dirt from one place to another, they regarded them as willful children, pretty children, but never as real adults capable of handling the real problems of the world.
>
> White women were ignorant of the facts of life—perhaps by choice, perhaps with the assistance of men, but ignorant anyway. They were totally dependent on marriage for male support (emotionally or economically). They confronted their sexuality with furtiveness, complete abandon or repression. (64)

While Morrison emphasizes significant differences in the social experiences of the races, she does not take into account the differences between white individuals, based on other factors such as class.

Throughout this one hundred-year period, some Southern women writers, both black and white, have attempted to undermine racial stereotypes by depicting a common bond between black and white women. In *Black and White Women of the Old South* Gwin has pointed out that this bond was often based "on an acknowledgement of common womanhood and common humanistic values" (24). This bond,[2] however, was never depicted as one of friendship and equality. Because of the times in which Alice Walker and Gail Godwin live, they are able to push further than their literary foremothers in imagining relationships between black and white women. Each creates a protagonist who discovers not only some similarity but the individuality in a woman of a different race. Then, each becomes better able to understand the other's difference. In Walker's *Meridian,* a Southern black civil rights worker, Meridian, discovers that a Northern white coworker, Lynne, is not simply a superficial white girl looking for adventure but a hard worker, just as committed to the movement as Meridian is. In Godwin's

A Mother and Two Daughters, Lydia, a genteel young white "lady,"
enrolls in a women's studies class at the University of North Carolina at
Greensboro and discovers that her black sociology professor, Harvard-
graduate Renee, shares her own tastes and interests. The black writer,
then, has her black protagonist realize that racial difference is not a
matter of simplistic opposition, and the white writer has her white
protagonist make the same realization. Thus the struggle that each
main character has in overcoming racial stereotypes reflects the struggle
that each writer imagines is the experience of readers of her own race.
But readers whose race is not the same as the author's also gain knowledge about the complex functioning of racial stereotypes. For example,
in reading *Meridian* many of my white female students were surprised
by Meridian's biased opinions about white women, a discovery that
made them think differently about themselves and their interactions
with black women.[3]

     The 1960s' civil rights movement brought black and white women
together in the South as equals for the first time. In *Meridian,* Alice
Walker explores such a relationship between Lynne and Meridian.
Despite their liberal politics both women at first have difficulty relating
to each other as individuals; both are preoccupied with racial difference.
     Although Lynne does not think of blacks as inferior to whites (she
ardently supports equal rights and marries a black man), she is preoccupied with race. Lynne feels guilty because she is a representative of the
race that discriminates against blacks, so she treats them as special
people. Walker suggests that Lynne's fascination with blacks is a romantic response to a people and a way of life different from her own:

> To her eyes used to Northern suburbs where every house looked sterile and
> identical even before it was completely built, where even the flowers were
> uniform and their nicknames were already in dictionaries, the suburbs
> incapable of strong odor or surprise of shape, and the people usually
> stamped with the seals of their professions; to her nestled in a big chair
> made of white oak strips under a quilt called The Turkey Walk, from
> Attapulsa, Georgia, in a little wooden Mississippi sharecropper bungalow
> that had never known paint, the South—and the black people living
> there—was Art. (130)

Such a romantic view involves perceiving the exotic otherness of blacks,
seeing them as objects rather than awarding them the full dignity of
human beings with emotions and thoughts. Certainly, the blacks who
had known the squalor and degradation of living in the sharecropper's
shack that Lynne describes did not find it quaint, nor did they call the

house a "bungalow." Instead of denigrating difference as Southern whites had, Lynne romanticizes it. Captivated by the differences between the races and blinded by her belief that all blacks are passive sufferers, Lynne fails to recognize the differences that exist between black individuals: "She had insisted on viewing them all as people who suffered without hatred; this was what intrigued her, made her like a child in awe of them" (162). Consequently, Lynne does not see the rage of black men like Tommy Odds, who feels powerless under white oppression. Nor does Lynne notice the anger of black women like Meridian, who has lost her boyfriend to a white woman.[4]

Misunderstandings arise on both sides because of racial difference. Walker suggests that Meridian's inability to understand the attraction her boyfriend Truman feels for Lynne originates from the black woman's feeling of sexual superiority over the white woman, the feeling that Toni Morrison described in her *New York Times Magazine* article. Although Meridian had originally liked Lynne and appreciated her liberal politics, Meridian is bewildered when Truman, the handsome black man whom she has been dating, shows an interest in Lynne. Because of this triangle, Meridian is forced to confront her prejudice against white women. She realizes that her mother and grandmother had taught her "that nobody wanted white girls except their empty-headed, effeminate counterparts—white boys. . . . As far back as she could remember it seemed something *understood:* that while white men would climb on black women old enough to be their mothers—'for the experience'—white women were considered sexless, contemptible and ridiculous by all" (107). This stereotype breaks down, however, when Meridian applies it to Lynne. Although at first Meridian rationalizes Truman's interest in Lynne as a fascination with her color, Meridian is forced to acknowledge that the attraction is much more complex. In her analysis of the novel, Barbara Christian suggests, "Because [Truman] is an intellectual as well as a man, he expects his mate to be worldly as well as virginal" ("Novels" 223). A pregnant teenager forced by school authorities to drop out of high school, Meridian does not have these qualifications.

Meridian, however, likes to think of black women as women who did "something unheard of. Outrageous" and white women as "frivolous, helpless creatures, lazy and without ingenuity. . . . useless except as baby machines" (108). Actually as Walker presents the facts of Lynne's and Meridian's lives, she inverts the stereotypes. In her teenage marriage to Eddie, Meridian resembles the white women she derides: "she knew she had lacked courage, lacked initiative or a mind of her own" (109). And Lynne, rather than conforming to Meridian's narrow notion of the white woman's fate, more nearly fits Meridian's image of the black woman, who escapes from her family and home town to do something adventurous, "to become something unheard of" (109). Although her motives are far from pure, Lynne leaves home and parents to work for the civil rights movement during a violent time in Southern history. She marries Truman, bears a child by him, and is subsequently disowned by her parents.

While Walker shows how race can separate women, she uses gender as one similarity to unite them. The brutal slaying of Lynne's daughter Camara brings the two women close together. As Lynne and Meridian mourn the death of Camara, whom they both loved, they begin to relate to one another as women, rather than as white or black. Both have experienced the loss of a child. Both have experienced the loss of Truman, who expressed his racial and sexual insecurity by breaking up with Meridian when the civil rights movement made white women more accessible and by leaving Lynne when the "Black is beautiful" movement made black women more desirable than white. Watching a television program in Lynne's New York apartment about the strain of race relations in the South, Meridian and Lynne feel that they have "temporarily solved" the race problem. Meridian reads Margaret Walker's poems to Lynne, Lynne attempts "to cornrow Meridian's patchy short hair," and they talk "intimately, like sisters" (173). During this time in New York they ask forgiveness of each other, acknowledging the harmful stereotyping that fosters hatred between the races.

But resolution does not come so easily. Society's stereotypes lie latent but potent in the consciousnesses of all of Walker's characters. A year later Lynne, still in love with Truman, tracks him to Meridian's house in Georgia. Although Meridian is not sexually involved with Truman, he continues to visit her. Lynne, in an attempt to hurt Meridian and to boost her own self-esteem, explains Truman's behavior by using racist cliches:

> "Tell me, how does it feel to be a complete *flop*" (this said with a Bette Davis turn of her wrist) "at keeping your men?"
> "You know, I could—yes, fat ass 'n' all, walk up the street anywhere around here and Hey Presto! I'd have all y'all' men following after me, their little black tongues hanging out." (150)

After Truman leaves, Lynne apologizes to Meridian, saying she has insulted her out of jealousy. Her motives are more complex. Walker suggests that overcoming hatred of "the other" first requires overcoming hatred of self.[5]

Rejecting white racism, Lynne has tried to reject her whiteness and has allied herself with black people, but she finds herself the victim of black prejudice, as the rape by Tommy Odds and the ensuing rejection by Truman prove. The rape episode dramatizes Walker's concern with the tenacious hold stereotypes have, even on people who know they are false. Lynne's experience with Tommy subsequently causes her to generalize that all black men are "savages" (161) and in doing so to dredge up a stereotype that lies not very far beneath her liberal activism. Ironically, then, Lynne's initial romanticism of blacks leads to the racism that denigrates them. In attempting to protect Tommy Odds from white injustice by not telling the police, Lynne has not made Tommy responsible for his actions, and she has unwittingly encouraged him to think stereotypically about her. For in Tommy's eyes Lynne becomes both the Northern liberal who "felt sorry for me because I'm black" (164) and the stereotypical white woman who secretly desires a dark-skinned lover—"She didn't even fight. She was just laying back waiting to give it up" (163).

Despite attempts to perceive each other without racial stereotypes, both Lynne and Tommy are trapped within the stereotypical images their society has promoted, images that render them incapable of responding to each other as distinct individuals. Furthermore, stereotypical thinking about "the other" transforms Lynne into a stereotype herself. For example, after the rape and subsequent sexual relationships with black men, Lynne perversely enjoys the resulting rage of black women, and she uses their rage

> as acknowledgement of her irresistible qualities. It was during this time that whenever she found herself among black women, she found some excuse for taking down and combing her hair. As she swung it and felt it sweep the back of her waist, she imagined she possessed treasures they could never have. She began to believe that men fucked her from love, not from hatred. For as long as they did not hate her she felt she could live. She could bear the hatred of her own father and mother, but not the hatred of black men. And when they no longer came to her— and she did not know why they did not—she realized she needed them. (166)

No longer a member of either the white or the black community, Lynne feels very much alone, and she envies Meridian her place and her purpose in life: " 'It's just that you have everything. I mean, you're so strong, your people love you, and you can cope. I don't have anything. I gave up everything for True and he just shit on me' " (151). To try to figure out her problem, Lynne reviews her life. When she tells Meridian about the rape, the bond that Lynne feels should have been there between the two women is strained. Race interferes. It is significant that Walker has the usually saintly Meridian react so insensitively here, saying that she cannot listen to such a story, much less believe it.

Meridian's difficulty in listening to Lynne arises because Lynne's story is too much like the stories white women traditionally told about being raped by black men, men who were never allowed to tell their own stories. Meridian defensively believes that white women have always lied about black men raping them. But Lynne tells Meridian her story anyway. And Alice Walker makes sure that both sides get told—the white woman's and the black man's—devoting separate chapters to each viewpoint. For only in the telling of each side can readers, both black and white, understand that though the behavior may appear stereotypical, the motives are more complex. Tommy does not rape Lynne out of lust, as the old white myth might purport, but out of rage—at white racism, at having his arm shot off by white bigots. Lynne does not allow him to take advantage of her because of the white woman's desire for the black man, as stereotypical thinking would have it, but because of guilt for being a member of the race that has victimized him and fear that he will not get a fair trial if she cries rape.

The significance of Walker's use of interracial rape as a pivotal point in the relationship between black and white women in *Meridian* can be better understood by considering the short story, "Advancing Luna—and Ida B. Wells," which Walker completed while she was writing the novel. Like Meridian, the black narrator of this story is pulled between two parts of her identity—being black and being female. The narrator (presumably Walker herself) refers to writing about interracial rape in a novel and begs to be forgiven by fellow black woman Ida B. Wells, who investigated some of the so-called rapes that led to lynchings during and after Reconstruction. Wells became convinced that the majority of these "rapes" had actually been affairs between consenting adults (Sterling 60–117). In the story, Walker's narrator says that "whenever interracial rape is mentioned, a black woman's first thought is to protect the lives of her brothers, her father, her sons, her lover" (93). The narrator explains "that a history of lynching has bred this reflex in her. . . . I grew up believing black men literally did not rape white women" (93–94). Like Meridian, the narrator is forced to confront her prejudiced beliefs when her white roommate and friend, Luna, confesses something she has told no one else—that while working in the civil rights movement down South, a black man had raped her.

Like the narrator in "Advancing Luna—and Ida B. Wells," Walker rebels against Wells's imaginary injunction to "write nothing" that will be used against black men ("Luna" 94). Instead, in *Meridian* she writes with sensitivity and complexity about an episode potentially damaging to black men. Perhaps Walker has her characters confront what she calls "the stumbling block" ("Luna" 101) of interracial rape because she hopes the time has come when both black and white versions of the story will be "unprejudicially heard" ("Luna" 102). Certainly in her novel she creates the "solidarity among black and white women" ("Luna" 102) that she says is so rare.

The understanding to which Meridian and Lynne come is born out of storytelling. Through telling her story to Meridian, Lynne realizes that her tendency to romanticize blacks has led to misunderstandings. Furthermore, memories of the white prejudice a New York Jewish family encountered when they moved South force Lynne to reflect on her own ethnicity, and she realizes that her religious group has been victimized as well as the black race, although certainly not in the same way. Her conclusion that "black folks aren't so special" (181) is evidence of her growing awareness of self and "other." Just as Lynne begins to see some of her self in "the other," Meridian does also: equating the oppression of blacks with that of Jews. Meridian's remark, "maybe . . . the time for being special has passed" (181), is a signal of her ability to accept blacks and whites as individuals. Finally she views Lynne as a person, not simply as a white woman. Walker insists that whether this sense of being special results from a tendency to romanticize differences or to criticize them, it causes one race to misunderstand the other and to dehumanize individuals in the process.

The humor with which Walker concludes Lynne's storytelling is hopeful because the women are able to make fun of the racial stereotypes that they have too long guarded so closely:

> "Good God, this [talk of oppression] is depressing," said Lynne. "It's even more depressing than knowing I want Truman back."
> "That *is* depressing," said Meridian.
> "Oh, I know he's not much," she said. "But he saved me from a fate worse than death. Because of him, I can never be as dumb as my mother was. . . . No, Truman isn't much, but he's instructional," said Lynne. "Besides," she continued, "nobody's perfect."
> "Except white women," said Meridian, and winked.
> "Yes," said Lynne, "but their time will come." (181)

In *Meridian* and in "Advancing Luna—and Ida B. Wells," Alice Walker suggests that listening to each other's stories helps to loosen the hold that stubborn myths and harmful stereotypes have had on the imaginations of both black and white women. Walker seems to agree with

Barbara Christian that to listen to another's stories or to read them is "not only to validate the self but also to participate in 'the other's' view of the world" (34).

Gail Godwin sets her novel, *A Mother and Two Daughters,* in North Carolina about fifteen years after the 1960s civil rights movement. Lydia, one of the two daughters of the title, is a 1980s version of the nineteenth-century Southern lady. Graceful, modest, refined, and well-mannered, she has devoted her life to her husband and children. When the novel opens, Lydia fits the stereotype that Godwin described in her 1975 *Ms.* article, "The Southern Belle": "soft hands and soft voices; first concern for others, not self; refusal to dwell on subjects of ugliness, unpleasantness, violence, tension, strife; suave short-circuiting of all 'embarrassing questions'; cultivation and veneration of traditional and beautiful things; impeccable manners; 'spotless reputation' " (52). But in fulfilling this role, Lydia has not been fulfilled. To find another self hidden behind the social mask, Lydia leaves her husband and her home and returns to college, where she discovers sociology, feminism, and a black friend, Renee.

Establishing a friendship with Renee plays a central role in Lydia's break with traditional Southern values and in her emerging sense of self, although the interracial friendship is not as prominent in Godwin's novel as it is in Walker's. Lydia's thrill in telling her sister Cate about her new friend comes as much from the fact that Renee is highly educated as from the fact that she is black. Cate, an English professor, has mercilessly criticized Lydia's country-club friends as superficial and her suburban life as trivial. But Lydia considers her new friend as evidence of the reverse—of her widening horizons and of her growing interest in a life of the mind. When she explains the impact her friendship with Renee and Renee's friend Calvin have had on her life, Lydia reveals her previous racial prejudice. She says she used to assume that all robbers and muggers were black and that all victims were white. Now she resents the "bad publicity" (482) that an individual black criminal brings to the race. While Lydia has yet to realize that the "bad publicity" comes not from individual blacks who commit crimes but from whites who see such behavior as a sign of racial inferiority, she is learning that all blacks are not alike by getting to know two black individuals.

In contrast to the relationship between Lynne and Meridian, which emerges after a long struggle, there is little conflict between, or within, Lydia and Renee as they become friends. In part the ease of developing their friendship, despite Lydia's racial prejudice, has to do with their positions in life. Lydia, newly separated from her husband, is eager to prepare for a career; Renee, a Harvard graduate about to have her first book published, has a successful career. So Lydia sees Renee, who is also younger than she is, as a role model, a woman to admire: "Renee's office door was open. She was sitting at her desk, reading an aerogram with an English stamp and smoking a little brown cigar. Framed by shelves full of glossy books and wearing a twill pantsuit with a low-necked cerise silk blouse, she was the advertiser's dream-image of the woman who has 'made it'" (145). Godwin chooses the details carefully here. They not only reflect the worldly working woman dressed for success but also counter the Southern white stereotype of the black woman. The books, aerogram, and slim cigar indicate that Renee is hardworking, educated, and sophisticated. Lydia is fascinated by Renee because she has never met an upper middle-class black woman. Indeed, Lydia acknowledges Renee's "superiority over her in many of the areas the world values" (158). In this pairing of white and black women, Godwin inverts the traditional Southern racial hierarchy by making the black character superior to the white.

A more significant factor in establishing their friendship as well as in emphasizing similarities between the two women is that their tastes and values are alike, something Lydia discovers when Renee asks her home to lunch. In Renee's home Lydia finds a similarity in tastes: a gray frame house on a "genteel old street" (149), rooms filled with plants and antiques, damask napkins and cut glass. In Renee's conversation Lydia discovers, to their mutual delight, a similarity in interests: French cuisine, sociology, children, the nature of love, the significance of social classes, snobbery. Race is not an issue in their friendship, though social class certainly is. Lydia feels neither hidden guilt, as Walker's Lynne does, nor a desire to confirm liberal views, either of which might cause her, as a white woman, to seek a friendship with Renee *because* she is black.

Godwin uses the relationship between Lydia's mother's friend Theodora and her black maid, Azalea, as a contrast to the friendship between Lydia and Renee. Godwin underlines the generational change in Southern race relations by juxtaposing Lydia and Renee's lunch with a luncheon Theodora gives the same day. Lydia's mother Nell describes it this way: "'There the three of us sat around the dining table, me and Theodora and Wickie Lee. And Azalea sat in the kitchen having *her* lunch. Theodora spent most of the time hollering back and forth with Azalea, and Wickie Lee and I sat in silence, picking at our shrimp salad'" (158–59). This brief scene depicts both the inequality and the irony of relationships between black maids and their white employers in the South. The conversation between Theodora and Azalea reveals that they have more to talk about than Theodora and her two white friends. When Wickie Lee deserts Theodora, it is Azalea, and not her white friend Nell, whom Theodora goes to for comfort. Yet Godwin makes her readers painfully aware that Theodora's relationship with Azalea is patronizing and self-centered. In giving Azalea her old clothes and jewelry and having her move into the house with her, Theodora appears generous. But such gestures are easy to make; they do not signify friendship, as Azalea understands:

> [Theodora] said to Azalea, "The old order changes, Azalea. Why, look at us. Who would ever have thought you and I'd be coughing each other to sleep on the opposite sides of our wall?"
>   Azalea gave Theodora a level look. "You perfectly capable of winning any argument all by yourself, Miss Thea, but you know and I know there's still that wall." She settled back in her chair with a dark smile, looking for all the world as if *she* had won. (580)

Unlike Theodora, Lydia is conscious of the racism that still exists in the interracial relationships in Southern society. Thus she is proud of the difference between her relationship with Renee and Theodora's relationship with Azalea. And yet for Lydia, the only embarrassing moments in their friendship come when she is reminded that Renee is black, a difference she no longer thinks about. Godwin indicates that similarities in feminist politics and social class have made Lydia forget about racial difference. But Godwin has Renee remind Lydia of this difference. Renee uses the word *nigger* in class, and she frequently drops her refined Southern drawing-room drawl and turns on her down-home Southern black dialect. Renee enjoys slipping into black dialect because the use of the two languages allows her to assert both similarity and difference. Lydia can only equate such language with Azalea, and yet at first Lydia cannot equate Renee with Azalea, even though they have the same skin color. However, Renee's continued use of Azalea's language makes Lydia conscious of the difference in skin color and therefore heritage between herself and her friend, at the same time that Lydia has decided there is no difference.

At first Lydia avoids this issue. Seeing class similarities between blacks and whites has allowed her to move beyond racial stereotypes. She does not want to consider racial differences. Eventually Renee's language switch catches Lydia off guard, and she giggles at the contrast. Like Meridian and Lynne, Lydia and Renee end up laughing together. But they indirectly acknowledge difference rather than directly confront it the way Meridian and Lynne do. There is a mannerliness about their relationship that does not exist in the relationship between Lydia and her sister Cate or between Meridian and Lynne. Lydia and Renee's friendship is much like the one Godwin imagines in her essay "The Southern Belle" between a black woman and her white friend who would probably hesitate to ask "embarrassing questions" (85). Lydia remains too much of a polite Southern lady to ask Renee embarrassing questions. However, as Lydia becomes more at ease with difference, she becomes more comfortable with Renee, and she expresses an interest in Renee's family history.[6] Godwin implies that only after black and white Southern women discover some similarities will they be able to begin to understand racial differences, not as innate or uniform, but as variably conditioned by a variety of social and cultural experiences.

Even though Renee may dress and act a part that previously few black women had filled, she transcends any stereotype, white or black, as Lydia's observation shows: "There was something wickedly arrogant about it, when Renee did it [drop into black dialect], as if she were showing her listeners that, though she was equally at home in both worlds, she was actually above both" (129). Godwin does not want readers to mistake Renee for a black woman trying to act white, a mistake Lydia's sister Cate makes when Lydia first tells her about Renee and Calvin. Cate too easily equates their upward mobility with insensitivity to racism and to the plight of their own race. Renee's teaching techniques and her decision to become a civil rights lawyer prove Cate's view false.

In the course of the novel, Godwin further dismantles racial stereotypes by having Lydia discover that in addition to Renee's having traits Lydia has thought of as "white," Lydia herself has characteristics she has attributed only to blacks. Her marriage to Max has lacked sexual passion, a characteristic she has stereotypically equated with the black race. On a vacation to New Orleans with Max the year before, she had hoped they would be freed from their "tight, civilized" lives by "some Negro playing a saxophone" (274), but "not the faintest throb of the jungle drum beat in their veins" (275). After her separation from Max, Lydia finds sexual passion with a podiatrist named Stanley, but she has difficulty integrating this newly discovered part of her self into the old definition of the Southern lady. To Lydia a lady is not a lover; she is an "amiable bed partner" (268). For a while Lydia tries to compartmentalize her life (mother, student, respected friend of Max, secret lover of Stanley), deciding that if she is a lover in private, she can still be a lady in public. Eventually though, the contents of one compartment of her life spill into another, and she is forced to come to terms with all parts of her self. She discovers that the passion of "the other" is in some respects a repressed part of her self.

In *Black and White Women of the Old South,* Gwin argues that in the nineteenth century women of both races, bound by dualistic thinking, "often viewed one another as missing pieces of a female identity denied them by the patriarchal culture. Female narrators of the slave narratives reveal their yearning for the chaste respectability of their white sisters, while the diaries and memoirs of the white women show their intense jealousy of the stereotypical sexuality of the slave woman. Each is only one half of a self" (11). In *A Mother and Two Daughters,* Gail Godwin brings these two halves together in both Lydia and Renee. At the same time that Godwin confers sexuality on Lydia, she gives Renee upper middle-class respectability with all its virtues and flaws. When Renee speaks derisively of the lower class whites who could not appreciate the weimaraner that she bought from them, Renee shows that upper middle-class blacks can be as snobbish as upper middle-class whites.

By the conclusion of *A Mother and Two Daughters,* Lydia feels in some ways "closer to Renee than to her own sister" (397). As testimony to this friendship, Godwin ends the novel with a symbolic marriage. Lydia's son Leo marries Renee's daughter Camilla, who Cate says is just like Lydia. At first, despite her new racial awareness, Lydia is shocked by the prospect of an interracial marriage in her own family, but she quickly acquiesces when she forces herself to think of Camilla as an individual. For as Carolyn Rhodes has noted, "The concept of the lady in the South of 1984 (the date of the epilog) has been quite detached from concern with color, although not from beauty and grace and demeanor. Camilla, the bride, impresses her white mother-in-law as 'a perfect lady' and the matriarchal Aunt Theodora agrees" (64).

If Gail Godwin's ending seems too pat and idealized, it does not totally depart from realism. In a traditional comedic resolution the harmony between a man and a woman symbolizes a larger harmony within the society. In Godwin's novel, however, the harmony that exists between black and white individuals is not extended to racial groups. Racism still exists in her fictional Southern world, though it is relegated to the background: a woman in a supermarket says she pities the children that Leo and Camilla will have, the Klan still marches in Greensboro, Calvin's life is threatened and he heads north, and the prejudiced white father of a "D" student in Renee's class firebombs her house and kills her dog. And yet the reader is not left without hope. Stereotypical thinking exists in Gail Godwin's world but not between blacks and whites who know each other personally.

Neither Godwin nor Walker suggests that interracial friendships will eliminate prejudice between groups, nor do they subscribe to "the mystical belief that the category 'woman' is the most natural and basic of all human groupings and can therefore transcend race division," a phenomenon that Gloria Joseph and Jill Lewis warn against in *Common Differences* (40). Although Godwin's portrait of the dynamics of interracial friendships is not as satisfyingly complex as Walker's, both writers suggest that if black and white women would only listen to each other's stories and find out about each other's lives, perhaps we would discover similarities that might allow us to better understand differences, as well as give us common goals. Both Gail Godwin and Alice Walker try to provide readers with such an experience through these novels. They make what we felt was strange about "the other" more familiar at the same time that they challenge our own sense of self. By imagining, as Audre Lorde calls for, some new "patterns for relating across our human differences as equals" (355), Alice Walker and Gail Godwin enable us to see that unity need not depend on homogeneity nor difference mean separation or simplistic opposition.

NOTES

1. See Anne Goodwyn Jones, *Tomorrow Is Another Day: The Woman Writer in the South, 1859–1936,* for an excellent summary and analysis of historians' speculations about the origins of these stereotypes (9–13). They range from the importation of the Western patriarchal tradition from Europe to racial slavery as an institution, to Southern anxieties about societal order before and after the Civil War, to white male anxiety about miscegenation.

In *Reconstructing Womanhood: The Emergence of the Afro-American Woman Novelist,* Hazel Carby argues that ideologies of white womanhood rigidified at the same time that the miscegenation laws were extended and importing slaves was outlawed: "That the slave followed the condition of his or her mother necessitated the raising of protective barriers, ideological and institutional, around the form of the white mother, whose progeny were heirs to the economic, social, and political interests in the maintenance of the slave system" (30–31).

2. In *Within the Plantation Household, Black and White Women of the Old South,* Elizabeth Fox-Genovese argues that although nineteenth-century black and white women shared emotional intimacy, they did not share a "sisterhood" because race and class were more important in their relationship than gender. While some critics have thought that the evidence Fox-Genovese cites suggests otherwise, Carby agrees with Fox-Genovese that "the social relation of slavery, which the ideology mystified, determined that the interests of the mistress lay with the slave master, not with the slave" (31).

3. For a discussion about race and reading, see Minrose C. Gwin's "A Theory of Black Women's Texts and White Women's Readings, or . . . The Necessity of Being Other" and Barbara Christian's "Response to 'Black Women's Texts.' "

4. In "Women's Consciousness and the Southern Black Movement," historian Sara Evans discusses the historical causes that underlie Walker's fictional event: "Interracial sex was the most potent social taboo in the South. The struggle against racism brought together young, naive sometimes insensitive, rebellious and idealistic white women with young, angry black men, some of whom had hardly been allowed to speak to white women before" (240). In *When and Where I Enter,* journalist Paula Giddings explains the racial conflicts within the civil rights movement this way: "The presence of white female students brought another, and sometimes emotional, dimension to the organization's sexual tension [between black men and women, struggling uneasily to share power in the movement]. The significance—and even the number—of interracial liaisons varies according to whom one talks to, but in an organizational context the weight of sex/race history was bound to be explosive" (296).

5. In "Stereotypes: Conceptual and Normative Considerations," Judith Andre explains that a "stereotype—which we retain in the face of contradictory evidence—must function in one of the following ways: it may be relatively fundamental to our conceptual scheme; it may protect our self-esteem; it may help bring about some desirable situation; or it may shield us from facing an unchangeable, unpleasant fact" (259).

6. See Elizabeth Schultz for another view of Godwin's representation of the relationship between Renee and Lydia. In "Out of the Woods and into the World: A Study of Interracial Friendships between Women in American Novels," Schultz reads Renee's absence in the epilogue as evidence that "when race does become an issue the friendship wanes" (75). However, Godwin explains Renee's absence by her enrollment in law school, and in no scene between the two women does Godwin imply a cooling off of the friendship.

WORKS CITED

Andre, Judith. "Stereotypes: Conceptual and Normative Considerations." In *Racism and Sexism.* Ed. Paula S. Rothenberg. New York: St. Martin's Press, 1988. 257–62.

Bartlett, Irving H. and C. Glenn Cambor. "The History and Psychodynamic of Southern Womanhood." *Women's Studies,* 2 (1974): 9–24.

Carby, Hazel. *Reconstructing Womanhood: The Emergence of Afro-American Woman Novelist.* New York: Oxford University Press, 1987.

Chesnut, Mary. *A Diary from Dixie.* Ed. Ben Ames Williams. Cambridge: Harvard University Press, 1980.

Christian, Barbara. "Novels for Everyday Use: The Novels of Alice Walker." In *Black Women Novelists: The Development of a Tradition, 1892–1976.* Westport, Conn.: Greenwood Press, 1980. 180–238.

———. "Response to 'Black Women's Texts.'" *National Women's Studies Association Journal* 1, no. 1 (1988): 32–36.

Clinton, Catherine. *The Plantation Mistress: Woman's World in the Old South.* New York: Pantheon, 1982.

Evans, Sara. "Women's Consciousness and the Southern Black Movement." In *Speaking for Ourselves.* Ed. Maxine Alexander. New York: Pantheon, 1977. 232–45.

Fox-Genovese, Elizabeth. *Within the Plantation Household: Black and White Women of the Old South.* Chapel Hill: University of North Carolina Press, 1988.

Gates, Henry Louis, Jr. "Writing 'Race' and the Difference It Makes." *Critical Inquiry* 12, no. 1 (1985): 1–20.

Giddings, Paula. *When and Where I Enter: The Impact of Black Women on Race and Sex in America.* New York: William Morrow, 1984.

Godwin, Gail. *A Mother and Two Daughters.* New York: Avon Books, 1983.

———. "The Southern Belle." *Ms.* 4 (1975): 49–52, 84–85.

Gwin, Minrose. *Black and White Women of the Old South.* Knoxville: University of Tennessee Press, 1985.

———. "A Theory of Black Women's Texts and White Women's Readings, or . . . The Necessity of Being Other." *National Women's Studies Association Journal* 1, no. 1 (1988): 21–31.

Hurston, Zora Neale. "What White Publishers Won't Print." In her *I Love Myself When I Am Laughing.* Ed. Alice Walker. Old Westbury, N.Y.: Feminist Press, 1979. 169–73.

Jones, Anne Goodwyn. *Tomorrow Is Another Day: The Woman Writer in the South, 1859–1936.* Baton Rouge: Louisiana State University Press, 1981.

Joseph, Gloria I., and Jill Lewis. *Common Differences.* Garden City, N.Y.: Anchor, 1981.

Lorde, Audre. "Age, Race, Class, and Sex: Women Redefining Difference." In *Racism and Sexism.* Ed. Paula S. Rothenberg. New York: St. Martin's Press, 1988. 352–59.

Morrison, Toni. "What the Black Woman Asks About Women's Lib." *The New York Times Magazine* 22 August 1971: 14–15, 63–64, 66.

Rhodes, Carolyn. "Gail Godwin and Southern Womanhood." In *Women Writers of the Contemporary South.* Ed. Peggy Whitman Prenshaw. Jackson: University Press of Mississippi, 1984. 55–66.

Schultz, Elizabeth. "Out of the Woods and into the World: A Study of Interracial Friendships between Women in American Novels." In *Conjuring: Black Women, Fiction, and Literary Tradition.* Ed. Marjorie Pryse and Hortense Spillers. Bloomington: Indiana University Press, 1985. 67–85.

Scott, Anne Firor. *The Southern Lady: From Pedestal to Politics, 1830–1930.* Chicago: University of Chicago Press, 1970.

Snyder, Mark. "Self-Fulfilling Stereotypes." In *Racism and Sexism.* Ed. Paula S. Rothenberg. New York: St. Martin's Press, 1988. 263–69.

Sterling, Dorothy. *Black Foremothers.* New York: Feminist Press, 1979.

Walker, Alice. "Advancing Luna—and Ida B. Wells." In *You Can't Keep a Good Woman Down.* New York: Harcourt Brace Jovanovich, 1981. 85–104.

———. *Meridian.* New York: Washington Square, 1976.

3. Individual Voices

Mary Ann Wimsatt

Caroline Hentz's Balancing Act

Time has not been kind to the reputation of Caroline Lee Whiting Hentz (1800–1856), once among the most prominent Southern writers of her era. In the general rise of interest in writing by women, the novels of her contemporaries such as Mrs. E. D. E. N. Southworth and Augusta Jane Evans Wilson have been resurrected, reprinted, studied, and commended, whereas her books, except for *The Planter's Northern Bride,* remain in eclipse, virtually forgotten today. Her contemporaries found her "one of our most dramatic of female writers," and her fiction, which was popular well into the 1890s, was hailed as among the "most exciting, interesting, and popular" work "that has ever emanated from the American Press"; commended for its "faithful delineations of Southern life, society, and scenery"; and praised for its "action and healthy excitement."[1] But today her books, if remembered at all, are dismissed, in a fairly typical assessment, as containing a "romantic vision of southern plantation life—of refined ladies and gentlemen, contented slaves, and rustic backwoods farmers" (Watson 222).[2]

This assessment of Hentz's work might be justified if Hentz had written only *Marcus Warland* (1852) and *The Planter's Northern Bride* (1854), each of which centers on an ideal Southern planter and his family and constitutes a reply to the antislavery discourse of the age through familiar arguments that appear annoyingly condescending to twentieth-century readers. Like Southern authors of tracts, essays, sermons, speeches, poetry, and novels—from Thomas Dew and James Henry Hammond to William J. Grayson and William Gilmore Simms—Hentz insists that slaves are children of a lower culture who have benefitted from connection with advanced white Christian civilization. She states that slavery imposes great discipline and responsibility upon owners and insists that most owners do not tax slaves beyond their endurance.

To the advantage of the South, she compares its agrarian economic system to the system of wage labor in the North, meanwhile stressing that the best slaveowners minister compassionately to their servants. She denounces the slave trade but insists that blacks are not ready for freedom; and she passionately urges her readers to preserve the Union by desisting from antislavery agitation.

As impassioned Southern answers to *Uncle Tom's Cabin, Marcus Warland* and *The Planter's Northern Bride* should interest the student of Southern history and literature. But Hentz deserves to be remembered for more than her romantic defenses of slavery. Her fiction, perhaps particularly her long fiction, has numerous features to recommend it. In a reconsideration of the female imagination in Southern literature, four of these features seem particularly noteworthy: Hentz's participation in the general tradition of romance; her vivid characterization, consonant with that tradition, of her leading figures and her inventiveness in balancing, comparing, and contrasting them; her use of fairy tale and folklore as structural elements in one of her best novels; and her sometimes spirited feminism, which enables her to devise unexpected, skillful turns in character development and narrative emphasis.

Even a cursory reading of Hentz's books reveals their clear relationship to the centuries-long tradition of romance as described by twentieth-century theorists such as Northrop Frye (*Anatomy of Criticism* 195–203; *Secular Scripture* passim). All Hentz's long fiction exhibits a clearly delineated moral and religious framework that bolsters her firm distinctions between right and wrong. Like most romance, her fiction upholds the ideals of the ruling class through its depictions of the well-born heroines and heroes representing the ideals; the marriage of these figures generally signifies, in the symbolizing tendency characteristic of romance, the union of desirable elements in antebellum Southern culture. Her narratives unfold against the rural or pastoral settings typical of romance, and their generally happy endings reflect the providential or wish-fulfillment movement frequently found in the genre. Finally, her emphasis on women characters exemplifies Frye's observation that women are central figures in romance—a fact that enables us as readers to understand how the literary tradition behind Hentz's writing helps bolster its sociocultural dimensions.

Frye and other writers such as Frederic Jameson note the close connection of romance with popular writing, an observation that is useful for understanding much of the literature—high, low, and middlebrow—of the antebellum era (*Secular Scripture*; Jameson Chaps. 2, 5). Like other early nineteenth-century authors, Hentz uses the traditional plot structures of romance as well as its conventional character types. The majority of her narratives, like narratives from Greek romances onward, center on young lovers who are brought together, separated, tested by misfortune, and reunited at the end of the book (Frye, *Secular Scripture;* Scholes and Kellogg Chap. 3). Her character types include the conventional, reasonably tradition-minded romance heroine and hero; the equally conventional dark or Byronic heroines and heroes who must learn to control their passions, often with the help of lovers or guardian figures; rebellious "good-bad" girls, sometimes blended with the figure of the dark lady, who descend from Di Vernon in Walter Scott's *Rob Roy;* and selfish parents or stepparents who try to control their children's lives, wreaking various kinds of havoc in the process (Fiedler 178).

Much romance employs a two-sided or dialectic structure that reflects the forces in conflict from which the plot structures usually spring (Frye, *Secular Scripture* Chap. 2; Bettelheim intro.). The pairing and contrasting of characters that make palpable that structure is, as Frye observes, a prominent feature of the "mental landscape" of romance (*Secular Scripture* 53). William Gilmore Simms, John Pendleton Kennedy, and other male romancers of the antebellum period who were concerned with historical action in the public sphere used the convention of character contrast to make the system of oppositions in that sphere apparent. But in the romances of Hentz and other antebellum women authors, the dialectic is, in a manner of speaking, domesticated. The source of conflict, even when male characters are dominant, usually lies within the domestic realm; and it is in portraying that realm and the problems to which it gives rise that Hentz cleverly employs—and refines—the character contrasts standard in the genre.[3]

In all her novels, Hentz uses the principle of character balance and contrast to define her thematic concerns and enhance the vigor and variety of her characterizations. This principle animates her first successful novel—*Linda; or, the Young Pilot of the Belle Creole* (1850)—the story of a plantation heiress who leaves her home rather than marry her rough, bold stepbrother, Robert Graham. Linda, who is impetuous, generous, warm, and friendly, is played off against her unpleasant stepmother, whose "smooth, cold countenance" and "thin, compressed lips" bespeak her unfeeling heart (22). Even more structurally significant in the narrative are the contrasts between Linda's suitors Robert Graham and Roland Lee, who serve to dramatize the domestic conflict on which the novel is based. A man whose moral and spiritual progress lags behind his intellectual development, Robert is initially a Byronic hero, darkly handsome, with "strong precocious passions and headstrong will" (110). Though he has a countenance of "striking beauty," his eyes burn with an "intolerable brightness" when he is enraged; and

Linda associates his "dark, violent passions" with storm and rain (135, 133, 141). Roland Lee, the "young pilot" of the subtitle who twice saves Linda's life, is by contrast firm, manly, ingenuous, frank, gentle, and dignified. At the end of the novel, Roland marries Linda, whereas Robert, chastened by his mother's fatal illness and also by false rumors of Linda's death, is converted to Christianity and learns to subdue his unruly passions.

This novel, like many of Hentz's later books, makes plain her conviction that deeply held moral and religious values enable human beings to learn discipline or transcend suffering. She elaborates upon this point in *Robert Graham* (1855), the sequel to *Linda*. Though separated by five years, the two books form, as it were, a single story. In the sequel, Hentz portrays how Robert, having lost Linda to Roland, has become a Christian minister and how, after various setbacks, he finally triumphs in love. During the course of the main plot, Roland is killed in a wreck at sea; and Linda, badly shaken by this misfortune, eventually marries Robert and prepares to become a missionary. Hentz thus gives primacy to the Christian values that are an animating feature of much nineteenth-century popular romance.

It should be noted, however, that the happy ending characteristic of most such romance is muted in this book by the tragedy of Roland's death and Linda's remarriage, which one cannot help but feel is more satisfactory for Robert than for Linda. Described another way, if *Linda* is a story about young lovers that shows a maturing heroine triumphant, *Robert Graham* is a book about the vicissitudes of mature life that not even the most courageous men and women can control. Firmly and clearly, it illustrates Hentz's conviction about the superiority of religious faith to any kind of earthly love.

In the subplots of *Robert Graham,* Hentz introduces a new group of young lovers whose relationships demonstrate her management—more sophisticated than in *Linda*—of the romance conventions of character balance and contrast. Early in the novel, she introduces two Northerners who are traveling in the South: Henry Bellenden, Robert's friend from college; and Julia, Henry's invalid sister whom he has brought to the South in hopes that her health will improve. Shortly thereafter, Nora Marshall, a childhood friend of Robert and Linda, bounds into the story; and the set of characters whose fortunes Hentz is occupied in tracing is complete.

As if to emphasize her methods of character contrast, Hentz is careful throughout *Robert Graham* to note the similarities and differences among her chief figures. In so doing, she also examines several types of complementary personal attributes that motivate love or friendship in actual life. Graham, cured of the uncontrollable passions that had marked his young manhood, devotes his "energy, vitality, and fire" to the cause of religion; and he has become an eloquent, affecting preacher (7). Henry Bellenden, who has a "bright, animated countenance" and a "slight, spirited figure," possesses a "sunny and unclouded" disposition that is the antithesis of Robert's; and, Hentz says, he is attracted to Robert precisely because of those "qualities entirely opposite to his own" (13, 20). Their contrasts in temperament are especially apparent in their attitudes toward love. Robert vows that he will never marry; but Henry, who is a widower, says his own nature is so elastic that it "rebounds from the pressure of grief with a resilience that is almost miraculous"; and he hopes to wed again (22).

Henry's sister Julia and Nora Marshall form another set of counterpoints. Julia is a shy, delicate girl threatened by tuberculosis who on first appearance is "shawled, bonneted and veiled" (11). Julia, "all grace and refinement," combines, says Hentz, "the innocence of childhood with the grace of womanhood." Like many blonde heroines in nineteenth-century literature, she possesses a complexion "transcendently fair" and golden hair that seems "literally to gild this fairness" (27, 14). Nora is a mischievous "good-bad" girl and a lighthearted version of the nineteenth-century dark lady who is one of Hentz's most appealing figures. These contrasts between Nora and Julia are even sharper than those between Robert and Henry. As Hentz observes, "They each seemed the personification of their opposite latitudes." Nora with her "quick-dancing, dark eyes" and the "purplish blackness of her thick clustering hair" seems "a representative of the vigorous and blooming North," while Julia with her "sapphire" eyes and her "slight and delicate form" seems "an emblem of the mild and sunny South" (26).

In the oppositions and intertwinings developed among Nora and the Bellendens, Hentz constructs a delicate series of movements among the friends that she playfully labels "first impressions." When Julia sees for the first time the "bright flashing glance of Nora," she muses to herself, "I shall admire her, but I fear I shall not love her." Nora for her part thinks that Julia is "a pretty, gentle creature" but fears "she lacks spirit" and concludes that she "may win love, but not admiration." Henry finds Nora handsome and brilliant but too "dashing and independent" for him, whereas Nora mentally notes that Henry "seems very intellectual, very animated . . . but he is too slight, too feminine, to suit my tastes" (29, 27–28). During the course of the narrative, Hentz repeatedly demonstrates the ways in which these first impressions are succeeded by other, quite different assumptions. In particular, she develops the friendship of Julia and Nora to the mutual advantage of each.

She does so first by emphasizing the extremes of conduct of which each woman is capable and then by stressing how each learns from the other. She contrasts, for instance, Nora's bold, callous behavior with Julia's timidity through scenes that portray the restrictions Julia's delicate health place upon her activity. It is possible, in fact, that Hentz uses Nora to undercut the stereotype, widespread by the mid-nineteenth century, of the excessively fragile antebellum woman (Bakker 11–13). Certainly this seems the import of early sequences in the novel. At first, Julia is "almost annihilated by the vehemence of Nora's convivial spirits"; she feels "very much as if a young colt had broken into the house, and that there was danger in its wild antics" (28). Her premonitions about Nora are soon confirmed. While Julia is walking in the woods, Nora impishly drapes her with some dead moss, besprinkling her "head and upturned face . . . with the dust of the dry and brittle lace-work" as she cries, "What a pretty nun you would make!" (30). Immediately afterward, Nora splashes water on Julia as the young girl stoops to drink from a spring. Julia slips into the water and in climbing out sprains her ankle. Nora, reproaching herself for having been "such a rough, Greenland bear," thereafter treats her friend with more compassion (33). But she also weans Julia from her tendency to excessive languor; and, by insisting that Julia exercise, she helps her friend overcome the constitutional timidity connected with her fragile health. Eventually Julia grows as "expert, agile, and graceful as her teacher," while Nora, correspondingly, is softened and sweetened by Julia's gentle influence (40).

Each of Hentz's major characters in *Robert Graham* is in fact permanently influenced by contact with the others, and the first impressions formed during their initial encounters fade in the light of their subsequent experience. During the narrative, the likable but somewhat prissy Henry is gradually attracted to Nora, and his sensitive spirit is emboldened by her fearlessness. In a scene that establishes his developing assurance, he rescues Nora when her wild horse, Thunderbolt, plunges into a river. Though she laughs at his fears, she begins to admire his courtesy, and she finds herself in imagination "winging her way" to his home on "New England's granite shore" (88). Julia, meanwhile, falls deeply in love with Robert Graham; and he, despite his devotion to Linda, develops an affectionate interest in Henry's delicate sister—so that finally, encouraged by Linda, he proposes to Julia.

Appropriately enough, the love of Henry for Nora and Julia for Robert culminates at Linda's plantation home, Rosaville, a natural paradise of jessamine and orange blossoms that, as Nora says, is a "second edition of the garden of Eden" (109). As in Eden, however, tragedy occurs: delicate Julia suddenly sickens and dies. Her death is the first stroke of sorrow that merry-hearted Nora has ever had to bear, and it helps her learn the importance of maturity and responsibility. The novel's final picture of Nora is of a young woman who has achieved considerable balance and sobriety. She agrees to marry Henry, who notes with satisfaction that in her character the "discipline of life had subdued the exuberance of animal gayety." With her spirits "never effervescing too boisterously, or sinking too despondingly, . . . she retained all the warmth and vitality and individuality he had so much admired, with the added graces of gentleness, sweetness, and womanly dependence" (237).

Midway through *Robert Graham,* Hentz enunciates the principles of balance and character contrast upon which she has based the book. After Robert, Nora, and the Bellendens join Linda and Roland Lee at Rosaville, Hentz observes that it "is very seldom that six beings with individuality so strongly marked are thrown together, as those who were assembled for the first time under the same roof" (103). After noting that Nora is "at times too turbulently gay" and Julia "too languidly pensive," she observes that Linda, by contrast, possesses "the golden mean of uniform elasticity. Her gayety was so chastened by refinement, her reflections so enlivened by cheerfulness, and her sensibility so free from morbidness, it was impossible to wish her otherwise than she was" (104). The three men, Hentz continues, are likewise "types of three distinct classes of character." Henry with his "bright, hopeful, inter-changing spirit" communicates "light to every surrounding object"; Robert in contrast is "the emblem of those who, . . . supported by a sublime enthusiasm, wrought out their destiny in the loneliness of intense thought"; and Roland stands between them "as a representative of that noble class of men" who are "the bone and sinew, the strength and reliance of the land" (104–5). Hentz's comments suggest that a major point of *Robert Graham* has been to demonstrate the extremes of action or sentiment of which several of her characters are capable and to establish the golden mean—the ultimately desirable state—through her portraits of Linda and Roland. By her talent for balancing and contrasting characters, Hentz makes distinctive contributions to a central convention of romance.

Between *Linda* and *Robert Graham,* Hentz published a lively novel titled *Eoline; or, Magnolia Vale* (1852), in which she depicts contrasting heroes who reverse some familiar fictional types in antebellum romance. She also contrasts three noteworthy women figures, in the process revealing a wide range of female temperaments. Like Linda, Eoline Glenmore (named for the eolian harp) forsakes her comfortable home rather than marry the man her father has chosen for her. In early sequences in the novel, that man, Horace Cleveland, seems indeed an unpromising prospect for a mate; he is reserved, cold, and indifferent, largely because "the pure intellectuality of his existence" has kept him from developing either deep feelings or social aplomb (165). At Magnolia Vale Seminary, where she has found work as a music teacher, Eoline is approached by St. Leon, a handsome Creole who—smooth, charming, and ingratiating— at first resembles the typical rake in eighteenth- and nineteenth-century fiction. With his "pale alabaster face, brilliant eyes, and romantic-waving hair," he is "adorned with every grace that can captivate the eye of woman" (174).

But in a surprising reversal of stereotypes, St. Leon proves considerably less rakish than he appears at first glance. He refuses to try to seduce Eoline; indeed, he is weaker physically and emotionally than she. Vivacious Eoline, who has more than a trace of the Byronic in her disposition, insists that she was "born to look up—up—high as the eagle's eyrie" (157). A "child of the elements," she takes great pleasure in the electrical storm that prostrates St. Leon, who suffers from "uncommon delicacy of constitution" (90, 162). Anticipating certain of Kate Chopin's portraits, Hentz locates the source of St. Leon's effeteness in his Creole blood. The race from which he springs, she observes, is "more distinguished for beauty of person, grace of manner, quickness and ardor of feeling, and gentleness of disposition, than for the stern and hardy virtues." And "even if nature had planted in his mind the germs of a firmer character," she continues, "the indolence and luxury of his life had never allowed their expansion" (162).

As St. Leon's power over Eoline diminishes, Horace's attractions increase, called forth in part by his maturation through experience, in part by Eoline's "gay, frank, and genial" disposition, and in particular by Eoline's music, which awakens in Horace passions "intense as the lightning, and almost as scorching" (15, 174). Finally, moved by Eoline's generosity, he develops a warmth and tenderness to match her own. By the end of the novel, the two have learned to love each other—"as we always would have done," says Horace, "had we been left to our own free will" (250).

More striking than the contrasts between Horace and St. Leon are the contrasts among Eoline and two other women in Hentz's novel. The first of these women is Louisa More, a close friend of Eoline and one of the teachers at the seminary, who, poor, sick, and pious, seems destined for an early death. But in another surprising reversal of stereotypes, Louisa recovers her strength, marries the son of a minister, and, as befits the submissive type of heroine in nineteenth-century romance, eventually becomes the center of a "charming domestic circle" (216). An even more illuminating foil to Eoline is Amelia Wilton, whose plight Hentz uses to warn both characters and readers of the dangers of marriages arranged by parents, a central issue of the book. Amelia, who secretly loves St. Leon, has been forced by her parents to marry another man, and in her unhappiness she succumbs to a paralyzing despair that is lifted only after Eoline befriends her. When Amelia's husband unexpectedly dies, she is free to wed St. Leon, who learns to love her under Eoline's tutelage. In typical romance fashion, the novel exhibits a providential or wish-fulfillment movement by concluding with its three main women figures matched with appropriate mates.

Various writers, among them Frye, Joseph Campbell, and Bruno Bettelheim, note the general resemblances among myth, romance, fairy tales, and folklore and the ways in which these literary forms can help people cope with difficulties in actual life. Bettelheim's well-known study, *The Uses of Enchantment,* for example, demonstrates how fairy stories can help disturbed children negotiate life's perils by providing them with examples of children in fairy tales who successfully escape numerous dangers. Anticipating Bettelheim, Hentz's writing reveals certain generic resemblances between fairy tales and romance, especially those of dialetic structure, character contrast, and happy endings. Moreover, in it she shows how folk legends may be used to entertain children while warning and instructing them. All of her long fiction, whether centered on male or female figures, depicts the young central characters successfully negotiating the perils of existence—unfeeling parents, poverty, inappropriate lovers, physical danger—while winning through to the satisfying happy ending; and several of her narratives reveal a direct relationship to fairy legends. More specifically, *Linda* recalls tales like "Snow White" in its picture of a lovely young girl victimized by a cruel stepmother, while *Helen and Arthur* (1853), which of all Hentz's work reveals the closest ties to folk or fairy legend, is a carefully developed initiation story in which the author provides the timid young heroine with helpful guardian figures to guide her through real and imaginary perils.[4]

In the latter novel, which is largely a study of child and adolescent psychology, young Helen is influenced by two older characters, Miss Thusa and Dr. Arthur Hazleton; and as part of her necessary maturation she moves from the occasionally threatening influence of the one to the benevolent protection of the other. Miss Thusa, her childhood friend and tutor, is initially an ambiguous character, a woman at once benign and sinister. Vaguely witchlike, she is tall, with a beaked nose; and she is consistently associated with a spinning wheel that seems to have marvelous properties. A single woman who makes her living by spinning marvelously fine thread, she has, says Hentz, "a heart naturally warm, defrauded of all natural objects on which to expend its living fervor," and a mind "naturally strong" but confined within "close and narrow limits" (103). These aspects of her character have apparently contributed to the extraordinary flowering of her imagination. Gifted with great storytelling ability, she has an unfortunate influence upon the impressionable Helen, whose own imagination becomes preternaturally developed from listening to Miss Thusa's horrific tales of an ogre who kills and devours children and of a "worm-eaten traveler" who carries a lonely woman resembling Miss Thusa to the grave (16).

As if in illustration of Emerson's dictum in *Nature* that "nature always wears the colors of the spirit," Hentz emphasizes that because Helen tends to project elements of her inner life onto nature, the physical world wears a divided aspect for her: depending on her moods, it can be either exquisite or terrifying. She can, for instance, see "angels cradled on the glowing bosom of the sunset clouds, angels braiding the rainbow of the sky. Light to her was peopled with angels, as darkness with phantoms" (33). Through Helen's exceptional sensitivity, Hentz develops the mythic and supernatural overtones that constitute the most intriguing aspect of her novel. Helen goes to gather strawberries for her dying mother in a setting that, as Hentz describes it, evokes both the Eden of the Biblical story and the legend of Proserpina gathering flowers before she is kidnapped by Hades. Helen finds herself in a lovely meadow, where she forgets "there were such things as night and darkness in the universe"—but through which, ominously, "a clear blue stream" glides "like an azure serpent in glittering coils" (35). Shortly thereafter, she sees a real serpent among the reddening berries; and forgetting her promise to her mother, she drops her basket and runs away.

Helen must obviously be weaned from her childish fears, and it is the task of her preceptor and future husband, Arthur Hazleton, to help her mature to the point that the beneficent rather than the sinister side of nature dominates her perceptions. Interrupting her flight from the meadow, he returns with her to get the strawberries and prove the snake is harmless. Later he helps her overcome her fear of darkness by sending her into the woods to get his sister Alice, who has fallen asleep under a tree, and later still he requests her to remain all night in an isolated cottage with Miss Thusa, who is dying.

Frequently in literature that has roots in folklore, an originally sinister figure who may inhibit or restrain the protagonist undergoes a transformation once the heroine or hero has mastered obstacles preventing maturation. The prototype of such literature, perhaps, is Homer's *Odyssey*, in which Circe changes from a destructive witch into a benevolent goddess after Odysseus successfully confronts her. The folk roots of Hentz's story are indicated by a similar metamorphosis in Miss Thusa. For after Helen has freed herself from the malign aspects of Miss Thusa's influence by successfully completing the tasks Arthur sets for her, Miss Thusa changes from a mildly sinister witchlike figure to a benevolent fairy godmother who bestows the gold that is hidden in the spinning wheel upon Helen and her brother Louis. At this point, through the minds of her leading figures, Hentz emphasizes the elements of supernaturalism in her narrative. Helen, pondering the gold "so strangely acquired, so mysteriously concealed," is reminded of "the tales of the genii, more than of the actualities of every day life" (200). And when the fairly prosaic Arthur sees the money in heaps upon the table, he likewise wonders, "Was Miss Thusa a female Midas or Aladdin? Was the dull brass lamp burning on the table, the gift of the genii? Was the old gray cabin a witch's magic home?" (207).

Besides using folklore to embellish her portrayals of Helen and Miss Thusa, Hentz employs it as an indispensable structural element in her subplot. In pointed contrast to Helen stands her sister Mittie, who is dark-haired, beautiful, and cold. Mittie's parents scold her for her callousness, and Miss Thusa, who has formidable powers of prophecy, delivers a stern admonition. She tells a folk story of a lovely but heartless girl who refuses to help a little child in the woods and shortly afterward meets a horseman dressed in black who takes her upon his steed. As they ride, "his long black hair got twisted all around her, and every time the wind blew, it grew tighter and tighter, till she could scarcely breathe." When she begs him to release her, he cuts the hair and flings her to the ground; but as she lies in the road she feels her "heart's blood . . . oozing out through every wound his dagger had made, for . . . his locks had taken root in her heart, and he cut the cords when he slashed about among his own long, black hair" (72–73). Miraculously healed by the child she had spurned, she is chastened and redeemed; and she vows to love all children for the holy child's sake.

As Miss Thusa intends, Mittie identifies herself with "the cruel maiden, and in after years she remembered the long sweeping locks of the knight, and the maiden's bleeding heart" (74). The tale, in fact, foreshadows her own subsequent misfortune as well as her eventual reformation. Selfish and unfeeling, she has never known passion until her brother's friend Bryant Clinton, an obnoxious Byronesque type, appears in the village. Helen, with her vivid sense of foreboding, instinctively associates Clinton with Lucifer as well as with "that terrible snake in the strawberry patch"; and indeed Clinton eventually proves to be a kind of devil to Mittie (140). After gaining her love he betrays her by courting Helen; and, "remembering . . . Miss Thusa's legend of the Maiden's Bleeding Heart," Mittie involuntarily puts "her hand to her own [heart] to feel if it were not bleeding, too" (187). She falls ill, but suffering serves to reform her as it had the maiden in the legend. Nursed by Alice and Helen, she learns to love unselfishly; and, sobered and chastened, by the end of the narrative she is beginning to be drawn to religion.

As analyzed thus far, Hentz's narratives seem to pose standard—and in the main nonfeminist—solutions for her several types of young heroines. Her ideal women, such as Eoline and Linda, mature and marry appropriate mates; her dark heroines needing discipline either learn it easily and marry happily, like Nora, or are forced into it through suffering and reform, like Mittie. Even timid, childlike Helen becomes a secure adult who wins the enlightened love of Arthur. What is not immediately obvious upon a first reading of Hentz's books is the degree to which she enables several of her young heroines to attain before marriage a nineteenth-century type of feminism involving independence, maturity, self-control, and influence over others. Linda, who is originally a wayward, spoiled child, learns discipline and fortitude first through education and then through a series of harrowing experiences, including shipwreck, kidnapping, and widowhood. Eoline, who at the beginning of her story is already largely mistress of herself, attains physical and emotional distance from her overbearing father as well as considerable economic security through her work at Magnolia Vale. But it is nevertheless true, as Nina Baym notes in *Woman's Fiction*, that the feminism of Hentz and other nineteenth-century authors—at least as expressed through young heroines—seems limited by twentieth-century standards because it is subordinated to other concerns (18–19).[5] Chief among these concerns for Hentz, as is evident in *Robert Graham* and most of her other books, is an orthodox nineteenth-century version of Christianity with a patriarchal cast.

Yet in reevaluating antebellum women's writing, one should look beyond the main narratives and the leading characters to see what is implied through subordinate characters or subplots. In other words, as Susan K. Harris observes in her study of nineteenth-century American women's novels, although the "cover plots" of many books seem antifeminist insofar as they appear to support the idea that women need men and marriage for happiness, the more radical "underplots" suggest how determined women can achieve physical, emotional, and financial independence with or without a man (20–21). Linda and Eoline attain such independence before marriage; several striking women figures in Hentz's work achieve it without having to wed. Foremost among these women is Miss Thusa; other such figures include Linda's boarding-school teacher Miss Reveire and the imposing Miss Manly, Eoline's supervisor at Magnolia Vale. A likable, memorable character, Miss Reveire—whose name suggests the reverence she inspires in her pupils—is balanced, compassionate, and controlled. She serves as substitute mother as well as role model for motherless Linda, and she also imposes sensible discipline upon a group of wayward girls at the institution. Though a secondary character, in terms of romance conventions she constitutes one of Hentz's ideal figures.

Altogether more formidable, and ostensibly somewhat less ideal, is the aptly named Miss Manly, the headmistress of Magnolia Vale. Of "iron frame and . . . iron spirit" (137), Miss Manly imposes stern discipline on the students at the school, drilling them in history and geography while they are at meals. (The dauntless girls repay her by styling her "the Colonel" behind her back.) Stating that she abandoned ease and pleasure when she became head of the school, Miss Manly styles herself "a missionary in a great and holy cause" (152). "Let others seek happiness in the exercise of domestic virtues," she says in pointed reference to Eoline's marriage; "I have entered a broader, and I say it with modesty, a nobler, more exalted sphere" (260).

Character balance and contrast, cleverly modified romance narrative structures, folktales, and a covert feminism—Caroline Hentz's novels contain enough variety in content and literary method to intrigue even the most jaded twentieth-century student of nineteenth-century fiction. An enlightened revisionist reading of her fiction indicates that she deserves to be remembered as something other than a writer of vapid plantation romances. Her work merits the commendations heaped upon it by her contemporaries—one of whom observed, "we defy anyone to read aloud" her fiction without complimenting its "truthfulness, pathos, and power."[6]

NOTES

1. These remarks appear in the collection of press notices of Hentz's fiction reprinted as part of the front matter to her collection *The Lost Daughter, and Other Stories of the Heart.*

2. Among the few extended treatments of Hentz's writing, particularly helpful are Baym, *Woman's Fiction: A Guide to Novels by and about Women in America, 1820–1870,* intro. and chaps. 1, 5; Seidel, *The Southern Belle in*

the American Novel, which notes that Hentz was "one of the three most popular American authors as late as 1892" (11); Shillingsburg, "The Ascent of Woman, Southern Style: Hentz, King, Chopin" 127–40; and Bakker, " ' . . . the bold atmosphere of Mrs. Hentz' and Others," a paper delivered at the Popular Culture/American Culture Association Conferences in Cincinnati, March 1981. Professor Bakker kindly let me read a typescript of his paper. Though it does not treat Hentz, Harris's *19th-Century American Women's Novels: Interpretative Strategies* is useful for its revisionist readings of women's fiction as well as for its theoretical premises.

3. Seidel discusses how antebellum Southerners believed that Victorian values of domesticity could help counteract the growing materialism of the nineteenth century (4–6).

4. Frye, *Secular Scripture* chaps. 1, 6; Campbell, *The Hero With a Thousand Faces* Part I, chaps. 1–3; Part II, chap. 3; Bettelheim, *The Uses of Enchantment* intro. and passim. Seidel notes that Linda's unkind stepmother resembles the evil stepmothers in "Cinderella" and "Snow White" (11).

5. Baym also observes that in women's fiction of this era, independence rather than marriage is the primary goal (38–39). Several of the literary conventions she analyzes, such as the contrast of the flawed and the flawless heroine (35–36), derive from the romance tradition.

6. From the collection of press notices in *The Lost Daughter.*

WORKS CITED

Bakker, Jan. " ' . . . the bold atmosphere of Mrs. Hentz' and Others: Fast Food and Feminine Rebelliousness in Some Romances of the Old South." Paper delivered at the Popular Culture/American Culture Association Conferences, Cincinnati, March 1981.

Baym, Nina. *Woman's Fiction: A Guide to Novels by and about Women in America, 1820–1870.* Ithaca: Cornell University Press, 1978.

Bettelheim, Bruno. *The Uses of Enchantment.* New York: Alfred A. Knopf, 1976.

Campbell, Joseph. *The Hero with a Thousand Faces.* New York: Bollingen Foundation, 1949.

Fiedler, Leslie. *Love and Death in the American Novel.* Rev. ed. New York: Stein and Day, 1966.

Frye, Northrop. *Anatomy of Criticism: Four Essays.* Princeton: Princeton University Press, 1957.

———. *The Secular Scripture: A Study of the Structure of Romance.* Cambridge: Harvard University Press, 1976.

Harris, Susan K. *19th-Century American Women's Fiction: Interpretative Strategies.* Cambridge: Cambridge University Press, 1990.

Hentz, Caroline Lee. *Eoline; or, Magnolia Vale; or, The Heiress of Glenmore.* New York: F. M. Lupton, 1869.

———. *Helen and Arthur; or, Miss Thusa's Spinning-Wheel. A Novel.* Philadelphia: A. Hart, 1853.

————. *Linda; or, the Young Pilot of the Belle Creole. A Tale of Southern Life.* Philadelphia: A. Hart, 1853.

————. *The Lost Daughter, and Other Stories of the Heart.* Philadelphia: T. B. Peterson, 1857.

————. *Marcus Warland; or, the Long Moss Spring. A Tale of the South.* Philadelphia: A. Hart, 1852.

————. *The Planter's Northern Bride.* 1854. Introduction by Rhoda Coleman Ellison. Southern Literary Classics Series. Ed. C. Hugh Holman and Louis D. Rubin, Jr. Chapel Hill: University of North Carolina Press, 1970.

————. *Robert Graham: A Sequel to Linda.* Philadelphia: T. B. Peterson, 1855.

Jameson, Fredric. *The Political Unconscious: Narrative as a Socially Symbolic Act.* Ithaca: Cornell University Press, 1981.

Scholes, Robert, and Robert Kellogg. *The Nature of Narrative.* New York: Oxford University Press, 1966.

Shillingsburg, Miriam J. "The Ascent of Women, Southern Style: Hentz, King, Chopin." In *Southern Literature in Transition: Heritage and Promise.* Ed. Philip Castille and William Osborne. Memphis: Memphis State University Press, 1983. 127–40.

Seidel, Kathryn Lee. *The Southern Belle in the American Novel.* Tampa: University of South Florida Press, 1985.

Watson, Ritchie D. "Caroline Lee Hentz (1800–1856)." In *Southern Writers: A Biographical Dictionary.* Eds. Robert Bain, Joseph M. Flora, and Louis D. Rubin, Jr. Baton Rouge: Louisiana State University Press, 1979. 221–22.

Susan V. Donaldson

Songs with a Difference:
Beatrice Ravenel and the Detritus of Southern History

Like a good many other modernist women poets of the 1920s, Charleston poet Beatrice Ravenel made an early strong impression on critics and readers alike and then gradually seemed to disappear, partly because of her own retreat from the public eye and partly because scholars of the Southern Renaissance simply overlooked her. In the late 1960s Ravenel and her shimmering, elusive poetry were briefly resurrected in a volume called *The Yemassee Lands,* selected and edited by Louis D. Rubin, Jr., who included in the collection an introductory essay on the poet's life and work. To his credit, Rubin hailed Ravenel's work as "better than any other poetry being written in the South during the 1920s outside of Nashville" (5). But his enthusiasm seems to have attracted little subsequent attention to Ravenel and her work.

The scant notice Ravenel and her work have received, I would suggest, reveals a good deal about the primary concerns, exclusions, and restrictions required in the making of Southern literary history and its interpretive community. For interpretive communities, as Elizabeth Meese cogently pointed out a few years ago, "like tribal communities, possess the power to ostracize or to embrace, to restrict or to extend membership and participation, and to impose norms—hence their authority" (9). Major revisionist approaches undertaken in the past several years by Michael O'Brien, Richard King, Daniel Joseph Singal, and Michael Kreyling have certainly made us take a longer and harder look at the most revered figures of the Southern Renaissance, especially the Fugitives in Nashville, but by and large they have limited their scrutiny to white male writers, to the very figures, in fact, who brought attention to the flowering of Southern letters between the wars in the first place.

For Allen Tate, John Crowe Ransom, Donald Davidson, Robert Penn Warren, and William Faulkner that flowering was defined in one way or another by its preoccupation with history, tradition, and the boundaries between what is Southern and what is *not* Southern. Scholars who have turned their attention to these writers as representative figures of the Renaissance echo—unwittingly or not—those concerns. Richard King, for one, defends his decision to limit *A Southern Renaissance* to white and mostly male writers by arguing that the interests of blacks and women are incompatible with the theme he examines. Region, he declares, "does not lie" at the center of their imaginative visions" (9).

Such exclusions, however, depend on the way history and politics are defined, as does the "centrality" of region, for that matter. Michel Foucault, after all, would remind us that history and its comforting images of unity and identity are made by expelling the contradictory and the anomalous. From his perspective, an alternative to history can be found in the practice of genealogy, a critical approach he defines as a concerted effort to recover memories of struggles and "illegitimate" forms of knowledge arrayed against "the claims of a unitary body of theory which would filter, hierarchise and order them" (83). Genealogy, Foucault argues, rejects the association of history with origins, unchanging truths, and progress and concentrates instead on subjection and conflict (Dreyfus and Rabinow 109). Rather than starting with leadership, prominent institutions, and the most conspicuous concentrations of power, then, the genealogist by Foucault's lights should start at the "bottom," at the most local area, for on the lowest levels of society and culture one can examine "how the mechanisms of power have been able to function" (Foucault 100).

Beatrice Ravenel, I would suggest, employs a similar strategy in her poetry of the Carolina Low Country, and that approach may account in part for critical neglect of her work and even the somewhat puzzled tone characterizing the accounts of those contemporary reviewers—and Rubin himself—who expressed enthusiasm for her work. For like a good genealogist, Ravenel turns her sights not on the making of a central tradition or dominating images and figures of the past but on the detritus of history—voices that have been silenced, figures that have been scorned or forgotten. She takes her cues not from the Thomas Sutpens or Porgys of Southern history, literature, and mythology but from the Yemassee Indians who have long since disappeared, pirates clapped into prison by the solid citizens of Charles Town, mothers of missing soldiers or famous poets, and octoroons wistfully contemplating the mysteries of their bodies. From these muted voices, shards, and forgotten odds and ends she constructs a private poetic self, one that does not lament the loss of tradition, as does Allen Tate's Aeneas at Washington, but probes, questions, and considers alternative visions, voices, and readings of the past. It is, ultimately, a poetic self identified with otherness, finding allies among those who serve as figures in someone else's story, and in this respect, her concerns do indeed fall outside the purview of chroniclers of the traditional Southern self.

These genealogical concerns, though, are all the more difficult to probe and ponder because Ravenel resorts in her poetry to subterfuge, deception, disguise, and half-glimpses. In this respect, she belongs to a long, submerged tradition of double-edged writing by white Southern women. Confronted by the pressures of the "cult of true womanhood," family obligations, and quite frequently the hostility of male writers, Southern women writers tended, in Anne Goodwyn Jones's apt phrase, to speak "through the mask" (37). What rebellious feelings they expressed were more often than not veiled with pious affirmations of woman's role, tradition, and the Southern sense of community. Indeed, the great bulk of writing by white Southern women in the nineteenth century certainly *appeared* to bow to the needs of a region determined to defend its borders in the political arena, the battlefields, and literature. As the Baltimore-based *Southern Review* observed with no little wonder in 1867, most poems celebrating the Confederate war effort "were composed by Southern women" ("Southern War Poetry" 276).

Still, women writers did have to contend with the hostility of a good many male literati in the South whose complaints about their female colleagues strongly resembled Nathaniel Hawthorne's famous reference to "scribbling women." One reason why artists in general were neglected by an insensitive Southern public, huffed the editors at *Russell's Magazine* in antebellum Charleston, was the average reader's tendency to confound "the false with the true, the nonsense of newspaper 'Floras' and 'Matildas,' with whatever is grand or beautiful in the works of acknowledged genius" ("Editor's Table" 559). Twenty years later Paul Hamilton Hayne, one of the writers associated with the short-lived *Russell's* venture, was still complaining about popular women writers in the South, a group he curmudgeonly labeled "The Fungous School." They are, he argued, "the worse enemies of the intellectual advancement and repute of their section" (651). Let "the exceptional reader" offer a dissenting view of "a literary *lioness*" in this school, he warned, and "all her adherents male and female, the whole body of her enthusiastic *'claqueness'* will descend upon the disagreeable critic" (652).

Women writers themselves appeared to be all too sensitive to this sort of opposition. In an extraordinary 1859 article titled "How Should Women Write?" for *Southern Field and Fireside,* a young Georgia journalist named Mary Bryan caustically observed: "Men, after much demur and hesitation, have given women liberty to write, but they cannot yet consent to allow them full freedom. They may flutter out of the cage, but it must be with clipped wings; they may hop about the smooth-shaven lawn, but must, on no account fly." Those women who did "seek to go beyond the boundary line," she added tartly, "are put down with the stigma of *'strong-minded.'"* [1]

As critics like Jones, Sandra Gilbert, Susan Gubar, and Alicia Ostriker have noted, women more often than not responded to expectations threatening to bind them with literary strategies of subterfuge, obscurity, and disguised rebellion. Even a poet with as much public acclaim as Margaret Preston, proclaimed the "Queen of Southern Song" by the *Southern Review,* occasionally expressed exasperation with the hostility greeting women's venture into the public arena of art ("Southern Poetry—A Sketch" 31). In a poem titled "Woman's Art," included in her 1881 collection *Cartoons,* Preston manages to cloak her anger, though, by portraying a confrontation between male and female artists in the distant reaches of the Italian Renaissance, a confrontation that offers, not incidentally, a genealogical perspective of the making of art history.

Addressing the reader as an American tourist in Bologna, Preston's persona directs attention to an artist mentioned in the tourist's Baedeker, "a girl, whose thought, / carved on the stone of a plum, survives / The volumed records of thousand lives" (70). This was an artist, the poem tells the tourist-reader, whose work was summarily ignored and dismissed by a male rival. Women's art, he declares, is unworthy of marble:

> The stone
> Of the quarries was meant for men alone,
> Whose genius had gift to shape it: walls
> Of churches, basilicas, palace halls,
> Only were ample enough to yield
> To limitless skill, the nobler field:
> But woman! . . . a cherry-stone might well
> Hold whatsoever *she* had to tell! (71)

Driven by pride, though, the "maiden" sculptor resorts to olive and apricot pits to produce "Marvels of frost-like carvings," and it is these diminutive works of art that survive the passage of time, not the frescoes of the arrogant rival who refuses to acknowledge her work as art (71).

All in all, Preston's poem offers a sly plea for rebellion and subversion, a plea with which Beatrice Ravenel, two generations younger, would have sympathized. Like those writers who preceded her, Ravenel was acutely sensitive to the pressures and boundaries defining women in the late nineteenth- and early twentieth-century—and just as covertly resentful. As a student at the Harvard Annex, later Radcliffe, in the 1890s, she made a vivid impression on her contemporaries as a forceful, strong-minded young woman rather contemptuous of the niceties of polite society (Rubin 8–9). According to a 1927 review of her book *The Arrow of Lightning,* she was known "for her ambition to be the widow of a very fashionable bishop. 'Then,' she said, 'one could get away with anything' " (qtd. in "A Promising Southern Poet").

Certainly in the fiction she wrote during her Cambridge sojourn, she occasionally gave voice to unexpected and rather iconoclastic remarks. In one of the stories written in the 1890s, a character about to enter her novitiate in a New Orleans convent offers a startling critique of patriarchal images of divinity. "Did you ever feel," the young novice asks a friend, "that it put a barrier between God and you—if you are a woman—by calling Him *He*—as though he were a man?" Such speculation was probably "wrong," she admitted. "But God ought to be called God, quite simply, or else one ought to have made a special pronoun. If only the writers of the Bible had thought of that—but then they were all men" (Witte [Ravenel], "Madonna Mia" 71).

Yet for the most part Ravenel appears to have kept sporadic impulses of rebellion well under wraps and to have conformed outwardly to the expectations of conservative Charleston. To readers writing to express appreciation and to inquire about her life and work, she more often than not simply replied, "As for my life, I am a Southerner, born in Charleston, South Carolina, and most of my poems deal with Southern scenes."[2] Born in 1870 to Charles Otto and Charlotte Witte, Beatrice Witte grew up in a stately Rutledge Avenue mansion famous for its garden and aviary (Waring 5, 7).

A youthful interest in literature led her to Harvard Annex in Cambridge. Originally planning to stay for a year or two, she eventually remained for five and pursued subjects that interested her—especially literature and philosophy—but never earned a degree. There she began to write, and her poems and short stories found ready acceptance in the *Harvard Monthly,* other college publications, and even *Scribner's Magazine.*[3] By her third year in Cambridge, Witte's work had already caught the eye of Thomas Wentworth Higginson, who applauded her for what he saw as the "promise of a new literary talent."[4]

As Rubin observes in his introduction to the 1969 collection of her poetry, a good deal of Beatrice Witte's early poetry and fiction seems to echo the concerns and poetic conventions of the day (9–10). Occasionally, though, her apprentice poems, like a few Beardsleyesque drawings in her college sketchbook, hinted at a vibrant and turbulent inner life that the young woman kept hidden from public view. In a poem titled "Half-Confessions," probably written in 1894, Witte's persona asks:

> Is your self like a hot-house, too troubled and warm,
> Starred, half with exotics with agate-smooth claws,
> And sulphurous breathing, ophidian bark;
> And half with the commonest daisies and haws
> Whose pets and prickles are turned every one
> To yearn from this reeking, luxurious dark
> To the openings, covered with crystal and sun?
> *(The Yemassee Lands* 99)

What could have come of such promising early beginnings, though, remained to be seen. Witte left Cambridge in the mid-1890s, and by 1900 she had married Francis Gualdo Ravenel, a fellow Charlestonian. If her papers and manuscripts are any indication, she wrote very little for the next seventeen years while she devoted herself to her husband and her daughter, born in 1904 (Rubin 10, 11).

In early 1918 Ravenel's "long silence was broken," as her friend DuBose Heyward put it, with the publication of a poem called "Missing" in *The Atlantic Monthly* (Heyward 474). Heyward tended to see the poem in the light of wartime patriotism, but what is particularly striking is the vividly rendered voice of the speaker, the mother of a missing soldier. In rather daring tones, she addresses God as both deity and reader and forcefully observes that she is "a creator even as Thou" (*The Arrow of Lightning* 66). And if the loss of young men in war is lamented in the poem, so too is the pain of women who see themselves in opposition to destructive armies. They form "a phantom wall, / Barring the way with desperate, futile hands. / The first charge tramples them, the first of all!" (*The Arrow of Lightning* 67).

However "conventional" a poem it may be in many respects, "Missing" is nevertheless a work that insists on the importance of giving voice to the powerless, a notion that seems to have been much on Ravenel's mind in 1917 and 1918. For included in her unpublished manuscripts were several poems, dated 1917, that contemplated the subservience of women to men and the inner worlds that women create in retaliation. The "seacoast" of women, one poem titled "Bondswomen" reads,

> is a smiling fierce republic,
> Their hinterland is a man-ruled suzerainty.
> Who would not mourn for women? I am fearful
> That men should know this truth concerning women.

> Therefore let no man dare to read these verses. (Ravenel Papers)

These were sentiments, though, that Ravenel rarely voiced openly in the next several years, a time when she began to write fast and furiously. Pressed first by financial need and then by the death of her husband in 1920, Ravenel, in the tradition of earlier white Southern women writers, apparently took up the pen again largely to support herself and her daughter. By 1919, she was writing editorial columns and then nearly the entire Sunday editorial page for the Columbia *State,* as well as a slew of short stories for magazines ranging from *Ainslee's* to *Harper's.* [5] By the late 1920s she had published about fifty short stories and eighty poems in magazines and journals, along with a volume of poems, *The Arrow of Lightning* ("Beatrice Ravenel, Poet and Short Story Writer").

Given that she was dependent on her writing for her livelihood, it is not surprising that Ravenel's articles in the Columbia *State* expressed opinions compatible with the audience of a white South Carolina newspaper of the period. In response to a visiting contingent of suffragists, Ravenel voiced sharp criticism in one article about the group's apparent silence on "the negro question" and suggested that South Carolinians by and large were more concerned with issues about race than about women and the vote ("The Silence of the Suffragettes"). But occasionally poems written at the same time suggested a deep ambivalence about the audience that awaited her efforts. In a 1920 poem called "Fear," her persona observes:

> I am only afraid
> Of the cold dull lids of eyes,
> And the cold dull grain of sand in the soul,
> Indurate, insensate, not to be made incandescent
> Even by God.
> I am afraid of the stupid people. (*Yemassee Lands* 77)

Ravenel's awareness of audience probably also had a good deal to do with the Charleston milieu in which she wrote, one that emphasized the close bond between the artist and society. Unlike the Fugitive group in Nashville, whose very name, after all, suggested something of the alienation they felt from their surroundings, writers of the so-called Charleston Renaissance in the 1920s tended to identify strongly with their community. One wag even went as far as to assert that the Poetry

Society of South Carolina, the center of Charleston writers, was made up of "one-tenth poetry and nine-tenths society" (qtd. in Cox 21). Since the society did include nationally known writers like Josephine Pinckney, Hervey Allen, DuBose Heyward, and Ravenel herself, the characterization was in some respects unfair, but certainly white Charleston writers as a group tended to be rather suspicious of literary modernism and quite conscious of their own literary heritage, defined by nineteenth-century writers like Henry Timrod, Paul Hamilton Hayne, and Sidney Lanier (Cox 76, 73). In the early 1920s Hervey Allen and DuBose Heyward even took care to specify the aims of the Southern artist in terms startlingly reminiscent of William Gilmore Simms and other nineteenth-century Southern literati. Since the South, they argued in Harriet Monroe's journal *Poetry,* was still based on "the economic, vital unit" of "the plantation of one kind or another," it was to be "expected that when the plantation poet speaks, it will not be from the necessity of introspectively asserting his existence as an individual apart from the crowd, but of objectively reflecting in simple measures the patriarchal life remnant about him" (36–37).

Ravenel herself was a respected member of this group, a figure who won prestigious prizes awarded by the society and served on the executive committee during the society's opening year in 1920–21.[6] But somehow Ravenel always managed to remain something of a solitary presence in the society. She did not, for one thing, participate in the regular critical discussions led by Heyward and Allen, and more to the point, her experiments in free verse and blank verse were more daring than anything attempted by other members of the society (Cox 30, 76). She seemed to draw much of her poetic vocabulary not from that "patriarchal life" of which Allen and Heyward spoke so reverently, but from the concrete imagery and uncomfortable incongruities characterizing avant-garde Anglo-American poetry. Amy Lowell shrewdly sensed as much when she first started reading the Charleston poet's work. "I rather imagine," Lowell wrote Ravenel in 1922, "that you have been writing off and on all your life, but that in the new poetry movement you have found your true expression—am I right?"[7]

Ravenel's poetry was indeed marked by the excitement of discovery in the early 1920s, and no doubt the energy the poet drew from that discovery had a good deal to do with her intense creative production in the first half of the decade and finally with the publication of her only volume of poetry, *The Arrow of Lightning.* For what she seems to have discovered in *The Arrow of Lightning* in particular are the possibilities of doubleness and duplicity inherent in language. Earlier American women poets, as Cheryl Walker has pointed out in *The Nightingale's*

Burden, might have turned to the nightingale as an enticing and elusive figure for the poetic self, but in the title poem of Ravenel's volume (reprinted in *The Yemassee Lands*), the Charleston poet explicitly rejects the nightingale whose "music drags me from sleep" and offers "a ready-made rapture" of inherited words and phrases. She turns instead to the mockingbird, the arrow of lightning claimed as "flashing totem of the Yemassee" Indians. It is, the poem suggests, a much more appropriate poetic voice because it has little to do "With English woodrides, / Trees pampered like the horses in a stall." Instead, Ravenel's mockingbird is a daring and resourceful thief, a "Trick-tongue" that steals the music of others and deceives its listeners:

> You are a conjurer.
> You sing the songs of all birds with a difference,
> Bringing the drop of blood, the touch of dead man's fingers,
> That makes the alchemy. (*The Yemassee Lands* 31)

Ravenel's choice of the mockingbird as poetic self, the thief and singer of songs with a difference, is a particularly witty one because the poet is herself something of a subtle thief. *The Arrow of Lightning* is sprinkled with phrases and words stolen from the work of an imposing nineteenth-century male predecessor—William Gilmore Simms's *The Yemassee*, an antebellum novel about the 1715 Yemassee War fought in South Carolina's Low Country. In particular, Ravenel borrows Simms's infrequent references to the mockingbird as totem and symbol of the Yemassee, whose call the Indians frequently use to deceive their enemies and whose mark of "lightning" represents their arrows. For Simms the mockingbird is very much of a marginal figure, as are the Yemassee, for that matter, in his story of the beginnings of white South Carolinian identity. His novel, after all, is about the passing of the Yemassee to make way for the whites—a development that his white characters defend again and again—and significantly enough, Simms's representative Indian figure usually falls silent in the intimidating presence of whites.

In Ravenel's hands, though, the mockingbird moves to the center and thus, in a sense, substitutes genealogy for history, "illegitimate" knowledge for unity and hierarchy. For the mockingbird makes it possible to recapture lost words of the past:

> There must be words of Catawba
> Barbed musical words of the Seminole,
> Words of the wind
> Weaving its Indian baskets of russet trash at the foot of the pine-
>   tree,
> To tell of the passing of nations,

Of the exquisite ruin of coasts, of the silvery change and the flux
    of existence,
And of the love that remakes us—
Trick-tongue! (*The Yemassee Lands* 32)

Singing its songs with a difference, the mockingbird challenges the authority of Simms's account of South Carolina history and of the white voices who have silenced the Yemassee. Suddenly, "the passing of nations" no longer seems quite so inevitable or irreversible. Their presence can be captured in the echoes of the mockingbird, and those echoes in turn suggest the possibility of acknowledging more than a single, dominating voice, the sort of voice, in fact, that characterizes the end of Simms's *The Yemassee,* once the Indians have been defeated and dispersed.

Ravenel's persona of the mockingbird, echoing, deceiving, and disorienting, anticipates to a startling degree the deconstructive strategies counseled by feminist critics today who call for the dismantling of patriarchy and its dominating voice. For Ravenel's mockingbird, like a good deal of current feminist criticism, borrows songs from an existing tradition in order to disrupt and subvert them. They are, after all, the only songs that are available, so the mockingbird must resort to theft to find a voice. Similarly, Hélène Cixous writes in "The Laugh of the Medusa": "It's no accident: women take after birds and robbers just as robbers take after women and birds. They (illes) go by, fly the coop, take the pleasure in jumbling the order of space, in disorienting it, in changing around the furniture, dislocating things and values, breaking them all up, emptying structures, and turning propriety upside down" (258).

Moreover, this sort of disorientation resists the reestablishment of a unitary voice, just as Ravenel's mockingbird, singing its songs of difference, resorts to a series of voices, never settling on one. If Ravenel questions the "voice" and history bestowed upon her by Simms, she nonetheless resists substituting her own version of truth and authority. Like feminist critics today, she resorts to a de-centering strategy that "constantly takes itself apart as it takes others into itself" (Meese 148). Her poems, like the songs of the mockingbird, echo with the voices of others, sometimes captured within quotation marks, as in the ghostly voices of vanished Indians in "The Alligator," and sometimes in monologues, as in the lamentation of "Poe's Mother," frightened and abandoned in Charleston.

In the former poem, for instance, the roar of the alligator, "Cry of the mud made flesh, made particular, personal," gives way to the voice of the ghostly medicine man, teaching the alligator to speak with the voice of the Yemassee's collective memory (*The Yemassee Lands* 33). Anticipating the disappearance of the Yemassee, the medicine man offers to the alligator the guardianship of the tribal war cry. Hence the final bellow of the poem resonates with doubleness: it is both the cry of the alligator and of the departed Indians, and for that reason it seems particularly unsettling:

> For two hundred years—
> Will, without inflexion—
> The bull alligator
> Roars from the swamp
> In the Spring. (*The Yemassee Lands* 36)

Less disturbing, perhaps, is the poem that attracted the most popularity in the twenties—"Poe's Mother"—but it is nonetheless a poem that directs attention to muted voices, in this case, that of Elizabeth Arnold Poe, who had reputedly once performed in a Charleston theater (Cox 170). The voice of the poem, after all, is not that of the South's most celebrated nineteenth-century poet but of his shadowy, remote mother, a young woman trying for a time in Charleston to make ends meet. Separated from her husband and scuffling with the stage company manager who both repels and attracts her, she ponders male contempt and her own inability to leave her mark, either in writing or in memory:

> Women he scorns, they barely save themselves
> By being mothers. Once, he said, some poet
> Proclaimed the sea the chariot of nature.
> Was I, sea-born, meant only for the bringer,
> The chariot of children? (*The Yemassee Lands* 68)

To her strange young son, though, she does leave a legacy of sort—the conviction that "The only bearable things in life are dreams"—and songs "of cities in the water, just like this, / And flowers that bloom when everyone's asleep"—references, of course, to poems that Poe himself would write (*The Yemassee Lands* 67, 71). She may be "only" a mother, but her songs and dreams will later live on in her son's art.

It is this identification with silenced and muted voices lying in the margin—with otherness, if you will—that informs Ravenel's work in the twenties. This sort of identification makes her sympathize with figures who have been swept aside in the making of history, like, for instance, the buccaneers of "The Pirates," brought to trial in early eighteenth-century Charles Town. In the written record they exist simply as shadows in another's story, the making of Charleston, but in popular memory they hold a much more prominent place. For the common folk, the poem concludes,

> once loved you,
> The humble, whose very life is in some sort a piracy,
> Maurauding the sun and air from the well-found and solid
>   citizen. . . . (*The Yemassee Lands* 53)

In these muted voices, the detritus of history and tradition, Ravenel finds her own voice, one that like the song of the mockingbird resonates with the sounds of others. These are the voices that have been ignored and overlooked in the making of art, South Carolina, and by implication Southern history. Defender of the status quo Ravenel might have been in the editorial pages of the Columbia *State,* but in her poetry she retained her iconoclastic bent and cast her lot with the silenced and the forgotten. Sensing something of this alliance, Harriet Monroe in her review of *The Arrow of Lightning* shrewdly observed: "She says nothing about her Charleston neighbors; perhaps she knows the old-southern aristocrat too well to treat him familiarly" (289).

By the late 1920s, though, Ravenel herself began to slip quietly from public view into the quieter corners of Charleston life. In 1926 Ravenel married Samuel Prioleau Ravenel, a distant relation of her first husband, and in ensuing years traveled a good deal and published less and less, perhaps in part because *The Arrow of Lightning,* generally well received by critics, did not attract the large audience for which she might have hoped.[8] She continued to write and even to publish, but by and large privacy seemed increasingly important to her. She even reacted with a certain measure of irritation to the short biographical description accompanying her contribution to a 1938 anthology. "I was rather surprised," she wrote the editor, "to find myself mentioned in the book as a 'social and intellectual leader' of Charleston. I do not claim either of these distinctions. As a matter of fact, I lead the quietest of lives and for some years have taken practically no part in social activities."[9]

It comes as no surprise, then, that Ravenel found Emily Dickinson a particularly sympathetic figure. A 1933 poem titled simply "Emily Dickinson" suggests that Ravenel saw in Dickinson a similar appreciation of a rich inner life and the dazzling possibilities of language wielded as weapon and shield. The poem is worth quoting in its entirety:

> You shut your doors on small intrusions.
> You chose your cage: a garden and the swap
> Of seaward-flung horizons free of bounds;
> Intensive secrets of your winter greenhouse;
> And words—the cutting wizardry of words,
> Sword-dance of dictionaries, patterning

> With more and more distinctiveness, finer painted grace,
> The rhythms flung between yourself and life.
> Bird in the dark, your wine-gold venturous eyes
> Pierced with a fiery needle; you must sing
> To night's vast world suffused with unseen stars;
> Beauty without topography or limit,
> Sufficient beauty, waiting for the sun
> No longer, all the promises of night
> Fulfilled in radiant darknesses of song. (16)

Ravenel herself knew something of "rhythms flung between yourself and life," for like so many women poets before her and particularly modernists of her generation, she was well aware that words could be used to say one thing and mean another, to reveal and to conceal (Ostriker 6). And as a poet who found alliances among those discarded in the making of stories and histories, she was particularly sensitive to the possibility of "Beauty without topography or limit."

It is, in fact, the possibility of new definitions of beauty resistant to confining categories that she celebrates in her last major sequence of poems—a series on the West Indies. Written largely in the voices of black Creoles, the poems evoke a rich and sensuous subterranean life struggling with the white world seeking to contain and domesticate it. Admittedly, resistance to white-imposed order seems at times improbable and distant, as in the poem "Judge Achille Fontaine." White-dominated ways determine the nuances of everyday life: "We wear long-tailed coats, we specialize forks, / We flatter Americans. Hé, we behave ourselves." But the veneer of whiteness is ultimately too thin and insubstantial to offer much protection against "The only god of the blacks who has power over the whites." When the "Radi drums shall shatter the Champ de Mars," the god of the blacks will have his day: "And the ancient ways, the ways of the ancient folk / They would be ours once more" (*The Yemassee Lands* 89).

In other poems, though, boundaries between white and black, between the orderly and the sensual, simply seem to vanish in the presence of urgent vitality, and nowhere more emphatically than in "Jeune Fille Octoroon":

> At the Sacré Coeur in Paris
> They took me for white.
> I sat with the daughters of ducs and maréchals.
> One day Soeur Marie-Martre made us swear in the chapel
> Never to work in a life class
> Where the models went without robes.
> We bathed in a chemise.

But the air of tonight is pressing against my body,
Insistent, harsh as a thorn-bush,
Saying, What can be this?
This is the enemy. This is between us.
And the Radi drums are abroad in this air,
Crying! Crying! Tearing the gauze of dusk
In the grove of the plunging shadows. (*The Yemassee Lands* 85)

Seemingly docile and submissive, the speaker of the poem nevertheless takes little heed of the boundaries between white and black, propriety and impropriety. What remains with her is not the admonition of the good sister but the moment of physical sensation and sensuality too vibrant to be contained. And it is that moment of transgressed boundaries that Ravenel celebrates, a moment linking black persona with white poet despite historical and social constraints.

In many respects, then, one hardly wonders that so many Southern literary historians have overlooked Ravenel's perplexing and unsettling poetry of otherness and disrupted boundaries. For writers and students of the region have been absorbed with the task of defining the *interior* and *boundaries* of the region and its literature, not its hinterlands and shadows. From Montrose Moses to Fred C. Hobson, students of Southern writing have faced, in Richard Gray's words, "the problem of deciding exactly where the South begins and ends, just what its geographical dimensions are" (ix). This problem in turn leads inevitably to exclusions and the marking of boundaries: what is Southern writing and what is not? What is, moreover, *proper* Southern art and what falls beyond the pale? In answering these questions scholars of the Southern Renaissance have all too often followed the lead of the very writers they have submitted to scrutiny. "Indeed, the temptation . . . ," Fred Hobson admits in *Tell About the South*, "especially if the author is a Southerner, is that he will try to do what his subjects have done—to make his own case for or against the South" (16).

Ultimately, Ravenel's poetry reminds us that this is a temptation to be resisted. Those boundaries that scholars have used to frame their definitions of the region, its history, and its literature may after all be quite arbitrary and perhaps even harmful at times. For the lament of Allen Tate's Aeneas at Washington, the displaced Southerner mourning his lost past, has long muffled dissenting and discordant voices, particularly those of women and other marginal figures. In Ravenel's slender opus and in the poetic self she constructs they find a place once again and remind us of "the other within" Southern history (Gallop 320).

NOTES

I would like to thank Scott Peeples for helping me track down fleeting references to Beatrice Ravenel. For direction and aid in manuscript collections, I would also like to thank Harlan Greene at the South Carolina Historical Society in Charleston and Patricia Gantt at the Southern Historical Collection at the University of North Carolina at Chapel Hill. Thanks go to Carol Manning, Robert Gross, Deborah Morse, Susan Schultz, and Elsa Nettels for reading and commenting on earlier versions of this essay. Finally, I gratefully acknowledge the University of North Carolina Press for permission to quote from Ravenel's *The Yemassee Lands* and the Library of the University of North Carolina for permission to quote from Ravenel's papers.

1. A brief summary of Bryan's life can be found in the *Dictionary of American Biography*, 1929 ed.

2. Beatrice Ravenel to Mrs. J. W. Tarwater, 5 May 1934, Beatrice Ravenel Papers, Southern Historical Collection, Library of the University of North Carolina at Chapel Hill.

3. Ravenel to Mrs. J. W. Tarwater, 5 May 1934, Beatrice Ravenel Papers; and "Beatrice Ravenel, Poet and Short Story Writer, Has Read Deeply in Books and People," Charleston *News and Courier* 5 Feb. 1939, newspaper clipping, Beatrice Ravenel Papers.

4. T. W. Higginson to Beatrice Witte, 2 April 1892, Beatrice Ravenel Papers.

5. Headley Morris Cox, Jr., "The Charleston Poetic Renascence, 1920–1930" (Ph.d. diss., University of Pennsylvania, 1958), 168; and "Beatrice Ravenel, Poet and Short Story Writer, Has Read Deeply in Books and People," Beatrice Ravenel Papers.

6. "Beatrice Ravenel, Poet and Short Story Writer, Has Read Deeply in Books and People," Beatrice Ravenel Papers; and *Year Book of the Poetry Society of South Carolina 1921* (Charleston: Poetry Society of South Carolina, 1921) 47.

7. Amy Lowell to Beatrice Ravenel, 15 April 1922, Beatrice Ravenel Papers.

8. Beatrice St. Julien Ravenel, letter to the author [postmarked 18 July 1988].

9. Beatrice Ravenel to Carlyle Straub, 24 June 1938, Beatrice Ravenel Papers.

WORKS CITED

Allen, Hervey, and DuBose Heyward. "Poetry South." *Poetry* 20 (1922): 35–48.
"Beatrice Ravenel, Poet and Short Story Writer, Has Read Deeply in Books and People." Charleston *News and Courier* 5 Feb. 1939. Newspaper clipping. Ravenel Papers.
"Bryan, Mary E." *Dictionary of American Biography.* 1929 ed.
Bryan, Mary E. "How Should Women Write?" *Southern Field and Fireside* 21 Jan. 1860. n.p.
Cixous, Hélène. "The Laugh of the Medusa." Trans. Keith Cohen and Paula Cohen. In *New French Feminisms: An Anthology.* Ed. and Introd. Elaine Marks and Isabelle de Courtivron. New York: Schocken Books, 1981. 245–64.

Cox, Headley Morris, Jr. "The Charleston Poetic Renascence, 1920–1930." Ph.D. diss., University of Pennsylvania, 1958.

Dreyfus, Hubert L., and Paul Rabinow. *Michel Foucault: Beyond Structuralism and Hermeneutics.* 2d ed. Chicago: University of Chicago Press, 1983.

"Editor's Table." *Russell's Magazine* 1 (1857): 559.

Foucault, Michel. "Two Lectures." In *Power/Knowledge: Selected Interviews and Other Writings, 1972–77.* Ed. Colin Gordon. Trans. Colin Gordon et al. New York: Pantheon, 1980. 78–108.

Gallop, Jane. "Reading the Mother Tongue: Psychoanalytic Feminist Criticism." *Critical Inquiry* 13 (1987): 314–29.

Gilbert, Sandra M., and Susan Gubar. *The Madwoman in the Attic: The Woman Writer and the Nineteenth-Century Literary Imagination.* New Haven: Yale University Press, 1979.

Gray, Richard. *The Literature of Memory: Modern Writers of the American South.* Baltimore: Johns Hopkins University Press, 1977.

Hayne, Paul Hamilton. "Literature at the South: The Fungous School." *Southern Magazine* 14 (1874): 654–55.

Heyward, DuBose. Introduction to poems by Beatrice Ravenel. *The Library of Southern Literature.* Eds. Edwin Anderson Alderman, Charles Alphonso Smith, and John Calvin Metcalfe. Vol. 17. Atlanta: Martin & Hoyt 1923. 473–75.

Higginson, T. W. Letter to Beatrice Witte. 2 April 1892. Ravenel Papers.

Hobson, Fred. *Tell About the South: The Southern Rage to Explain.* Baton Rouge: Louisiana State University Press, 1983.

Jones, Anne Goodwyn. *Tomorrow Is Another Day: The Woman Writer in the South, 1859–1936.* Baton Rouge: Louisiana State University Press, 1981.

King, Richard H. *A Southern Renaissance: The Cultural Awakening of the American South, 1930–1955.* New York: Oxford University Press, 1980.

Kreyling, Michael. *Figures of the Hero in Southern Narrative.* Baton Rouge: Louisiana State University Press, 1986.

Lowell, Amy. Letter to Beatrice Ravenel. 15 April 1922. Beatrice Ravenel Papers.

Meese, Elizabeth A. *Crossing the Double-Cross: The Practice of Feminist Criticism.* Chapel Hill: University of North Carolina Press, 1986.

Monroe, Harriet. "The Old South—Review of *The Arrow of Lightning.*" *Poetry* 30 (1927): 288–90.

Moses, Montrose. *The Literature of the South.* New York: Thomas Y. Crowell, 1910.

O'Brien, Michael. *The Idea of the American South, 1920–1941.* Baltimore: Johns Hopkins University Press, 1979.

Ostriker, Alicia Suskin. *Stealing the Language: The Emergence of Women's Poetry in America.* Boston: Beacon Press, 1986.

Preston, Margaret J. "Women's Art." In *Cartoons.* Boston: Roberts Brothers, 1881. 70–71.

"A Promising Southern Poet." Chicago *Post* 28 Jan. 1927. Newspaper clipping, Scrapbook No. 4. Ravenel Papers.

Ravenel, Beatrice. *The Arrow of Lightening.* New York: Harold Vinal, 1926.

Ravenel, Beatrice. *The Arrow of Lightening.* New York: Harold Vinal, 1926.

————."Bondswomen." Vol. 2, ms. poems. Ravenel Papers.

————. "Emily Dickinson." *The Carillon* 4, no. 4 (1933): 16. Ravenel Papers.

————. Letter to Carlyle Straub. 24 June 1938. Ravenel Papers.

————. Letter to Mrs. J. W. Tarwater. 5 May 1934. Ravenel Papers.

————. Papers. Southern Historical Collection, Library of University of North Carolina at Chapel Hill.

[————]. "The Silence of the Suffragettes." Scrapbook No. 3. Ravenel Papers.

————. *The Yemassee Lands: Poems of Beatrice Ravenel.* Ed. and introd. Louis D. Rubin, Jr., Chapel Hill: University of North Carolina Press, 1969.

Ravenel, Beatrice St. Julien. Letter to the author. 18 July 1988.

Rubin, Louis D., Jr. Introduction. *The Yemassee Lands: Poems of Beatrice Ravenel.* Chapel Hill: University of North Carolina Press, 1969. 3–28.

Simms, William Gilmore. *The Yemassee: A Romance of Carolina.* 1835. Introd. Joseph Ridgely. Boston: Twayne, 1964.

Singal, Daniel Joseph. *The War Within: From Victorian to Modernist Thought in the South, 1919–1945.* Chapel Hill: University of North Carolina Press, 1982.

"Southern Poetry—A Sketch." *Southern Review* [Baltimore] 25 (1879): 5–32.

"Southern War Poetry." *Southern Review* [Baltimore] 1, no. 2 (1867): 273–86.

Walker, Cheryl. *The Nightingale's Burden: Women Poets and American Culture before 1900.* Bloomington: Indiana University Press, 1982.

Waring, Laura Witte. *The Way It Was in Charleston.* Ed. Thomas B. Waring, Jr. Old Greenwich, Conn.: Devin-Adair, 1980.

Witte [Ravenel], Beatrice. "Madonna Mia." *Harvard Monthly* 14, no. 2 (1892): 68–71.

Year Book of the Poetry Society of South Carolina 1921. Charleston: Poetry Society of South Carolina, 1921.

Anna Shannon Elfenbein

A Forgotten Revolutionary Voice: "Woman's Place" and Race in Olive Dargan's *Call Home the Heart*

Reviewing the "proletarian" fiction[1] produced in the early 1930s, E. A. Schachner, an influential Communist journalist and editor, announced in 1934 that the South, mirabile dictu, had "suddenly made a manly bid for a place in the cultural sun with four important novels, three of them written by women" (28). Still more marvelous, according to Schachner, whose loaded use of the word *manly* implied the effeminacy and hence the inferiority of the Southern "bozart" of previous decades, was the fact that Sherwood Anderson's treatment of the bloody Gastonia, North Carolina, textile strike of 1929 had been "surpassed" by novels on the same subject by three women novelists, Fielding Burke (Olive Tilford Dargan), Grace Lumpkin, and Myra Page. Attempting to explain the paradoxical idea that "a manly bid" for literary preeminence had been made by genteel white Southern women, Schachner wrote: "Who but the most sensitive, the most cultured and the most progressive of Southerners were in a position to write the novels that demanded to be written about Gastonia? And who, in the South, are more progressive, more sensitive to oppression, and more equipped with the necessary culture than those Southern nonproletarian women who are themselves enslaved by bourgeois man-made codes, and who see a promise of their own emancipation in the Southern working class's fight for freedom?" (60). These observations were remarkably insightful for their time. Unfortunately, however, Schachner had nothing more to say about the ways in which gender was inflecting the new genre of proletarian fiction in the South.

Schachner's failure to elaborate upon his insights is hardly surprising. The Communist party of the 1930s, which was "a masculine preserve— male-dominated in person, in politics, and in metaphor" (Rabinowitz, "Women" 5), concerned itself primarily with issues of class struggle and hardly at all with gender issues.[2] Moreover, party literati held that proletarian fiction should be written exclusively by men. The well-known Communist editor and writer Michael Gold, for example, described the proletarian author as a "wild" working-class youth who "works in the lumber camps, coal mines, steel mills, harvest fields and mountain camps of America" ("Go Left" 4; rpt. in Folsom 188). The masculist thrust evident in Gold's words engendered the terms of the discussion of radical fiction carried on in the 1930s and thereafter. Male literary radicals like Gold often employed aggressively sexist and even homophobic tropes of proletarianism, invoking masculinity, as Paula Rabinowitz points out, in order "to stake a claim within 'The Great Tradition,' one that echoed Hawthorne's desire to distinguish himself from the 'damned mob of scribbling women'" ("Female Subjectivity" 11). Although most of the critics of succeeding generations disputed the greatness of radical fiction, labeling it "'desolate wastes'" on maps of the literary landscape (Rideout 171),[3] they generally accepted the male radicals' exclusive claim to this particular piece of literary territory. Even those few heterodox critics who found merit in works of radical protest generally subscribed to the masculist account of proletarian fiction.[4]

It is now time to pick up where E. A. Schachner left off more than fifty years ago. Since the fulsome masculist prescriptions for and descriptions of proletarian fiction put forward by Michael Gold and his successors obviously apply neither to the radical women authors of the 1930s nor to their female protagonists, feminist critics must now replace them with a more balanced and more accurate account of the radical literature of the period. In this essay I will examine a fine but largely forgotten proletarian novel by a Southern woman, Olive Tilford Dargan's *Call Home the Heart.* This neglected work, which Schachner praised as the best of the Gastonia novels (61), provides a telling example of the "different voice" (see Gilligan) of radical white Southern women authors of the 1930s and evidence that they occupy an important place in the Southern female tradition of literary protest against oppressive man-made codes. Dargan's novel attacks the constraints imposed on women by traditional notions of "woman's place" and problematizes female heterosexual desire, the call of the heart, by demonstrating it to be a divisive force that imperils female revolutionary solidarity. In addition, *Call Home the Heart* courageously condemns racism and classism as forces that, like sexual desire, prevent women from uniting to end their oppression. In publishing the novel, Dargan added her voice to the chorus of progressive Southern women who had joined together in a campaign against lynching (see Hall, *Revolt*).

Despite its enlightened treatment of racism as an impediment to revolutionary action, it must be acknowledged that the depiction of racial prejudice in *Call Home the Heart* is contaminated by what would now be recognized as racist rhetoric and stereotypes. But this is not a valid reason, in my view, to perpetuate the neglect of *Call Home the Heart;* on the contrary, the novel's exploitation of the rhetoric and conventions of racism is one of the factors that render it worthy of reconsideration.

With almost three decades as a publishing poet and dramatist already behind her, Olive Dargan turned her hand to novel writing in 1929 and published *Call Home the Heart* three years later. She wrote the novel to lend support to the cause in Gastonia, where women workers—many of them mountain whites—were playing central roles in an explosive strike at the Loray mill. As unlike the "ideal" proletarian novelist envisioned by Gold as anyone could be, this sixty-three-year-old white Southern woman and fellow traveler wrote *Call Home the Heart* under a gender-neutral pseudonym, "Fielding Burke," probably in part to ward off criticism from those who believed that the proletarian novelist should be a man who had worked in the coal mines and steel mills. Having lived in the mountains for many years herself and having provided a refuge for homeless and abused poor white women in her home in Asheville in the late 1920s, Dargan knew women like those who were striking in Gastonia.[5] And she believed passionately that such women should participate fully in the historic changes going on around them. She therefore wove a feminist protest against their narrow and oppressed lives into her story.

The novel's plot is one of individual rebellion and retreat: Dargan's Ishma Waycaster Hensley, a poor white and a mountain woman, rebels against the confines of her life as a woman and later retreats before achieving liberation. Dargan's description of her heroine's conversion to Communism, however, transvalued this plot by merging Ishma's personal quest with the larger struggle of her class, which at that moment in history seemed capable of transforming society itself. Dargan also reconstructed the male-centered master plot of revolutionary fiction by choosing a female protagonist rather than a proletarian hero. In addition, she revised the "happy ending" of romance fiction by presenting the South and Ishma in realistic terms, racism and all. Through her heroine's failure to escape both the enforced immanence of her "place" as a woman in a male-dominated society and the racial prejudices of that society, Dargan demonstrated that class struggle for women must begin at home and in the heart.

One of Dargan's most important achievements in *Call Home the Heart* is her moving depiction of sexual dependency and gender oppression as defining experiences for women and as catalysts for their revolutionary consciousness. At a time when the Communist party's chief goal was to have women fighting " 'side by side' or 'shoulder to shoulder' with men against capitalism" (Shaffer 79), she identified a potentially powerful source of division and contention between men and women of the working class. *Call Home the Heart* thus extended the reach of radical critique in a feminist direction and introduced feminist complications into the calculus of revolutionary theory. Of equal importance is Dargan's portrayal of racism as a means by which the ruling class can divide and conquer the working class. Through her heroine's failed struggle to transcend sexism and racism, Dargan exposed, with what today seems artistic clairvoyance, two forces that were to fragment the women's movement in the 1960s and 1970s.

Not surprisingly, the few critics who have read *Call Home the Heart* over the years and compared it to the other Gastonia novels have found it to be the best crafted and most moving of them all.[6] The editors at the Feminist Press, which reprinted the novel in 1983, regarded it so highly that they gave it first place in their "Novels of the Thirties" series. In spite of its merit, however, *Call Home the Heart* has inspired little interest and virtually no comment since being reprinted. By 1989, according to Florence Howe, publisher of the Feminist Press at the City University of New York, the press had not yet sold-out its first printing of four thousand copies of Dargan's novel (telephone interview, 7 June 1989). And except for an essay by Joseph R. Urgo and a book review by Kathy Cantley Ackerman, *Call Home the Heart* has apparently been the subject of no published scholarship since 1983. Earlier criticism of the novel is equally scanty. The neglect of the novel by feminist critics is especially puzzling in light of its strong feminist message and aesthetic merit.

The reason for the virtual silence of feminist critics concerning Dargan's novel may be that it contains some racist rhetoric, which, despite its attack on the ideologies of oppression, may have discouraged some readers who would otherwise have written about it. Paula Rabinowitz, for example, in "Female Subjectivity in Women's Revolutionary Novels of the Thirties," not only chooses not to discuss *Call Home the Heart* but also questions its entitlement to be counted as a revolutionary work. Evidently revolted by its racist language, Rabinowitz asks, "Is a novel like Fielding Burke's *Call Home the Heart* really 'revolutionary' just because it advocates class struggle, when its rhetoric, form and, to some extent, content are truly reactionary?" (18).

Despite the racist rhetoric of the novel, Dargan's personal racial views, which she expressed repeatedly to her friends, were extremely liberal, especially for a white Southerner of the 1930s. Aware, however, that the times were perilous for those who spoke out against racism, she found it necessary to conceal both her views on racial issues and her friendships with blacks.[7] In 1944 when a fellow Southerner, Lillian Smith, published *Strange Fruit,* a novel of interracial love and betrayal, Dargan praised Smith for speaking out in support of the cause of racial justice. An enthusiastic subscriber to Smith's racially enlightened journal, *South Today,* Dargan marveled at the success of Smith's novel, which had been banned in Boston only to become a bestseller, and remarked, perhaps wistfully, "Lillian goes right on saying and doing what she thinks should be said and done for the Negroes with no diminution of respect or patronage" (qtd. in Shannon 441).[8] Dargan's awareness that a public position on the race question posed risks to herself and others may have contributed to her decision to mask her identity with a pseudonym when she published *Call Home the Heart.*

It is clear that Dargan's decision to make race pivotal in her novel was advanced for its time. It was not until 1935, three years after *Call Home the Heart* appeared, that the Communist party, representing the avant-garde of progressive racial opinion, issued its "Call for an American Writers' Congress," which exhorted writers to combat through their fiction "white chauvinism" and the "persecution of minority groups and of the foreign-born" (314). By making racism one of her white heroine's primary flaws, Dargan was broaching a topic many of her readers would have preferred not to consider at all. Moreover, by showing racism to be a serious impediment to class unity and hence to revolutionary action, she was calling racially bigoted white Southerners to account, years before it became fashionable, even on the Left, to do so.

Dargan's account of Southern town and country life in *Call Home the Heart* issued a bold challenge not only to the Communist party hierarchy but also to a second virtually all-male group whose ideology was essentially masculist: the Vanderbilt University Agrarians. In *I'll Take My Stand* (1930), the Agrarians had valorized the Southern past, prescribing traditional Southern values as an antidote to "Progress," which they saw as the national disease. The Agrarian dream, as adumbrated in *I'll Take My Stand,* provided an escape for those Southerners who, like the Mandarin class of ancient China, saw the world, in Dargan's words, as " 'a seething torrent,' " believed that there was " 'no hope for it,' " and wanted their compatriots simply to " 'dig, and plant, and die in peace' " (293). Seeking to preserve or restore rural values, such as leisure, stability, and spirituality, in the South, the Agrarians also recommended the Southern genteel model to a nation convulsed by the onset of the Great Depression. In so doing, however, they failed to acknowledge the inhumanity of slavery, which provided a few wealthy whites with an easy existence at the expense of millions of blacks and poor whites. In his essay in the volume, Frank Lawrence Owsley went so far as to argue that slavery was legitimate because it was the only available means of protecting civilized whites against savage blacks, "some of whom could still remember the taste of human flesh," and most of whom were "hardly three generations removed from cannibalism" (62). Anticipating present-day repudiation of the Agrarians' romanticization of Southern aristocratic life and of their rationalization of the South's crime against humanity, *Call Home the Heart*, in its account of rural life, industrial expansion, and race relations, took a stand of its own that refuted *I'll Take My Stand* virtually point for point.

First, rather than follow the Agrarians in romanticizing rural Southern life, Dargan attempted to portray the South realistically. Having lived in rural North Carolina for a quarter of a century, she knew the region, both the beauty of its mountains, on the one hand, and the classism, racism, and poverty of its people, on the other. In her indelible portraits of mountain folk, Dargan foregrounded Southern women who fail to achieve solidarity with each other because they fail to surmount the barriers of class and race. She also depicted the backbreaking labor required to wring subsistence from farming. Moreover, in what appears to be a pointed reference to the Agrarians, many of whom were academics, Dargan has a successful piedmont farmer scoff at college professors for their impractical remedies for farm problems and their romantic visions of pastoral retreat.[9]

Second, in paeans to human progress, Dargan attacked the Agrarians' aversion to industrialism, which they had defined as "a program under which men, using the latest scientific paraphernalia, sacrifice comfort, leisure, and the enjoyment of life to win Pyrrhic victories from nature at points of no strategic importance." She had seen firsthand, as had the Agrarians, "the human catastrophe which occurs when a Southern village or rural community becomes the cheap labor of a miserable factory system" (Ransom 15, 23). Nevertheless, speaking through her heroine Ishma, Dargan testified to her belief that industry would become a liberating force in human history. Thus, when a worker confronts Ishma with the news that a nearby town has brought in " 'a new machine where they can put one man to 'tendin' a hundred and eighteen looms,' " Ishma advises him against forming a vigilante group to smash the machine, declaiming: " 'We're going to get together till there's not a working man left out, white, black, yellow or brown, the world over. When a new machine is put in, we'll not merely install it and run it. We'll own it. That machine, instead of making profits for one family up in Pawtucket, will shorten the working day for a hundred families in North Carolina, and do it without cutting down their bread supply. You'll have time to play a game of horse-shoes after work, maybe' " (306, 307).

Third, in polemical statements prophesying racial solidarity the world over, like the foregoing declaration by her heroine, Dargan rejected the backward glance and racism of the Agrarians. In opposition to these men, who had never even entertained the possibility that their racial attitudes were a problem that needed to be addressed, she showed her heroine's racism to be a crippling disability symbolic of the atavistic impulses preventing her (and, by extension, the South and the nation) from finally realizing democratic ideals.

Although explicitly concerned with the issues raised by the Agrarians and with class oppression, *Call Home the Heart* is implicitly concerned with the omnipresence of gender oppression. In her very first sentence, which identifies Ishma Waycaster as a member of "the class of burden-bearers" (1), Dargan begins to establish the theme of feminist protest that runs throughout the novel. *Call Home the Heart* underscores the ubiquity of women's subordination by showing that they occupy a second-class status both in the mountains, with their clean air and water and their fascinating, ethnically homogeneous folk culture, and in the starkly contrasting mill town, Winbury, with its polluted air and brown lung and its distinctions of race, ethnicity, and social class. Everywhere in the world of the novel, male-dominated relations of reproduction perpetuate an oppressive sexual order. Mountain folk wisdom has it that " 'a gal she must marry,' " and " 'a wife she must carry' " (63, 115). This saying proves to be as true, and probably even truer, for women who live in town as for those who live in the mountains, since, in addition to the physical hardships of childbearing and -rearing, women living in town risk becoming casualties of the "second shift" (see Hochschild). "No man in Spindle Hill could support his family on his own wages alone" (216), and no mill wife could escape "helping out," thereby doubling her drudgery. Thus, although several of the original reviewers of *Call Home the Heart* complained that a disjuncture was created in the narrative by Ishma's flight from the mountains and by the emergence of Marxist polemic in the depiction of class struggle in the mill town,[10] the novel is in fact unified, as Sylvia Jenkins Cook points out, by a "pattern of feminist discontent" (104).

Dargan complicates this pattern by exposing Ishma's racism at the novel's climax, where it emerges with blinding fury, forcing her to acknowledge its power as "something unguessed within her" (432). Ishma's racial antagonism impels her to flee political engagement and prevents her from transcending her primal biological drives to mate and have children. Sexual drives and racist programming, Dargan implies, are the kinds of forces that have interacted historically to ensure women's subordination. In naming her heroine Ishma, which means "waste" (*A Stone Came Rolling* 381), Dargan made her emblematic of the waste of women's talents that inevitably results from such subordination.

Although the depiction of Ishma in *Call Home the Heart* reveals the odds against her becoming more than another faceless and wasted woman, Dargan allows her to yearn for more and to imagine that she has a great destiny before her. Initially, Ishma believes that she can escape "the class of burden-bearers" (1). " 'Why does everybody think a girl's got to marry?' " she asks. " 'I'm going to have something else' " (49). Despite her vow, however, Ishma falls in love with and marries Britt Hensley, a mountain musician, only to find that she has been trapped by her passion into an endless cycle of childbearing and -burying. Eventually, though pregnant with a fourth child, she flees the mountains (and the privation her repeated pregnancies will inevitably cause) with a relatively affluent former suitor, Rad Bailey.

In leaving her husband and children, Ishma violates all the traditional norms governing woman's place in male-dominated society. On the eve of his own departure to enlist in the military, Ishma's brother Steve invokes these norms in an attempt to dissuade her from leaving the mountains herself: " 'A woman's a woman,' " he says. " 'She's bound to carry the baggage in this life. They's no gittin' out of it for her. A man can walk off any time, but a woman kain't. God, or Nature, or something we kain't buck against, has fixed it that way. You make up your mind it's all right. That's all you can do right now' " (149). The effect of this speech, however, is to intensify Ishma's resolve to escape, even though she recognizes that her leaving will cause her to lose the husband she loves and to incur the condemnation of her mountain neighbors.

When she arrives in Winbury with Rad, Ishma discovers that the double standard invoked by Steve is also in force there. In the town she meets Derry Unthank, a Communist physician who dispenses birth-control information to the husbands of his women patients but withholds it from the women themselves. Having overheard fragments of a conversation between Derry and Rad, Ishma is tantalized by the possibility of learning how to prevent future pregnancies. Recognizing her potential as a convert to Communism, Derry opens the door of revolutionary theory to her but at the same time blocks her access to birth-control information. The repeated frustration of Ishma's desire to discover the secret of contraceptive practice, which Dargan emphasizes through calculated shifts of narrative focus that repeatedly draw attention to the male monopoly of medical knowledge and the complicity of men in preventing women from controlling their biological destinies, is emblematic of Ishma's ultimate failure to realize her revolutionary aspirations. Ishma's failure in both areas stymies her desire "to count, to be part of something real" (227).[11]

For Ishma and the other women in the novel, motherhood is a fate rather than a choice, and one that makes them dependent on men and limits their opportunities for personal fulfillment through political action or artistic endeavor. Because Ishma is pregnant when she flees the mountains, her choices thereafter are bound to be severely limited, even if she finds out how to prevent future pregnancies. Having little to say about whether she will bear children or will care for Vennie, the daughter born to her in Winbury, Ishma, though a strong and independent woman, must rely on Rad for support. Ishma's responsibility for Vennie and her dependence on Rad weigh her down like a " 'ball and chain' " (192). " 'Just a little scrub of a kid,' " she tells herself. " 'That's all I'm living for' " (196). When Rad asks her whether she thinks she can be happy with their arrangement, Ishma can only say, " 'I'm going to be' " and, probably to herself, " 'I've got to be' " (179).

After Vennie is run over by a car, Ishma, who has risked her own life in a futile attempt to save the child, has an epiphany concerning the way in which her biology has controlled her destiny. She remembers that once, after climbing a mountain in anticipation of being able to "see the far world," she found herself looking instead into the branches of a "stunted loblolly," a spindly, unhealthy little pine tree, that "hid the far valleys, the sunlit peaks, the long, dreamy ridges, and the pale path of rivers" from her view. Ishma perceives an analogy between the tree and her "little stunted child, doomed from her birth to insignificance" (231). Encapsulating the hauntingly brief life of Vennie, the loblolly trope implies the right of a mother to seek fulfillment even at the expense of her ailing child. This trope is one of the devices through which Dargan attacks the unfair relations of reproduction and the disempowering reality of women's heterosexual desire.

After Vennie's death Ishma is, of course, still subject to physical desire. The "aching . . . within her," which "had nothing to do with the new world" of revolutionary promise, ties her "to the stern, begrudging earth with bonds of flesh that no dream could break" (334). Moreover, alongside the familiar pull of sexual desire, a new and unfamiliar force emerges: classist and racist revulsion and antagonism. In Winbury she confronts blacks for the first time in her life and finds herself wishing "they were all back where they came from, [going] on with their own kind of civilization, whatever it is" (354). In the mill town, classism and racism pervade and shape daily existence. The workers are prone to especially intense racial and class animosities because of having to endure the rigors of the "speed up" and the "stretch out" and having to compete for a dwindling number of jobs (219). Ishma comes to understand the divisive nature of capitalist competition. "What a strange system, she thought, where to do your best meant hurting your neighbors!" (272).

While living in the mountains, where class and race distinctions were far from salient in her daily life, Ishma believed that by freeing herself from her domestic roles and routine, she could obtain a much larger measure of personal freedom. The constraints of social class that she experiences for the first time in Winbury soon teach her, however, that the belief is unfounded. As the "wife" of a man who has managed to keep out of the mills, Ishma is accorded a privileged social status. She finds this status to be as irksomely confining and isolating as her arrangement with Rad, the more so because he has been infected by bourgeois class-consciousness and has come to regard her as a trophy to show off to his friends.

Ishma's relationships with the other women in the novel—such as Leta Unthank, her replacement in Rad's bed; Virginia Grant, the wealthy wife of the mill owner; and Gaffie Wells, a poor black woman—further demonstrate the workings of classism and racism. Ishma conspires with Leta to marry Rad off to her, and Leta then repays Ishma for the gift of Rad by betraying to her his involvement in a plot to lynch Butch Wells, a black strike leader and Gaffie's husband. Shared class values enable Ishma and Leta to make common cause by conspiring together and trading favors. In contrast, Ishma's relationships with Virginia and Gaffie show that distinctions of class and race alienate women from one another. Although Ishma befriends the aristocratic Virginia, the friendship never matures because Ishma discovers that Virginia has cultivated her only for her entertainment value as a teller of mountain stories. In the case of Gaffie, Ishma is unable even to initiate a relationship because she finds her race and poverty to be repulsive.

Long before her racist response to Gaffie Wells, Ishma perceives that her racism may make her a liability to the Communist cause. She therefore rationalizes her antipathy toward blacks by asserting that, as a mountain woman, she cannot help feeling as she does. " 'Mountain people are always *white,* ' " she explains. In response, Derry Unthank admits that he, too, has wrestled with racist impulses but blames his attitudes on his upbringing, noting that " 'when a child gets his prejudice from the woman he most admires on this earth [his mother], he has a long, hard fight before he can leave it behind him' " (353). Derry confesses that he fears that white racism and the backwardness of Southern blacks " 'are a handicap that may yet defeat us.' " " 'We have enough to do to save ourselves without a race question to entangle us,' " he observes (354).

Derry's premonition of defeat foreshadows Ishma's racist response to Gaffie Wells and Ishma's flight from the scene of her attack on the black woman at the end of the novel but hardly prepares the reader for the racist rhetoric that scars those pages. Derry and Ishma describe blacks as " 'strong earth-currents,' " " 'intuitive,' " and " 'rhythmic with nature' " (352, 355), thus intellectualizing the problem of racism in a way that suggests their inability to deal with its reality. To a disturbing degree, the novel echoes and amplifies these stereotypical and essentialist views in its final pages, where, in passages narrated in the third person, it describes Butch Wells's mother as wailing "with the vigor of her forest ancestry" (381). Similarly, Gaffie is described as a minstrel type having no capacity for genuine human emotion: "It was impossible to associate [Gaffie] with woe, though tears were racing down her cheeks. As her fat body moved she shook off an odor that an unwashed collie would have disowned" (383). These repellent descriptions of Butch's mother and Gaffie plunge racism not merely into the heart of Dargan's protagonist but also into the heart of the novel itself, which thus unconsciously enacts the racist ideology it consciously attacks.

Although the novel contains a few passages tainted by racist rhetoric, its conscious design makes Ishma's failure to control her racist impulses a decisive obstacle to her personal and political growth. When the gathering storm of labor unrest in Winbury offers her the opportunity to show which side she is on, she finds that her racism prevents her from taking her stand as a revolutionary. Because she has merely rationalized and repressed her racial antipathy, it can only return with horrific force. In the climactic scene of the novel, after her single-handed rescue of Butch Wells and her imagined victory over racism, "that final error in her blood," Ishma recoils from the grateful Gaffie, who has embraced her, mumbling, " 'We'll al be in heaben togeddah! Sistah! sistah! Yo' sho' got Jedus in you!' " Stifled by Gaffie's odor and fleshy embrace, Ishma responds by hitting her with one "wild blow, followed by another," and watching her as she falls, "striking the hearth cruelly hard, and uttering no cry" (382, 383). Following this episode Ishma obeys her programming and flees home to the mountains, where race is not an issue, yielding to her "uncontrollable revulsion" and deserting the movement for human equality that once promised her a transcendent purpose in life (383). As the trigger for Ishma's flight back to the mountains and the locus of the racist rhetoric in the novel, Ishma's brutal attack on Gaffie seems to have been designed to tell, but also unconsciously shows, the bitter truth about racism in the South of the 1930s—that even the most committed white opponents of racism were tainted by it.

Ishma learns this bitter truth by living it. After the fulfillment of her long-denied passion for Britt, her former husband, she reflects on the irrational forces that have called her home, her racist revulsion and sexual passion, and acknowledges that "something unguessed within her" "had voraciously made itself known" (432), something that can never be buried or denied but must be confronted and conquered. As a result of confronting this "something," Ishma becomes both more capable of effective revolutionary action and more committed to the movement for social justice. In *A Stone Came Rolling* (1935), the sequel to *Call Home the Heart,* Ishma at last succeeds in her struggle to conquer the impulses of her heart. Having acted on the basis of blind prejudice and passion and having learned from her mistakes, she is no longer hampered in her political efforts by the delusion that she is an exceptional woman or by a superior attitude toward the workers, an attitude that manifests itself in *Call Home the Heart* when she exhorts them to disregard their racial differences and to " 'get together till there's not a working man left out, white, black, yellow or brown, the world over' " (307).

Had someone pointed out to Olive Dargan that her otherwise brilliant depiction of Ishma's fatal flaw was marred by the exploitation of racist rhetoric, I think that she, like Ishma, would have acknowledged the presence of "something unguessed within her" and would have cleansed *Call Home the Heart* of its pernicious effects. It appears, however, that none of Dargan's friends was sufficiently advanced in thinking about the race question to do so. In fact, though almost certain to offend modern readers, the novel's racist descriptions of Butch Wells's mother and Gaffie Wells appear not to have occasioned a single comment from Dargan's contemporaries, who were no doubt inured to the rhetoric of exotic primitivism that had proliferated during the Harlem Renaissance. Given the prevailing racial discourse of the early 1930s, Dargan may have been constrained, despite the best of intentions, to resort to racist language and conventions in order to mount her attack on racism.

If this is true, even in part, Dargan's predicament as a white Southern woman author seeking to resist racism and to advance the cause of women prefigured that of the feminist critic of today, who seeks to overthrow patriarchal literary canons and to rediscover and reinstate a woman's literary tradition but finds this revolutionary enterprise impeded by the language of critical analysis, a language engendered by patriarchal politics and praxis. The disturbing presence of racist rhetoric in *Call Home the Heart,* like the disturbing presence of racist, classist, and heterosexist rhetoric in feminist criticism, admonishes us to pursue our revisionary work while keeping Audre Lorde's maxim always before us: "The master's tools will never dismantle the master's house" (112).

NOTES

1. The literary history of the term *proletarian* stretches back at least as far as 1901, when it appeared in the *Comrade,* a Socialist journal. The term did not enter American literary-critical discourse, however, until 1930, when Michael Gold launched his inflammatory attack on Thornton Wilder as "the poet of the genteel bourgeoisie" in the *New Republic* ("Wilder" 266; rpt. in Folsom 199; Rabinowitz, "Female Subjectivity" 31).

2. Although Frederick Engels had observed that the first class oppression was "that of the female sex by the male" (75), the American Communist party of the 1930s failed to see sexual oppression as primary or to give priority to what it characterized as the "woman question." Robert Shaffer argues that the party was "an important institution of struggle for women's liberation in the United States in the 1930s," concedes that women encountered "sexism" in the party and that "most of [its] leadership was male," and blames the lack of a strong women's movement during that period for the "*relative* unimportance" that "issues of women's oppression" had within the party (74).

3. Obviously shaped by the same historical dialectic as less politically engaged modernist fiction, proletarian fiction of the 1920s and 1930s became quite simply bad art, defined by critics in contradistinction to the safe, apolitical aestheticism of fiction that staked its claim to greatness on its many kinds of irony, ambiguity, complexity, and stylistic and formal novelty.

4. In *The Radical Novel in the United States, 1900–1954* (1956), an examination of left-wing fiction, including works by women authors in which the protagonists are women, Walter B. Rideout described the proletarian author as a generic male who "imaged himself as plunging into the surge of a mass movement" and his protagonist as a "worker" who "attempts to rise from his class, only to find that his struggles are thwarted" (180). Rideout's claim that "the explicit linking of political revolution and sexual freedom rarely appears" in radical novels of the 1930s (219) is impossible to reconcile with the works of many women radicals of the period, for those works clearly depict the sexual

double standard and the second-class status of their women characters as impediments to the overthrow of the existing political order.

5. In a letter to a friend in 1927, Dargan wrote: "This winter I seem to be building up an official employment bureau. There is so much need. And if it is so in this favored region what must it be in other places! I've been helping young girls find work—They come here, so young, so helpless, so pretty, and not a place to lay their heads" (qtd. in Shannon 440).

6. Six novels in all were written about the Gastonia strike: Mary Heaton Vorse's *Strike!* (1930), Olive Tilford Dargan's *Call Home the Heart* (1932), Grace Lumpkin's *To Make My Bread* (1932), Myra Page's *Gathering Storm* (1932), Sherwood Anderson's *Beyond Desire* (1932), and William Rollins's *The Shadow Before* (1934). Schachner says that *Call Home the Heart* "contains far and away the best writing" of the three Gastonia novels by Southern women (61). Rideout writes that of the works by Dargan, Page, and Lumpkin, Dargan's is "the most proficiently written" (174). Sylvia Jenkins Cook asserts that Dargan's novel is "by far the best" of those about Gastonia, and that the problems with which it deals are of "a universal nature" (98). Joseph R. Urgo's opinion is that "*Call Home the Heart* stands apart" from the other Gastonia novels "as a work of considerable artistic merit" (77). And Jacquelyn Dowd Hall, while faulting historians for failing to tell the story of the women workers, praises the proletarian novelists and singles out *Call Home the Heart* as especially noteworthy ("Disorderly Women" 355 n.4).

7. In 1919 Dargan decided to keep secret her long-term friendship with William Stanley Braithwaite, a well-known black intellectual and literary critic, and urged her editor at Scribner's not to mention Braithwaite's admiration for her work to a Southern reviewer because "all I could say in this part of my country would only pull the roof down on us both" (qtd. in Shannon 440–41).

8. Dargan was also an admirer of Smith's racially progressive camp for girls in Clayton, Georgia, and hoped to found a camp herself that would serve impoverished Appalachian youth. Her dream was realized in part when Don West, her young friend and fellow poet, founded the Appalachian South Folklife Center at Pipestem, West Virginia, in 1965. According to West, the summer program of this camp is still serving the young people of Appalachia (telephone interview, 23 February 1989).

9. " 'Now they're beginnin' to talk about a live-at-home cure. . . . Strange how some people, who think they're intelligent too, can go on believing they can team up the first age of man with the last and get anything out of it but tangle and trouble' " (345–46).

10. Perhaps the most striking description of the supposed disjuncture in the novel occurred in a review by Elmer Davis, who noted that *Call Home the Heart* "is, for the first half of its considerable length, one of the finest of American novels"; that it has "pity, passion, elevation, a long list of characters clearly and plausibly realized"; and that "carried along on the current," he "completely surrendered to the illusion." Davis deplored the effect produced by its second

half, however, and recalled that while reading it, he had found himself "absorbing a communist missionary sermon that lasts for eight solid pages" and feeling "as if the second act of 'Tristan' ha[d] been embellished with a long interpolation by a Salvation Army band" (662). Many of the critics who took this view also applauded the return to the mountains that occurs at the end of the story because they believed that it "redeemed [the novel] into art" (Cook 104).

11. In her examination of the Gastonia novels by women authors, Cook observes that their "repeated guarded attempts to discuss birth control, the open portrayal of the anguish of each pregnancy, and the grisly tales of amateur abortion efforts sometimes suggest that Margaret Sanger rather than Marx might have been the hero they sought" (99).

WORKS CITED

Ackerman, Kathy Cantley. "Feminist Affirmation in Appalachia: Fielding Burke's *Call Home the Heart.*" Humanity and Society 13, no. 2 (1989): 227–32.

"Call for an American Writers' Congress." Appendix. *New Masses: An Anthology of the Rebel Thirties.* Ed. Joseph North. New York: International Publishers, 1969. 313–15.

Cook, Sylvia Jenkins. *From Tobacco Road to Route 66: The Southern Poor White in Fiction.* Chapel Hill: University of North Carolina Press, 1976.

Dargan, Olive Tilford [Fielding Burke]. *Call Home the Heart.* 1932. Old Westbury, N.Y.: Feminist Press, 1983.

———. *A Stone Came Rolling.* New York: International, 1935.

Davis, Elmer. "The Red Peril." *Saturday Review of Literature* 16 Apr. 1932: 661–62.

Engels, Frederick. *The Origin of the Family, Private Property, and the State.* 1884. New York: Pathfinder Press, 1972.

Folsom, Michael, ed. *Mike Gold: A Literary Anthology.* New York: International Publishers, 1972.

Gilligan, Carol. *In a Different Voice: Psychological Theory and Women's Development.* Cambridge: Harvard University Press, 1982.

Gold, Michael. "Go Left, Young Writers!" *New Masses* Jan. 1929: 3–4. Rpt. in Folsom 186–89.

———. "Wilder: Prophet of the Genteel Christ." *New Republic* 22 Oct. 1930: 266–67. Rpt. in Folsom 197–202.

Hall, Jacquelyn Dowd. "Disorderly Women: Gender and Labor Militancy in the Appalachian South." *Journal of American History* 73 (1986): 354–82.

———. *Revolt Against Chivalry: Jessie Daniel Ames and the Women's Campaign Against Lynching.* New York: Columbia University Press, 1979.

Hochschild, Arlie. *The Second Shift: Inside the Two-Job Marriage.* New York: Viking Press, 1989.

Lorde, Audre. "The Master's Tools Will Never Dismantle the Master's House." In *Sister Outsider: Essays and Speeches.* Trumansburg, N.Y.: Crossing, 1984. 110–13.

Owsley, Frank Lawrence. "The Irrepressible Conflict." Twelve Southerners 61–91.

Rabinowitz, Paula. "Female Subjectivity in Women's Revolutionary Novels of the 1930s." Ph.d. diss., University of Michigan, 1986.

———. "Women and U.S. Literary Radicalism." In *Writing Red: An Anthology of American Women Writers, 1930–1940*. Ed. Charlotte Nekola and Paula Rabinowitz. New York: Feminist Press, 1987. 1–16.

Ransom, John Crowe. "Reconstructed but Unregenerate." Twelve Southerners 1–27.

Rideout, Walter B. *The Radical Novel in the United States, 1900–1954: Some Interrelations of Literature and Society.* Cambridge: Harvard University Press, 1956.

Schachner, E. A. "Revolutionary Literature in the United States Today." *Windsor Quarterly* 2 (1934): 27–64.

Shaffer, Robert. "Women and the Communist Party, USA, 1930–1940." *Socialist Review* 9, no. 3 (1979): 73–118.

Shannon, Anna W. Biographical Afterword to *Call Home the Heart*, by Olive Tilford Dargan. Old Westbury, N.Y.: Feminist Press, 1983. 433–46.

Twelve Southerners. *I'll Take My Stand: The South and the Agrarian Tradition.* 1930. Baton Rouge: Louisiana State University Press, 1977.

Urgo, Joseph R. "Proletarian Literature and Feminism: The Gastonia Novels and Feminist Protest." *Minnesota Review* n.s. 24 (1985): 64–84.

Jill Fritz-Piggott

The Dominant Chord and the Different Voice: The Sexes in Gordon's Stories

John Alvis calls it the "dominant chord" of Caroline Gordon's work (93), and Andrew Lytle remarks that "Miss Gordon rarely departs" from it. It is—in Lytle's terms—"the stress between the sexes" (8), and it is indeed a subject central to Gordon's *Collected Stories.* Three critics in particular—Alvis, Jane Gibson Brown, and Thomas Landess—have set the tone for consideration of the roles and relations of the sexes in Gordon's short fiction.[1]

Brown reads "The Captive," Gordon's long account of a woman's daring escape from a band of Indians, as a lesson in "the essential helplessness of women without men" (79). According to Brown, frontier woman Jinny Wiley falls victim to a brutal Indian attack primarily because she has refused her husband's protection. The band burns her home, murders her children, and holds her hostage. But, Brown argues, when Jinny wisely welcomes the "guidance" of a dead white boy who appears to her in a dream and recognizes him as her "only help," she is saved. She has learned that "she must remain true to the providential scheme of things" (83), what Brown calls the "basic order of nature," which acknowledges the "feminine need for protection" (78) and asserts the "masculine role" of the "guardianship of women" (79). Thus, Brown argues that the men "who hold [Jinny] captive and threaten her most severely teach her the most important lesson of her life": "an acceptance of her proper place in creation" (80).

In Brown's view of "The Captive," Gordon's tale reveals the "proper" and "providential" submission of the female to the male, a surrender essential for survival itself. In such a reading, woman is betrayed by her own will to power, her own refusal to accept her feminine, dependent role. Alvis agrees, writing that Gordon is "most concerned with the relative roles of man and woman, with that fundamental need of woman to find a source of strength in the man" (86). He points to "Tom Rivers" and "The Petrified Woman" as stories about failures in marriage based on failures to recognize and assume "appropriate" gender roles.

Tom Rivers's fiancee, Barbara, refuses to marry him unless he agrees to abstain from drinking. He chooses to leave. According to Alvis, Rivers's decision is "admirable" because it "appears to involve a recognition and affirmation of a condition of his manhood the denial of which would entail the negation of his proper sexual role" (95). In "The Petrified Woman" Tom Fayerlee's wife Eleanor ridicules her drunk husband and ignores his sexual demands. He can do little more than call her names. Alvis argues that Tom Fayerlee lacks Tom Rivers's "manhood and self-sovereignty" (97) and is "not capable of exercising the kind of masculine sovereignty which marriage requires of the husband and which the woman expects even though, as with Eleanor, she may dispute it" (95).

Hence, unlike Brown, who focuses on a female character's failure to conform to traditional gender roles, Alvis emphasizes Gordon's interest in the failure of both genders to embrace and embody the basic "demands" of sexuality that call men to be courageous, assertive, spirited, and sovereign and women to be "warmly sympathetic, spirited though modest, gentle, and single-minded in their devotion" (108). According to Alvis, "Miss Gordon seems to imply" that these qualities are not "simply those we naturally associate with the proper enactment of the masculine and feminine roles," but are instinctively taught by nature (109).

But, as Alvis immediately notes, "despite the accessibility of instructive norms which indicate the way to succeed, Miss Gordon's stories all depict the frustration of love and nature, and one must ask why they persistently do so." Alvis's answer is that "the timeless cause of love's frustration is connected in Miss Gordon's mind with the doctrine of original sin" (109). Brown also argues that sexual tension results from woman's willful rejection of her natural submission and resolves itself only through grace. Both critics suggest that Gordon considers personal and impersonal nature unnatural until it is redeemed by supernatural grace.

But there must be an answer to the question of the stress of the sexes closer to the action than original sin and more accessible to the reader than Gordon's mind. If we clear away extratextual terminology about gender and grace and return to the stories themselves, the most general fact about gender in Gordon's fiction is that the tales are told in different—that is, in male and female—voices. And, as Anne Boyle notes, for Gordon, "voice, rather than plot, is essential in fiction" (75). In *How To Read a Novel,* Gordon discusses voice or point of view as "the most difficult question that confronts a writer of fiction" (73), and she describes it in an appendix to *The House of Fiction* as "the primary secret of the art of fiction" (628).

Attention to Jinny's voice as the narrator of "The Captive" dramatically alters Brown's analysis. Jinny's painstaking attention to the everyday details of Indian life reveals her resourcefulness rather than any weakness. Her frank assessment of her situation—"I can't do nothing" (*Collected Stories* 196)—refers to her enforced passivity, not her natural ability. For the story to be understood, Jinny's voice must be heard. She is the teller of her own tale: both captive and captivator. Her speech attests to her survival; her style explains her escape. Throughout the story, Jinny notes details with precision; she emphasizes her task ahead, not her trouble behind; and she analyzes and assimilates the Indians' knowledge of nature. Her ever-present self-reliance is evident in her confident assessment of her strength and skill, in her increased wisdom and ability. Following the Indians carefully, Jinny masters the arts of campmaking—cooking, curing pelts, and smelting lead for bullets. After days of long labor, she lies awake, listening to the Indians describe their bearings. And from them, she learns how to cover her trail, stick close to waterways, and find her way through the woods. When the old chief offers her to a brave as a bride, she has provisions and plans in place for her escape. This is a story of survival, not a lesson in submission.

Brown argues that the entire text moves toward a moral. She believes Jinny's final statement, " 'Lord God . . . I was lucky to git away from them Indians!' " (209), "acknowledges her newfound humility and the wisdom of nature" because Jinny takes no credit for her escape and realizes it was all luck—"a kind of grace" (84). Actually, at the close of the story it seems quite clear that Jinny chooses guts over grace. When she and the old man from the fort find their raft splitting and the Indians "swarming down to the water," the man drops to his knees to pray. Jinny drops to her knees to pull the logs together. Then she grabs his pole: " 'Go on and pray, you old fool,' " she snaps. " 'I'm a-going to git across this river' " (209). And she does.

Indeed, Jinny's understatement—" 'I was lucky to git away' "—says less about her savior than it does about her style. Jinny doesn't need the bolster of boasts any more than Davy Crockett needs frills to fill out his tales. Gordon's decision to imitate Crockett was a conscious one: "and if you don't think that's hard," the writer confessed in a letter, "try it some time." The narrative is stripped of excess emotion and exaggeration. Jinny's "sensational escape"—the words are Gordon's—is left as statement enough of the character's strength (Waldron 98).

A female character also narrates "The Petrified Woman," but John Alvis reads the story as Jane Brown reads "The Captive," emphasizing what is said, rather than who says it. He argues that the action is "filtered through" a first-person consciousness "only to give it the added weight and significance of felt experience" (93). But by making "The Petrified Woman" young Sally Maury's story, Gordon draws our attention from Tom and Eleanor Fayerlee's strained marriage to Sally's growing awareness of her own sexuality.

Sally is attracted to Tom and to his interest in her. When he greets her at a family reunion, she thinks he is going to kiss her: "He is a man that you don't so much mind having him kiss you, even when he has whiskey on his breath" (*Collected Stories* 6). She notices that "He is not awfully old," and in a dream, she sees Tom waiting for her until she is able to approach him as an equal: "I saw Cousin Tom. He saw me too, and he stood still till I got to where he was and he said, 'Sally, this is Tom.' He didn't say Cousin Tom, just Tom. I was about to say something but somebody came in between us" (5).

Tom's wife comes between the two cousins, attracting and repelling the girl. Although Sally tells the story years after its events, she still remembers Eleanor's diamond cross and earrings and the sound her long white dress made sweeping across the porch. "I thought that she was the prettiest person ever lived," she recalls (4); "I always thought that [her eyes] were like violets" (14). But Sally also remembers Eleanor's thin, black dress with the bow that Eleanor "sort of dusted . . . off, though there wasn't a thing on it" (13). Thinking of Eleanor's darker, haughty side, Sally remembers the woman staring at her husband while he humiliated her in front of his family: "I looked at her and then I wished I hadn't. . . . It was like the violets were freezing, there in her eyes" (14).

Sally thinks Eleanor is the prettiest woman she has seen, but Eleanor's groom grants the honor to the "petrified woman" on display near the reunion site, whose veiled eyes opened in their presence and whose bared "bosom was moving up and down": "I don't know when I've seen a prettier woman . . . lies quiet, too" (10; Gordon's ellipsis). According to the carnival man's claim, the petrified woman was "Sweet Sixteen a Hundred Years Ago / And Sweet Sixteen Today" (10). Veronica Makowsky argues that "Tom would like a woman to be frozen at the age of romantic idealism, before disillusionment and criticism emerge" (*Biography* 183). Surely he likes her passivity, her submission, her veiled eyes, but bared breast. " 'Some women are just petrified in spots,' " he tells his family at dinner. " 'She was petrified all over. . . . She just lay there and looked sweet' " (*Collected Stories* 14). Tom rises from the table to search for the petrified woman, but he is brought down by his two sources of trouble with Eleanor: women and drink. He gets tangled in a cousin's skirt and ends sprawled on the floor, his wine glass shattered, his forehead bloody. The story ends with Sally's lasting images of the later-divorced couple. She always thinks of Eleanor in white at the window, "where, on moonlight nights, we used to sit, to watch the water glint on the rocks," but she remembers Tom "still lying there on the floor" (15).

Alvis begins by assuming that Tom and Eleanor's failure in marriage is based on their failure to fulfill natural gender roles. In such a reading, Tom lacks the authority Eleanor disputes but "expects" (Alvis 95). He is not adequately assertive and composed. But on her part, Eleanor is an "overly-demanding woman," who ought to be able to accept her husband's drinking, which Alvis considers in part a "natural expression of his manhood" (96). Although Alvis acknowledges that Tom "demonstrates his lack of manhood and self-sovereignty" at dinner, he argues that Eleanor's response (her freezing, frozen stare) "is even more startling in its unnaturalness" (97). And although Alvis admits that "Tom's ineffectualness in the performance of his masculine duties" may have caused or aggravated Eleanor's estrangement, he finds Eleanor's "total lack of the most rudimentary of the feminine qualities, simple warmth or sympathy, . . . a more radical perversion of the natural sexual order" (98).

Alvis hopes that Sally learns from Eleanor's negative example, particularly since Sally "demonstrates the germ of similar propensities in the earlier stories which deal with her disinclination to accept womanhood." But Alvis cannot find evidence in "The Petrified Woman" that "Sally realizes the salutary lesson which is there to be learned" (98). Actually, Sally's attention is drawn to the ways traditional gender roles can isolate individuals. Tom (literally, it seems) embraces the petrified woman who remains passive and self-prostituting. And he rejects Eleanor, who cannot—will not—stay still. For Sally, this once romantic character becomes a mere caricature, collapsed on the dining room floor with a drink in his hand and blood on his face. And in Sally's mind, Eleanor stands forever fixed at the window, searching for romance, but never finding it.

In this reading, the story suggests that sexual stereotypes petrify women and men, fix and freeze them in ridiculous roles: the hard-drinking man, demanding and purchasing female passivity; the white-robed romantic woman on the porch or at the window; the bitch in black. Perhaps the "real" petrified woman is the story's teller, the quickly maturing Sally Maury, who is frightened by the lessons she learns on her way.[2]

A male character narrates "Tom Rivers," and two male critics share the narrator's attitude toward Tom, the story's central subject. Like Tom's cousin Lew, critic Thomas Landess emphasizes Tom's "assertive manhood," his "masculine integrity," and his "pride" in the "purity" of his manhood (57, 61, 59). These qualities lead Tom to leave home when his girl makes what the critic Andrew Lytle considers "an impossible demand" on him: she makes their wedding contingent on Tom's promise that he will never drink again (8). "She is asking him to surrender his sovereignty," Lytle writes, something Tom will not do (8). He rejects this "overly-demanding woman" (Alvis uses the term to describe both Tom Fayerlee's wife and Tom Rivers's fiancee, 96) and enters what Lytle calls a "masculine world of horses and whores" where Tom must wander, but may retain his "integrity" (9). Critics and narrator approve of Tom's decision. Tom is a "dispossessed aristocrat," according to Lytle (9), a "heroic sacrificial figure," according to Landess (57), and an "utterly fearless" "hero" in Lew's eyes (*Collected Stories* 29, 33).

But Landess argues that masculine integrity is not the "true subject" of the story. Tom refuses to submit to a woman's wishes; he confronts and conquers other men—the armed and angry poker player in the saloon, the band of "twenty or thirty" night riders in the cotton fields (40). But he willingly renounces his comfort and stability for the cousin he barely knows. Landess believes Lew embodies the "social order Tom has publicly abandoned and yet privately continues to cherish" (60). Tom shows signs of attachment to his family and home: he reminisces about Kentucky, he names his horse after the woman he left behind, and he "immediately recognizes in [a] man's features a kinship" to a family from his home county (59). His only remaining connection is his cousin Lew, and he chooses "to sacrifice the glory of [his] manhood and the status and security it has bought him to reaffirm an ultimate commitment to family" (61).

Whatever his reasons, Tom goes out to the cotton fields to protect Lew, who has drunkenly boasted that he can pick the crop despite the interference of night riders. The gang attacks, and Tom shoots one of the men in the arm. When the shooting is traced to Tom, the sheriff asks him to leave town. Landess argues that resisting the sheriff's order would be the more honorable, "more practical and convenient choice" because Tom is established in town and has supporters (60). But the sheriff has deputized Lew to arrest his cousin if he resists the order.

Hence, "in order to remain Tom would have to confront his own kinsman and those values he most respects." He leaves town immediately, barely saying a word. Because Tom acts on his "ultimate commitment to family" (61), Landess suggests the story "both contains the image of Tom's assertive manhood and effectively transcends it" (57).

Clearly, although Tom feels connected, he cannot make connections. Although he is proud of his relations, he cannot relate. If Landess is right and Tom achieves the "highest level" of being offered by the story—submission of self to family—why does he go off on his own? If Tom is ultimately committed to his kin, why does he never contact his fiancee, his family, or his cousin Lew again? Landess finds a "clear hierarchy" in the story: "desire for a woman" gives way to personal integrity which gives way to broader social ties (61). But he forgets that this is Lew's hierarchy, that these values are Lew's values. Lew prefers autonomy to adaptability. He considers a man who sacrifices for a man a hero, a man who sacrifices for a woman a coward.

Cousin Emily brings a different picture of Tom into the tale. She and Lew sit under the tree at the "old place" and swap family stories years after Tom had walked out of Lew's life (*Collected Stories* 24). Emily remembers a photograph taken of Tom at seven with "his hair roached on the top of his head." The photo had shamed Tom because it pictured him "so young." Lew imagines an "infantile" Tom wearing kilts, in the fashion of the day. But this girlish Tom, who wears skirts and rolled hair, seems to die like the "pretty little gal" in the song Tom sang both as a boy and a young man (26). Lew will not let this image live.

Yet once suggested, this version of Tom cannot be repressed, and it struggles to resurface during one of the story's most stereotypically masculine scenes. When Tom confronts the angry gambler in the bar, Lew notices that Tom's eyes look "as if they might spill over and run down his face." But Lew sees Tom's eyes "glittering," not crying; he associates the tears with "excitement," not fear. And moments later, when Tom takes a gun from the gambler's hand, Lew remembers a "ludicrous precision about the movement, a finickiness as of a lady being careful to hand a spoon to a guest, handle first" (32). Lew cannot accept a feminized image of his cousin; Tom's precision is "ludicrous" and finicky precisely because it strikes Lew as ladylike. As the story progresses and Lew takes on the drinking, boasting, and swaggering role of the "hero's friend" (33), he increasingly defines the hero by masculine stereotypes. In the end, Lew becomes "officially" responsible for Tom's image. He is "deputized" to offer Tom one choice only: to be jailed as a man who took justice into his own hands and risked liberty for male kin, or to ride free as the wanderer whose integrity isolates him from community and home. Jailed or freed, Tom remains bound by these typically masculine roles.

As the years go by, Lew often wonders why Tom left, "how it was that he disappeared, leaving nowhere any trace of his going" (25). Lew never considers that Tom may have left no trace because—out of flaw or fear—he followed so perfectly the tracks that Lew laid for him. And Lew never considers the possibility that Tom may have left to escape the life Lew had planned. Indeed, Lew started creating the myth of "Tom Rivers" when he first laid eyes on his cousin. Lew remembers himself as a boy, but Tom as a man at that meeting—despite the fact that Tom is only four or five years his senior. He considered Tom "the man" he was "looking for" and fixed an image of Tom in his mind: "I can see him always walking on his bandy legs across that lawn toward the waiting boy. And in the distance the strawberry mare, Winnie" (28). He saw Tom that day between his horse (the freedom of the individual) and himself, a cousin (the responsibility of family). The myth Lew uses to mold the story allows Tom to be both the father of the boy and the self-sovereign wanderer who has no home.

Lew's account of Tom takes shape under the shade of the family tree. Sitting there, Lew notices that the "light falls under and through the boughs to strike always in the same pattern" (25). Lew reproduces this dominant pattern in his version of Tom's life. But the pattern conceals as much as it reveals. The shadows cast by the tree "fall across" Emily's white skirt like black text on a white page. She produces her own version of Tom. Her shadow-text produces a more vulnerable and personal portrait of Tom, showing Lew a side of his cousin that he "never knew before" (26).

Perhaps this "minute, interlacing" of shadow with shadow (26) sheds light on the problem that concerns Lew from the opening of the story: "I have never been able to understand it though I think about it a great deal" (24). "It" may well be more than Tom's departure from town; it may once again be the identity and relations of the sexes. Attention to the narrator's gender reveals a story that is about a boy's creation of a male hero, not about heroism itself. Thus, Tom's actions and qualities are not to be abstracted from the story as explicit statements about proper gender roles. They are the qualities and actions that one man questions and remembers as he continues to consider what it means to be a person, a family member, a man.

Indeed, Gordon's sense of the variations between male and female narrative voices is strikingly similar to Carol Gilligan's conclusions concerning the different ways in which women and men define themselves. In her work on developmental psychology and moral choice, *In a*

Different Voice, Gilligan shows that "male and female voices typically speak of the importance of different truths, the former of the role of separation as it defines and empowers the self, the latter of the ongoing process of attachment that creates and sustains the human community" (156). Hence, readings that attempt to be accurate explorations of character demand attention to the gender of a story's speaker or central consciousness.[3]

In an early essay on Gordon's fiction, Louise Cowan argues that Gordon's men must choose between "perpetual flight" (17) and "withdrawal" (23), while her women "fall over the precipice into utter destruction" or join the "women on the porch" (16) for whom life "has stopped" (15). Frozen, fallen, or in flight, both sexes find only one other option in Gordon's fiction, according to Cowan: the "utter self-immolation" which all ought to practice to "prepare . . . the ground into which the gratuitous gift of grace can enter" (26).

The predominance of individual perspectives and single voices in Gordon's stories, at least, presents self-expression as an alternative to "utter self-immolation." Over half of Gordon's collected stories are told from an individual's point of view (seven from a man's perspective, six from a woman's).[4] In each of these stories, the individual—male or female—confronts a force (family or nature) as the other against which the self is defined. These self-definitions differ, and these responses remain descriptive, not prescriptive. As almost all her critics conclude, Gordon stresses not the attainment, but the difficulty of union or unity. In *The Collected Stories,* we hear not the choir or the harmony, but the single voices—the male and female, different voices—who speak to the reader on their own.

NOTES

1. All citations to Gordon's fiction are to *The Collected Stories.* A survey of Gordon criticism reveals a firm consensus regarding the hierarchy of traditional gender roles in Gordon's short fiction. For example, see Thomas D. Young, "Religion and Literature"; Howard Baker, "From the Top of the Tree"; Robert H. Brinkmeyer, Jr., "New Caroline Gordon Books"; and Ashley Brown, "Caroline Gordon's Short Fiction."

2. See Veronica Makowsky, who also argues that Sally is petrified (*Biography,* 183) and who posits (as Gordon's biographer) that the writer herself was "a 'petrified' woman in both senses of the word" ("Women's Writing" 48).

3. Two scholars—Anne Boyle and Makowsky—have recently turned their attention to this issue. Boyle looks at Gordon's later novels and exposes in *Green Centuries* and *The Women on the Porch* a "pattern in which the polyphonic or many-voiced story gives way to the monologic utterance of a single, male

protagonist" (79). In Gordon's final two novels—*The Strange Children* and *The Malefactors*—Boyle finds female characters increasingly mute and argues that "Gordon seems to endorse feminine passivity and silence as she allows the male to assume voice and power" (82). Because the stories in which women speak were all published before the appearance of *The Strange Children* in 1951, we may conclude with Boyle that "in Caroline Gordon's fiction, as we witness this artist's progression toward a traditional religious faith and her adoption of conservative family values, we also witness the gradual disappearance or devaluation of the female voice" (85). Makowsky, Gordon's most recent biographer, believes that Gordon devalued her own voice "because of the way she internalized her culture's attitudes toward women and writing, both in her life and in her work" ("Women's Writing," 43).

4. The seven stories written in male first person or with a male central consciousness are: "The Burning Eyes," "Tom Rivers," "Old Red," "One More Time," "To Thy Chamber Window, Sweet," "The Last Day in the Field," and "The Presence." The six stories written in female first person or with a female central consciousness are: "The Petrified Woman," "One Against Thebes," "Hear the Nightingale Sing," "The Captive," "All Lovers Love the Spring," and "The Waterfall."

WORKS CITED

Alvis, John E. "The Idea of Nature and the Sexual Role in Caroline Gordon's Early Stories of Love." Landess, *Short Fiction of Caroline Gordon* 85–111.

Baker, Howard. "From the Top of the Tree." *The Southern Review* 18, no. 2 (1982): 427–41.

Boyle, Anne. "The Promise of Polyphony, the Monotony of Monologue: Voice and Silence in Caroline Gordon's Later Novels." *The Southern Quarterly* 28 (Spring 1990): 71–87.

Brinkmeyer, Robert H., Jr. "New Caroline Gordon Books." *Southern Literary Journal* 14, no. 2 (1982): 62–68.

Brown, Ashley. "Caroline Gordon's Short Fiction." *Sewanee Review* 81 (1973): 365–70.

Brown, Jane Gibson. "Women in Nature: A Study of Caroline Gordon's 'The Captive.'" Landess, *Short Fiction of Caroline Gordon* 75–85.

Cowan, Louise. "Nature and Grace in Caroline Gordon." *Critique* 1 (Winter 1956): 11–27.

Gilligan, Carol. *In a Different Voice.* Cambridge, Mass.: Harvard University Press, 1982.

Gordon, Caroline. *The Collected Stories of Caroline Gordon.* New York: Farrar, Straus, Giroux, 1981.

———. *How to Read a Novel.* New York: Viking Press, 1964.

Gordon, Caroline, and Allen Tate. *The House of Fiction,* New York: Charles Scribner's Sons, 1950.

Landess, Thomas H. "Caroline Gordon's Ontological Stories." Landess, *Short Fiction of Caroline Gordon* 53–73.

————, ed. *Short Fiction of Caroline Gordon.* Dallas: University of Dallas Press, 1972.

Lytle, Andrew. "The Forest of the South." *Critique* 1 (Winter 1956): 3–9.

Makowsky, Veronica A. *Caroline Gordon: A Biography.* New York: Oxford University Press, 1989.

————. "Caroline Gordon on Women's Writing: A Contradiction in Terms?" *The Southern Quarterly* 28 (Spring 1990): 43–52.

Rubin, Larry. "Christian Allegory in Caroline Gordon's 'The Captive.' " *Studies in Short Fiction* 5 (Spring 1968): 283–89.

Waldron, Ann. *Close Connections: Caroline Gordon and the Southern Renaissance.* New York: G.P. Putnam's Sons, 1987.

Young, Thomas D. "Religion and Literature." *Mississippi Quarterly* 39, no. 2 (1986): 126–32.

Lisa Nanney

Zelda Fitzgerald's *Save Me the Waltz* as Southern Novel and *Künstlerroman*

"Atrocious," "aimless," "annoying"; or "carefully balanced," "fascinating," and "brilliant": these wildly divergent reviews suggest the critical controversy Zelda Sayre Fitzgerald's one novel in print has generated since its publication in 1932.[1] Its earliest critics primarily dismissed it—"shallow" and "unreal," the *Charlotte News's* 1932 reviewer asserted (Morrison 6). Upon its re-release in 1967, the faint praise it garnered was in effect equally as dismissive: "a literary curio," Harry T. Moore called the novel (vii), echoing Matthew Bruccoli's assertion that it was "readable" and, in fact, valuable "because anything that illuminates the career of F. Scott Fitzgerald is worth reading" ("Afterword" 206). The 1970s, however, saw the novel's reputation swing to the other extreme, when, unlike the biographical critics who had judged the author and her book solely in comparison to her husband and his work, a new set of critics evaluated the artist and the artistry in light of new insights about the canon. Feminist critics extolled the novel as brilliant, comparing the work to T. S. Eliot's *The Wasteland* in its ability to portray accurately twentieth-century despair and anonymity and to Charlotte Perkins Gilman's "The Yellow Wallpaper" for its pioneering feminist spirit (Wagner 206). Ironically, many of these critics still regarded Fitzgerald relationally—emphasizing her writing as a valiant reaction *against* her circumstances and her husband. None, of course, limited the parameters of his or her appraisal to the criteria Fitzgerald's husband, F. Scott Fitzgerald, applied to it when, protesting its publication, he labeled it "a bad book" (Buttitta 123). That remark resonates with the first controversy the book engendered, a conflict over whether Fitzgerald had the right to employ material in her writing that her husband regarded as his artistic territory—their life together—and a conflict that cast Zelda Fitzgerald inexorably in the role of the artist's *wife, not* the artist.

Obviously, *Save Me the Waltz* has been defined in many different ways by different people. Like its creator, like its protagonist, the novel has been cast in varying roles during its lifetime depending on the biases its readers have brought to it. In fact, the distortion, damage, and limitation resulting from the imposition of roles create the central problem within the text as well as the central problem historically attendant upon *evaluating* the text. Having pointed out the limiting roles critics have already assigned the novel—as associational curiosity, biographical background, feminist tract, wifely insurrection—and at the risk of falling into the same critical fallacy, I want to propose two new roles for *Save Me the Waltz*. The conjunction of these new definitions—of the novel as a Southern novel and as a *Künstlerroman*—can lead to a reading of the text that transcends any role, however, a transcendence both its protagonist and its creator devoutly wished. This analogy—among novel, character, and artist—that seems to arise persistently in critics'—and my—consideration of the work hints at the form in which the transcendence occurs, for in the inseparability of the text, its style and content, and its creator lies a paradigm of the *problem* of female creativity.

Although many of the critics—especially female critics—who have commented on *Save Me the Waltz* have accurately noted that the novel's conflict emanates from its protagonist's indoctrination into traditional female roles during the girl's upbringing in the turn-of-the-century deep South, none has taken what seems the next logical step in tying theme to structure: examining the novel as a Southern novel. Applying the very simplest definition of that genre—any novel produced by a writer "who was born and lived his formative years" (Bradbury 4) within the South—qualifies *Save Me the Waltz* easily; probably one of the best-known pieces of Fitzgerald lore is the story of how the young officer F. Scott Fitzgerald, stationed in 1918 in Montgomery, Alabama, fell in love at a country club dance with the belle of Montgomery, Zelda Sayre, daughter of a prominent judge. Less well-known is the plot of *Save Me the Waltz*, in which Zelda Fitzgerald transformed that Southern girlhood and her subsequent marriage to the ambitious young officer into autobiographical fiction. Her protagonist, Alabama Beggs, is shaped by her Southern girlhood into conventional roles reinforced by her marriage to David Knight, whom she, too, meets at a country club dance. David's career as a painter catapults Alabama into jazz-age New York and Parisian society but so dominates their life together that Alabama, hoping to forge an identity distinct from David's, embarks belatedly on a career in ballet. Finally winning a solo debut with a corps in Naples, Alabama first refuses the role out of deference to David's career and their daughter's needs, but ultimately reconsiders, against her husband's wishes. Alone in Naples, Alabama drives herself and succeeds; but almost immediately, an infected foot and the accompanying high fever require her hospitalization and result in surgery. Her foot is permanently damaged; she will never be able to dance again; and, equally sobering, she receives word that her father is dying. She returns to America's South to stand vigil with her mother and sisters at his deathbed and to try to come to terms with the traditions he represents. The novel's ending in the South, where the story and the conflict that propels it began, insures a poignant sense of unity in its structure and the protagonist's life.

By virtue of its author's origins and the structural significance of its Southern setting, then, *Save Me the Waltz* is a Southern novel in obvious ways; but in less obvious and perhaps more important ways as well, the novel embodies what Robert B. Heilman, in "The Southern Temper," defines as the distinguishing "temper" of Southern literature: "the coincidence of a sense of the concrete, a sense of the elemental, a sense of the ornamental, a sense of the representative, and a sense of totality" (3). Fitzgerald's sometimes overwritten concrete images of the natural world, of violence and entropy and decay, encompass all these senses; through the novel's imagery Fitzgerald conveys the archaic, moribund quality of the patriarchal traditions indoctrinating the protagonist during her Southern girlhood and suggests the corrosive, wounding effects of these traditions on her as her role indoctrination conflicts with her quest for identity.

In the novel's first half, Fitzgerald's imagery evokes the environment that molds Alabama into the gender roles it prescribes, an environment already defeated and past its time but still powerful in its ability to inculcate behavior. As early as the novel's fifth page, Fitzgerald identifies the girl's development with growth in nature—flowers, gardens, untamed weeds. "Incubated in the mystic pungence of Negro mammies" (17), the child Alabama is "already contemptuous of ordered planting" (19), Fitzgerald notes, establishing early on the girl's instinctive rebellion against internalized patterns of behavior that will undermine her attempt to establish her own identity and define herself by her creative efforts. As a girl, Alabama believes not in the efficacy of her own efforts but "in the possibility of a wizard cultivator to bring forth sweet-smelling blossoms from the hardest of rocks, and night-blooming vines from barren wastes" (19). She "wants to be told what she is like, being too young to know she is like nothing at all" (17). The girl does discover, when she reaches adolescence, that "all the old responses"—such as blushing at a beau's compliment—"were her proper heritage" (31), and she begins to define herself by these suitors' attentions just as she had previously defined herself in terms of her father. Alabama realizes "the necessity of being something that you really weren't was the same" (31) with a suitor as with one's father.

It is, in fact, Alabama's father who represents and imposes on the family the order in which the girl, lacking any image of herself, finds a comfortable identity. Fitzgerald associates the Judge primarily with inorganic images—impregnable structures such as castles and keeps— suggesting the stultifying nature of his influence on the girl. Fitzgerald calls the Judge "a living fortress" whose "towers . . . of intellectual conceptions" leave "no sloping path near his castle open" (15); she thus associates him with the old feudal order of the South, which he dog- gedly tries to preserve, shielding his family from the world that is invading and changing the South. His old-fashioned concept of family, his insistence on reigning as "lord of the living cycle" for his family, robs them of their ability "to meet the changing exigencies of their times" (15); the result, Fitzgerald continues, foreshadowing her pro- tagonist's fate, is that they are "crippled, . . . [clinging] long to the feudal donjons of their fathers" (15). Their home "[hangs] pendent on his will" (21), Alabama realizes, and accepts the correctness of his dominant will as unquestioningly as she accepts the male domination implicit in the anachronistic old order the Judge represents and defends.

Alabama regards her mother "as she [is], part of a masculine tradition" (193), perceiving her entirely in relation to the Judge, much as critics regarded Fitzgerald's work in relation to her husband's. But where the Judge is structure and accepted order, the mother, Millie, is all feminine adaptiveness to that male-imposed structure. Fitzgerald signals Millie's difference from the Judge by associating her with images of the natural Southern world in chaotic abundance, poised on the brink of overripeness; this imagery, associated with Alabama herself, establishes a pattern that foreshadows Alabama's ultimate recognition of her "otherness" from her husband when she articulates her creative dilemma in dis- tinctly nonlinear, nonmasculine patterns. From Millie, Alabama and her sisters learn unquestioningly "the attributes of femininity, seeking respite in their mother . . . as they would have haunted a shady protec- tive grove to escape a blinding glare" (17). As a child, Alabama "presses against her mother in an effort to realize some proper relationship" (17) as they sit on their front porch, amid the shadows of the Southern night that Fitzgerald describes as being "like heavy impregnated mops soaking [the night's] oblivion back to the black heat whence it evolved" under the "melancholic moonvines . . . over the string trellises" (17). From her mother's example, Alabama learns the necessity of "feminine tolerance," sees that the woman is "a less closely knit thread in the pattern" of life than the man, and internalizes the method her mother suggests of circumventing rather than confronting male dominance to get her way: " 'Why do you bother your father?' " Millie asks; " 'You could make your arrangements outside' " (22).

The Judge, Millie, and Alabama's older sisters all provide role models for this youngest daughter who, in her childhood, finds her identity in the family structure. So strongly does she identify herself in terms of her family that when she recognizes family characteristics in herself, it is "like finding she [has] all five toes when up to the present she had been able to count only four. It was nice to have indications about yourself to go on" (29–30). As the image suggests, without her identity in the family structure, she would feel abnormal somehow, an indication of the power this externally-imposed self-image will have over her as she later tries to free herself of it. Alabama's whimsical analogy between her feeling of normalcy within the family and finding all her toes present also anticipates, with sinister overtones, her later, pervasive sense of abnormality for having given career precedence over family after her damaged foot actually does cripple her, ruining her career in ballet.

By her seventeenth summer, however, Alabama begins to perceive dimly "the sense of suffocation . . . eclipsing her family" (38), a sense conveyed in this first section of the novel by images of decay and stagnation. She complains to her father that she is tired of " 'sitting on the porch and having dates and watching things rot' " (40). Her restlessness coupled with her "strong sense of her own insignificance" (40) create in her an unsettling desire to escape. The imagery of decay intensifies, reflecting the enervating effect of the South's culture on the protagonist, who feels "her life's slipping by while June bugs covered the moist fruit in the fig trees with the motionless activity of clustering flies upon an open sore" (40).

Thus the young blond Midwestern lieutenant David Knight, who courts Alabama while stationed in her town, seems to represent to her a way to escape this suffocation, seems to represent a more vital society. But in spite of the romantic hyperbole infusing the images describing him, those images hint that in David, Alabama has perhaps unconsciously chosen a man who will exert the same kind of influence over her as her father does: Fitzgerald describes David in terms of structures and order, as she described the Judge. David's blond hair, for instance, lies over his forehead "in Cellinian frescoes and fashionable porticoes" (44). Alabama may imagine that David is a kind of rescuing "knight in shining armor," as his very name suggests, but that name connects him inexorably to the imagery of feudal enclosures that characterizes Alabama's father. David intends flattery when he writes to her, "My dear, you are my princess and I'd like to keep you shut forever in an ivory tower for my private delectation" (48). Both he and the Judge impose roles on Alabama that restrict her development and precipitate the crisis that undermines her creative efforts.

This creative quest, the focus of the novel's second half, provides another way of defining *Save Me the Waltz*—as a *Künstlerroman*. Certainly, placing the novel in this context, reading it as a work concerned with a female artist's development, yields a more contemporary perspective on it than does viewing it as the product of early twentieth-century Southern culture. But this latter critical perspective seems in fact a necessary precondition to understanding *Save Me the Waltz* as a *Künstlerroman*, because it is the South's role expectations of women, inculcated through the family structure, that determine the outcome of Alabama's creative quest; and further, it is Fitzgerald's imagery of the Southern natural world as overripe, past its time, and decaying that sets the tone and the pattern for the imagery conveying the struggle and, finally, the outcome of Alabama's attempt to be a dancer.

The alternatives available to female protagonists in *Künstlerromane*, as in *Bildungsromane* and in romance plots in general, are determined— or, more accurately, limited—by the culture that produces the narrative, as critics such as Rachel Blau du Plessis and Susan Gubar have written. Traditionally, the female protagonist confronted a choice between "romance"—love, marriage, domesticity—and "quest"—education, achievement, or creation in the world at large (du Plessis, *Writing Beyond the Ending* 3–4). Nineteenth-century authors of fiction concerning women made sure that the two options were mutually exclusive, impossible to integrate, and, in fact, that if a woman opted for the quest, she often paid with her life. Twentieth-century women writers have sought to create new options for female protagonists, options that transcend the nineteenth century's cultural strictures and offer the possibility of romance and quest. To expand the woman character's set of choices, modern women writers have identified or developed nontraditional narrative "acts," in du Plessis's terms, "writing beyond the ending" (4) of the traditional romance.

Fitzgerald's *Künstlerroman* plainly deals in nineteenth-century cultural values, the values that determine the roles Alabama internalizes. Yet the novel was published in 1932, by a woman who had lived in America and in France in the 1920s among some of the foremost innovators of modernist art. Some critics have even called *Save Me the Waltz* a strongly modernist novel on the strength of its structure (Wagner 203). But, again conversely, the novel's structure depends on the continuity and intensification of the imagery of flowering and decay, imagery inexorably rooted in the turn-of-the-century South. And the novel's resolution—the crippling surgery that ends Alabama's career, and the Knights' return to the South to live when Alabama's father dies—seems a denial of Alabama's quest typical of nineteenth-century fiction. Most feminist critics of the novel have regarded the forced termination of Alabama's dancing as a negation of the identity she has established via that art. Likewise, Fitzgerald's husband's insistent editing of and control over her effort to publish *Save Me the Waltz* undermined the identity Fitzgerald had defined for herself by producing this book despite tremendous obstacles. Once again, the analogy among author, character, and work seems natural in evaluating the degree of success—or lack of it—all three found in establishing autonomous identities.

But what if, given that analogy, a truly independent, separate identity for all three—and, thus, success in the quest—lies not in socially, professionally quantifiable terms, but in a more subtle, intrinsic, permanent sphere: the discovery of an individual voice capable of conveying the self? Returning to the text's central unifying strategy, its image patterns, and discovering how that imagery changes in the novel's second half, as Alabama struggles to establish her own identity through her profession, may lead to a revelation about the nature of the means of artistic self-expression Fitzgerald's protagonist finds.

The imagery accompanying David's courtship of Alabama, for instance, suggests even *before* their marriage the danger of Alabama's loss of identity in David, prefiguring the violent natural imagery that conveys her later struggle. Once Alabama and David become engaged, spring arrives, "shatter[ing] its opalescent orioles in wreaths of daffodils" (47); summer follows, "flood[ing] the South with sweat," "tangles of goldenrod shred[ding] the sun" (48). The first three years of their marriage bear out the foreboding of this imagery: as nature in entropy falls into decay and destruction, so the Knights' marriage disintegrates, and, along with it, Alabama's sense of herself. Finally, living amid David's artist friends in Paris, she realizes that the roles she has internalized as daughter and belle and wife offer no substantial purpose. She rejects also the stereotypes their avant-garde circle seems to expect of her, declaring that she wants neither to "sleep with the men or imitate the women" (118). David's friends, cosmopolitan as they are, find her behavior "peculiar" (114). But when Alabama proposes a career in ballet, they condescendingly agree that "an art would explain" (114) her quaint insistence on a meaningful life.

Once Alabama determines to forge a meaningful life, the imagery conveying her "impressions" (118) almost immediately attains a sinister quality. Her efforts to succeed are associated with disease, mutilation, and death. For instance, a paragraph of setting preceding Alabama's first lesson with a famous Russian ballerina describes "the typhus-laden waters of the Seine," the "people with tuberculosis wait[ing] in the damp bowels of the earth for the Metro," and the "pulse [of life]" in Alabama "like the throbbing of an amputated leg" (118), a premonitory simile. One of Fitzgerald's most perceptive and recent critics, Elizabeth Robertson, notes that these images and especially the images of flowers associated with Alabama's career, extending the pattern established in the novel's first half, suggest "the frightening aspects of artistic endeavor" (134). To her Russian ballet instructor, for instance, Alabama brings gifts of "pink tulips like moulded confectioner's frosting, . . . malignant parrot tulips . . . with their jagged barbs, ... [and] threatening sprays of gladioli" (136–37). But Robertson finds the "negative aspects of art raised here . . . in conflict with the temporal structure of the book" as established by the imagery because "at this stage Alabama has nothing but hope about her career" (134). However, what Robertson perceives as a schism between structure and intention in the novel—and as a flaw—is actually further indication of the paradigmatic quality of Alabama's—and Fitzgerald's—struggle for artistic identity. For the very anxieties about creativity that produce this seeming disjunction between style and meaning, anxieties rooted in role indoctrination expressed by image patterns, determine the form the work of art will assume and emerge in the creation of a new narrative strategy to express the new identity, a "writing beyond the ending."

Given the role indoctrination whose effect Fitzgerald conveys through her image patterns, Alabama could hardly escape anxiety about her quest. Even in the early twentieth century, the South in many ways still clung to its antebellum identity. In the nineteenth-century culture that provides the basis for the values Alabama's family and husband impose on her, such a quest could only end in death or repression for the fictional heroine of the *Künstlerroman*. Indeed, the progress of Alabama's struggle for artistic identity as Fitzgerald creates it provides a paradigm of the problems the woman artist confronts in her quest, anticipating by almost half a century Sandra Gilbert and Susan Gubar's definitions of that paradigm in such works as their 1979 *The Madwoman in the Attic* and Gubar's 1981 " 'The Blank Page' and the Issues of Female Creativity."

The syndrome begins, as Gubar writes, when the woman receives through her socialization and her close relationships an image of herself "as text and artifact" (295). Certainly, we have seen that Alabama is an artifact of Southern culture. Her husband regards her as his own creation, his "aesthetic theory" (56), as he reminds her. Then, feeling "her lack of accomplishment" (Fitzgerald 108) and having no sense of autonomy, Alabama makes the second paradigmatic step toward realizing her creativity: she finds a medium of expression. Like many ambitious women historically, like the royal princesses in Isak Dinesen's story, Alabama has few options in this area; consequently, as Gubar defines the paradigmatic pattern, Alabama experiences her own body "as the only available medium" (Gubar 296) for her art. As she considers beginning a career in ballet, she thinks of her firm body as being "like a quill" (121) and "like a lighthouse" (115), both images involving methods of communicating. She wants her body to be "a channel through which [her emotions] might flow" (Fitzgerald 124) and emerge. Because her body serves as her artistic medium, "the distance between the woman artist and her art is . . . radically diminished" (296), as Gubar points out. She becomes her own text, her body her instrument of expression; likewise, the autobiographical nature of Fitzgerald's chosen instrument anticipates Gubar's observation that women writers' "attraction . . . to personal forms of expression like letters, autobiographies, . . . and journals points up the effect of a life expressed as an art or an art experienced as a kind of life" (299).

But when Alabama finally achieves an autonomous artistic identity, given her role indoctrination it seems that she *must* self-destruct. What happens, of course, is that an infected foot lands Alabama in a hospital in Naples, feverish and delirious, her creativity as a dancer ended. But, in fact, in Gubar's terms, "the creation of female art *feels* like the destruction of the female body" (302), since for many women such creativity begins as a reaction against the identities, the selves, that men have constructed for them. Whether the male constructs the woman as a literary text or a sexual object, that construction must necessarily penetrate the boundaries of "the [woman's] passive self" (Gubar 302). In many women's stories of creativity, the very physical evidence of actual physical violation—blood—is also, as Gubar reminds us, an accurate metaphor for the "issue"—creativity—that verifies the existence of a woman's life. Alabama's infection, harming her body and career inseparably, necessitates the cutting of tendons so that, it appears, her artistic identity is irreparably destroyed: she can no longer dance. But when the body is cut, it bleeds, producing an issue—and even though Alabama can no longer create as a dancer, Fitzgerald's text suggests that the true "issue" or product of Alabama's "wounding" is another means of expression: her own voice.

Once Alabama is crippled, Fitzgerald finds that the only way for her to express accurately this new Alabama is to dislocate language, dissociating signifier from signified to create a voice for the "other" that Alabama now knows she is. In Shoshana Felman's terms, Fitzgerald " 're-invent[s]' language" (10). As an autonomous being, finally "wounded" into art, Alabama must "relearn how to speak . . . to establish a discourse . . . no longer defined by . . . masculine meaning" (Felman 10).

Alabama's "re-invention" of language begins, significantly, after the incision and when David arrives at her bedside. Her discovery of her own identity is still associated with images of mutilation and illness that seem punitive. But this very illness, a fever that seems almost like a descent into madness, releases her into the realm of her imagination, almost as if the illness is the price she must pay for her own voice. Suddenly, her imaginative world seems far more real to her than does her doctor or her now-attentive husband. Because she has defied the role expectations of her Southern upbringing and her traditional marriage, it is not surprising that she now feels she cannot make herself understood to the men who now attend her illness. They seem "of a different world" with a different "tempo" (187) than the one she danced to. They cannot "hear what she [is] saying" (185) now that she tries to express her own identity rather than the one her patriarchal culture has prescribed for her.

Moreover, the narrative pattern of her ideas is now distinctly different from the traditional linear conception of language that shapes the dominant forms of speech and of canonical writing in patriarchal culture. She breaks with these traditional uses of language, "break[s] the sentence," thus rejecting the "structuring of the female voice by the male voice" (du Plessis, "Breaking" 474). Words now take their own life, abandoning conventional meaning in a passage such as this: "The word 'sick' effaced itself against the poisonous air and jittered lamely about between the tips of the island" (187). The word "turned and twisted about the narrow ribbon of the highway" bisecting this new world, "gouging at her eyeballs with the prongs of its letters" (187). This new linguistic territory is a kind of "no man's land," which constitutes precisely what men fail to understand of her as she tries to speak "in her inevitably alienated language," as Claudine Herrman (169) characterizes the world of women's writing. As Fitzgerald's imagery shows, Alabama cannot inhabit this new land, cannot express her own identity, without great pain and guilt, given her role indoctrination. When she begins to try to express her nascent identity, she is "estranged from language" (Kristeva 166), as the protagonists women create often are. Thus, like her creator, in her brief possession of her own voice, Alabama anticipates the thinking of feminist critics. Both literally and metaphorically, her attempts to find her own voice place her among those women artists who in their struggles for identity are, in Julia Kristeva's phrase, "dancers who suffer as they speak" (166).

And Alabama does suffer. The images conveying her discovery of her own voice reveal that it is the violent pain of being compelled to label her difference as "sick" that ultimately forces Alabama to follow the "narrow . . . straight . . . white road" (187)—the *linear* path—that leads her back to "normalcy," where her husband and her doctors can understand her once again. She may have "[broken] the sentence," but she has not entirely succeeded in breaking the hold of "male expectations . . . and existing conventions of gender" (du Plessis, "Breaking," 474) that have shaped her youthful identity and undermine her adult effort at self-expression. The painful literal impression on her vision of the disembodied word "sick" finally goads her to follow that twisting "highway" out of her state of "otherness."

Soon, David is attending her recovery "like a parent supervising a child who is learning to walk" (Fitzgerald 188). The simile, echoing earlier imagistic links between David and the Judge, makes clear that the persistent power of her role indoctrinations has dissolved her briefly glimpsed autonomous identity. As the couple receives word that the Judge is dying back in America, David assumes a paternal role in their relationship, denying Alabama's adult identity. Nor does she seem likely to be able to recover the ground she has lost. When they return to her hometown in Southern America, as her father dies Alabama fits herself dutifully back into the roles expected of her by her own family and by her husband. *Save Me the Waltz* ends with an image of Alabama playing the hostess, picking up after a cocktail party. Just as she now devotes herself to restoring order to the household she has settled into with David and her daughter, Alabama herself has been restored by her husband and family to "sense." In the same way, traditional critics have dealt with the expression of the "Other" in women's writing, as Felman notes, by trying to "obliterate[ ]" it, "curing" or "normalizing" the texts by imposing on them critically a "reassuring closure" (10). Certainly, this closure is what critics have sought in Fitzgerald's *Save Me the Waltz,* attacking its language, its structure, its form as amateurish or incomprehensible when they could not "normalize" the novel.

Although this woman's *Künstlerroman* was published in the twentieth century, its identity as a Southern novel links it to the tradition of the nineteenth-century *Künstlerroman*. The roles that doom Alabama's quest for artistic identity are the essentially nineteenth-century expectations that Southern culture continued to impose on women of Zelda Fitzgerald's time. These same restrictive roles are those that defined and limited the options of the female protagonist in the nineteenth-century *Künstlerroman*, effecting a traditional narrative closure whether she chose "romance" or the "quest" that, punitively, usually cost her her life. But critics—and I—do not find a closure or resolution in Fitzgerald's autobiographical *Künstlerroman* because *Save Me the Waltz* is poised between the nineteenth-century and the twentieth-century *Künstlerroman:* Alabama's marriage is reaffirmed, but images at the end suggest its ultimate failure; Alabama has failed in her "quest" for autonomy through a career in ballet, but she *has* found her own voice, if only fleetingly. Inevitably, when we recall how Alabama's quest for her self requires her to try to reinvent language to express that newly discovered self, we step back from the protagonist, back from the text where this discovery occurs, to see the text as the voice of its creator, Zelda Fitzgerald: even if Fitzgerald's protagonist has failed as an artist at ballet, she has enabled her creator to find her own voice for the first time. The conflicts embodied in Alabama's struggle against her roles as Southern daughter and as wife and in her subsequent quest and breakdown are the conflicts of the woman artist; they were Zelda Fitzgerald's conflicts; and they prefigure the paradigm we now accept of female creativity.

NOTES

1. For these reviews, see "Of the Jazz Age" 7; *"Save Me the Waltz";* Pinckard; Cary 66; Tavernier-Courbin 23; and Sullivan 33.

WORKS CITED

Bradbury, John. *Renaissance in the South.* Chapel Hill: University of North Carolina Press, 1963.

Bruccoli, Matthew J. Afterword. Fitzgerald 206.

Bruccoli, Matthew J., Scottie Fitzgerald Smith, and Joan P. Kerr. *The Romantic Egoists.* New York: Charles Scribner's Sons, 1974.

Buttitta, Tony. *After the Good Gay Times.* New York: Viking Press, 1974.

Cary, Meredith. *"Save Me the Waltz* as a Novel." *Fitzgerald-Hemingway Annual* (1976): 65–78.

du Plessis, Rachel Blau. "Breaking the Sentence." In *Essentials of the Theory of*

Fiction. Ed. Michael Hoffman and Patrick Murphy. Durham: Duke University Press, 1988. 472–92.

————. *Writing Beyond the Ending: Narrative Strategies of Twentieth-Century Women Writers.* Bloomington: Indiana University Press, 1985.

Felman, Shoshana. "Women and Madness: The Critical Phallacy." *Diacritics* 5 (Winter 1975): 2–10.

Fitzgerald, Zelda. *Save Me the Waltz.* New York: Charles Scribner's Sons, 1932.

Gubar, Susan. " 'The Blank Page' and the Issues of Female Creativity." In *The New Feminist Criticism: Essays on Women, Literature and Theory.* Ed. Elaine Showalter. New York: Pantheon Books, 1985. 292–313.

Heilman, Robert B. "The Southern Temper." In *Southern Renascence: The Literature of the Modern South.* Eds. Louis D. Rubin, Jr., and Robert D. Jacobs. Baltimore: Johns Hopkins University Press, 1953. 3–31.

Herrman, Claudine. "Women in Space and Time." Trans. Marilyn R. Schuster. In *New French Feminisms.* Ed. Elaine Marks and Isabelle de Courtivron. New York: Schocken Books, 1981. 168–73.

Kristeva, Julia. "Oscillation between Power and Denial." Trans. Marilyn A. August. In *New French Feminisms.* Ed. Elaine Marks and Isabelle de Courtivron. New York: Schocken Books, 1981. 165–67.

Moore, Harry T. Preface. Fitzgerald vii.

Morrison, Jane. "Modern Story by Fitzgerald Seems Unreal." *Charlotte* [N.C.] *News* 27 Nov. 1932: B6. Rpt in White 167.

"Of the Jazz Age." *New York Times* 16 Oct. 1932:B7. Rpt. in Bruccoli, Smith, and Kerr 190.

Pinckard, H. R. "Fitzgerald's Wife Presents Her First Book." *Huntington* [W.V.] *Advertiser* 30 Oct. 1932. Rpt. in White 166–67.

Robertson, Elizabeth. "Speaking from the Place of the Other: Identity and Narrative Form in the Life and Art of Zelda Fitzgerald." *The Denver Quarterly* 19 (Summer 1984): 130–39.

"Save Me the Waltz" (Review). *New York Herald Tribune.* Rpt. in Bruccoli, Smith, and Kerr 189.

Sullivan, Victoria. "An American Dream Destroyed: Zelda Fitzgerald." *College English Association* 41 (ii): 33–39.

Tavernier-Courbin, Jacquelin. "Art as Woman's Response and Search: Zelda Fitzgerald's *Save Me the Waltz."* *Southern Literary Journal* 11 (Spring 1979): 22–42.

Wagner, Linda W. *"Save Me the Waltz:* An Assessment in Craft." *Journal of Narrative Technique* 12 (Fall 1982): 201–9.

White, Ray Lewis. "Zelda Fitzgerald's *Save Me the Waltz:* A Collection of Reviews From 1932–1933." *Fitzgerald-Hemingway Annual* (1979): 163–68.

4. From Life to Art

Ruth M. Vande Kieft

The Love Ethos of Porter, Welty, and McCullers

Since love is a central theme in much fiction, especially that of women writers, it is not surprising to find the theme dominant in the fiction of Katherine Anne Porter, Eudora Welty, and Carson McCullers. What is surprising, given their time and place in the most conservative part of the country, the South (Texas, Mississippi, Georgia) in the first half of the twentieth century, is the extent to which each writer, though she could not totally escape conventional codes and attitudes toward love, essentially subverted them in her life as a fiction writer. Their contrasting lives and fictional projections of love reveal how as artists they individually fulfilled their destinies and escaped from the common female destiny, the stories society might have written for them, and they for their characters, as lovers, wives, and mothers.

In my essay, I analyze and relate these two sets of stories, the biographical and fictional "love lives" of the three writers. I am aware of the hazards of my undertaking: chiefly its magnitude and the impossibility of sorting out facts from fiction. For in what other area of a woman's life is reality more infused with fantasy, is language more "loaded" and ungovernable, are assumptions, actions, values more charged and elusive in their meanings?

I face these difficulties squarely and attempt to deal with them in two ways. First, I use the term *mythos* because it implies a pattern of attitudes and experiences that are both individual and yet shared with others in smaller or larger groups. For each of the three writers, there is, in addition to a unique personal history, a set of "conventional" (religious, archetypal, literary) sources of the mythos that the writer either wholly or partially accepts or rejects. Each has her own relationship to "the truth," each a different way of conducting her life and using it in her fiction, a different mix of the realistic with the fantastic. Each writer's "mythos of love" is the intricately woven pattern of several components: (1) her early experiences within the family setting; (2) her "love history" as a woman; and (3) her imaginative assimilation of both traditional and modern attitudes toward love acquired through formal education, reading, observation. Each component is to some extent cloaked in its own language and reference system, the community's encoding of attitudes and assumptions. Since I cannot treat all elements consistently or at equal length, I shall stress what seem the most important formative influences on each writer.

Second, I have limited my study to the fiction itself and material essentially biographical rather than critical. Fortunately, for two of the writers we have long, definitive, authorized biographies written by sympathetic women: Joan Givner's of Porter and Virginia Spencer Carr's of McCullers. In Welty's case, we have a slender autobiography, *One Writer's Beginnings,* itself a work of art, though not, I think, another of her works of fiction, for I believe it to be as honest as it is beautiful, moving, and amusing, however selective in its personal revelations. These biographical sources being different from each other in kind and approach, I make no claims for their comparative objectivity, or that of my own conclusions. Since the territory I hope to survey is thickly wooded, I intend to be wary, flexible, and suggestive rather than definitive or doctrinaire.

1

Porter's mythos of love seems the most perilous of the three to describe because, though convoluted, it is easiest to reduce to a formula: the Freudian one of the wholly determining effects of early childhood on all of a writer's work. In an extraordinary feat of fact-gathering and reconstruction, Givner has told Porter's life story and revealed her life-long habit of interweaving fact, fantasy, and fiction. Porter invented for herself a Southern aristocratic past and early family history. She assumed and played out the dual roles of Southern belle modernized and liberated, and legendary femme fatale. Her beauty, love of finery in clothing and decor and exoticism in food and drink, her four marriages and countless love affairs, her self-infatuated conversations, her restless traveling and adventures, her uncanny timing in being in the right place at the right time to involve herself with important historical persons and events—all this is the stuff of a legend she self-consciously created, a legend more usually associated with Hollywood stars than one devoted to a craft that invites what Welty once referred to as "the intimacy of strangers."

Givner's "uneasy sense," expressed in the prologue to her biography, "that the revelations about [Porter's] life constituted some cruel kind of exposure" (22), seems justified, for it is an often vain, selfish, capricious, exploitive, irresponsible, deceitful character that emerges. Yet Givner salvages respect and admiration for Porter, whose actual life she found "more heroic than anything [Porter] invented" (23), for it is the story of a sensitive child named Callie whose mother died when she was two years old; who was raised in miserable poverty and overcrowding in a large household by a strict Methodist grandmother; who was neglected, erratically treated and unloved by a weak and self-indulgent father; whose amorous adventures were the compulsive attempts of a love-starved woman to find what she could not possibly attain. Givner's commissioned biography seems the fruit of Porter's decision to "come clean," make a truthful final confession, not only to a priest but to the world. Yet whatever her relation to the truth, in her personal legend making, Porter was exhibiting a characteristically Southern trait.

The encoded rhetoric that lies behind Porter's ethos of love has both a popular and a traditional source, each of which I think she had unconsciously assimilated, insofar as the rhetoric fed some impossible idealism about romantic love that she seems never to have lost. The popular source is best illustrated by excerpts from letters Porter's father, Harrison, wrote shortly after the death of his wife, Alice, samples of the kind of sentimental graveyard rhetoric satirized by Mark Twain in *Huckleberry Finn.* The first letter, to his oldest daughter, was sent with a picture:

> Gay: This is your mother. She is buried near Brownwood. It is a holy place for us all. There I saw the star of all my earthly hopes go down in an endless darkness and there is no light in my heart even at noonday. In this strange twilight I try to trace the narrow road I must walk to reach this city of the dead and lie down in the long night beside my love. But this star is not extinguished altogether for it shed the rays of its purity and love over the waste landscape of my life, gave meaning to Nothingness and left memories that not time nor death itself can take away. (Givner 40)

To a close friend of Alice he wrote: "I loved her better than my own life, aye, better than I did my God.... If there is, after this turmoil, a halcyon period, a golden place somewhere 'en vista' of the golden dawn, I know my spirit will seek hers there, though but a season. Hell thenceforth with the companionship of the Dragon of the Apocalypse will not torment me worse than the pangs that now rend me" (Givner 40–41).

From this graveyard rhetoric it is a short leap to that of the poem Uncle Gabriel writes to memorialize his beloved Amy in "Old Mortality" ("A singing angel, she forgets / The griefs of old mortality" [Porter, *Stories* 181]). Noteworthy about Harrison Porter's rhetoric, in addition to its self-indulgence, is its "literary" pretension and the mixing of religious language with that of human love. Harrison plays out his drama as mourner on a cosmic stage against a backdrop of time and eternity, heaven and hell, salvation and damnation. And Porter played out her drama on the same cosmic stage.

The other encoded rhetoric is that of the ancient noble literary tradition of Courtly Love, the Age of Chivalry. The love ethos is often adulterous, thriving most when unconsummated, product of fevered imaginations, high codes of morality and tests of bravery, celebrated by poets of stature from the Middle Ages to the nineteenth-century Romantics. Actually, this noble tradition reached the South, and doubtless Porter, more by way of Sir Walter Scott than Dante, Shakespeare, and Keats. Porter had little formal education and was not an inveterate reader as a child. Her fictional portrayal of what had become of the Western world's and the South's version of love is negative: she shows love traduced and betrayed, relentlessly exposed and rejected, yet also as inescapable and hopelessly victimizing. The romantic and antiromantic are constantly at war in Porter's fiction; her pages are strewn with the combatants wounded, dying, and dead of that mortal struggle.

It is instructive to look closely at the battle in its formative stages, to Miranda's, that is, Porter's generation as it appears in "Old Mortality." Miranda and her sister Maria, eight and twelve years old, are deeply impressed by the story of Aunt Amy, who, though now only a "ghost in a frame," had once been "beautiful, much loved, unhappy, and had died young." Though somewhat skeptical about the romantic legends told by their elders, the little girls enjoy "patching together . . . fragments of tales that were like bits of poetry, and music . . . with the theatre." The romance of their Uncle Gabriel's "long, unrewarded love for [Amy], her early death," was a story linked for them with books they thought of as "unworldly . . . but true, such as the Vita Nuova, the Sonnets of Shakespeare and the Wedding Song of Spenser; and poems by Edgar Allan Poe" (178). Thus an ancient and noble lineage of love poetry is provided for Porter's fictional counterpart, Miranda, though there is little to indicate that these greatest of love poets were early a seriously formative part of Porter's actual reading and thinking. Yet as central to her fictive world, they provided her with the norm for the lofty and unattainable ("unworldly") ideal of love she saw everywhere traduced.

Amy is presented as willful, capricious, a type of La Belle Dame Sans Merci. She dresses and behaves scandalously, has many beaus while resisting the courtship of Miranda's profligate Uncle Gabriel, has a duel fought over her and compensates for life's dullness by running off, half-sick, on a three-day lark to the border with her brothers. She perversely accepts Gabriel when he loses his family inheritance, marries him in a gray wedding gown, and dies within ten days, not only of chronic illness, but, it is hinted, an overdose of medication. Miranda is impressed by this history, and although she already knows how far reality is from the romantic legends enshrined in the family memory, she persists in her addiction to the romantic gesture, as in her rebellion against conventional morality. Her alternately strict and indulgent rearing makes satirical comedy of the emphasis on character training taught by the nuns in the convent school in which Miranda and her sister are "inured." Their father reinforces the superficiality of the Catholic moral codes by stressing his daughters' need to be good chiefly in order to win the reward of being swept off to the races on certain "blessed Saturdays."

Miranda elopes from out of the convent at sixteen and flees from the marriage within two years. Desperately in love, Porter herself married at sixteen in a double wedding with her sister, a civil ceremony conducted by a Methodist minister. Though the marriage lasted nine years, the longest of her marriages, the relationship was a disaster. Porter later referred to her husband, John Koontz, as a "monster"—a term she applied to all her husbands and lovers. Givner speculates that Porter's "inability to find any pleasure in sex . . . aggravated furthermore by her discovery that she was not able to bear a child" (92) was the cause for her romantic disillusionment. In the final section of "Old Mortality" Porter has Miranda think, after her divorce, "I hate loving and being loved. I hate it," and then suffer "a shock of comfort from the sudden collapse of an old painful structure of distorted images and misconceptions" (221).

Yet Miranda rejects also her ugly, chinless, peppermint-breathed feminist cousin Eva in Eva's reductive assessment of Amy's romantic history as "just sex!" What else but desire for romantic love—with its rich fantasy, brief and ambiguous pleasure, and almost inevitable disillusionment and pain—could have induced Porter's fictional characters to act as they did? "Old Mortality" ends with Miranda's thinking, "I don't want any promises, I won't have false hopes, I won't be romantic about myself. . . . At least I can know the truth about what happens to me, she assured herself silently, making a promise to herself, in her hopelessness, her ignorance" (221). The final word shows how little Porter believed that Miranda, or anyone, *could* find the truth for herself, unshackle herself from the past or even settle for the bleak reductions of the present. Porter found her truth only in the realm of what she created, the means and end of her integrity and her personal salvation, her fictional art. And in her choice of the free, bohemian existence and refusal of the traditional roles of strong, supportive wife and mother, she became a prototype of the modern woman artist.

The Miranda stories tell a bitter story about love—with one exception, "Pale Horse, Pale Rider." But that story presents romantic love as mythical, Edenic. Miranda's soldier-lover is named Adam—obviously prelapsarian; he is described as being round, firm, and beautiful as an unbitten apple; he is even compared to the sacrificial lamb. The pale horse and rider of the Apocalypse, death, carries him off sinless, and before his and Miranda's love is consummated. There is no grand passion: only the sweet elusiveness of an ideal lost love. The encoded language is religious—hymns, prayers, the Bible—from Genesis to Revelation, Eden to the fourth horseman of the Apocalypse (death) to a viewed and missed Paradise beyond; the love language is innocent—that of simple Western ballads.

The finality of death is the seal on a perfect love that might be viewed as Porter's imaginative reenactment of the love of her mother and father. In later life Porter idealized the young man on whom she modeled Adam—apparently a young English soldier who lived in the same rooming house, looked after her before a hospital bed could be found, kissed her once, and died of influenza while she was ill. She made of this casual acquaintance the man she might have trusted and been happy with all her days. "This lifelong devotion," says Givner, "should properly be seen as the love of a writer for a favorite character, the love of an artist for the created object. There is, therefore, an ironic truth in her assertion that he was the one man she could have loved" (129).

Miranda, the survivor, denied her bright vision of death, is seen in the end as a silver-gray ghost, though a very smartly dressed one, with her beautiful smooth gray gloves. Salvation through style: that too was Porter's modus vivendi as she took up her life after her rub with death. In stories based more purely on her own experience, Porter achieves a group of painfully authentic, psychologically acute portraits of the failures of modern love. Givner describes how the patterns of confusion, tension, and dissolution developed from a "fatal ambivalence" in Porter's nature. She craved an adoring, protective kind of masculine love she never got from her weak father, or for a great length of time from any of her husbands and lovers, since it would have been one requiring a docile and obedient wife or mistress to complete on the receiving side. Yet she also had the desire to be a strong, dominant and independent woman like her grandmother. Her apparent distaste for the sexual relationship and her apparent inability to bear children further threatened her fragile sense of her femininity and desirability (Givner 89–93).

In story after story, Porter presents stormy quarrels between lovers and the unconvincing calms or reconciliations that follow them; she shows destructive fury striking out blindly. To the heroine of "Theft," survivor of many painful love affairs, the loss of a beautiful, golden cloth purse reflects "the long patient suffering of dying friendships and the dark, inexplicable death of love" in a landslide of remembered losses" (*Stories* 64). In the end she thinks, "I was right not to be afraid of any thief but myself, who will end by leaving me nothing" (65). In these stories love is elusive and illusionary yet eternally revived as though in answer to some demon of obsession.

This misanthropy and cynicism about love reaches a series of frenzied peaks in *Ship of Fools*. The feeling between David darling and Jenny angel passes quickly and irrationally from loving passion to fierce hatred, the flux of emotion touched off by the slightest impression, such as the couple's reactions to Jenny's appearance in a fresh white dress. When David sees her as lovely, and tells her so, the narrator says, "She believed it with all her heart, and saw him transfigured as he always was in these mysterious visitations of love between them—reasonless, causeless, having its own times and seasons, vanishing at a breath and yet always bringing with it the illusion that it would last forever" (*Ship of Fools* 422). Yet, after seeing Jenny drunk in another man's embrace, David comes to think that "the girl he thought he knew had disappeared so entirely he had almost to believe he made her up out of the odds and ends of stuff from his own ragbag of adolescent dreams and imaginings. . . . There never was, there couldn't possibly be, any such living girl as he had dreamed Jenny was" (450).

Dr. Schumann, the ship's physician, loves La Condessa but does not comfort her by giving any sign of his love until very shortly before she leaves the ship in political custody. The irony is that he is illicitly feeding the Condessa's drug addiction and thus killing her. A Mrs. Treadwell, divorced and bitter, remembers her "despairs, her long weeping, her miserable grief over the failure of love" (481). She unleashes such mindless fury against aggressive male sexuality that she makes pulp of the face of a young man with the sharp pointed heel of her evening slipper when he comes to the cabin in lustful pursuit of her young cabin-mate. All three of the "heroines" of *Ship of Fools*, as

Givner points out, are avatars of Porter at some state of her life in a typical love relationship.

Whereas this psychologically acute fiction is painful, often self-lacerating in its personal revelation, in other stories Porter makes the imaginative leap into persons unlike herself, relating their experiences with empathy and compassion as well as fidelity to the particulars of their time and place. In "Flowering Judas" she shows the plight of a modern young woman who has lost the Catholic faith of her childhood and can replace it neither with the Socialist faith of the Mexican Revolution nor the personal faith and purpose of romantic or maternal love. In "Noon Wine" she portrays a weak poverty-stricken woman, Mrs. Thompson, testifying against her conscience, in support of her morally weak husband. She is defeated by fate and social codes in a society as dominated by male supremacy as is Sicily or Mexico.

In other of Porter's stories, however, women are far from weak and defeated in relation to their men. Maria Concepcion accomplishes her own revenge on her sexual rival by killing her and taking the girl's child as her own. "Granny Weatherall" nourishes a life-long grievance against the man who jilted her and risks hell rather than surrender that hatred, even on her deathbed. These women are strong enough to take risks that may cost them their lives, for time and eternity. In their fight against male hegemony, they might appear to be champions of female independence until one looks closely at what each of these women desires. It is the love of her man, the fulfillment of the promise or vow he made and broke; it is position in the community, marriage, the child by him she expects. These are women who embrace traditional feminine roles with a vengeance. Porter knows much of woman's consciousness and dilemmas in love but nothing of their cure, and she does not fictionalize her own personal "cure" of self-realization through her art.

What fascinates in Porter's personal and fictional love experiences, finally, is the tension between extreme idealism and scepticism, traditional romance and realistic modern attitudes. A clear-eyed appraisal of herself told her how foolish and brief were her many affairs, how much based on fictions spun out of the imagination. And yet she had a faith that there was also, in the love object, an actual love and beauty that answered her need and capacity for discovering and offering her own; and that, when this idealization was mutual in a relationship, it was wonderfully transforming. When she fell in love, her partner was "instantly transfigured with a light of such blinding brilliance all natural attributes disappear[ed]" and an "archangel" appeared, "beautiful, flawless in temperament, witty, intelligent, charming, of . . . infinite grace, sympathy, and courage." This is the golden god of romantic love.

It was inevitable that such great expectations should again and again suffer disillusionment. She called it " 'probably the silliest kind of love there is, but I am glad I had it. I'm glad there were times when I saw human beings at their best, for I don't think by any means I lent them all their radiance' " (Givner 336).

Porter was a fierce and often intolerant woman, requiring impeccable manners but failing in trust and fidelity. Legendary in all things, she was above all that in her primary dedication to her art. Admired and hated with equal fervor, she has been accused of many character flaws but never of being a less than committed and formidably gifted fiction writer.

2

That Porter should have approved of Eudora Welty and her fiction is not surprising. This shy and gentle woman with her obvious artistic talent evoked Porter's praise. Porter was an early supporter of Welty's work, which she encouraged by writing an introduction to Welty's first collection of stories, *A Curtain of Green.* Many years later Welty repaid that debt with her discerning lecture on Porter's work, which she made the title essay of her collection of nonfictional writing, *The Eye of the Story.* In it, she comments on Porter's antiromantic vision of love, stating, "All the stories she has written are moral stories about love and the hate that is love's twin, love's imposter and enemy and death. Rejection, betrayal, theft roam the pages of her stories as they roam the world. . . . all this is a way of showing to the inward eye: Look at what you are doing to love" (*Eye* 33–34).

Welty's comments about Porter's stories are indicative of the contrasts between the two writers' ethos of love and the experiences that lay behind them. Instead of the poverty-stricken, love-starved, motherless Callie, we find, in Welty's account of her childhood in *One Writer's Beginnings,* a child secure in the love and protection of parents who loved each other deeply and her with the special care and concern of a couple who had lost their first born and themselves had lost parents at an early age. She describes her habit of half-listening in on her parents' intimate conversations after she had been put to bed, feeling herself "present in the room with the chief secret there was—the two of them, father and mother, there as one." This made her feel included, exercising when young "the turn of mind, the nature of temperament, of a privileged observer . . . [of] the loving kind" (21). One might say that her parents and their love are the muses of Welty's art: she seems almost to invoke them in her epigraph to her autobiography, which she also dedicates to them. Such parental influence is beneficent, except for the necessary loss of independence anyone much loved experiences, especially when that love is strongly reciprocal, when the child is shy, and (though she does not say so) the protection is especially strong because it is of a girl in that Southern place and time. She experienced a feeling of guilt as she gradually broke away from her family's sheltering, though without ceasing to love them deeply.

The necessary independence was accomplished by her being away at college, then for a year in New York City (where she studied advertising at Columbia University); traveling around the state of Mississippi doing publicity work for the Works Projects Administration; continuing to make frequent trips to New York trying to sell her photographs and stories. But already as a child she had begun to achieve her inner freedom and sense of adventure through her wide reading and active imagination, her fascination with stories of all kinds—fairy tales, myths, children's fiction, family stories, and local histories and legends, which were as indigenous to her southern region as the landscape. At Wisconsin, as an English major, she studied literature and came to know many of the great "canonical" writers, including the moderns, such as Yeats and Chekhov. All this made for breadth in Eudora Welty's love ethos, as ancient fictions were assimilated to the lives and experiences of people she saw and knew. She tapped the mythical and archetypal—their symbols and personifications—a dimension always evident in her work, sometimes boldly, as in *The Robber Bridegroom,* sometimes more subtly, as in *The Golden Apples.*

Classically "romantic" attitudes about love are seen in an autobiographical story in which the narrator tells about her own experience of first love, "A Memory." Here, she describes the two worlds in which she lived as a child: as observer, making frames with her hands to look out at and identify everything, imposing order on confusion; as dreamer, in her feelings for a small blond classmate. "I was in love then for the first time: I had identified love at once" (*Stories,* 76). The love, brought into being by an accidental touching of wrists on the stair, exists entirely in her dream world, since the two children are not even friends and the boy knows nothing about the passion he has innocently evoked. Significantly, the love is *protective*—the girl is fearful about the dangers that might befall her beloved; she faints when he has a sudden nosebleed in class: only thus does the imagined and threatening "real world" of the boy darken her dream of love. And that dream, in turn, is crashed into by an "unwelcome realism" of a group of fat, ugly, vulgar bathers in the violence they perpetrate on their own and each others' bodies and the beach. Of the dreamer's love, Welty says in *One Writer's*

Beginnings, "Amorphous and tender, from now on it will have to remain hidden, her own secret imagining" (89).

The two images—of the frame (rigid, removed, objective yet coercive in her hands, imposing order where life always threatens chaos) and the dream (amorphous, boundless, vagrant)—are equivalents of the polarity evident in Welty's love ethos at its two extremes: at once highly romantic yet realistic. That we have no knowledge of Welty's later personal experience of love beyond that first love described as "hopelessly unexpressed within me and grotesquely altered in the outward world" (*Stories,* 76)—subjective, internal, unrealistic—means no more than that Welty has always been reticent about the private life that lay behind the shy but gracious manner of a writer who remained single, practiced her craft and stayed mostly at home (much of the time with a widowed mother), made frequent trips to New York, traveled often to Europe and around the United States, and became a publicly honored and widely loved American fiction writer. A single remark dropped incidentally in *One Writer's Beginnings,* by way of her differentiating her actual self from the fictional character she feels closest to because of their shared passion for their art (Miss Eckhart of *The Golden Apples*), about having not "miss[ed] out in love" (101), suggests what no one might have reason to doubt from her fiction: firsthand experience of love. But she does not use that experience directly, as Porter did. Nor could she write about people to whom she was close—"those known to you in ways too deep, too overflowing, ever to be plumbed outside love." Instead, she states, "what I do make stories out of is the *whole* fund of my feelings, my responses to the real experiences of my own life, to the relationships that formed and changed it, that I have given most of myself to, and so learned my way toward a dramatic counterpart" (100).

Considering Welty's love ethos as it emerges in her fiction after Porter's is like bursting out of heavy storms into sunshine. The comic intrudes almost everywhere in her fiction (even in so tragic a work as *The Optimist's Daughter*), providing balance, lending perspective. In Welty's fiction we have a complete and completed world of love: complete in that the full spectrum of *kinds* of love, both perennial and modern, is presented; completed in that characters are not usually left both betrayed and betraying, as they are in Porter's fiction, or (as we shall see) loose and unfinished, as in Carson McCullers's fiction. The theme being central to Welty's fiction, and her approaches to it so varied, some radical selection is necessary.

Welty's characters are often in some sort of predicament when it comes to love. They may be dimly aware of the need for fulfillment in love but are denied access to it. Clytie is thwarted by the members of her

decaying aristocratic family, and Livvie by being married to her dignified old husband Solomon, whom she tends like a baby through his
terminal illness. While Clytie concludes her search for the elusive face
like her own by drowning herself in a rain barrel, Livvie is released and
fulfilled when Solomon surrenders his life and Livvie to Cash, Solomon's
field hand, young and beautiful to her. Livvie, ripe for sexual passion,
requires no initiation. For young Jenny in "At the Landing," it proves a
harrowing experience as her tenderly evolving virginal love endures the
rough seizure of Billy Floyd, and finally, multiple rape by violent river
men.

Yet an almost worse predicament is one in which a male character is
ignorant of his overwhelming need for "A marriage, a fruitful marriage.
That simple thing. Anyone could have had that" (*Stories* 129). This is
the tragic realization of traveling salesman Bowman when he encounters such love in the primitive, back-country Sonny and his pregnant
wife ("Death of a Traveling Salesman"). Exclusion seems to kill Bowman as much as does his failing heart. Tom Harris, the traveling
salesman of "The Hitch-Hikers," seems compelled to maintain his
freedom from personal ties and commitments; his unattached love
contents itself with pity and small acts of compassion such as he
performs for the two tramps with whom he becomes involved. Harris is
wary of domination, which leads him to automatic gestures of rejection,
directed even at the nonthreatening and sweet young Carol. By refusing
a relationship with her, he is helplessly resigning himself to his empty,
rootless life on the road, a hitch-hiker who catches rides on other
people's experiences. Yet there is no bitterness in Welty's two salesmen—
mostly perplexity and weariness, the wistful sadness that comes from
hope constantly denied or quelled.

Welty's fiction often explores the conflicting claims of the self and
the other, even when love is fulfilled in marriage. Her lovers and mates
are shown as fighting attrition and overfamiliarity in love, refusing to
make a dreary set of habits of what began as excited discovery. Her
women in particular are independent, asking to be seen as always
changing, not taken for granted, inviolable in their center of self. In
"The Wide Net," Hazel causes her husband William Wallace to respect
the mystery of her changing body in pregnancy, the secret of her coming
motherhood and his fatherhood; and Ruby Fisher, in "A Piece of News,"
wants her dullard husband Clyde to see her in the alien fantasy role she
toys with in her casual adultery, as the victim of his passionate
jealousy—"beautiful, desirable, and dead" (*Stories* 14). If individual
mystery must be protected, so must joy: in "The Bride of the Innisfallen"
this is called "primal joy," "the kind you were born and began with"

(*Stories* 517). In "Bride" a young American wife runs away from her husband in London's grayness to Ireland's Cork in all its springtime glory, to rediscover the exhilaration of private selfhood, of people and places, fresh as dawn. For "love with the joy being drawn out of it," she feels, has "nearly destroyed" her (*Stories* 517). These women will not be "killed" in their spirits by the dullness or dominance of their mates. They subvert the conventional codes of male supremacy as well as common wisdom about threats to the marital state.

Welty's characters tend to be hopeful and resilient, for example, Virgie Rainey at the end of *The Golden Apples*. A woman in her early forties, she once supposed, like so many other young girls, that personal fulfillment lay in sexual pleasure, and so made love on a bare mattress with her sailor boyfriend in an abandoned house, then ran away with him to Memphis, and in so doing rejected her old piano teacher Miss Eckhart along with her Beethoven—and a special gift, the potential to become a great pianist. But Virgie had come back and had felt herself "undestroyed" walking across the golden fields toward her home town and her widowed mother. After her mother's death and many years of self-discipline, Virgie is now freed to begin a life of her own. In *One Writer's Beginnings* Welty says of Virgie: "Passionate, recalcitrant, stubbornly undefeated by failure or hurt or disgrace or bereavement, all the while heedlessly wasting of her gifts, she knows to the last that there is a world that remains out there, a world living and mysterious, and that she is of it" (102).

It is in her novels that Welty most fully explores the theme of love. *Delta Wedding* presents a large "extended" family with strong loyalties and traditions in a variety of love predicaments. Among these characters are two through whom Welty creates an ideal of love in action, Ellen and George Fairchild. They are not, however, a married couple but brother and sister-in-law. Ellen has married the oldest son in the Fairchild family, Battle, and does the mothering not only of her own large brood but of anyone who needs it, not through domineering nor coddling but through a deep understanding of individuals, seeking always in quiet, tactful ways to help those about her toward responsible maturity and personal fulfillment. She wisely shows how most conflict, including marital, lies within ourselves, not *between* us, and is "not over people" but "things like the truth, and what you owe people" (*Delta Wedding* 163). Her own center of self, appearing so fragile and feminine, is tough and durable, resembling the delicate, spiritually poised woman in Frost's "The Silken Tent" or Mrs. Ramsay in *To the Lighthouse;* most of all perhaps the famous portrait of *agape* in I Corinthians 13. All this is without benefit of a visible religious faith, though rising clearly from a

Christian morality and reflecting, one might guess, the morality of Welty's own parents.

If Ellen Fairchild seems that not impossible she, George Fairchild does seem that impossible he. Welty tried to make him as credibly human and faulty as she made him heroic, ideal, charismatic, but it was a perilous undertaking. That is, as I see it, because she tried to graft a type of *agape* onto human love outside the framework of the Christian faith. George is made to be and act much like Christ—or at least the St. George who slew the dragon—while often resembling neither, but rather Dionysus, Pan, or King McLain of *The Golden Apples.* He also appears to have the psychological complexity and sophistication of a modern man.

The initiating action of the novel is George's saving an idiot niece from an oncoming train, the Yellow Dog. This heroic risk taking is related to what the love ethos of the novel presents as life's greatest risk, marriage; George has compounded that risk by "marrying down"—a pretty girl, Robbie, who worked in the plantation store. His double risk precipitates Dabney Fairchild's decision to marry Troy, the plantation overseer, a man twice her age with a mountain country background: she too is "marrying down." To Robbie, George's heroism on the train track reveals what she regards as his thralldom to the Fairchilds, his greater concern for the idiot daughter of dear dead Dennis, the family hero, than for her and their possible (unborn) child.

But sensitive members of the family know that not only devotion to the Fairchilds and their traditions motivates George's love. Dabney perceives that though "the very heart of the family," he is "different from them." His risk taking includes separating two little Negro boys fighting dangerously with knives, embracing them as well as family members. Dabney had protested against that—"all the Fairchild in her had screamed at his interfering . . . caring about anything in the world but them." She is awed at the kind of sweetness that "could be the visible surface of profound depths—the surface of all the darkness that might frighten her. . . . George loved *the world,* something told her suddenly. Not them! Not them in particular" (*Delta Wedding* 36, 37). The language evoked here is clearly biblical: "For God so loved the world." George's love is as universal as divine love in its confrontation of all that is dark and terrifying in human life, in its selfless sacrifice and detachment, though with its capacity also for special attachments. Its end product is an active, courageous participation in all human life, a life of suffering sustained, terrors met and subdued. George the beloved, the peace maker, is apart from the family that mothers him indulgently and yet relies upon him as its conscience and protector. He has the quality of waiting or withholding, curbing his strength while some frail or tentative life asks to be nurtured. The motherless child Laura sees this quality and responds with ardor. George's wife, Robbie, learns, with pain and humiliation, that his love can never be exclusive. George *must* love the whole world—not her exclusively.

One brief mysterious incident helps to fill out Welty's concept of the nature of George and his and Ellen's love. Though both are loyal spouses and harbor no secret adulterous passion for each other, their deep mutual understanding makes them sister souls. Ellen is searching in the woods for her lost garnet pin when she comes upon a half-wild lost girl who seems to *"shed beauty,"* nymph-like, "a creature not hiding, but waiting to be seen" (70). Ellen tries to warn this nymph of the danger of her unprotected position, but the girl wants to know the road toward Memphis, "the old Delta synonym for pleasure, trouble, and shame." Ellen says, "I'm not stopping you," and the girl says comfortably, "You couldn't stop me" (70–71). But someone apparently can.

Later, when Ellen tells George about meeting the girl, he says, "Yes, I took her over to the old Argyle gin and slept with her." Ellen is shocked but withholds judgment, mulls over George's action and failure to excuse or explain what he has done, and finally concludes that he was "the one person she knew in the world who did not have it in him to make of any act a facile thing or to make a travesty out of human beings—even, in spite of temptation at a time like this moment, of *himself* as one human being. . . . Only George left the world she knew as pure—in spite of his fierce energies, even heresies—as he found it; still real, still bad, still fleeting and mysterious and hopelessly alluring to her" (79–80). Ellen sees that her fear for the whole family has been projected onto the girl. So George has absorbed not only the lost girl's sexual need but Ellen's anxiety about her own daughters' sexual rites of passage, with no excuses for his act. He has slain the dragon both for Ellen and the lost girl (whose desire for passion and adventure is fulfilled). But clearly, *heresy* is the right word for it, as for what Welty has done with that character in that act. And Welty disposes of the girl rather too conveniently by having her killed by the Yellow Dog. Since George seems too paradoxically idealized a character— half Christian, half pagan—to be quite credible, he might be thought of as Welty's fictional projection of a complex ideal of modern manhood— what Adam was to Porter. Much of George's generous and universal human love *(agape)* is also to be found in the young hero of *Losing Battles*, Jack Renfro, though he lacks George's intelligence and sophistication.

Welty's most mature vision of love is to be found in the last and most autobiographical of her novels, *The Optimist's Daughter*. The background of the wife and mother of the novel, Becky McKelva, is identical to that of Welty's own mother. In the McKelva family, Welty shows the same kind of ardent and protective love she herself had known at home, though with important differences: Laurel Hand, the McKelva's daughter, is an only child (Welty had two younger brothers); Laurel was briefly married to Philip Hand during World War II and soon widowed; and Judge McKelva, the father, is a Southerner, unlike Christian Welty (from Ohio, a Northerner like Philip). Welty shows the characters' protecting and protesting in their deep love and concern for each other, to the point where it becomes limiting of personal freedom, and finally, under the blight of illness (literal sight problems become symbolic of inner loss of vision), almost abusive. Judge McKelva's protective love leads to a need to indulge women (a possible indictment on Welty's part of superficial Southern male gallantry). This turns into a form of self-indulgence as he marries his second wife, the cheap, self-centered Fay Chisom. The result, as Laurel perceives, is her father's suffering then from too little rather than too much love. And in the last years of her life Becky—blind, half-crazed from desperation, her reason crippled by strokes—feels abandoned by her husband and daughter. Laurel's tragic discovery is that love can remain perfect only when it has been frozen in time by the early death of the beloved (thus Laurel with Philip). Subject to the hazards of time, chance, sickness, death, no human love can remain perfect. Yet in memory it can be renewed, given continuity, even a form of permanence. This is the wise and weathered love of a survivor.

So far the vision of the child of "A Memory" has come. How very far from the vision of Porter in the work of her late maturity, *Ship of Fools;* for though Welty always combined a clear-eyed realism with deep romantic sympathies, and recognized how subjective and ephemeral love could be, her work is untouched by cynicism. For all the external restrictions of her life, in comparison with Porter's broad experience, she seems to have known and believed more about love and its potentials than did the legendary and glamorous Katherine Anne.

3

Though born only eight years after Eudora Welty in a Southern town (Columbia, Georgia) with codes and attitudes essentially like those of Welty's Jackson, in her love ethos Carson McCullers seems to have come from a totally different place and to have taken a giant step in time into the postmodern era of sexual liberation and tolerance of many kinds of sexual orientation. The paradox of McCullers is that she seems to combine the sophisticate with the ingenue or waif, as though she'd been born both old and innocent, achieved her full growth by adolescence (this she did literally, being so tall and lanky as a girl that she thought of herself as a freak), yet had never quite grown up. Like Porter and unlike Welty, she seems to have lived her life self-consciously, dramatically, intermingling the world of fiction or fantasy and reality.

Although Virginia Spencer Carr, in her biography of Carson McCullers, *The Lonely Hunter,* does stress what is unusual in the childhood of Lula Carson Smith, there is no immediate way to get from the facts to a small body of fiction that begins when she is in her late teens; opens with a pair of deaf mute homosexuals strolling arm in arm; and includes a man who drives a nail through his hand and fastens it to the table, a sexually frustrated woman who cuts off her nipples with a pair of garden clippers, and a love match between a powerful, mannish woman and a dwarf. There isn't even a way to anticipate McCullers's central theme, which Carr identifies as "loneliness, isolation, and estrangement," a condition in which "reciprocity in a love relationship seemed impossible" and in which "the norms were normlessness, meaninglessness, purposelessness, powerlessness, and alienation" (2). Surely she was loved but by a strong, ambitious, dominating mother who was convinced that her child was a genius and who showed tendencies to nonconformity and the flouting of convention. McCullers's father, a jeweler, seems to have been more conventional, and rather distant from his daughter. This lack of a solid paternal influence may have contributed to McCullers's sexual ambivalence, as her mother's dominance contributed to the ambivalence she always felt about her two paradoxical needs: to be separate, independent, uniquely gifted; and to belong, be dependent, a member merging her identity with that of others. What Porter seized for herself in the absence of parental guidance and restraint, what Welty's mother granted Eudora so fearfully and reluctantly—the freedom to develop in her own way as an artist in the wicked and dangerous outside world—Carson's mother seems almost to have urged upon her daughter. At seventeen Carson left home for New York.

The succeeding months of being "loose" in New York, moving about and supporting herself with odd jobs, undoubtedly fed her sense of loneliness. And her morbid imagination, her sense of the frailty and tenuousness of life and love, was deepened by her battle with serious illness that began when she was fifteen: rheumatic fever, heart disease, a cerebral vascular accident, breast cancer, a gradual deterioration of the body, and after a final massive stroke, death when she was fifty. These chronic afflictions were aggravated by chain smoking and heavy drinking.

McCullers's formal education extended only through high school, and though she became an avid reader of modern fiction, especially the great Russian novelists, her fiction shows little of the kind of encoded language, the biblical, classical, or romantic allusions to be found in the fiction of Porter and Welty. Carr describes her as having been "steeped" in Freud (39), which may partially account for her liberated attitudes about sex. However, Carson's sixteen-year marriage to Reeves McCullers, a sensitive and intelligent but ineffectual young man who shared his wife's aspiration to be a writer, as well as her bisexuality (they once fell in love with the same man), obviously affected her fictional portrayal of love. The marriage was romantic but stormy, competitive, and largely miserable, falling into a pattern of quarrels, separations (including a divorce), and reconciliations. There were suicide attempts, and Reeves finally shot himself in a state of despair.

Throughout her life, Carr shows, McCullers developed infatuations for persons of both genders, though rarely was her love returned in kind or intensity. No more than Porter does she seem to have been chiefly interested in the sexual relationship, which served mostly as a route to the intimacy and adoration both women craved. Though any deeply sympathetic person, like a psychiatrist, could unleash a surge of confessional love in her, McCullers's crushes seem usually to have been inspired by artistic talent, and she apparently conceived such a passion for Katherine Anne Porter when both writers were at Yaddo, the artist's colony in Saratoga Springs. Carr describes how, in the summer of 1941, Carson laid seige to Katherine Anne, following her around adoringly saying, " 'I love you, Katherine Anne' . . . with unabashed candor" (155). Once she is supposed to have "sprawled across the threshold" of Porter's door in an effort to see and talk to her, but Porter "merely stepped over her and continued on [her] way to dinner" (156), disliking lesbians, and feeling an especially strong antipathy for the strange young woman who so idolized her.

The question of sexual identity is crucial in McCullers's fiction, which often takes place in some unsettled no-man's land, nor woman's either. Yet her most successful work deals with the one period in the life of most people when sexuality is ambiguous, "in solution," so to speak—that of early adolescence. Because sexual ambivalence—with all its attendant yearnings, anxieties, explorations, idealism, hopes and despairs—is all but universal in that brief moment out of a life span, McCullers achieves her most convincing and appealing heroines in

Mick Kelly of *The Heart is a Lonely Hunter* and Frankie Addams of *The Member of the Wedding.*

McCullers presents homosexual yearning, attachments, and frustrations with great sympathy and insight, especially in the characters of John Singer and Biff Brannon in *The Heart is a Lonely Hunter.* No doubt partly because these relationships were then widely regarded as pathological, partly because of McCullers's embracing of alienation, homosexuals are made to appear freakish or miserable in their attachments, which are neither reciprocal nor, for any length of time, fulfilling. The kind, all-absorbing Singer is a deaf-mute whose love for Spiros Anatonopoulous is thwarted from lack of response; and Cousin Lymon of *The Ballad of the Sad Cafe* is a hunchbacked dwarf scorned by the man he loves. The loves of that strange, circular round of lovers in *Ballad* seem to break with definite psychosexual labels. Miss Amelia is like a grown-up tomboy, though more male than female in her assumed sexual roles; and Marvin Macy, adored by Cousin Lymon, wants Miss Amelia only because she does not make the easy target he has made of the soft country girls he has left in the path of his destructive sexual relationships. He seems embattled with another man of strength superior to his. By allowing for the possibility of a sexual relationship between Miss Amelia and Cousin Lymon, McCullers gives the story another grotesque twist.

If the theme of the quest for sexual identity lends itself to modern psychological terms, McCullers's projection of that yearning of the self for completion in the other, what Frankie calls "the we of me," lends itself to more ancient mythical terms—to the view of love presented in Plato's *Symposium,* within a social and historical context of homosexuality. In that dialogue the view is presented, first by Aristophanes, that originally three sexes existed rather than two, the third being that of the hermaphrodite. These wonderfully furnished creatures (McCullers might have called them "finished") constituted a threat to the gods in their strength and pride. Socrates explains how Zeus executed the plan of cutting each of them in two, which accounts for the three varieties of sexual orientation. Love is the desire and pursuit of the whole. Whenever a half-lover has the good fortune, after long search, to encounter his or her other half, he or she experiences an ecstasy of fulfillment.

Something of this eager, tireless search of the split pairs of Plato's myth seems to drive both Carson and her characters, for the heart is a lonely hunter, and seeks that form of access to love that is communication. Plato tends to idealize homosexual love, especially when the sexual passion was mastered heroically through strength of mind and will and purity of spirit (illustrated by Socrates). This discipline freed the soul to ascend through the various stages of love, a love that led to the only valid form of immortality, through the mystical vision of God.

McCullers's ethos of love does not include such Platonic reaches, though she does show these strange loves of hers as attended by a beneficent overflow. The selfless, sympathetic presence of Singer, though uncomprehending and mute, is absorbent of much human need and frustration. Yet his capacity for receiving is dependent upon his own private escape hatch, in the form of the fat, nonabsorbent presence of his beloved Spiros, a narcissist who seems to live only to eat. Singer can no longer live when Spiros dies; his own despair and suicide result in the cutting of the lines of imagined communication with the four persons who use him as a confidante. As for Miss Amelia's love for Cousin Lymon, at first it leads wonderfully to the flowering of the sad cafe. There is an abundance of sociability: Cousin Lymon enjoys his new role as king of conversation and commander of the once penurious Miss Amelia, now dispenser of largess; her liquor flows freely, she applies her healing arts to the needy, especially children, and many a timid or shrunken soul emerges from hiding in the pleasurable ambiance of the cafe in its happy phase. But these loves are as vulnerable and ill-fated as the romantic attachments of Porter's characters, as much subject to destructive jealousy and hatred; and after the terrible fight between Marvin Macy and Miss Amelia, with her crushing defeat brought on by the decisive weight of Cousin Lymon, the cafe becomes once more, and this time permanently, the sad cafe.

The circle of loves in McCullers's fiction is always short-circuited, whether as result or source of the theory she imposes on the nature and functioning of love. In her own voice as narrator, she sets this theory forth at length in *The Ballad of the Sad Cafe:*

> First of all, love is a joint experience . . . but it is [not] a similar experience to the two people involved. . . . The lover and the beloved . . . come from different countries. Often the beloved is only a stimulus for all the stored-up love which has lain quiet within the lover for a long time hitherto. . . . He must create for himself a whole new inward world . . . intense and strange. . . . The most outlandish people can be the stimulus for love. . . . A most mediocre person can be the object of a love which is wild, extravagant, and beautiful as the poison lilies of the swamp. A good man may be the stimulus for a love both violent and debased, or a jabbering madman may bring about in the soul of someone a tender and simple idyll. Therefore, the value and quality of any love is determined solely by the lover himself. It is for this reason that most of us would rather love than be loved. . . . The beloved fears and hates the lover. . . . For [he] is forever trying to strip bare his beloved. The lover craves any

possible relation with the beloved, even if this experience can cause him only pain. (*Ballad* 26–27)

These theories have a ring of truth for more than McCullers's characters in *Ballad:* they apply to adolescent lovers, whose passionate attachments are often entirely subjective, unexpressed, and completely out of touch with reality (like that of the young girl in Welty's "A Memory"); they apply to any person in the grip of a compulsive attachment that is unreciprocated and may be masochistic; they doubtless applied to many of McCullers's own attachments. But they do not apply to the love relationships of most mature adults. Being so unrealistically founded, one-sided, and often grotesque, the love of McCullers's fictional characters is inevitably thwarted, leading to bitterness and defeat rather than the nobility of character so highly valued in Plato.

In an essay titled "The Flowering Dream: Notes on Writing" in *The Mortgaged Heart,* McCullers has this to say about *Ballad:* "The passionate, individual love—the old Tristan-Isolde love, the Eros love—is inferior to the love of God, to fellowship, to the love of Agape—the Greek god of the feast, the God of brotherly love—and of man. This is what I tried to show in *The Ballad of the Sad Cafe* in the strange love of Miss Amelia for the little hunchback, Cousin Lymon" (281). The explanation is unclear, but perhaps McCullers means that in Miss Amelia's love and its beneficent effect on the cafe, McCullers was trying to present some merging of Greek and Christian love, as did Welty in *Delta Wedding.* In each case, generous impulses seem to be at work: a highly personal, nondoctrinaire love ethos that includes and embraces all sorts and conditions of men and women, rejoicing in all sorts of love feasts.

One can only guess the extent to which McCullers's views on love were shaped by her own bisexuality and then-current attitudes toward it. She cultivated and almost seemed to enjoy the idea of being a "freak" and the special outrage as well as the special sympathy that it evoked. Had she lived and written in the present era, she might have been able to imagine and project in fiction a love both reciprocal and mature, whether homosexual or heterosexual, but that does not seem likely. In temperament, she was too much the child, always retaining her child-like ways, and she appears to have been most content with mothering, sheltering figures who prized and adored her, such as her mother Marguerite, Tennessee Williams, Mary Mercer (a psychiatrist, McCullers's therapist and life-long friend), and Ida Reeder (her black housekeeper, nurse, secretary, and close companion in the last decade of McCullers's life). She remained always, as Tennessee Williams once described her in a poem, "the little boy . . . with sorrows older than Naishapur" (Carr

537), the mysterious half child, half adult, always in search of another part of a divided self who never appeared.

Tracing the components of the love ethos of the three writers—childhood experience, personal "love life," reading and observation—we find much contrast and paradox. Porter's childhood was blighted by early loss of her mother, neglect of her father, strict rearing of a Methodist grandmother, poverty, ugliness, confinement of surroundings. She escaped through fantasy and an adventuresome, bohemian way of life. Callie renamed herself Katherine Anne and gave her fictional counterpart, Miranda, an aristocratic, slaveholding Catholic family with a romantic, chilvarous past. Welty's childhood was happy and carefree, sheltered in middle-class comfort by loving, nurturing parents within the codes of small-town Southern morality. She found her love models right within her family. McCullers's childhood was marked by the influence of an unconventional, strongly dominating mother who was convinced that her daughter was born to greatness. Carson adopted this notion, with the modification that she was also a freak, and therefore lonely, alienated, excluded from the support of human community while enabled by the perils and potentials of her gifts.

Porter's love life was a long history of largely disastrous marriages and affairs resulting in a paradoxical attitude of disillusionment about romantic and sexual passion together with a desire for it that often seems more like a compulsion or addiction than a perennial hope or idealism, though both of those qualities are to be found in the early, romantic stages of her affairs. Welty's early love life appears to have been very much like her family life—"normal" for an unusually imaginative, impressionable young woman—but we know little about it because of her insistence on privacy. McCullers's love life was blighted by a rocky marriage to a weak and competitive husband who only aggravated her own neurotic tendencies. For her as for Porter, love seems to have been to a great extent compulsive, causing her to "fall" for men and women who seemed to complete her own unfinished self. The paradox in these relationships was that by throwing herself slavishly at this strong, independent, artistic type of person she was all but insuring her rejection.

Books do not appear to have been as central to Porter and McCullers as they were to Welty, an inveterate and omnivorous reader from her earliest years. Fairy tales, myths, legends, the great works of fiction—all these were nutrients to the rich soil of her imagination and the development of her love ethos, as was her more extensive formal education. Welty also showed greater powers of empathy and imagination than the other two, who usually wrote more limitedly from their own immediate experience.

In quite different ways, I would regard both Porter and Welty as having "completed" love stories, both in and out of their fiction, whereas McCullers's personal story seems to fall short of completion. Her husband died a suicide; she seems never to have achieved much joy in her marriage nor other love attachments; her theory of love—lonely, unreciprocated, and incapable of durance—made it hopeless. She seemed as craving of attention, of gifts and all tangible signs of affection, as a child. Her life was continually afflicted by illness and terminated in early death; her last novel, *Clock Without Hands,* was unfinished and should probably not have been published.

McCullers not only seems "unfinished" in her personal life but also in her fictional theorizing about it seems never to have changed, developed, or even imagined some avatar of an ideal love, as did Porter and Welty. Late in her life, in ill health, she participated in an international symposium on "Sex in Literature" at the Cheltenham Literary Festival in England. Her contribution was to read, with great difficulty, her love thesis from *Ballad,* and the coda of the chain gang (Carr 517). To love irrationally and obsessively without hope of return, to fear and resist being the object of such love, to assuage grief and alienation by becoming a member of some real or imagined intimate group: she never envisioned beyond that poignancy.

Porter's life, extending into her nineties, seems to me a classic example of what is known as the self-fulfilling destiny. For all her misery, she got what she wanted: love, glamor, literary success, fame, and wealth. She became a legend. In one of her lovers she found an adoring, discriminating, emotionally stable man sympathetic to her nature and appreciative as well as supportive of her art—an ideal husband. But too late, she learned he was already happily married. In her eighty-seventh year she found an adoring, reliable attendant and lover in a forty-seven-year-old retired naval officer; the relationship was romantic and affectionate but asexual. She created a fictional ideal of love for Miranda in a character named Adam, who died young. Through all these experiences she retained the essentials of the Catholic faith to which she had converted as an adult, however little she seems to have practiced it.

Of the three writers only Welty, from limited experience but rich imaginative powers, has created images of love in many stages and conditions, from first love to mature conjugal love. Her comic spirit has provided perspective and balance, an essential part of the warm, tolerant humanism evident in her love ethos. If at times confusion results from her attempts to fuse the classical love ethos (pagan, mythical) with the Christian (*agape*), in her last novel she does present a clear image of love's *durance,* its power to survive the tests of sickness and death, to maintain continuity in the memory of a survivor. The depth, variety, and authenticity of her fictional portrayals of love speak for the great power of story through the ages—fairy and folk tales, myth, fiction of all kinds to which Welty has always been addicted—to generate *more* stories. Her success also shows the power of observation and a fertile imagination to conceive what personal experience cannot alone supply.

None of the three writers was a domesticated wife or loyal mate, and none had children. For all three, the art of fiction was a care and a passion, a first and last love, the means through which they tested their integrity. In that intense dedication they broke with the social codes that, in the South of their era, might have put them on a pedestal or made them slaves to their husbands and provided them narrowly circumscribed roles for developing their interests and talents. All three were masters of their craft; and thus, in and through their fiction, all three will live happily ever after.

WORKS CITED

Carr, Virginia S. *The Lonely Hunter.* Garden City, N.Y.: Doubleday, 1976.

Givner, Joan. *Katherine Anne Porter, a Life.* New York: Simon and Schuster, 1982.

McCullers, Carson. *The Ballad of the Sad Cafe.* New York: Bantam, 1969.

————. "The Flowering Dream: Notes on Writing." In *The Mortgaged Heart.* Ed. Margarita G. Smith. Boston: Houghton Mifflin, 1971. 274–82.

Porter, Katherine Anne. *The Collected Stories of Katherine Anne Porter.* New York: Harcourt Brace Jovanovich, 1965.

————. *Ship of Fools.* Boston: Little, Brown, 1962.

Welty, Eudora. *The Collected Stories of Eudora Welty.* New York: Harcourt Brace Jovanovich, 1980.

————. *Delta Wedding.* New York: Harcourt Brace Jovanovich, 1946.

————. *The Eye of the Story: Selected Essays and Reviews.* New York: Random House, 1978.

————. *One Writer's Beginnings.* Cambridge: Harvard University Press, 1984.

Doris Betts

Daughters, Southerners, and Daisy

On the content of *Little Women,* Louisa Mae Alcott said, "We really lived most of it."[1]

Many of us women writers seem more willing than men to admit to practicing that very partnership we used to read off the cover of a typical high school textbook, *Literature and Life.* Women writers often endorse Gail Godwin's statement: "I believe our lives shape our fiction just as much as our fiction gives shape to our lives. . . . All my protagonists—slapstick, allegorical, disguised by gender, species, occupation, social class, or hardly disguised at all—are parts of myself" (75).

Born the year before Thomas Wolfe died and with memories of a rather different Asheville, North Carolina, Godwin recalls writing her first story at age eight or nine, about a henpecked Ollie McGonnigle who, after falling into a manhole, climbs out and whacks a guffawing spectator with his umbrella; but later learns he must dine that very evening with that very same spectator who turns out to be—Gasp!—THE MAYOR OF THE TOWN! When she wrote this story, the Godwin household was entirely female; her knowledge of henpecked husbands was derived from Jiggs and Dagwood in the comics, and the rebellious little man facing embarrassment represented her own insecure self wearing trousers. In later stories, she continued to assign male names to young Gail as well as to small rebellions—sometimes her protagonist was even a male dog—until she reached adolescence. Then, overly restricted young women determined despite society to make independent choices surfaced in Gail Godwin's plots and began standing up there for themselves (71–72).

Because misuse and oversimplification are so likely ("Clearly Edgar Allen Poe *is* Arthur Gordon Pym"), autobiographical criticism has an uncertain reputation. While Adrienne Rich stresses the importance of writing as an act of looking back to see one's life with fresh eyes, feminist critics remain wary of emphasizing women's backward looks at perhaps restricted lives, lest this method congeal for male readers their work into limited (even boring) domestic fiction and poetry. Colette concluded that men make fun of women's writings because women "can't help being autobiographical," as in Woolf's *To the Lighthouse* St. Ives becomes the Hebrides while Leslie and Julia Stephen become the Ramsays. But when male writers use direct experience, as Ernest Hemingway does in rewriting his marriages and friendships, many male critics consider their content reveals greater breadth or meaning. Even in literary criticism there are better-half assumptions, such as the way one would read Anais Nin in order to get to Henry Miller, Aline Bernstein and Zelda Fitzgerald for glimpses of Thomas Wolfe and Scott, or the wife's eye view of Jean Stafford on Robert Graves, Mary McCarthy on Edmund Wilson, Caroline Gordon on Allen Tate, and so on. As Mary Gordon has warned, readers and book reviewers sometimes assume that "Hemingway writing about boys in the woods is major; Mansfield writing about girls in the house is minor" ("The Parable of the Cave" 132–33).

Specific girl characters in their fictional houses certainly can be traced directly to the writer herself. Jean Rhys always called her work autobiographical; Rita Mae Brown describes Molly in *Ruby Fruit Jungle* as "a nice version of me." Joan Williams's novel *The Wintering* fictionalized her love affair with William Faulkner. Evelyn Scott's first two novels are clearly autobiographical. Laura Wilder began her "Little House" stories at the age of sixty-three, but they recall her own remembered pioneer childhood. Surely Mary Lee Settle's protagonist, novelist Hannah McKarkle, is at least a kissing cousin. Elizabeth Bowen called *Seven Winters* a "fragment of autobiography," adding that after early childhood no subsequent years ever proved "so acute."

Other creative women have found candid exploration of their own lives difficult or unappealing. Anne Tyler writes for the pleasure of living *other* lives, she says, not reliving her own; and Jayne Anne Phillips agrees that a writer's goal is to get beyond oneself. She thinks having one's work called autobiographical is basically the praise of a responsive reader convinced that the author has "really lived" the work. There are women, too, who, because they are still embedded in family life, postpone recording it and exposing its dark side; especially do they delay satirizing it. Women writers with husbands, children, parents, and the extended web of kinfolk still typical in the South seldom enjoy that light of exposé in whose glare a writer like Erica Jong turns her best profile toward the lens.

Very few contemporary writers, male or female, however, can entirely elude contemporary speculation about the mixture of their private lives, public roles, and published fiction, as Salinger and Pynchon have done. Today's Emily Dickinson will be followed to her upstairs drawing room by reporters; Christina Rossetti's love poems would today be tried on for size by various lover-candidates. Even if, like the reserved Anne Tyler, today's woman writer writes at home and abstains from public appearances, nobody's privacy can be renewed long-term like copyright. As Merle Oberon and Cornell Wilde once hyped on film the love life of George Sand, Meryl Streep has popularized Izak Dinesen's in a technicolor Africa. Would Virginia Woolf have told Leon Edel her dreams; can we imagine Willa Cather answering Barbara Walters's prying speculations about Edith Lewis?

And in a world inhabited not only by exploiters but also by earnest graduate students, once a writer is safely dead, any wall of privacy will probably crash more loudly than at Jericho, and whatever autobiography she may have consciously omitted from her fictions will get dredged up and applied nonetheless. When Joyce Carol Oates reviewed for the *New York Times* a 1988 biography of Jean Stafford, for instance, she commented on the new literary genre, "pathography," her term for writers' biographies so "cruel and merciless that the only surviving mystery is 'How did a distinguished body of work emerge from so undistinguished a life?' " ("Adventures" 3).

One Southern woman writer, Eudora Welty, avoids dichotomy between art and life by making clear that what happened in her past was only a springboard for the imagination, that memory became attached to her later vision, that while she *was* an optimist's daughter, she was never identical to Laurel McKelva. Though she had always been writing about "the structure of the family" (Welty 86), her fiction does not merely record life experiences nor make them prettier for public display nor even rearrange them for emotional effect; Welty insists that fiction results after the artist's imagination has acted upon raw material both lived and observed. While Welty acknowledges her own "literal memory" of specific sights and sounds, she adds quickly that her work is not autobiographical, just "very personal; they aren't the same thing at all." When, from the decade of her seventies, she looks back on her life and that of both parents, she sees continuities invisible when her parents were still alive, and admits that writing fiction has "developed in me an abiding respect for the *unknown* in human life" (90, italics mine).

When the known facts of the lives of other women writers are laid alongside their best imaginative work, their work, too, is seen as "personal"—not private, not merely autobiographical nor confessional.

For example, a young North Carolina novelist, Kaye Gibbons, credits her own writing urge to her mother, Shine, a "good country women who kept crocheted doilies pinned to the backs of chairs," and who coped with her husband's drinking by "going and doing despite my father's Snopesian not going and not doing." Gibbons admits that she writes under the burden of memory; but when as a University of North Carolina undergraduate she showed Professor Louis Rubin thirty pages of manuscript that began, "When I was little, I would think of ways to kill my daddy," her verisimilitude of memories was already being altered by imagination into the themes of her first novel, *Ellen Foster;* and in 1989 her second, *A Virtuous Woman,* transformed by imagination Shine from Gibbons' mother into a fictional character larger than life.

Coleridge called imagination that creative function of the intellect by which the small jigsaw parts of human experience get synthesized into a new whole, different from and transcending its small components, into, for instance, a poem as personal (but not autobiographical) as "Kubla Khan." When Hortense Calisher defined the novel as "rescued life," she might have added that what rescues life is not video nor audio nor print reproduction, but the transforming imagination that can reveal the very truths, as Jessamyn West added, "that reality obscures." Jayne Anne Phillips, who wrote about, never fought in, Vietnam, has said that what fiction does for history is "to make what happened real."

Welty put it this way:

> Writing a story or a novel is one way of discovering *sequence* in experience, of stumbling upon cause and effect in the happenings of a writer's own life. This has been the case with me. Connections slowly emerge. Like distant landmarks you are approaching, cause and effect begin to align themselves, draw closer together. Experiences too indefinite of outline in themselves to be recognized for themselves connect and are identified as a larger shape. And suddenly a light is thrown back, as when your train makes a curve, showing that there has been a mountain of meaning rising behind you on the way you've come, is rising there still, proven now through retrospect. (90)

Thus, any fascination with writers' childhoods is not concerned with those molehills of old events, but with that mountain of meaning later to be discerned in the work.

I had not yet realized this when, as a child planning to grow up and be a writer myself, I started on the other end through avid reading to learn from the trivial details of writers' biographies what decisive childhood preparations I should undertake. If Amy Lowell had smoked cigars I planned to try them; it might be worth infections to become Katherine Mansfield or Elizabeth Barrett Browning. I did not really pay attention, then, to the advice of writers to apply imagination to whatever childhood was at hand. Katherine Anne Porter was not much interested in anyone's personal history after the tenth year: "Whatever one was going to be was all prepared before that." Willa Cather would have added five more years; she believed that a writer's basic material was acquired before the age of fifteen.

Perhaps it is just as well that the details of many writers' lives remained unknown to me and beyond my imitation. During those formative years that Porter and Cather cite, for instance: Louise Bogan survived a household of quarrels with a mother who had love affairs and periodically disappeared; Sarah Teasdale, a late child, felt smothered by worried, overprotective, controlling parents; Nadine Gordimer, at ten, became a cardiac semi-invalid (and became as voracious a reader as Walker Percy had after tuberculosis); Maya Angelou was raped at age eight by her mother's boyfriend; Olive Higgins Prouty's nervous breakdown at age twelve foreshadowed the future of her future.protégée Sylvia Plath; and Phyllis Wheatley, probably from Senegal, sold as a slave in 1760 in Boston, opened her mouth to an owner who estimated by her teeth that her age was seven.

Writers as Daughters

The easy assumption for those doing biographical study of women writers has usually been that women writers—like Alcott's Jo March, like Kaye Gibbons—became creative almost by default, because their lives did not reveal to them that creativity was normally assigned to males. Supposedly they had strong role-model mothers or grandmothers, weak or absent fathers; the cultural pattern became distorted for them in houses where women had rooms of their own.

Some biographies of women writers do, of course, reflect this pattern. Anne Sexton's father was alcoholic; Diane Wakoski's father was almost continually absent. Marianne Moore's father abandoned the family; so did Kate Millett's, and her mother sold insurance to support them. The poet Anne Spencer of Virginia, illegitimate daughter of a slave woman and a Reynolds family tobacco heir, was reared by her mother, who finally left her Seminole husband. In contrast, Ellen Glasgow had a strong father who "never changed his mind or admitted he was wrong," but she became disillusioned with him when as a teenager she watched her mother have a breakdown after learning of his black mistress.

Among writers with strong role-model women in the family: At sixty-seven Sarah Teasdale sighed that her superwoman mother still seemed to have "as much strength in her little finger as I have in my whole body." Gail Godwin's spunky mother was a writer. Mary Mebane's strong woman was her Aunt Jo, without whom she could never have gone to college nor written her story of growing up poor and black near Durham, North Carolina. For Josephine Humphreys, the strong woman was her grandmother Nita. Bobbie Ann Mason and her mother traveled together as groupie fans of recording stars during the 1950s. Margaret Mitchell's bright and humorous mother worked for women's suffrage. Four generations of women reared Kate Chopin, whose handsome father died in a train wreck when she was four. After Rita Mae Brown left the orphanage, her mother kept them going on hambone soup cooked and recooked for days; now her mother crusades for gay rights. And the mother of Edna St. Vincent Millay got rid of her gambler husband when Edna was seven and supported her three daughters by working as a practical nurse. She was such a vivid role model that in 1920 Edmund Wilson said she had anticipated the Bohemianism of her daughters, smoked heavily, and though she looked like a New England school teacher, "sometimes made remarks that were startling from the lips of a little old lady."

Some biographers can even claim that women in the family had a direct influence on the woman writer's career or writing. Lillian Hellman modeled most of her characters on her mother and her mother's family. For Katherine Anne Porter, the grandmother in Kyle, Texas, who reared her from the age of two became the heroine of many stories. Alice Walker, eighth child of a sharecropper father who earned three hundred dollars a year, has said, "Many of the stories that I write are my mother's stories," and she enlarges this life experience to a general black woman's aesthetic in *In Search of Our Mothers' Gardens.* Ellen Douglas (Josephine Haxton) uses as her pseudonym the name of her unpublished writer-grandmother. Elizabeth Madox Roberts, a frail girl nurtured on family stories, especially loved those about her great-grandmother who had come to Kentucky by the wilderness road. Elizabeth Spencer's mother encouraged her to write; her father wanted the whole nonsense stopped. Mona Simpson was given a typewriter by her mother, the financing to write a novel by her grandmother. Florence King, Pamela Frankeau, Rachel Carson have all acknowledged their debts to their mothers.

Other researchers have explained women writers' creativity by whatever positions in the family constellation would produce independence and self-reliance. While a student at Radcliffe, Rosellen Brown did research showing that female achievers were often the oldest or only daughters in families. Eudora Welty's memoir shows how with Edward, three years younger, and then Walter, three years younger still, she acquired an audience. And consider: Willa Cather, oldest of seven; Margaret Mead, oldest of five; Jessamyn West, oldest of four; Elinor Wylie, oldest of five; and only children Madeline L'Engle, Mabel Luhan, Flannery O'Connor, May Sarton, Ann Beattie.

The tunnel vision that produces such easy patterns is surely one reason biographical criticism needs to be read with a whole box full of salt. In 1988, Leo Schneiderman's *The Literary Mind* placed nine modern writers, including Southern women Lillian Hellman and Flannery O'Connor, on his own procrustean bed and demonstrated that "deep personal suffering is an essential ingredient in creating great literature" (jacket copy). O'Connor's Catholicism becomes here merely the expression of Freudian parental conflicts; all the words written by Lillian Hellman (another only child) spring from chronic rage resulting from maternal deprivation, and so on. Remember those "little did they know" biographies we read in childhood, in which 20-20 hindsight spotted, like some omniscient Paul Harvey, the pimply boy with an earache who would grow up to write the Ninth Symphony?

No, the easy post hoc effects of writers' girlhoods must allow for pro-daddy patterns, too. Adrienne Rich, born into a household of books with a father who encouraged her to read and write, wrote for twenty years with him as her chief audience. Nancy Leman traces her love of eccentrics to her father. Mary McCarthy's father taught her to read before she went to school, and when he died, her father had been reading to her a long fairy story that they never finished and she never forgot. There were favored academic upbringings with two supportive parents for Alice Adams, Ursula K. Le Guin, Anne Morrow Lindburgh, and Anne Tyler. Caroline Gordon was tutored by her father until she was ten, then attended his all-boys classical school. Gene Stratton Porter spent her youth outdoors with father and brothers. Harper Lee, like her fictional Scout, watched proudly from a courtroom balcony the jury speeches of her lawyer father. Grandfathers were important for Mississippi writers Berry Morgan and Elizabeth Spencer.

When Toni Morrison wrote *Song of Solomon,* she was in a rage because her father was dead and she wanted to figure out "what he may have known." Her own view of memory as it informs fiction is similar to Welty's:

The act of imagination is bound up with memory. You know, they straightened out the Mississippi River in places, to make room for houses and livable acreage. Occasionally the river floods these places. "Floods" is the word they use, but in fact it is not flooding; it is remembering. Remembering where it used to be. All water has a perfect memory and is forever trying to get back to where it was. Writers are like that: remembering where we were, what valley we ran through, what the banks were like, the light that was there and the route back to our original place. It is emotional memory—what the nerves and the skin remember as well as how it appeared. And a rush of imagination is our "flooding." (119)

Out of good and bad memories of the past, imagination produces art. Mary Gordon has written: "Everywhere I have been I have thought at least once a day of my dead father. He has been dead for over thirty years. In a book he inscribed for me are these words, in his handwriting, a translation of a line of Virgil: 'Among the dead there are so many thousands of the beautiful' " ("Notes from California" 198).

Southern Girlhoods

History, of course, is memory on a larger scale—and in the South those thousands of the beautiful dead have been assumed to be Confederate forefathers, the famous Lost Cause of the Civil War a standard stimulus for the imagination of regional writers. In *A Writer's America*, Alfred Kazin has said that no Southern boy or girl becoming a writer would ever lose that intervention into history that Faulkner wrote about near the end of his career:

For every Southern boy fourteen years old, not once but whenever he wants it, there is the instant when it's still not two o'clock on that July afternoon in 1863, the brigades are in position behind the rail fence, the guns are laid and ready in the woods, and the furled flags are already loosened to break out and Pickett himself with his long oiled ringlets and his hat in one hand probably and his sword in the other looking up the hill waiting for Longstreet to give the word and it's all in the balance, it hasn't happened yet. (quoted in Kazin 144)

If women writers apply their imaginations to wildly varied girlhoods, perhaps in the South their individual memories might nonetheless share an overarching and archetypal regional history? There is little indication that female Southern writers sat on moss-draped verandas and listened to veterans' grisly recollections of Pickett's charge; perhaps the sisters of Faulkner's deep-South audience were out in the detached kitchens baking pies at storytime. Eudora Welty, for example, says she hates the Civil War, claims to be ignorant about it, and had kinfolks fighting on both sides. She has written only one Civil War story, "The

Burning." Bobbie Anne Mason's characters go to Shiloh today for reasons unlike Shelby Foote's.

If their personal histories fit no universal pattern, their gender histories will spill out of the usual file folders marked "Fugitives" or "Agrarians." Mary Lee Settle has made her own Yoknapatawpha in the coal-mining region of West Virginia and traced it back into prehistory, but she is not much interested in slaveowner guilt. In her introduction to *Women Writers of the Contemporary South*, Peggy Prenshaw notes that the South reflected in women's fiction today differs from that portrayed during the much-touted renaissance of the twenties and thirties. The South that contemporary women remember was less rural than the one Ransom and Tate and Porter and Faulkner recalled; the South they grew into is urban, mobile, transient, electronic. They may have a sense of place and community, but it is a woman's place, often a woman from the middle or lower economic class, the granddaughter of yeoman farmers or slaves rather than plantation owners—not the same South as that where Donald Davidson and Cleanth Brooks spent their childhoods. These women grew up reading the large body of serious Southern literature that came out of the period between two world wars, but the youngest ones also grew up under the shadow of another war with guilts of its own and Saigon as its Appomattox, and more extensive lost causes in national racism and environmental filth.

Since Appomattox, too, the age of puberty has dropped from seventeen to thirteen. Near-babies know where babies come from now, and their older sisters are off the pedestal and on the pill. Since Hiroshima, one Southern Democrat has become president while the solid South has solidly switched parties. The land of cotton is the integrated, urbanized, crowded land of the computer. In the K–Mart checkout line, Dilsey's descendants and those from the Compson and Sartoris clans are all wearing jeans.

The usual literary motifs historically classified as "Southern" are being modified by contemporary male and female, black and white, Southern writers: race, religion, nature, concreteness, family, a sense of evil, history, and so on. *Oldest Living Confederate Widow Tells All*, a first novel by Allan Gurganus, recalls the Civil War with horror more than pride, and ends with the very old lady flying over today's Georgia, still able to see from her airplane window the lightning zig-zag line of greener vegetation stretching down to Atlanta that marks the route of Sherman's army and its 1865 torches. In most Southern literature today, the mark of that great conflict may still be visible from far enough aloft, but as the passenger across the airplane aisle remarks when he points out the scar upon the land, "They claim it'll fade on us in a few years." The fact is, as the elderly widow observes, "people recover."

That very optimism—perhaps better described as stoicism with its teeth in view—seems one of the characteristics of the heroines of Southern novels by many women, all the way from Scarlet O'Hara's "Tomorrow will be better" at the end of *Gone with the Wind* to the identical mood of Maggie Moran at the end of Anne Tyler's *Breathing Lessons* and, indeed, at the end of most of her novels, or Laurel McKelva's at the end of Welty's *The Optimist's Daughter,* understanding the confluence of rivers and of life.

How do Southern women writers handle other themes thought to be specific to their region? The natural setting is still a meaningful locale for Annie Dillard's speculations, for characters like Sylvia Wilkinson's Cary or Ramy, or Lee Smith's mountain women. At the end of Smith's *Oral History,* the unsullied human spirit of the mountain people has been vandalized and Hoot Owl Holler is being sold out to a commercial theme park called Ghostland. Even so, the "ghost" of the dead granny still haunts the commercialized despoilment and invisibly moves her old rocking chair on the artificial porch. The regional emphasis on nature seems for many current women writers linked now to feminism, to the traditions of earth goddess folk wisdom, instinct—and in this area a trust in concrete experience rather than abstraction or fact seems to fuse the frequent preoccupations of writers who are Southerners, blacks, and feminists.

Religion? Though the Bible Belt appears to be more religious still than northeastern metropolitan America, and while a recent biographical dictionary of Southern writers cited the church denomination of many, Walker Percy was correct in setting *The Second Coming* in Linwood, North Carolina, a spiritual wasteland surrounded by a plethora of busy bee churches. Not many Southern choirgirls have grown up to profess in 1980s' novels the commitments of Flannery O'Connor.

Though racial conflict and pain remain a Southern subject for women writers, too, many of these writers are also black. Those genteel Southern guilts lived out by fine old families whose sons went to Sewanee, where they worried like Hawthorne about inherited sin, have proved irrelevant to black anger, energy, and ambition. Nor do the Southern Agrarians have many white female counterparts. Though Gail Godwin is correct in asking whoever heard of a Northern or Midwestern "belle," young Southern women today talk more like Belle Watling than Aunt Pitty Pat, and have their best girlfriends at the economic levels portrayed by Harriet Arnow, Jill McCorkle, and Lee Smith. "Today's Southern women," says Reynolds Price, are "Mack trucks disguised as powder puffs."

If the South itself is no longer defined by its Delta or low-country plantation subsouth, if Southern history has shifted to include women's history and slave narratives, the new stereotype for women—and for many female characters in novels—is the equally oversimplified category of Sharon McKern's title, *Redneck Mothers, Good Ol' Girls, and Other Southern Belles*. McKern sees modern Southern women as stage managers who apply only those parts of feminism that suit their machinations. Daphne Athas in her essay, "Why There are no Southern Writers," says these are the new characters of Southern women's fiction, from the farm, the mill, the new city, named Vicki or Elizabeth rather than Norma Rae, in novels by Lisa Alther, Rita Mae Brown, Bertha Harris, Shirley Ann Grau, and others. She thinks there is little similarity in content or theme in Southern women's writing; what they may still have in common is a particular prose style, sometimes musical, usually oblique, increasingly plebian.

There may be one other distinctive quality in Southern women's fiction, even when it deals in its local drawl with broader American themes such as feminism. Flannery O'Connor put her finger on "the business of being a storyteller" when, on a panel with Caroline Gordon, Madison Jones, and Louis Rubin at Wesleyan College in 1960, she said that language alone did not correlate with Southern identity in literature. "I have Boston cousins and when they come South they discuss problems, they don't tell stories," she said. "We tell stories" (71).

In its early stages, the women's movement understandably dissected problems and produced thesis fiction. Marilyn French's *Women's Room* seems as didactic as any of the illustrative homilies Charles Dwight Moody invented to illustrate his sermons. And Southerners who grew up reading the Bible knew how often sermons needed an accompanying pious anecdote, since the mysterious Bible stories themselves were often morally ambiguous and strange. You might get a rags-to-riches story in which the hero was a cheat and liar, like Jacob; by turning a few pages you could leave the Good Samaritan behind and watch Jael pound a tent peg through a sleeping man's skull. Even today, when fewer of the South's women writers look back on girlhoods spent memorizing verses in Sunday School, something must survive of the puzzlement with which children tried to grasp why Jepthah needed to pacify God by killing his own daughter and why this story now was meant to produce their moral edification. Whatever the source, to an audience nurtured on television's disease-of-the-week documentaries—where "theme" is defined as the suggested social solution to Aids, Drug Abuse, or Apartheid—Southerners of both genders still seem to know that a story is not a prescription, that the artist reveals with amazement how things are, rather than sending the world telegrams about how things should be.

Stories, novels, poems do not solve problems so much as gaze upon mysteries and secrets. In Welty's memoir, she recalls long weeks of pestering her mother to tell her in detail where babies came from. Then one day she found a small cardboard box containing two polished buffalo nickels, and learned these had weighted the cold eyelids of a stillborn baby brother years before. "She'd told me the wrong secret," Welty writes—"not how babies could come but how they could die, how they could be forgotten about" (17).

For Southern boys, the discovery that ordinary lives were full of secrets might have been made about slavery or Gettysburg or Pickett's charge. Battles as time-worn as Adam's with Eve and Mom's with Dad stirred mystery for others, since imagination always stretches toward those parts of any story somebody lived but could never fully tell. The three parts of Welty's memoir seem to summarize this process of the boyhoods and girlhoods of future writers: "Listening." "Learning to See." "Finding a Voice."

Daisy

For me, at the heart of a happy childhood, lay one such secret, first to overhear as fact, then to see and now to tell as story.

Like so many future writers, I was before first grade already reading feverishly, making bad rhymes, acting out long, complicated dramas with a neighborhood cast, and spying on adult mystery. Unlike my playmates, I had three grandmothers—two with the usual surnames, and a more mysterious third stranger who visited us rarely from another city and whose coming made my parents polite and tense. Daisy Cloninger Turner was a plump, red-haired woman who stayed an occasional afternoon and stared too hard at me and each time left a limp dollar bill hidden under my dresser scarf. In separate conversations, my parents told me with anxiety and warning, "She writes poems, too!" as if poetry could develop into a debilitating, possibly genetic, disease.

Years passed before I learned that Daisy was my father's "real" mother, that he had been born out of wedlock in 1911, adopted in 1915 by childless sharecroppers, the Waughs of Iredell County, North Carolina, who then were promptly surprised by four successive babies of their own.

"Well, so what?" was my half defensive, half-delighted reaction. I could not wait for Daisy's next visit to see if something dissolute showed between the wrinkles of her face.

My mother, fearing that since I owned scrapbooks of passionate poems I might also become like Daisy in other ways, gave me her version of a lecture on sex hygiene; she read me the first confusing six verses of Psalm 51.

Thereafter, in steamy holiday kitchens, I slowly picked up crumbs of the story from judgmental women; the family males were down by the barn discussing Hitler and baseball and hay. They only had one Civil War story, involving family treasures buried for fear of Sherman and the location then lost; after a century, this wealth had grown vast somewhere underground. I was more interested in Daisy Cloninger, sixteen, who had named her baby boy William Elmore after her own father, had kept him until age four when her money ran out. There had never been a legal adoption, just an agreement among farm people used to raising calves, foals, and sons able to pick cotton. The Waughs took Will asleep, from Daisy in the middle of the night, so that he woke crying in a strange place, and strangers gave him jar lids to play with.

A hole in the story occurs here partly because, from delicacy, I never asked my father what he remembered from his boyhood on that farm. I wanted Grandmother Waugh to be the unreliable narrator—tired, overworked, poor, overwhelmed by a late flux of babies.

When Will is school age, he begins to stutter. He develops a temper, too—inherited, everybody thinks. Though small for his age, and destined always to be short, he fights boys who say bad things. His adopted mother breaks a cake of hot cornbread over his head because she has heard that such a shock is a guaranteed cure for stuttering.

Another hole, years-long, intrudes. Then, when he has at last become a happy farm boy, speaking smoothly without a snag, well adjusted, age twelve and black-haired, eldest of five, four of whom have red hair and blue eyes, his Mama says to him abruptly one day, "Your *real* mother is in the front room; wash your hands and go see her."

He edges in, holding clean hands away from his field overalls, to stare at a young woman unknown to him. He will remember nothing of their struggle to converse. Afterwards, his stuttering recurs.

But, no, Daisy was not just a sentimental betrayed country virgin from solid peasant stock. Despite even larger holes in her story, I know she also bore a second child out of wedlock, a girl, and by a different father. My own natural grandfather was said to have been a traveling machinery salesman out of Greensboro, married and with sons of his own, very different from Daisy's struggling kinsmen farming these red clay fields in piedmont North Carolina.

Meantime, William Elmore Waugh, who nowadays would have been aborted in the first trimester after a brief clinic conference, grew up poor and working hard, finally joined the Navy at sixteen, where he injured his back, and after discharge came home to marry in August 1931 a shy, religious girl from a neighboring farm, Mary Ellen Freeze, who had a cleft palate. The Freezes were also poor, but at least they owned their seventy acres.

Because she was unwilling to say much in her nasal, noticeable voice, Mary Ellen had made a youthful promise—like Hannah's in the Old Testament—that if God ever gave her a child she would return that child, like Samuel, to His service; perhaps that child, like the voluble Aaron, would become an orator for God? The bride and groom were not quite twenty. The next June, God sent her me.

Now my loving, only-child girlhood begins, with William being to me the devoted father he'd never had, with Mary Ellen marveling that words seemed essential to the daughter of one who spoke them only timidly, who disliked being asked if she had a terrible cold, who, in fact, hated to get thirsty in public and cope with fountains that sent their icy water streaming from her nostrils. And she puzzled, perhaps, over why those words seemed destined for secular purposes, verses and stories. *Entertainment*—not what she nor Hannah had had in mind.

Dad worked hard, in the Depression as a cotton weaver, later as a post office maintenance man. I suppose we were poor, though well-loved children seldom feel poor. Both parents were thrifty enough and inspiring enough to guide me toward the college opportunity they had lacked. They saved as much of the tuition and costs as possible, my mother by then working in the mill herself in a metallic din that would eventually cost her hearing. It bothered her that William Elmore would not join her in steady church attendance, but her prayers and example wore him down. In the end Dad became a Sunday School teacher, an elder in the conservative Associate Reformed Presbyterian Church in Statesville, the church treasurer.

As the years passed he finally rediscovered Daisy, who had married and lived in Lincolnton. Though he began visiting her regularly, I was by then in college, later married, then a mother living across the state, and did not share this new relationship, though Daisy and I did occasionally correspond. She sent me her picture—a rather homely woman in a flowered hat with teeth that had not been tended in time. With age she had grown so deeply religious that even my mother felt uneasy, and now instead of poems wrote regular letters about Jesus to convicts in Central Prison. She had also begun, rather tentatively in case I might mind, to tell people I was her granddaughter, a writer. I did not mind. Once my father had been bitter because she had given him away. Now he no longer minded, either.

A widow and a non-smoker, Daisy had beaten lung cancer after surgery in her sixties and lived on. When finally she died in her late eighties, the boy she hadn't been able to keep kept vigil by her hospital bed. He grieved for her. He gave to me what little and unremarkable furniture she had left. And all these years he remained a devoted son to his adopted mother as well.

Not until after Dad's death in 1983 did distant kin send me a browning early photograph of Daisy, age fifteen, taken the year before my father was born to her, taken three months before she was even pregnant. She stands there forever—and stands there for no time at all, as Anne Tyler and Rainer Maria Rilke know—young and beautiful in her pure white dress. She looks like me. Her very dark eyes look like mine, like my children's.

I set forth, then, to locate and identify the unknown salesman who had changed so many lives, whose name Daisy had finally told me in a letter. After a surprisingly simple search through newspapers and death certificates, I finally stood in High Point, North Carolina, by the grave of the grandfather who never even dreamed of me, much less of my children and grandchildren farther along. My father had never even gotten his true surname right, perhaps because he was outdoors listening to menfolk argue over squirrel hunts and war, while indoors we women spelled things out for one another.

Though I had expected to feel some feminist anger, by then I knew too much—how the obituary showed he and my Dad had died of the same heart ailment, the son's life prolonged by medication maybe eight years longer; how volunteer firemen had been his pallbearers; where his legitimate sons had lived and worked; that they became parents, too.

This late, who could be blamed? Is blame even a question? So do most omniscient novelists conclude if their stories cover enough time and lives, or if they work long enough at their trade.

But the true secret of any human life is not what happened during its span, not mere facts or names or dates; the true secret here and everywhere remains emotionally as unsolved as ever. Unknown feelings rise up off history like vapors and evaporate like steam. Did Daisy hate him? Did he even know there was a boy in the world who maybe had his temper? Was her next man a cure, a revenge, a despair, a triviality? Her eventual marriage an economic compromise or a joy? How did she remember her twelve-year-old son with a changed face and fresh-washed hands? And the grandfather—how did his marriage turn out, and those of his children? And me—Do I favor free choice on abortion? If I had been Daisy, I would have chosen no. But then I have the 20-20 hindsight that knows how the story ended; Daisy had no choice at all.

Though this is my first time to mention Daisy Cloninger in print or in public, my stories have drawn on her mysterious life for years. In the first novel, *Tall Houses in Winter,* as Jessica, she bears a boy named Fenwick whose fatherhood is ambiguous. In *The Scarlet Thread* Esther is betrayed, perhaps pregnant, runs away North and vanishes for years but makes a success of her unknown life. In a short novel, "The Astronomer," she is like Eva whose abortion causes guilt and a possible religious conversion based on the book of *Hosea.* In *Heading West* Nancy Finch is the daughter of an older Daisy, this one embittered, who confides that premarital sex was never that important after all.

Yet of course none of these characters is Daisy; all are only my response to her mystery. I agree with Welty, "Writing fiction has developed in me an abiding respect for the unknown in a human lifetime" (90).

The Chinese have a saying, "It is easier to paint a dragon than a horse." We have seen so many horses; seen pictures of horses; people have told us far too much about horses. But the imagination is still able to act on mystery, on the idea of a dragon.

Whether our childhoods were lived through in the North or South, one crucial element for potential writers is that their maps of memory contain uncharted terrain, secret treasure, mystery, possible dragons. For certain Southern writers, the mystery lay in Vicksburg, Chicamaugua; the mystery lay in owning slaves, or being them. Women growing up in the same latitude heard in the kitchen less of battles or emancipation, more of fevers and bastard babies and deathbed sayings. Even the Sunday School teachers who told us stories of Goliath perishing before a shepherd boy's slingshot throw, and hurried past our questions about why God wanted Abraham to sacrifice Isaac in the first place, lingered longer on King David wandering through his palace crying, "Absalom, my son. My son, Absalom!"

And so we concentrated less on Saul's contest for the throne than on Bathsheba's feelings when a very patriarchal God killed her baby for spite. Or we imagined how Mrs. Jefferson Davis managed. Facts are like horses everybody's seen, but the dragon's lair is the heart. Welty says it is our "inward journey that leads us through time—forward or back, seldom in a straight line, most often spiraling. As we discover, we remember; remembering, we discover, and most intensely do we experience this when our separate journeys converge. Our living experience at those meeting points is one of the charged dramatic fields of fiction" (102).

The girl still smiling in her white dress in 1910 could have been me as a teenager, and then my daughter; and soon she will stand fixed there the age and size of my grandchildren; and still I cannot rescue her from anything nor whisper to her that it all turned out all right, that people do recover, that even the scorched long scar to Atlanta has healed over now with green. "All that is remembered," wrote Welty at the end of her memoir, "joins, and lives—the old and the young, the past and the present, the living and the dead" (104). Writers claim access by means of imagination even to all they cannot directly remember but seem to know, as I seem to know how it was to be a pretty black-haired teenager named Daisy Cloninger during that long night she packed everything that belonged to her four-year-old son and watched him sleep for the last time.

NOTE

1. I have not documented every brief quotation because the sources are so varied that constant notation would be less an aid than a hindrance. Instead, I cite sources used extensively and sources for substantial quotations. In a separate list I indicate additional sources consulted but generally omit sources for biographical information readily available in standard reference guides or in a number of places.

WORKS CITED

Athas, Daphne. "Why There Are No Southern Writers." In *Women Writers of the Contemporary South.* Ed. Peggy Whitman Prenshaw. Jackson: University Press of Mississippi, 1984. 295–306.

Godwin, Gail. "The Uses of Autobiography." In *The Writer's Handbook.* Ed. Sylvia K. Burack. Boston: The Writer, 1988. 71–75.

Gordon, Mary. "Notes from California." *Antaeus* 61, no. 2 (1988): 196–98.

———. "The Parable of the Cave or: In Praise of Watercolors." In *First Person Singular: Writers on Their Craft.* Comp. Joyce Carol Oates. Princeton: Ontario Review Press, 1983. 132–35.

Gurganus, Allan. *Oldest Living Confederate Widow Tells All.* New York: Alfred A. Knopf, 1989.

Kazin, Alfred. *A Writer's America.* New York: Alfred A. Knopf, 1988.

McKern, Sharon. *Redneck Mothers, Good Ol' Girls, and Other Southern Belles.* New York: Viking Penguin, 1979.

Morrison, Toni. "The Site of Memory." In *Inventing the Truth: The Art and Craft of Memoir.* Ed. William Zinsser. New York: Houghton Mifflin, 1987. 101–24.

Oates, Joyce Carol. "Adventures in Abandonment." *New York Times* 28 Aug. 1988, sec. 7: 3+.

O'Connor, Flannery. "Recent Southern Fiction: A Panel Discussion." In *Conversations with Flannery O'Connor.* Ed. Rosemary M. Magee. Jackson: University Press of Mississippi, 1987. 61–78.

Prenshaw, Peggy Whitman. Introduction. *Women Writers of the Contemporary South.* Ed. Peggy Whitman Prenshaw Jackson. University Press of Mississippi, 1984. vii–xii.

Schneiderman, Leo. *The Literary Mind.* New York: Human Sciences Press, 1988.
Welty, Eudora. *One Writer's Beginnings.* Cambridge: Harvard University Press, 1984.

ADDITIONAL WORKS CONSULTED

Faust, Langdon L., ed. *American Women Writers.* Abr. ed. New York: Frederick Ungar, 1988.
Jones, John Griffin, interviewer and ed. *Mississippi Writers Talking.* 2 vols. Jackson: University Press of Mississippi, 1982–1983. (Interviews of Ellen Douglas, Margaret Walker, Elizabeth Spencer, and others.)
McCaffery, Larry, and Sinda Gregory, eds. *Alive and Writing.* Urbana: University of Illinois Press, 1987. (Information on Ursula Le Guinn and others.)
Oates, Joyce Carol, comp. *First Person Singular: Writers on Their Craft.* Princeton: Ontario Review Press, 1983. (Information on Adrienne Rich, Mary Gordon, Anne Tyler, and Joyce Carol Oates.)
Polak, Maralyn Lois, ed. *The Writer as Celebrity.* New York: M. Evans, 1986. (Interview of Rita Mae Brown and others.)
Paris Review. Interview Series.
Prenshaw, Peggy Whitman, ed. *Women Writers of the Contemporary South.* Jackson: University Press of Mississippi, 1984. (Information on Lisa Alther, Shirley Ann Grau, Mary Lee Settle, Elizabeth Spencer, Anne Tyler, Ellen Douglas, Gail Godwin, Lee Smith, and others.)
Profile of Kay Gibbons in Chapel Hill *Triangle News Leader.* December 1988.
Schumacher, Michael, ed. *Reasons to Believe: New Voices in American Fiction.* New York: St. Martin's Press, 1988. (Information on Jayne Anne Phillips, Nancy Leman, Mona Simpson.)
Todd, Janet, ed. *Women Writers Talking.* New York: Holmes & Meier, 1983. (Information on Alison Lurie, Grace Paley, and others.).

Notes on Contributors

DORIS BETTS, Alumni Distinguished Professor of English at the University of North Carolina at Chapel Hill, is the author of seven books of fiction, including *Heading West*, a Book-of-the-Month Club selection. Her frequently reprinted story "The Ugliest Pilgrim" was filmed by the American Film Institute and won an Academy Award. In 1989, she received the Medal of Merit in the Short Story from the American Academy of Arts and Letters.

MARY HUGHES BROOKHART, associate professor of English at North Carolina Central University, has published on Eudora Welty, Ellease Southerland, and Margaret Walker and is interested in both Southern literature and cross-cultural studies of fiction by women.

JAN COOPER is the John Charles Reid Associate Professor of Expository Writing at Oberlin College. She has published on the teaching of writing and is currently working on a study of Zora Neale Hurston's *Seraph on the Suwanee.*

THADIOUS DAVIS is professor of English at Brown University. She has published extensively on Southern literature, including *Faulkner's "Negro": Art and the Southern Context,* and is currently researching a book on race, gender, and region in Southern women's writings.

SUSAN V. DONALDSON teaches in the English department and the American Studies Program at the College of William and Mary. She has published essays on Robert Penn Warren, William Faulkner, Eudora Welty, and Walker Percy and is currently working on two books, a study of the late nineteenth-century American novel (to be published by G. K. Hall) and a study of subversive and alternative traditions in modern Southern writing and painting.

ANNA SHANNON ELFENBEIN teaches American literature and women's studies at West Virginia University. She is the author of *Women on the Color Line,* which examines portrayals of mixed-race women by George Washington Cable, Grace King, and Kate Chopin, and a co-editor of *Engendering the Word: Feminist Essays in Psychosexual Poetics.* She has also written on Emily Dickinson, Elinor Wylie, and Toni Morrison.

JILL FRITZ–PIGGOTT teaches in the English department at Drew University, where she is completing a dissertation on Nadine Gordimer's fiction. She has published on Welty, Emerson, and Plato and frequently has written on African and American literature for *The Women's Review of Books.*

SUZANNE W. JONES is coordinator of the Women's Studies Program and associate professor of English at the University of Richmond. She has published articles in a number of journals that focus on the study of the South and Southern literature, and she wrote the preface for a recent University of Georgia reprinting of *The Grandissimes.* She is the editor of *Growing Up in the South,* a collection of stories, and *Writing the Woman Artist,* a collection of essays. She is currently working on a book on race relations in contemporary Southern fiction.

CAROL S. MANNING teaches in the English department and directs the Writing Intensive Program at Mary Washington College. She has published *With Ears Opening Like Morning Glories: Eudora Welty and the Love of Storytelling* and articles on Southern literature and women writers.

LISA LORRAINE NANNEY teaches twentieth-century American literature, American studies, and women's studies at Georgetown University. In 1990–91, she was a Fulbright lecturer in American literature and American civilization at the University of Valencia, Spain.

PEGGY WHITMAN PRENSHAW holds the Fred C. Frey Chair in Southern Studies at Louisiana State University. She is general editor of the University Press of Mississippi's *Literary Conversations* series, and she edited the *Southern Quarterly* from 1973 to 1991. Her monographs and edited books include *Elizabeth Spencer, Women Writers of the Contemporary South, Conversations with Eudora Welty,* and *Eudora Welty: Critical Essays.*

JOAN SCHULZ is associate professor in the English department and Women's Studies Program at the State University of New York at Albany, where she has long taught courses on twentieth-century Southern literature and women writers. Her research and writing have focused on feminist literary theory, and she plans more work with contemporary Southern women writers.

RUTH M. VANDE KIEFT, retired professor of English at Queens College, City University of New York, has devoted most of her critical writing for the past thirty years to the work of Southern writers. Her *Eudora Welty* (Twayne U.S. Author series 1962; revised 1987) was the first full-length study of Welty's work. She is editor of *Thirteen Stories by Eudora Welty*, now in its third edition. In recent years she has written on postmodern criticism of Welty's work, particularly feminist criticism.

LOUISE WESTLING is associate professor of English at the University of Oregon. She is the author of two books, *Sacred Groves and Ravaged Gardens: The Fiction of Eudora Welty, Carson McCullers, and Flannery O'Connor* and *Eudora Welty* (Barnes and Noble Imports), and a number of essays on Southern literature and women writers. She transcribed and edited *He Included Me: The Autobiography of Sarah Rice.*

MARY ANN WIMSATT, McClintock Professor of Southern Letters at the University of South Carolina, is the author of *The Major Fiction of William Gilmore Simms* and of many articles on Southern literature. She is editor of *Tales of the South*, associate editor of *The History of Southern Literature*, has been president of the Society for the Study of Southern Literature, and has served on the executive councils of the South Atlantic Modern Language Association, the South Central Modern Language Association, and the Southern Literature Discussion Group at MLA.

Index